THE

GREAT AMERICAN WILDERNESS

TOURING AMERICA'S NATIONAL PARKS

3RD EDITION

LARRY H. LUDMER

HUNTER

HUNTER PUBLISHING, INC,
130 Campus Drive, Edison, NJ 08818
☎ 732-225-1900; 800-255-0343; Fax 732-417-1744
hunterp@bellsouth.net

Ulysses Travel Publications
4176 Saint-Denis, Montréal, Québec
Canada H2W 2M5
☎ 514-843-9882 ext 2232; fax 514-843-9448

Windsor Books International
The Boundary, Wheatley Road, Garsington
Oxford, OX44 9EJ England
☎ 01865-361122; Fax 01865-361133

ISBN 1-55650-877-8

Cover photos: Top, Canyonlands National Park;
Middle, Everglades National Park; Bottom, Glacier National Park
All photos courtesy of the National Park Service,
with special thanks to Rosa Wilson
Maps by Kim André © 2000 Hunter Publishing, Inc.

1   2   3   4

www.hunterpublishing.com

Hunter's full range of guides to all corners of the globe is featured on our exciting website. You'll find guidebooks to suit every type of traveler, no matter what their budget, lifestyle, or idea of fun. Log on and join the excitement!

Adventure Guides – There are now over 40 titles in this series, covering destinations from Costa Rica and the Yucatán to Florida's West Coast, New Hampshire and the Alaska Highway. Complete information on what to do, as well as where to stay and eat, *Adventure Guides* are tailor-made for the active traveler, with a focus on hiking, biking, canoeing, horseback riding, trekking, skiing, watersports, and all other kinds of fun.

Alive Guides – This ever-popular line of books takes a unique look at the best each destination offers: fine dining, nightlife, first-class hotels and resorts. In-margin icons direct the reader at a glance. Top-sellers include: *The Cayman Islands, St. Martin & St. Barts,* and *Aruba, Bonaire & Curaçao.*

Our **Romantic Weekends** guidebooks provide a series of escapes for couples of all ages and lifestyles. Unlike most "romantic" travel books, ours cover more than charming hotels and delightful restaurants, featuring a host of activities that you and your partner will remember forever.

One-of-a-Kind travel books available from Hunter include *Best Dives of the Western Hemisphere; Golf Resorts; The African-American Travel Guide; Chile & Easter Island Travel Companion* and many more.

Full descriptions are given for each book, along with reviewers' comments and a cover image. Books may be purchased on-line using our secure transaction facility.

CONTENTS

INTRODUCTION

IN THIS CHAPTER

❖ General Planning ❖ Using This Book ❖

One of America's greatest treasures is the diverse beauty that nature has bestowed upon the its landscape. While many parts of the world may contain majestic mountains, eye-popping geological phenomena, rushing waterfalls, and more, nowhere is there a greater variety or concentration of such wonders as in the United States. The very best of these have been set aside in parks, monuments, and other special areas administered by the National Park Service. They are truly the crown jewels of America. The national parks have been created to be seen, felt, touched and enjoyed by everyone.

And that is precisely what this book is about: seeing and enjoying nature at its most inspiring, its most unusual, and its most powerful. Nearly 400 separate areas are administered by the National Park Service, a great many of which are dedicated to people, places, events or ideas that have played a significant role in the development of our nation. Since the theme of this book is the scenic treasures of America, we have selected those that seemed especially worthwhile, regardless of how "popular" they are. This eliminates, for example, many heavily visited areas whose primary attraction is miles of beachfront for frolicking in the ocean. However, a brief look at dozens of other scenic NPS sites is given in the *Suggested Trips* section at the end of the book.

This book assumes you will be visiting the parks by car, which eliminates some highly inaccessible locations that are generally limited to "adventure" touring. While almost all of the places described in this book can satisfy the desires of the most ardent adventure traveler, they also appeal to a much broader public.

Most of the existing books on our nation's scenic areas may describe park features in exquisite detail, but they don't really tell you how to see what has been described. It also seems that

1

most books are aimed at people who will be spending a great deal of time hiking and camping in the back-country. Admittedly, this is the best way to see what the parks have to offer, but the reality is that many thousands of people have neither the time nor the inclination to "rough it" in the wilderness; or they may have physical limitations. The primary goal of this book is to show how to make the most out of your time in the park, detailing those highlights that should not be missed even if you can't spend days trekking through the back-country or hiding in a blind with binoculars waiting for a rare bird to appear.

The National Park Service has designated the areas it administers as National Parks, National Monuments, Recreation Areas, and so forth. (Actually, Congress is the only body that can designate an area as a National Park.) Frequently, but not always, national parks are large, famous, and have the greatest attraction for visitors. But there are a number of "non-park" areas that are every bit as worthwhile. In this book, 53 different areas are described. Three have non-scenic aspects that were of primary importance in establishing the area, but there is enough natural beauty to be seen there to have included them in this book. Four areas aren't administered by the National Park Service at all, but their beauty is such that they *had* to be included. It's of little concern which agency of the government has jurisdiction when the scenery is so marvelous.

GENERAL PLANNING

Some people like to do things on an ad hoc basis, and there is definitely something to be said for spontaneity. But unless your time is unlimited, proper planning is essential. The longer the trip and the more you wish to accomplish during your vacation, the truer this axiom becomes.

Some major decisions should be made in advance:

❖ What exactly do you want to see?

❖ How many miles are you willing to drive and how much time do you have to spend?

❖ What types of accommodations will suit you?

The first and most important step in the planning process is to write down your proposed itinerary. Block off each day's activities by how long they will take, allowing enough time for driving, rest stops and meal breaks. Once you have a basic outline, it's easy to make adjustments as you secure additional information and decide that you want to add or delete an activity.

When you actually begin your trip, the itinerary serves as your travel guide, and you can always alter it as you go along.

> ❖ **TIP**
>
> *Be sure to bring touring materials on additional sights that may be available should you find yourself running ahead of schedule with some extra time on your hands. Why not put that time to good use?*

The information in this book will enable you to create an itinerary for each park. This does not mean that you will not need or want other information. One source that is a natural partner to this book is the National Park Service itself. Each park or area has a superintendent's office that will be happy to furnish you with brochures. The information they send is generally clear, concise, and extremely useful. Moreover, most Park Service literature will include an excellent map. While narrative description is important, a good map is absolutely indispensable, except perhaps for the smallest of our national parks. The maps in this guide should be used as a base to draw from. When you arrive at the park, pick up the Park Service's map, usually found at the Visitor Center. It will help you keep "on track" once your trip actually begins. You will also need adequate maps of your routes to and from the parks. AAA maps are excellent, as are many state maps that can be purchased in book or travel stores or are available from state tourism offices. Do not rely on the small maps in pocket-sized road atlases.

> **❖ TIP**
>
> *Look for detailed maps. The more detail on a map, both in and outside the park destinations, the easier it will be to find what you are looking for without getting lost or going far out of your way.*

You also might want to consider picking up an Auto Tape Tour. These can be rented or purchased at many of the larger national parks or you can get them in advance (purchase only). The company that specializes in such tapes is **CC Inc.**, PO Box 385, Scarsdale, NY 10583. Tapes are not available for every area.

USING THIS BOOK

Each chapter begins with a brief narrative that introduces you to the park and its outstanding features. It is meant to spark your interest rather than provide a comprehensive description. Subsequent sections are as follows:

FACTS & FIGURES

LOCATION/GATEWAYS/GETTING THERE: Where the park is located and how to get there from the nearest large city or cities (which I refer to as the gateway).

ADMISSION FEES: The user fee per private passenger automobile is listed. This includes the driver and all passengers. Admission is for a specified number of days, depending upon the area. It is always at least three days and more commonly for a week or 10 days. Rates for trailers, where allowed, will be higher. Individuals entering via motorcycles, as pedestrians, or by bus are charged on a per-person basis, which is usually about half the private automobile charge.

SPECIAL PASSES

The Park Service provides three special forms of admission. One is the **Golden Age Passport**, available to any person over 62. It can be obtained from any National Park Service office upon presentation of proof of age and is good for a lifetime. The cost is $10. Besides admitting the senior citizen, anyone traveling in the same car will also be admitted at no additional charge. The **Golden Eagle Passport** is available for $50 to persons of any age and is good for one year. It also admits everyone traveling with the bearer in the same car. Certainly, if you are going to be visiting several park areas that have user fees, the Golden Eagle is well worth the small initial outlay. The **Golden Access Pass** is issued free of charge to any person who is disabled under federal program guidelines. Each passport is valid at all Federal fee areas. This includes, besides the National Park Service, areas administered by the Bureau of Land Management, Fish & Wildlife Service, Bureau of Reclamation, the Forest Service, and the Tennessee Valley Authority.

The daily user fee and the Passports admit you to the park only. In most instances, tours and other special activities, whether conducted by the Park Service or a private concessionaire, will involve an additional charge. If such a fee is charged, the cost will be indicated in the text. However, passports often entitle the holder to discounts on other activities. In the case of the Golden Age Passport, the discount can be as much as 50%.

CLIMATE/WHEN TO GO: Unless you are the hardy type and are interested in mushing through the snow in the bitter cold, most of your visits will be in summer. In fact, many of the most scenic park roads are closed in winter. However, summer is not always the best time to visit. The chapters that follow will give you information on climatic conditions in each park, along with road closings and the availability of services.

CONTACT INFORMATION: In the past couple of years many of the parks have instituted automated information systems where you can call at any time and, using a touch-tone telephone, hear recorded information on topics you select. The downside is that it can be more difficult to speak with a real live person!

AUTO TOUR/SHORT STOPS

This, along with the next section, forms the heart of each chapter. In this part the park roads and what can be seen from them will be described. There is also information on short walks (those that can be accomplished in under 20 minutes, round-trip), visitor centers, museums, the best scenic overlooks, and more. A minimum time allotment is suggested.

GETTING OUT/LONGER STOPS

This section is for those who have more time to spend at each park. It has useful descriptions of some longer walks that are well worth the time and effort they may require. Not included are any hikes that take more than half a day or that require unusual stamina or special skills, such as mountain climbing. These trips assume that you will be capable of walking up to several miles on terrain that isn't always level and is, generally, unpaved.

> ### ❖ TIP
>
> *If you have any health limitations, remember that many of the parks are located in higher altitudes, which makes even an apparently simple walk somewhat more difficult.*

NOTE: *Because some parks are small or otherwise not suited to the previous categories, for those we combine the Auto Tour and Getting Out sections into a single Touring section.*

SPECIAL ACTIVITIES

This section won't be found in every park description. Guided tours, unusual means of seeing a park (for example, river rafting or by horseback), and other activities not included in the preceding sections will be described here. Virtually all National Park Service areas in this book have nature walks, escorted hikes and campfire programs, conducted by Park Rangers. Information on these activities can best be obtained by contacting the park directly (either by mail or telephone). They will gladly send a listing and schedule, which often changes from year to year and depending on the season. Otherwise, inquire at any Visitor Center upon your arrival at the park.

ACCOMMODATIONS

This section deals with hotel/motel accommodations and camping. Places to stay are listed within the park and nearby.

❖ HOTELS & MOTELS

Price categories are indicated as follows:

$$$$ . . . . More than $125 per night
$$$ . . . . $100-125 per night
$$ . . . . $61-99 per night
$ . . . . $60 or less per night

All prices are for double occupancy. When two price ranges are shown it usually indicates that there is a wide variety of rooms available for different fees. There may be great differences as to the quality of these rooms. The price range is accurate at press time.

❖ CAMPING

Almost all of the areas covered in this book offer on-site camping. The few that don't aren't far from nearby commercial establishments. In-park campground information is listed under each

INTRODUCTION

locality. Some campground reservations can be made through the National Park Reservation Service, ☎ (800) 365-2267. The offices are open daily from 10 am to 10 pm, eastern time. You can write for reservations at PO Box 1600, Cumberland, MD 21502. Or, you can reserve online at http://reservations.nps. gov. Be sure to give a second and third choice of dates. If there is no NPRS indication, call the general park telephone number for information. Daily prices given are per site (not per person), unless specified otherwise. The number of people allowed per site varies but is rarely less than four and may be as high as 10. However, if you have more than four in your party it is best to inquire in advance about the campground you are interested in. Because of the popularity of camping in the national parks, advance reservations are almost essential where available.

> ❖ **TIP**
>
> *Many park campgrounds operate on a first-come, first-served basis. In such cases it is wise to arrive early in the day and claim your spot.*

Park campgrounds often have restrictions on trailers and large trailers are usually inconvenient in the mountain parks even if they aren't prohibited or restricted. The campgrounds we have featured are all considered to be developed.

The park service also maintains a number of primitive campgrounds (usually in the back-country). If you are interested in them, contact park officials for information. All of the information offered here is for individuals and families; group camping regulations are almost always different.

DINING

Information will be given on restaurants both inside and outside the park. A good choice of restaurants is usually found in nearby towns.

Prices are as follows:

```
$$$. . . . . . . . . . . . . . . . . . . . . . . . . . . . . $21 or more
$$ . . . . . . . . . . . . . . . . . . . . . . . . . . . . . . . . $11-20
$ . . . . . . . . . . . . . . . . . . . . . . . . . . . . . . $10 or less
```

Prices are for entrée and are exclusive of beverage, tax and gratuity, unless indicated otherwise.

WHERE DO WE GO FROM HERE?

This final section of each park chapter refers to the *Suggested Trips* found in the last part of the book. These trips focus primarily on parks that are near one another and that can be combined as part of a single itinerary. Many other outstanding scenic attractions found along the route are described here as well.

INTRODUCTION

1. Acadia National Park
2. Arches National Park
3. Badlands National Park
4. Bandelier National Monument
5. Big Bend National Park
6. Black Canyon of the Gunison National Monument
7. Bryce Canyon National Park
8. Canyon de Chelly Nat'l Mnmt
9. Canyonlands National Park
10. Capitol Reef National Park
11. Carlsbad Caverns Nat'l Park
12. Colorado National Monument
13. Crater Lake National Park
14. Craters of the Moon Nat'l Mnmt
15. Death Valley National Park
16. Denali Nat'l Park & Preserve
17. Devils Tower National Mnmt
18. Dinosaur National Monument

19. Everglades National Park
20. Glacier National Park
21. Glen Canyon Nat'l Rec. Area
    Rainbow Bridge Nat'l Mnmt
22. Grand Canyon National Park
23. Grand Staircase-Escalante
    Nat'l Mnmt
24. Grand Teton National Park
25. Great Basin National Park
26. Great Sand Dunes Nat'l Mnmt
27. Great Smoky Mtns Nat'l Park
28. Haleakala National Park
29. Hawaii Volcanoes Nat'l Park
30. Hells Canyon Nat'l Rec Area
31. Lake Mead National Rec. Area
32. Lassen Volcanic National Park
33. Mammoth Cave National Park
34. Mesa Verde National Park
35. Mount Rainier National Park

36. Mt Rushmore Nat'l Memorial
37. Mount St. Helens National
    Volcanic Mnmt
38. North Cascades National Park/
    Ross Lake National Rec. Area
39. Olympic National Park
40. Petrified Forest National Park
41. Rocky Mountain National Park
42. Saguaro National Park
43. Sawtooth Nat'l Rec Area
44. Scotts Bluff National Mnmt
45. Sequoia & Kings Canyon
    National Parks
46. Shenandoah National Park
47. White Sands Nat'l Monument
48. Yellowstone National Park
49. Yosemite National Park
50. Zion National Park

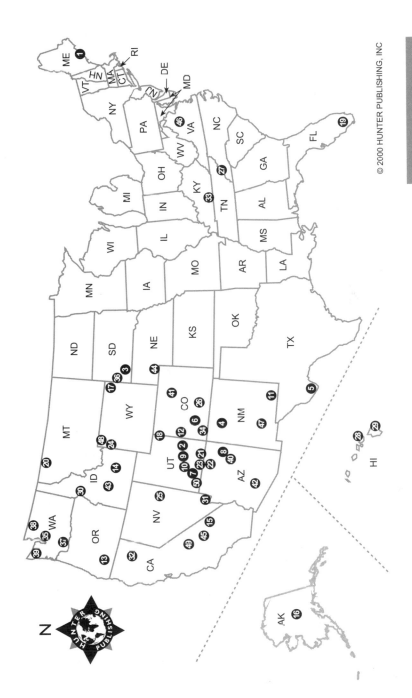

The Northeast

IN THIS CHAPTER

❖ Acadia National Park ❖

Acadia National Park

We'll begin our scenic journey with America's easternmost national park. Here, majestic cliffs rising sharply from the ocean are pounded constantly by the surf. Within the park is the highest point on the Atlantic seaboard, **Cadillac Mountain**, which rises 1,530 feet above sea level. Besides the park's beautiful cliffs and scenic coast, it is an area of great diversity in vegetation. Many types of trees and flowers dot the interior.

> **❖ DID YOU KNOW?**
>
> *Acadia used to be a part of the French Province of Acadia, hence its name.*

The park land occupies the greater part of **Mount Desert Island**. Many smaller patches of land are, however, in private ownership and the landscape is thus dotted with picturesque towns, their harbors jammed with fishing boats and other recreational vessels.

> **❖ TIP**
>
> *Take care when hiking to be sure that you are not violating private property.*

FACTS & FIGURES

Location/Gateways/Getting There: Along the coast of north-central Maine, Acadia is about 5½ hours from Boston. Take I-95 to Bangor and then US 1A and SR 3 for 47 miles to the town of Bar Harbor, gateway to the park.

Year Established: The island was first discovered by Champlain in 1604 and was settled about a decade later. It became a national park in 1919.

Size: 39,707 acres (or 62 square miles).

Admission Fee: $5.

Climate/When to Go: The park is open all year, although the Park Loop Road is closed in winter. Since spring and fall are a bit chilly for comfortable sightseeing, you should plan to visit during the summer months, even though it is much more crowded at this time. Crowds are at their peak in August, so June and July are the best months. If you don't mind the weather being somewhat brisk, fall is a very beautiful time to visit. It is generally dry, with the foliage putting on its annual display of color.

Contact Information: Superintendent, Acadia National Park, PO Box 177, Bar Harbor, ME 04069. ☎ (207) 288-3338.

AUTO TOURS/SHORT STOPS

The park has three separate sections. The largest is Mount Desert Island. The other two sections are Isle Au Haut (accessible only by boat) and the Schoodic Peninsula area, located approximately 40 miles east from the main section. We'll consider Mount Desert Island first.

Entering the park via SR 3, you will soon reach the Hull's Cove Visitor Center, where there are exhibits about the park and the history of the area, as well as information on activities within the park. Here, too, begins the 27-mile-long **Park Loop Road**, which passes many of the park's outstanding features. There are frequent turnouts for scenic views of the rocky coast. The road is one-way (south) for 20 miles from just below the Cadillac Mountain entrance to Seal Harbor.

About 10 miles south of the visitor center begins the primary concentration of scenic attractions along the Ocean Drive section of the Loop Road. They come along in quick succession, so drive slowly and be ready to stop. But before you begin this section we suggest stopping at Sieur de Monts Spring, on SR 3 about two miles south of Bar Harbor.

The craggy shoreline of Acadia National Park.

SIEUR DE MONTS SPRING

Sieur de Monts has a nature center (open Mid-May to late September, 9 am-5 pm, free) and a museum focusing on Native American cultures. The latter is open daily from 9 am to 5 pm during summer and from 10 to 4 during the spring and fall. It costs $2. ☎ (207) 288-3519.

The first sight along the Loop Road is **Great Head**, one of the largest rock headlands on the east coast. Next is **Sand Beach**, composed almost entirely of millions of tiny seashell fragments. Soon after is one of the most famous points in the park, the impressive **Thunder Hole**. Here, wave erosion has created a chasm that can, when wave and tide conditions are right, produce extremely loud reverberations that sound like thunder. Most any time, you are almost certain to encounter heavy surf crashing into the gorge – a very pretty picture. Finally, after Thunder Hole are the **Otter Cliffs**, where a heavily forested area extends right to the edge of the cliffs, more than 100 feet above the Atlantic Ocean.

The Loop Road then skirts the south shore of the island before heading north. Several miles down the road you will reach a side road that leads to the summit of **Cadillac Mountain**. Don't miss this short detour. The mountaintop offers fine views in all directions, but especially to the south and east where the terrain slopes sharply down to the sea.

A bit farther north from Cadillac the Loop Road reaches its end. However, there is a second loop, via SRs 233, 198 and 102, that visits the southwestern portion of Mount Desert Island. Although this part of the park is not nearly as scenic as the area you just came from, it does contain more picturesque seaside towns and coves.

The second loop leads you back onto SR 3. The driving tour of Mount Desert Island (both loops) covers 50 miles and you should allow about three hours to complete it, including stops.

Should you wish to see the **Schoodic Peninsula** portion of the park, follow SR 3 into US 1 northbound and then SR 186. The main attraction is **Schoodic Point**, a rocky headland that rises more than 400 feet from the ocean. It provides outstanding vistas of the Bay of Fundy and the Mount Desert Mountains across Frenchman Bay. This addition to your route will take about 2½ hours, including the drive to and from the peninsula.

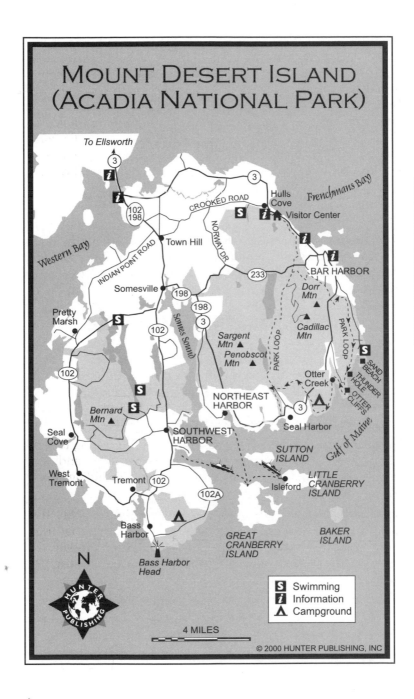

THE NORTHEAST

GETTING OUT/LONGER STOPS

❖ HIKING

The stops above are all just a short walk from the roadside parking areas. But the park contains many more miles of trails. The easiest are the graded carriage roads, originally designed for horse-and-buggy travel, but now ideally suited to strolling, hiking, jogging and bicycling. The 44 miles of carriage roads cross the Park Loop Road at numerous locations and give you a chance to explore more of the park's interior with its lush pine forests and flowers. The same general type of landscape can be seen from the many hiking trails, but the carriage roads are improved and so do not require any special effort – you can simply take a meandering journey over the gentle hills for as long as you like.

> ### ❖ TIP
>
> *Bar Harbor and Northeast Harbor have bike rental shops and this is another good way to explore the carriage roads. Try:* **Bar Harbor Bicycle Shop**, *☎ (207) 288-3886; or* **Acadia Bike & Canoe**, *☎ (207) 288-9605.*

SPECIAL ACTIVITIES

There are several **cruise** companies that take visitors to islands off the coast and a number of these have commentary supplied by a park ranger. Many of the cruises feature whale-watching (depending upon the season) and spotting wildlife is a year-round activity. The boat tours are easy to find – just ride around the towns of Bar Harbor, Southwest Harbor, Northeast Harbor and Bass Harbor. Two to try are the **Acadian Whale Watcher**, ☎ (207) 288-9794 and **Dolphin Cruises**, ☎ (207) 288-3322. Schedules and fares vary depending upon season, itinerary and length of the ride, but range from $25 to $45. You can also take the **Mink** **ferry** from Stonington (located east of Mount Desert

Island via SRs 176, 175 and 15) to Isle Au Haut. This tiny island has some very scenic ocean vistas, but the drive to Stonington is rather long and the scenery is not significantly different from that in other portions of the park. Call the ferry company at ☎ (207) 367-5193 (leaves daily at 10 am; $18, round-trip).

ACCOMMODATIONS

❖ HOTELS & MOTELS

Several nearby communities offer accommodations and are surrounded by park lands, including Bar Harbor, Northeast Harbor and Southwest Harbor.

ATLANTIC OAKES BY-THE-SEA ($$$$), SR 3, two miles north of Bar Harbor. ☎ (207) 288-5801. 151 rooms. Varied attractive accommodations with most rooms overlooking Frenchman Bay. Many patios and balconies.

BAR HARBOR INN ($$$$), Newport Drive, Bar Harbor. Located in center of town by the pier. ☎ (207) 288-3351. 153 rooms. Excellent views of the sea. Comfortably furnished rooms in pretty motor-inn style facility. Rate includes continental breakfast.

KIMBALL TERRACE INN ($$$), Huntington Road, Northeast Harbor, at the Municipal Pier. ☎ (207) 276-3383. 70 rooms. Older but quite attractive facility with good on-premise restaurant. There's no air-conditioning, but you probably won't need it.

MAINE STREET MOTEL ($$-$$$), 315 Main Street, Bar Harbor. Located near center of town on SR 3. ☎ (207) 288-3188. 44 rooms. Better-than-average rooms at a price that is relatively low for this area. Located in the middle of things, including restaurants and shopping.

SEACROFT INN ($$$), 18 Albert Meadow, Bar Harbor. Midtown location. ☎ (207) 288-4669. 6 rooms. Small, friendly and well-located motel with old-style New England charm.

❖ CAMPING

There is a 14-day limit at both campgrounds. RVs allowed. Reservations can be made through the **National Park Reservation Service**, ☎ (800) 365-2267.

CAMPGROUNDS AT A GLANCE			
NAME	LOCATION	SITES	COST
Blackwoods	6 miles east of Bar Harbor on SR 3	310	$14-16 per day
Seawall	2½ miles south of Manset on SR 102A	212	$10-14 per day

DINING

INSIDE THE PARK

JORDAN POND HOUSE ($$), Park Loop Road, two miles north of junction of SR 3. ☎ (207) 276-3316. $$. Excellent fresh fish and seafood served in a pleasant setting overlooking the pond. Patio dining in season. Great popovers are alone worth the trip.

NEARBY COMMUNITIES

GEORGE'S RESTAURANT ($$-$$$), 7 Stephens Lane, Bar Harbor; in mid-town. ☎ (207) 288-3708. Continental cuisine. In a town where seafood is king, the variety of well-prepared non-fish entrées is a welcome change. Good service and nice atmosphere.

MAGGIES CLASSIC SCALES ($$), 6 Summer Street, Bar Harbor; mid-town location. ☎ (207) 288-9007. Good selection of seafood, including specialty of the house – raw oysters. Also serves several pasta dishes. Attractive surroundings in former residence.

QUARTERDECK RESTAURANT ($$), 1 Main Street, Bar Harbor; mid-town. ☎ (207) 288-5292. One of the more reasonably priced full-service seafood restaurants in a mostly high-priced town. Nice view of harbor. Patio dining in season. Good early bird specials.

THE ROSE GARDEN ($$$), 90 Eden Street, Bar Harbor; set in the Bar Harbor Hotel-Bluenose just west of town center on SR 3. ☎ (207) 288-3348. Continental cuisine. The best restaurant in town offers attentive service and delicious cuisine in a beautiful dining room. What more could you ask?

WHERE DO WE GO FROM HERE?

As Acadia is not near any other national park, it is not included in one of the itineraries at the end of the book. However, both the **White Mountains** of New Hampshire and the **Green Mountains** of Vermont are very beautiful and have enough points of interest to make them worthwhile scenic vacation destinations. Large sections are either state parks or national forests. In addition, the famous Maine coastline along US 1 is filled with countless vistas of rocky shores and small islands.

THE NORTHEAST

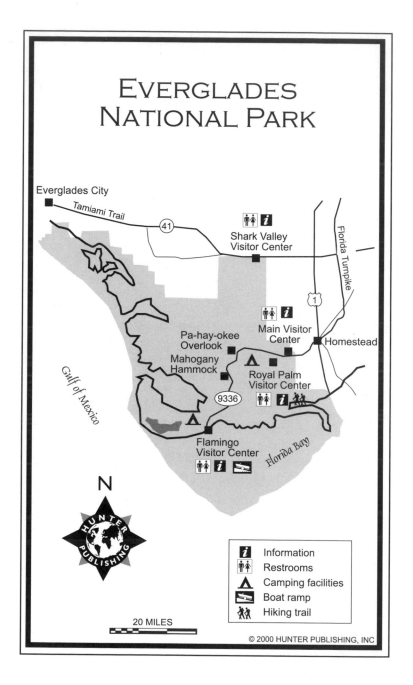

EVERGLADES NATIONAL PARK

Everglades City

Tamiami Trail

41

Shark Valley
Visitor Center

Florida Turnpike

1

Main Visitor
Center

Pa-hay-okee
Overlook

Homestead

Mahogany
Hammock

Royal Palm
Visitor Center

Gulf of Mexico

9336

Flamingo
Visitor Center

Florida Bay

N

Information
Restrooms
Camping facilities
Boat ramp
Hiking trail

20 MILES

© 2000 HUNTER PUBLISHING, INC

22

THE SOUTH

EVERGLADES NATIONAL PARK

One may wonder how a vast area with a maximum variation in elevation of less than 25 feet can be considered scenic. But the Everglades National Park has a unique tranquil beauty. It is the largest subtropical wilderness area in the nation.

> ❖ **DID YOU KNOW?**
>
> *The park is essentially a broad river (averaging some 50 miles wide) that is, remarkably, only a few inches deep.*

The very shallow freshwater, moving much more slowly than a normal river, contributes to the development of the unusual Everglades landscape: marsh and mangrove. It supports an enormous variety of flora and fauna, including many different species of palms and sawgrass. It is home for crocodiles and alligators, as well as a wealth of other animals.

Nowhere else in the continental states will you find a tropical world such as this. So, come along on our trip to a land from another era.

THE SOUTH

FACTS & FIGURES

Location/Gateways/Getting There: Everglades National Park is in the extreme southwestern corner of Florida, less than 40 miles from Miami via US 1 and SR 9336. It is the only national park of comparable size so close to a major city. The park can also be reached from the Tampa/St. Petersburg area, a distance of approximately 200 miles, by I-75 and US 41 (the Tamiami Trail).

Year Established: The remnant of what was once a much larger area of wilderness, the park was established in 1934 to prevent further encroachment of development.

Size: 1,398,937 acres (2,186 square miles)

❖ DID YOU KNOW?

The Everglades is larger than the state of Delaware and one of the biggest parks in the entire country.

Admission Fees: $10.

Climate/When to Go: Its location in southern Florida means it's possible to carry on outdoor activities at any time of the year. However, the summer is extremely hot and humid, despite cooling coastal breezes; mosquitos are another summer problem. From mid-September through mid-November certain activities may be subject to cancellation because of high-water conditions. This, too, is hurricane season in the Gulf and along the Atlantic seaboard. December through May is the ideal time to visit.

Contact Information: Superintendent, Everglades National Park, 40001 State Road 9336, Homestead, FL 33034. ☎ (305) 242-7700.

AUTO TOURS/SHORT STOPS

The park has three access points. Two of them (at Everglades City and at Shark Valley) are off of US 41 on the park's northern edge, away from the main sights.

> NOTE: *The northern edge of the park is not part of the Auto Tour, so activities and all other details about this section will be described under Special Activities.*

The main driving route into the park is via SR 9336, just east of Florida City on US 1. A road extends from the entrance station to Flamingo, a one-way distance of 38 miles. Along this route are most of the major attractions.

Baby alligators ride on their mother's back in the Everglades.

NOTE: *The stopping points have been listed in the order that you will reach them driving towards Flamingo. However, if you skip some on the way in, that will leave you something to see on the return trip.*

Begin at the **Ernest F. Coe Visitor Center** just inside the entrance. There is a lot of information on the park here, but even more is available at the nearby **Royal Palm Interpretive Center**, located at the end of a short side road. From this spot begins the **Anhinga Trail**, an elevated boardwalk that offers the best opportunity to view much of the wildlife (including alligators) found in the park. Also originating at this point is the **Gumbo Limbo Trail**, which highlights the abundant jungle-like plant life. The starting points for this trail and most of the others that will be mentioned are a short ride off the main road.

NOTE: *Some of these trails may take a bit longer than we usually allow in the Auto Tour, but since they are all level, easy trails, we are including them here.*

Soon after leaving the visitor center you come upon the **Long Pine Key Trail** and then the **Pinelands Trail**. Both have many trees that are native to the park.

Your next stop along the main park road is at the **Pa-hay-okee Overlook**. The 12-foot-high tower provides a panoramic view of the southern Shark River Basin, a vast wilderness area teeming with sawgrass.

❖ **DID YOU KNOW?**

The sawgrass plant gets its name from its razor-sharp leaves, which are sharp enough to tear your clothes or your skin.

A few miles further down the road is **Mahogany Hammock**. Here, you'll find another easy, elevated boardwalk; the trail will take you through an area of mahogany trees and various subtropical plant species. The last trail is at **West Lake**, where you can wander along the water's edge by a mangrove forest. About 15 miles later you reach the end of the road at Flamingo, where there are numerous recreational and other visitor facilities.

> ❖ **DID YOU KNOW?**
>
> *Flamingo is on Cape Sable, the south-ernmost point of the US mainland.*

As the trails are short and easy, your *Auto Tour* will take about five hours to complete, including round-trip driving time.

GETTING OUT/LONGER STOPS

Other than the trails mentioned above, there are really no other opportunities for walks along the auto route. Nature lovers may choose to extend their visit by staying a bit longer on the trails and scanning the surrounding area for signs of wildlife.

SPECIAL ACTIVITIES

There are a number of very popular activities in the Everglades. First, at the Shark Valley entrance along US 41, there's a 2½-hour guided tram tour of the **Shark Valley** area. This is one of the thickest areas of vegetation in the park (largely sawgrass), and a half-hour stop is made at a high observation tower so you can take in the scenery and look for wildlife. The view is much better here than the one described previously for the Pa-hay-okee Overlook.

> NOTE. *Private automobiles are never allowed on the 15-mile tram route. However, bicyclists find it an enjoyable way to explore the area.*

Tours operate daily all year long, but can be postponed because of adverse weather conditions or high water. Departure times

THE SOUTH

vary according to season so it is best to call for schedules and prices in advance. Reservations are recommended from December through March. **Shark Valley Tram Tours** can be reached at ☎ (305) 221-8455.

There are numerous **bicycle tours** and **canoe excursions** that begin in Flamingo. **Boat trips** also depart from Flamingo several times daily, with reduced operations from June 1st through the end of October. If you have your own canoe (or rent one), then you can explore several canoe trails at your own pace. **Nine-Mile Pond, Noble Hammock, West Lake, Mud Lake** and **Bear Lake** are among the more popular canoe trails that begin near the main road. The canoe trails range from four to 16 miles. Boat owners will also enjoy sailing on Florida Bay with its many islands and keys. A boat ramp is located at the very end of the park road.

The Everglades City entrance (junction of US 41 and SR 29) connects via a short road to the **Gulf Coast Visitor Center** and the visitor services at Chokoloskee. Launching ramps provide access to the waterways of the Everglades for those who have their own boats.

> **❖ TIP**
>
> *The labyrinth of canals can be very confusing. Plan your excursion carefully with the aid of charts from the Everglades City Ranger Station.*

One of the easier routes to negotiate is also the longest. The signed **Wilderness Waterway** extends for 99 miles from Chokoloskee all the way to Florida Bay near Flamingo. If you don't have your own boat you can still see many of the sights along the Gulf Coast portion of the park. National Park Boat Tours explore the extensive mangrove wilderness and the Ten Thousand Islands. Departures are from the park docks adjacent to the ranger station on the Chokoloskee Causeway. Three different tours are offered. Call ☎ (941) 695-2591 or (800) 445-7724 (in Florida only) for schedules and prices. Reservations are recommended during the winter months.

Finally, **airboats**, which skim along the water's surface, are a popular means of touring the Everglades interior. These trips are available from a number of private operators found along the Tamiami Trail from west of Miami to near the park. Such trips vary from a few hours to the better part of a day.

ACCOMMODATIONS

❖ HOTELS & MOTELS

INSIDE THE PARK

FLAMINGO LODGE ($$$) is at the end of the road in Flamingo, 38 miles from the park entrance. ☎ (941) 695-3101 or (800) 600-3813. Continental breakfast included only during the summer. 126 rooms. Not a great place, but adequate if you want to stay in the park. Small rooms in one-story lodge building as well as 25 cottages with kitchenettes. Restaurant on premises, but full meals are not available during the summer.

NEARBY COMMUNITIES

BEST WESTERN GATEWAY ($$), 1 Strano Blvd., Florida City; on US 1, just south of the end of the Florida Turnpike and about 10 miles from the park entrance. ☎ (305) 246-5100 or (800) 528-1234. 114 rooms. Attractive Colonial-style building with tastefully decorated rooms. Swimming pool with spa. Restaurant is close by.

HAMPTON INN ($$), 124 E. Palm Drive, Florida City; off US 1 and about 10 miles from the park. ☎ (305) 247-8833 or (800) 426-7866. Rate includes continental breakfast. 123 rooms. Modern structure with one wing only a few years old. Nicely furnished rooms are fairly spacious. Restaurants are within a short drive.

❖ CAMPING

Reservations can be made through the **National Park Reservation Service**, ☎ (800) 365-2267. The offices are open daily from

THE SOUTH

10 am to 10 pm, eastern time. You can write for reservations at PO Box 1600, Cumberland, MD 21502, or reserve online at http://reservations.nps.gov.

CAMPGROUNDS AT A GLANCE		
NAME	LOCATION	SITES
Long Pine Key	6 miles in from park entrance along main park road.	108
Flamingo	At end of park road.	295
Chekika	5 miles west of State Highway 997 in the northeast section of the park.	20

There is 14-day limit at all sites. $8-14 per day (free in summer). RVs allowed. NPRS reservations not applicable to Chekika site.

DINING

INSIDE THE PARK

FLAMINGO LODGE (see above) has a restaurant open only during the winter season. Snacks are available at other times.

NEARBY COMMUNITIES

MUTINEER RESTAURANT ($$), 11 SE 1st Avenue; at the junction of US 1 and Palm Drive. ☎ (305) 245-3377. American food. Pretty surroundings that include an indoor/outdoor fish and duck pond. A very large selection of entrées with emphasis on seafood and fresh fish. Also good steaks.

WHERE DO WE GO FROM HERE?

The Everglades is the only Florida park covered in depth in this book, so it isn't part of any of the itineraries in the final section. While Florida certainly isn't the most scenic state in the nation, the southern part of the state does have a number of interesting natural attractions that can be combined with the Everglades. These include **Biscayne National Park** (on several keys near Miami, ☎ 305-247-7275) and the **Big Cypress National Preserve** (☎ 941-695-4111), which sits above the northwest portion of Everglades National Park. The **Overseas Highway** to Key West is a beautiful drive. At the beginning, near Key Largo, is the **John Pennekamp Reef State Park**, ☎ (305) 242-7700. Boat rides to the **Dry Tortugas National Park**, 68 miles from Key West, are offered by Coral Reef Boat Rides. Reservations can be made at ☎ (305) 451-1621.

GREAT SMOKY MOUNTAINS NATIONAL PARK

This park is close to major population centers, but its lush greenery and pleasantly rounded peaks create a soothing aura of tranquillity. And, of course, there is the famous "smoke" that seems to perpetually hang over the land here.

❖ DID YOU KNOW?

The bluish haze above the mountains is the condensation of vapors from the thick vegetation. Even on the sunniest days you will probably see the haze that gives the park, and the Blue Ridge Mountains of which it is a part, its name.

Most of the park is at an altitude of 5,000-6,000 feet and there are about 20 peaks over 6,000 feet, making this one of the highest tracts of land in the east. The variety of plants and flowers that cover the mountains is extraordinary. Mountains without such cover are called, appropriately, balds.

THE SOUTH

FACTS & FIGURES

Location/Gateways/Getting There: The park's area is divided about evenly between Tennessee and North Carolina. It sits astride US 441 between Knoxville, Tennessee and Asheville, North Carolina. Knoxville is the larger of the two cities and, therefore, the best gateway. The southern terminus of the Blue Ridge Parkway at Cherokee runs directly into the south entrance of the park.

Year Established: The park opened in 1926, but was not officially dedicated until 14 years later. It took that long to buy up all of the land, which previously had been in private hands.

❖ TIP

Even today there are clusters of private land within the park. Please respect such private property if you come upon it.

Size: 520,269 acres (813 square miles).

Admission Fee: There is no entrance fee.

Climate/When to Go: The weather is delightful in spring and fall and even summer is not uncomfortable because of the elevation. Although the park is open all year, winter can be quite cold and many facilities are not available during the period from November through April.

Contact Information: Superintendent, Great Smoky Mountains National Park, 107 Park Headquarters Road, Gatlinburg, TN 37738. ☎ (423) 436-1200. For information on the Blue Ridge Parkway, contact: Blue Ridge Parkway Headquarters, 200 BB&T Bldg, 1 Pack Square, Asheville, NC 28801. ☎ (704) 298-0258.

AUTO TOUR / SHORT STOPS

The **Newfoundland Gap Road** (US 441) traverses the width of the park for 33 miles from Gatlinburg to Cherokee. There are also some 170 miles of other paved roads, some of which will bring you into areas of the park that should be seen in a comprehensive visit. The suggested route will begin at the northern entrance. If you are coming from the other direction, simply reverse the entire route.

At the park entrance look for the beginning of the **Roaring Fork Motor Nature Trail** (closed during winter). The unique one-way route covers six miles in an area that is particularly blessed with a variety of flora.

❖ DID YOU KNOW?

There are more than 1,500 different plant varieties within Great Smoky Mountains National Park.

Returning to the main road you will soon arrive at the **Sugarlands Visitor Center**, which has excellent exhibits about the park's history, animal and plant life, and the culture of the area.

Just beyond the center, turn off US 441 onto the **Little River Road**. This is the beginning of a 60-mile round-trip leading through the Cade's Cove section of the park, one of the most scenic areas. A one-way loop road at Cade's Cove passes through a recreated 19th-century agricultural community. A visitor center here is devoted to the surrounding historical village.

Returning to the main road we are now finally ready to embark on the first half of the Newfoundland Gap Road. There are frequent overlooks as the road climbs to its high point and you should definitely stop to take a better look at the **Chimney Tops** and **Mount Le Conte** pullouts. Soon you will arrive at Newfoundland Gap itself, the halfway point of the road and the border between Tennessee and North Carolina. This route is seven miles each way and has several scenic pullouts along the way. It ends just a half-mile short of **Clingman's Dome** (see next section for trail description).

> ### ❖ DID YOU KNOW?
>
> *At 6,643 feet, Clingman's Dome is the highest point in the park and in the state of Tennessee.*

Now you can head back to the main highway and continue on, negotiating some gentle switchbacks as you descend to the **Oconaluftee Visitor Center** at the southern end of the park. The **Pioneer Farmstead**, a living museum, is of interest here.

The route just described covers almost 120 miles. Great Smoky's proximity to major population centers makes it the most heavily visited facility in the National Park System. The resulting traffic, along with many turns, means that you should allocate six to seven hours for the Auto Tour, including the mentioned stops.

GETTING OUT/LONGER STOPS

❖ HIKES

There are hundreds of miles of trails in the park, virtually all of which are back-country hiking trails. There are two shorter trails for the more casual hiker.

The first is on the nature motor loop mentioned above. A trail leads to the very attractive **Grotto Falls**, and takes about 40 minutes.

The second one is a must. This half-mile trail is reached via a seven-mile spur road from Newfoundland Gap and leads to the **observation tower** at the top of Clingman's Dome. The view from atop the tower is the best of any in the park. Plus, you will be able to tell your friends that you literally climbed to the top of the Smokies! Allow one hour for the complete trip, which isn't that long but is steep in places. Several other trails of varying lengths also begin from Clingman's Gap.

The park has dozens of picturesque waterfalls. Several can be reached via longer trails. A 2½-mile round-trip begins on the Lit-

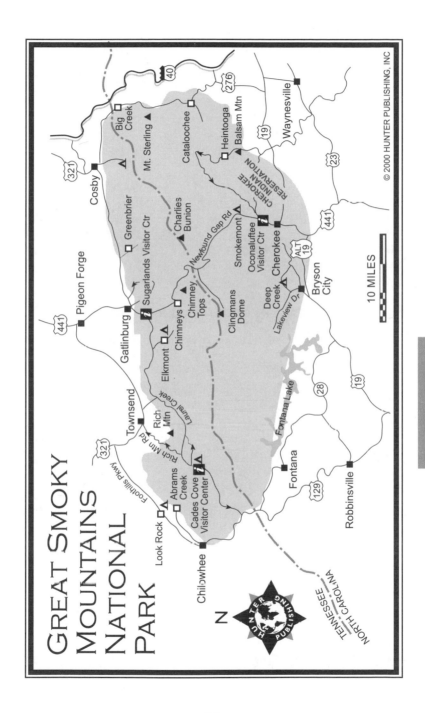

GREAT SMOKY MOUNTAINS NATIONAL PARK

© 2000 HUNTER PUBLISHING, INC

THE SOUTH

10 MILES

tle River Road about four miles west of the Sugarlands Visitor Center and takes you to **Laurel Falls**. A longer trail (five miles round-trip) begins at Cade's Cove and leads to **Abrams Falls**. Neither one is particularly difficult, but you should allow at least two hours because of their length.

SPECIAL ACTIVITIES

The previously mentioned Cade's Cove and Pioneer Farmstead have frequent craft demonstrations and other activities. Also, for those who want to take a break from driving, tours of the park are available from Gatlinburg from **Smoky Mountain Tour Connection**, ☎ (423) 436-2108. These trips (from $35) will not cover as much ground as you would on your own, but the informed commentary is interesting.

> ### ❖ TIP
>
> *Keep in mind that if you will be continuing your trip in the opposite direction south from Gatlinburg, you will have to drive through the park on your own in any event.*

Park Rangers conduct an extensive program of guided walks of varying lengths and difficulty. You can read about them in the seasonally published park newspaper, available at park visitor centers. Schedules are also posted.

There are other means of getting around portions of the park besides driving a car. **Bicycling** is especially popular on the Cade's Cove Loop Road. **Horseback riding** is an excellent way of exploring the park's interior from spring through fall. Rentals are available at several concession facilities, including Cade's Cove and Sugarlands. Expect to pay between $15 and $20 an hour. **Hayrides** and **buggy rides**, including some that are guided by park rangers, can be taken along the Cade's Cove Loop Road. The cost is $8 for adults. ☎ (423) 448-6286 for horseback and other rides.

ACCOMMODATIONS

❖ HOTELS & MOTELS

INSIDE THE PARK

LE CONTE LODGE ($), ☎ (423) 429-5704, which is the only hostelry inside the park, sits atop Mount LeConte. It can be reached from the nearest road only after a fairly difficult five-mile hike. And it barely meets the standards for inclusion in this book. If you're hiking and backpacking and want an interesting change from camping out, LeConte Lodge might well suit your interests.

NEARBY COMMUNITIES

BEST WESTERN GREAT SMOKIES INN ($$), located at the junction of US 441 and Acquoni Road, Cherokee, NC (about three miles south of the southern entrance of the national park). ☎ (828) 497-2020 or (800) 528-1234. 152 rooms. Typical modern roadside motel set in front of a tree-covered mountainside. Comfortable accommodations. Restaurant on the premises.

BROOKSIDE RESORT ($$-$$$), 463 E. Parkway, Gatlinburg, TN; three blocks east of the center of town on US 321 and just north of the park entrance. ☎ (423) 436-0039 or (800) 251-9597. 216 rooms. Very attractive complex of motel units and cottages. Swimming pool and recreational facilities. Nice streamside location. Restaurants within walking distance.

CRAIG'S MOTEL ($-$$), US 19, Cherokee, NC; three miles from the park's southern entrance. ☎ (828) 497-3821 or (800) 360-6869. 30 rooms. Basic motel lodging. Clean and comfortable and a fairly good value for such a popular tourist area. Restaurant adjacent.

MIDTOWN LODGE ($$-$$$), 805 Parkway, Gatlinburg, TN; just north of the park entrance. ☎ (423) 430-3602 or (800) 633-2446. Rate includes continental breakfast. 133 rooms. Convenient to many restaurants (one is opposite) and shopping as well as access to the park. Slightly better than average rooms.

THE SOUTH

ROCKY TOP VILLAGE ($$), 311 Airport Road, Gatlinburg, TN; off the main highway leading to the park. ☎ (423) 436-7826 or (800) 553-7738. 89 rooms. Attractive facility in quiet location away from hustle and bustle of The Strip leading through Gatlinburg. Clean and comfortable rooms, each with refrigerator. Several cottage units available. Restaurant is adjacent.

❖ CAMPING

National Park Reservation Service (NPRS) for Cade's Cove, Elkmont and Smokemont camps only. All others on first-come, first-served basis. Contact the **NPRS**, ☎ (800) 365-2267. The offices are open daily from 10 am to 10 pm, eastern time. You can write in for reservations at PO Box 1600, Cumberland, MD 21502. Or, you can reserve online at http://reservations.nps.gov.

CAMPGROUNDS AT A GLANCE			
NAME	LOCATION	SITES	COST
Abrams Creek	On the park perimeter.	16	$10 per day
Balsam Mtn.	On the park perimeter.	46	$12 per day
Big Creek	On the park perimeter.	12	$10 per day
Cade's Cove	On road to Cade's Cove.	161	$15 per day
Cataloochee	On the park perimeter.	27	$10 per day
Cosby	On the park perimeter.	175	$12 per day
Deep Creek	On the park perimeter.	108	$12 per day
Elkmont	On road to Cade's Cove.	220	$15 per day
Loon Rock	On the park perimeter.	92	$12 per day
Smokemont	Off the Newfound Gap Road, the park's only through-route.	140	$15 per day

There is a seven-day limit at all sites. RVs allowed at all campgrounds except for Big Creek.

DINING

INSIDE THE PARK

Snack bars and light meals can be found at two of the park's more developed areas – Sugarlands, near the visitor center and north entrance station; and at Cade's Cove. (Both $.)

NEARBY COMMUNITIES

HEIDELBERG RESTAURANT ($$-$$$), 148 N. Parkway, Gatlinburg, TN; on the main highway on the north side of town. ☎ (423) 430-3094. Excellent selection of German and Swiss cuisine with a smattering of American fare for those who find Teutonic cooking a bit too heavy. Listen to authentic German music while having your schnitzel or sauerbraten.

PARK GRILL ($$-$$$), 1100 Parkway, Gatlinburg, TN; located at the entrance to the national park. ☎ (423) 436-2300. American food. Good variety of dishes, specializing in locally caught trout and steak. Some vegetarian items. Pleasant atmosphere and service.

WHERE DO WE GO FROM HERE?

The logical extensions to this park are the **Blue Ridge Parkway** and **Shenandoah**, both a part of *Suggested Trip 1*. But if you want a shorter vacation, the many attractions in the park and nearby at Gatlinburg and Asheville can provide a compact but enjoyable trip.

THE SOUTH

MAMMOTH CAVE NATIONAL PARK

This is probably the largest system of caves in the world, but not even scientists are sure about that because not all of it has been explored yet. There are over 300 miles of mapped passageways on five different levels, which does make it the largest known cave. It is estimated that there are at least another 50 miles of unexplored passageways.

The cave and its colorful formations are the result of water seeping through the limestone rock above. While there are some caverns whose formations might be more delicate or beautiful than at Mammoth, no other cave can offer the sheer variety of sights displayed here. Its size alone is awesome; some rooms are so big and high that you will barely feel that you are inside a cave at all. Although evidence of human habitation in the cave goes back 4,000 years, white settlers discovered it only in 1798.

The Onyx Owl in Mammoth Cave.

❖ **DID YOU KNOW?**

Huge deposits of saltpeter found in Mammoth provided over 200 tons of gunpowder, primarily during the War of 1812.

A fascinating world in itself, Mammoth Cave and the attractive surrounding areas that have been set aside as national park lands are certainly ingredients for a trip to remember.

FACTS & FIGURES

Location/Gateways/Getting There: Not far from Blue Grass Country, Mammoth Cave is conveniently located off I-65 via SR 70 in southcentral Kentucky. Use the Cave City exit. It is just northeast of the larger town of Bowling Green. The major gateways are Nashville, approximately 1½ hours south via I-65, and Louisville, about 1¾ hours north, also by I-65.

Year Established: Though the cave's existence has been known for centuries, it became a national park in 1926.

Size: 52,390 acres (82 square miles).

Admission Fee: Although there is no fee levied on admission to the park, all cave tours are on a fee basis. Further information is presented in the *Special Activities* section.

Climate/When to Go: The park is open year-round and the cave itself has a constant temperature of 54°F, so a sweater or jacket is prudent at all times. This area of Kentucky is hot and humid in summer and fairly brisk in winter. The fall and spring are delightful, and the fall foliage, though not on the level of New England's famous colors, is quite beautiful.

THE SOUTH

NOTE: *Most park activities are available from April through October, so those are the best times for a visit.*

Contact Information: Superintendent, Mammoth Cave National Park, Mammoth Cave, KY 42259. ☎ (502) 758-2251 for general information. For cave information, ☎ (502) 758 2328.

TOURING

There are only a few miles of paved roads in the park and, although they traverse pleasant forests amid hilly, rugged terrain, there are no points of special interest along them. Similarly, the park is not geared toward the casual outdoor stroll. Across the Green River, a tributary of the Ohio River that cuts through 24 miles of the park, the road soon ends and there are miles and miles of trails through the picturesque bluffs of Kentucky's countryside. These trails are long and unimproved, attracting overnight hikers and wildlife enthusiasts. The cave is definitely the thing to see here, so we'll get on to that right now.

SPECIAL ACTIVITIES

The major activity in the park is taking one or more of the several ranger-conducted tours of the cave. These last from just over an hour to more than five hours. No self-guided options are available. Tour prices range from about $5 to $35, depending upon the length of the tour. Seniors holding Golden Age passports are admitted for half-price.

> ❖ **TIP**
>
> *It is wise to consider taking more than one tour, since they generally visit different areas of the cave. It is also advisable to make reservations in advance as many tours will be sold out if you wait until your arrival at the park. Reservations can be made up to three months in advance by calling ☎ (800) 967-2283.*

The 1¼-hour **Frozen Niagara Tour** covers about one mile and requires little effort on the part of visitors. It passes many of the cave's most famous and beautiful formations, including the one that gives this particular tour its name.

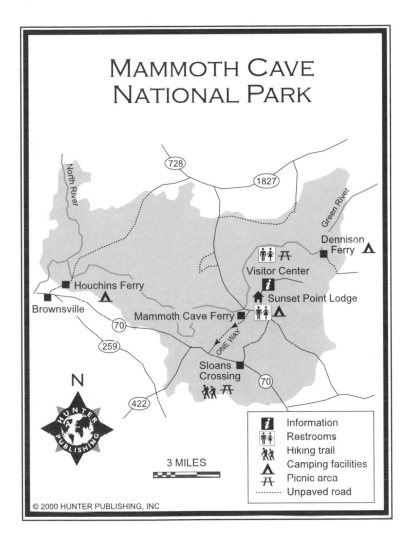

> ### ❖ TIP
>
> *This is a good introduction to the cave, but don't let it be your only venture underground, for the Frozen Niagara does not give you a real sense of how vast the subterranean rooms can be.*

The **Travertine Tour** is an even shorter version of the Frozen Niagara, and is especially well suited for the elderly and physically challenged. (There are also special tours for the disabled. Inquire at the visitor center.)

The **Historical Tour** takes about two hours and covers two miles. It, too, is not very strenuous, although there are a few parts that might be difficult if you are of very large build.

To really experience Mammoth Cave, you should take the **Scenic Tour** (sometimes called the Half-Day Tour). It lasts more than five hours and takes you through four miles of passages. There are several long climbs and descents but, unless you are disabled or really out of shape, the pace is not too strenuous. This tour makes a stop for lunch in a section of the cave known as the Snowball Dining Room.

> ### ❖ TIP
>
> *The Scenic Tour includes a large part of the Frozen Niagara Tour, so you need only take the Scenic and Historic tours to see the cave adequately. These two do not cover any of the same territory.*

Real caving enthusiasts can take one of several more difficult lantern tours through primitive portions of the cave system. The park's visitor center has interesting exhibits and will also provide you with information on tour departure points. Reservations can be made here as well.

An often overlooked but worthwhile attraction in the park is the hour-long cruise along the **Green River** aboard the *Miss Green River II*, which gives visitors a good idea of the terrain and countryside surrounding the cave. Trips leave from the boat dock adjacent to the cable ferry. Tickets must be purchased in advance at the visitor center, which is only a few miles from the dock. Trips depart daily from May through October. There are four to seven departures each day, with the higher number occurring during the peak summer months. The adult fare is $4.

ACCOMMODATIONS

❖ HOTELS & MOTELS

INSIDE THE PARK

MAMMOTH CAVE HOTEL ($$) is in the park headquarters area. ☎ (502) 758-2225. 110 rooms. A variety of lodging is available, ranging from rustic cabins (about a third of the units) to more modern motor inn-style accommodations. Attractive, tree-shaded grounds. Some recreational facilities, including tennis courts. Restaurant on premises.

NEARBY COMMUNITIES

HOLIDAY INN EXPRESS ($$), 102 Happy Valley Road, Cave City; off Exit 63 of I-65, about nine miles from the national park. ☎ (502) 773-3100 or (800) HOLIDAY. Rate includes continental breakfast. 105 rooms. Good-sized rooms furnished in a modern but rather undistinguished style. Nice public areas. Swimming pool. Several restaurants within a short distance.

SUPER 8 MOTEL ($$), 799 Mammoth Cave Road, Cave City; a half-mile east of I-65, Exit 63, and about 10 miles from the park. ☎ (502) 773-2500 or (800) 800-8000. Rate includes continental breakfast. 51 rooms. Nice, well-kept units in a two-year-old inn. Swimming pool and Jacuzzi. Only five minutes to park. Restaurants nearby.

❖ CAMPING

There is a 14-day limit at both areas. The Headquarters site allows RVs, while Houchins does not. Book through the main park telephone number.

CAMPGROUNDS AT A GLANCE			
NAME	LOCATION	SITES	COST
Headquarters Campground	Near the visitor center	111	$10 per day
Houchins Ferry Campground	2 miles east of Brownsville off State Highway 70	12	$5 per day

DINING

Since many of the cave tours are rather long you might well feel some hunger pangs while underground.

INSIDE THE PARK

MAMMOTH CAVE HOTEL DINING ROOM ($$), Mammoth Cave Hotel. See listing above. ☎ (502) 758-2225. American food. Attractive room with a good selection of dishes served in a professional and friendly manner.

The SNOWBALL DINING ROOM ($), inside the cave, has simple box lunches and sandwiches which, while definitely not gourmet, will keep your energy levels up during your cave visit.

NEARBY COMMUNITIES

HICKORY VILLA RESTAURANT ($-$$), 806 Sanders Lane, Cave City; located a half-mile from I-65, Exit 53. ☎ (502) 773-3033. American food. A friendly and casual place that's popular with locals. Their specialty is barbecued ribs and chicken, but you'll also find some steak dishes as well.

SAHARA STEAKHOUSE ($$-$$$), 413 E. Happy Valley Street, Cave City; just east of downtown. ☎ (502) 773-3450. American food. Delicious, well-prepared steaks as well as a decent selection of seafood. Good salad bar. Comfortable surroundings and attentive service.

WHERE DO WE GO FROM HERE?

As an extension to *Suggested Trip 1*, Mammoth Cave is relatively far from other parks in this book. But it is close to the scenic attractions of the Kentucky **Bluegrass country** as well as the rugged **Appalachian region** of eastern Kentucky.

SHENANDOAH NATIONAL PARK

Stretching 80 miles along one of the highest sections of the famous Blue Ridge, Shenandoah National Park offers some of the most beautiful scenery east of the Mississippi. The park's elevation varies from 600 feet at the northern end to 4,050 feet at Hawksbill in the south. The main feature of the park is the **Skyline Drive**, which hugs the crest of the ridge. To the west are views of the rolling Shenandoah Valley, while to the east are panoramas of fertile farmland far below the crest. The park is long and fairly narrow. Once you leave the crest, it becomes heavily wooded with a great variety of tree species and the wildflowers abundant practically all year, especially from spring through fall.

THE SOUTH

FACTS & FIGURES

Location/Gateways/Getting There: In northwestern Virginia, the northern entrance to the park is at Front Royal, a distance of only 60 miles from metropolitan Washington via I-66. The southern end of the park is at Waynesboro, 90 miles from Richmond via I-64.

Year Established: The park was established in 1926, although it had been well explored from late Colonial times.

Size: 195,072 acres (305 square miles).

Admission Fee: $10.

Climate/When to Go: The park is open all year and the weather is good for touring during much of that time. However, many of the facilities are closed from November through March, so it is best not to go during the heart of winter. Summer is not very hot because of the high altitude. The only negative in summer is that the park can be crowded.

Contact Information: Superintendent, Shenandoah National Park, Route 4, Box 348, Luray, VA 22835. ☎ (703) 999-2266.

AUTO TOUR/SHORT STOPS

Shenandoah is one of our national parks that can be seen almost entirely by car. **Skyline Drive** runs from one end of the long and narrow park to the other, a road distance of some 105 miles. The highest elevation along the road is 3,680 feet and there are 66 scenic overlooks, more than enough to satisfy even the most avid devotee of nature's beauty. We'll describe the route's highlights from north to south, not mentioning all of the overlooks, only those that are especially worthwhile.

> NOTE: *Points of interest along the Skyline Drive are well marked by numbered mileposts measured from the northern entrance at Front Royal. These numbers are indicated below for your convenience.*

Early along your drive, the **Shenandoah Valley** (Milepost 2.8) and **Signal Knob Overlooks** are certainly worth a stop. The road climbs gently in the beginning until it levels out and remains at about 3,000 feet. There are no steep grades or severe switchbacks on the Skyline Drive. Between the first two vistas you will

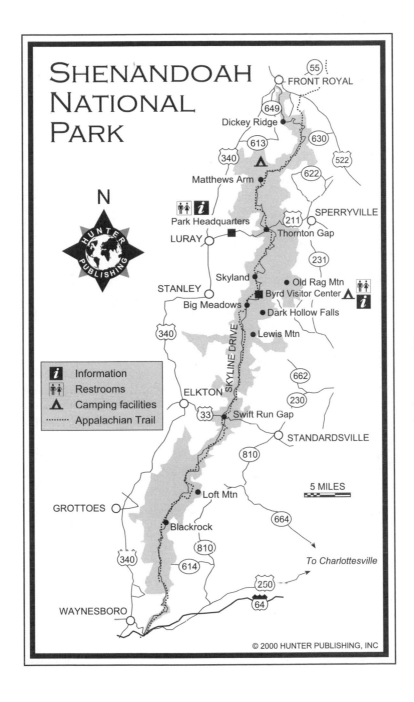

come to the **Dickey Ridge Visitor Center** (4.6), where you can obtain information on the park. Right after that there is the lovely, though unfortunately-named, **Hogback Overlook** (21), which offers views of the twisting Shenandoah River.

One of the main attractions of the Skyline Drive is its passage through **Mary's Rock Tunnel** (32.4), a distance of about 700 feet. An excellent overlook at the tunnel's south entrance provides a great view of the surrounding terrain.

Then comes the **Pinnacles Overlook** (36.7), followed by **Crescent Rock** (44.4), which affords the best view of **Hawksbill**, Shenandoah Park's highest peak. Soon after this you reach the **Harry Byrd Visitor Center** (51.2), where various exhibits document both the history of the park and the culture of the surrounding area.

South of the visitor center are two more grand vistas, at **Rockytop** (78.2) and **Big Run** (81.1). At that point you reach the end of the Skyline Drive and the park's exit.

Allow 3-3½ hours for traversing the Skyline Drive with stops at the viewpoints.

GETTING OUT/LONGER STOPS

❖ HIKING

> **❖ TIP**
>
> *Remember that all of the trails lead down from the narrow crest on which the road lies. As a result, every one requires a strenuous return climb.*

There are ample opportunities to hike on one of the trails that begin along the Skyline Drive. Among the best trails are:

Little Stoney Man (39.1), a 1½-mile round-trip offering some of the best views of the valley from anywhere in the park. Allow 90 minutes to two hours for this trail.

The **Whiteoak Canyon Trail** (42.6) leads to the first of six beautiful falls ranging from 35 to 86 feet in height. It is a half-day, five-mile trek.

Also at Mile 42.6 is a trail leading to the summit of **Hawksbill**. This is two miles, round-trip, and takes less than two hours to complete.

The **Dark Hollow Falls Trail** (50.9) leads to a beautiful 70-foot-high waterfall by that name. The 1½-mile trail can be accomplished in under 90 minutes.

Guides and maps to all of the trails can be found at the visitor centers. Several nature trails at Dickey Ridge, Matthew's Arm, Skyland, Big Meadow and Loft Mountain do not descend beneath the crest. Finally, almost 100 miles of the **Appalachian Trail** traverses the park. Access to it is easy from many of the parking areas along Skyline Drive.

SPECIAL ACTIVITIES

Horseback riding is available by the hour or as half-day trips at the **Skylands Stables** (Mile 41.7). Guided trail rides of 1 or 2½ hours are also available. Reservations can be made in person at the Skyland Lodge or by calling, ☎ (540) 999-2210.

ACCOMMODATIONS

❖ HOTELS & MOTELS

INSIDE THE PARK

All accommodations within the park are through **Aramark Sky-Line Company**, ☎ (800) 999-4714. The local number for all of their properties is (540) 743-5108 or (540) 999-3500. Open season is roughly from April through October, although it does vary slightly from property to property. Skyline Drive mileage markers are measured from the north entrance at Front Royal.

THE SOUTH

BIG MEADOWS LODGE ($$-$$$), Mile 51.3. 91 rooms. Accommodations are either in the historic main lodge, individual rustic cabins or suite lodges, all constructed of native chestnut trees and stone. Attractive and comfortable. Restaurant on premises.

LEWIS MOUNTAIN CABINS ($-$$), Mile 57.5. 20 rooms. Simple cabins with outdoor cooking facilities. Offers a basic vacation experience but not quite at the "roughing it" level. About a 10-minute drive to restaurants. General store on premises.

SKYLAND LODGE ($$-$$$), Mile 41.7. 177 rooms. Dating back to the 1890s, Skyland sits at 3,680 feet – the highest point on Skyline Drive – and affords magnificent views. Fully modernized, the lodge has a varied selection of rooms, cabins and suites. Recreational activities are offered and there's a restaurant on premises.

NEARBY COMMUNITIES

BEST WESTERN IN TOWN ($), 410 W. Main Street, Luray; located on US 211, about 10 miles west of the Thorntan Gap entrance to the park (Mile 31.5 of Skyline Drive). ☎ (540) 743-6511 or ☎ (800) 526-0942. 40 rooms. Fair-size rooms that are clean, comfortable and nicely furnished. Quiet location. Swimming pool. Restaurant on the premises.

INN AT AFTON ($$), US 250 and I-64 at the junction of Skyline Drive, Waynesboro; located off I-64, Exit 99, near the south entrance of Shenandoah. ☎ (540) 942-5201 or (800) 860-8559. 118 rooms. Attractive facility in a nice setting between the national park and the beginning of the Blue Ridge Parkway. The comfortable rooms are nicely kept. Friendly staff will make you feel at home. Swimming pool. Restaurant.

QUALITY INN ($$), 10 Commerce Avenue, Front Royal; at end of Main Street off US 522, near north entrance to the park. ☎ (540) 635-3161 or (800) 821-4488. 107 rooms. Better-than-average accommodations at a reasonable price. Swimming pool. The on-site restaurant might be among the best places to eat in Front Royal, a town definitely not known for its culinary delights.

❖ CAMPING

Reservations for Big Meadows can be made through the **National Park Reservation Service**, ☎ (800) 365-2267. Their offices are open daily from 10 am to 10 pm, eastern time. You can write in for reservations at PO Box 1600, Cumberland, MD 21502. Or, you can reserve online at www.reservations.nps. gov. All other campgrounds operate on a first-come, first-served basis. There is a 14-day maximum stay at all sites. RVs allowed, but no hookups.

CAMPGROUNDS AT A GLANCE			
NAME	LOCATION	SITES	COST
Matthews Arm	Mile 22.1	179	$14 per day
Big Meadows	Mile 51.3	217	$17 per day
Lewis Mountain	Mile 57.5	32	$14 per day
Loft Mountain	Mile 79.5	219	$14 per day

DINING

INSIDE THE PARK

In addition to full-service restaurants at **Skyland** and **Big Meadows**, Aramark also operates the **Panorama Restaurant** (Mile 31.5) and "**Waysides**," which offers lunch counters and snack bars at **Elkwallow** (Mile 24.1), **Big Meadows**, **Lewis Mountain** and **Loft Mountain** (Mile 79.5). Prices are $$ for the restaurants and $ at the wayside facilities.

> ❖ **TIP**
>
> *Any of the regular restaurants will prepare box lunches to go on request.*

NEARBY COMMUNITIES

PARKHURST RESTAURANT ($$), 2547 US 211, Luray; two miles west of the center of town. ☎ (540) 743-6009. American food. Good selection of steaks, seafood and fowl. Pleasant views. Attentive service and nice family atmosphere.

WHERE DO WE GO FROM HERE?

Suggested Trip 1 features Shenandoah National Park and continues with the Blue Ridge Parkway, which begins where the Skyline Drive ends. However, if that trip is not to your liking, the scenic **eastern highlands** of West Virginia are nearby. **Luray Caverns**, ☎ (540) 743-6551, is but a few miles west of the park and should be seen as part of any visit to Shenandoah.

The Midwest

Badlands National Park

Spanning 80 million years of geologic history, the biggest area of badlands in the nation is an outstanding example of erosion and weathering. The fossil-rich area is both awe-inspiring in its beauty and, at the same time, dark and forbidding, despite traces of color in a mostly grayish white and barren landscape. Deep ravines and highly jagged ridges dot the terrain, and there is much to see in this unusual area. Although the land appears inhospitable, the Badlands provide a home to an unexpected diversity of animals and plants. Fortunately, despite the impression of impenetrable natural barriers that one might get from its name, Badlands National Park is not difficult to see.

Facts & Figures

Location/Gateways/Getting There: In the southwestern portion of South Dakota, east of the famous Black Hills region, Badlands National Park is accessible via the Badlands Loop Road (SR 240) from exits 110 (Wall) and 131 (Cactus Flat) of I-90. It is just over an hour's drive on the interstate from Rapid City, the nearest city with regular air service. Sioux Falls is about six hours to the east, also via I-90.

Year Established: First opened as a national monument in 1929, the area was redesignated as a national park in 1978.

Size: 243,302 acres (380 square miles).

Admission Fee: $5.

Climate/When to Go: The park is open all year, but winters are cold and there is a lot of snow. Summers tend to be hot but dry; hence, they are not so bad that they make a visit at this time unpleasant. There are frequent afternoon thunderstorms, some of which can be quite severe. Although summer is a good time to visit, fall and spring are even better; the weather is very comfortable during these times and the roads are not as crowded.

Contact Information: Superintendent, Badlands National Park, PO Box 6, Interior, SD 57750. ☎ (605) 433-5361.

AUTO TOUR/SHORT STOP

Most of the park's major attractions are readily accessible via the **Badlands Loop**. This road is about 27 miles long and covers all but the park's isolated South Unit. You can choose either an east-west or west-east routing for your journey. For this discussion, we assume that you'll begin from the Cactus Flat (or northeast) entrance of the park. The road through the central section of the park is winding and hilly, but not difficult to negotiate. Only in the beginning, where it rises from the relatively flat plain up to the rim drive, does it have steep grades and switchbacks. Each turn and dip brings with it new and exciting vistas. At the western end, the road drops back to the level of the surrounding area, but not as sharply as at the eastern end.

Along the Loop Road there are 13 overlooks, spaced more closely together in the generally more scenic eastern half of the park. You will probably want to stop at each one as they all provide clear views of typical Badlands formations and are only a few feet from your car. In addition to these overlooks, there are some other attractions that you should not miss.

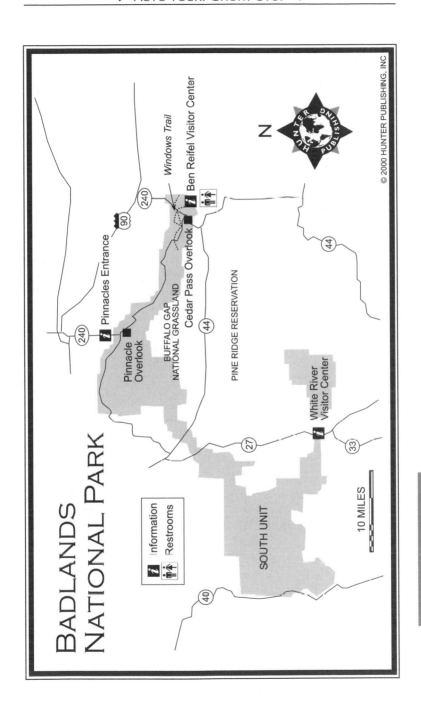

BADLANDS NATIONAL PARK

Information
Restrooms

N

© 2000 HUNTER PUBLISHING, INC

Pinnacles Entrance

Windows Trail
Ben Reifel Visitor Center

Cedar Pass Overlook

BUFFALO GAP
NATIONAL GRASSLAND

Pinnacle
Overlook

PINE RIDGE RESERVATION

White River
Visitor Center

SOUTH UNIT

10 MILES

THE MIDWEST

57

The **Cedar Pass Visitor Center**, reached after a thrilling drop in the road coming from the east, provides excellent information about the park's history and geology. A bit farther on is the **Fossil Exhibit Trail**, only a quarter-mile long and containing replicas of fossil remains that have been found throughout Badlands. It also has excellent views of distant Badland formations. Allow three hours for the Loop Road.

GETTING OUT/LONGER STOPS

❖ HIKING

Shortly after entering the eastern end of the park is the **Door Trail**, a popular and easy three-quarter-mile hike that leads to an opening (the door) in the rocky hill-like formation. Through the door is a magnificent view of the Badlands, possibly the best in the entire park. Allow about 90 minutes for the round-trip.

The **Notch Trail** comes soon after the Door Trail. This 1½-mile trail is much more difficult and involves climbing a ladder at one point. Be forewarned that this trail is not for everybody. If you do attempt this trail, it will take approximately two hours to complete.

SPECIAL ACTIVITIES

Although the vast majority of visitors to the Badlands restrict themselves to the main Loop Road and its accompanying trails, the South Unit of the park also has some fantastic Badlands formations. To reach the South Unit, exit from the Loop near its western terminus at Sage Creek. Follow this road to the small town of Scenic and then up to **Sheep Mountain Table** for an excellent overall panorama of the Badlands. This is the highest point in the park that is accessible by car.

> NOTE: *This graded road may be too difficult for drivers not accustomed to mountain driving. Also, it may be impassable in bad weather, no matter how much experience you have.*

One additional item of interest, and one that all can partake of, is the prairie dog town in the extreme western portion of the park's main unit. It's located five miles west of the junction of the Park Loop Road and the Pinnacles entrance road. If you are lucky, you might just catch a glimpse of one of these shy creatures as they scamper to or from their underground homes.

ACCOMMODATIONS

❖ HOTELS & MOTELS

INSIDE THE PARK

CEDAR PASS LODGE ($), 1 Cedar Street, at the park visitor center (SR 240), south of I-90, Exit 131. ☎ (605) 433-5460. 24 rooms. Closed during the winter. The comfortable individual cabins aren't great, but are a real bargain. The lodge sits on historic property operated by the Oglala Sioux tribe.

NEARBY COMMUNITIES

BADLANDS BUDGET HOST MOTEL ($), junction of SRs 44 and 377, two miles south of Badlands National Park. ☎ (605) 433-5335 or (800) BUD HOST. 17 rooms. Very basic accommodations that even the thriftiest traveler can afford. One shortcoming is that decent eating places are a fair distance away.

BEST WESTERN PLAINS MOTEL ($$), 712 Glen Street, Wall, off I-90, Exit 110. ☎ (605) 279-2145 or (800) 528-1234. 74 rooms. Closed during the winter. Simple motel-style facility with clean and comfortable rooms. Several restaurants are nearby.

SANDS MOTOR INN ($$), 804 Glen Street, Wall; off I-90, Exit 110. ☎ (605) 279-2121 or (800) 341-8000. 49 rooms. Closed during the winter. Cozy, attractively furnished rooms that are a little on the smallish side. Restaurants nearby.

❖ CAMPING

Reservations are not accepted at any of the following. There's a 14-day maximum stay at both grounds. RVs are allowed.

CAMPGROUNDS AT A GLANCE			
NAME	LOCATION	SITES	COST
Cedar Pass	State Highway 240, near the visitor center.	96	$8 per day
Sage Creek	State Highway 590, 11 miles west of the Pinnacles entrance station.	30	$8 per day

DINING

INSIDE THE PARK

The CEDAR PASS DINING ROOM ($-$$) is inside the Cedar Pass Lodge. See listing above. ☎ (605) 433-5460. American food. A casual and friendly little place with basic homestyle cooking served in generous portions. Overlooks the beautiful Badlands.

NEARBY COMMUNITIES

ELKTON HOUSE RESTAURANT ($-$$), South Boulevard, Wall; just off I-90 at Exit 110. ☎ (605) 279-2152. American food. A nice family-style restaurant with a good selection of entrées (including prime quality steaks) and an extensive salad bar.

WALL DRUG CAFÉ ($), 510 Main Street, Wall; off I-90, Exit 109. ☎ (605) 279-2175. American food, cafeteria-style. Good burgers and sandwiches. Famous throughout the world, not for its food, but for the crazy surroundings of Wall Drug, which include mechanical figures, bizzare stuffed animals and more. It's an experience!

WHERE DO WE GO FROM HERE?

Suggested Trip 2 in the last section of the book incorporates the Badlands National Park. If you are unable to do that entire trip, the proximity of the park to the beautiful **Black Hills** (including Mount Rushmore) makes a good, relatively short sidetrip. If you fly into either Sioux Falls or Denver, then your trip will involve much more driving with sightseeing possibilities available en route.

DEVILS TOWER NATIONAL MONUMENT

L ong before it gained additional notoriety from the motion picture *Close Encounters of the Third Kind,* Devils Tower was one of the most recognizable landmarks, not only in Wyoming, but in the entire country. It is not difficult to understand why. Rising 867 feet (1,267 feet above the Belle Fourche River), this gigantic monolith is visible, on clear days, from as far as 100 miles away! Other statistics are equally staggering. The tower is estimated to be 50 million years old. At its bottom it is almost 1,000 feet across, but it narrows as it rises so that at the very top it measures only 275 feet across.

Although many people climb it (we're told that it is much easier than it looks), you won't be doing so as a casual visitor.

> ❖ **DID YOU KNOW?**
>
> *Wondering what's on top (besides a view of the surrounding plain and the distant Black Hills)? The plateau atop the tower is covered with grass and sagebrush – something of an anticlimax.*

THE MIDWEST

The tower itself is quite beautiful, despite having been described most often as a gigantic stone tree stump (indeed, its many fluted columns do give that effect). It is certainly among the most unusual of the many geologic formations in the country.

FACTS & FIGURES

Location/Gateways/Getting There: In the northeastern corner of Wyoming, the tower is about 110 miles northwest of Rapid City, South Dakota via I-90 to Sundance, then by US 14 and SR 24. It is 300 miles from Billings, Montana via I-90 to Moorcroft, then US 14 and SR 24 again.

Year Established: The first ascent of the monolith was made in 1893. It became America's first national monument in 1906.

Size: 1,347 acres (two square miles), making it one of the smallest scenic attractions administered by the National Park Service.

Admission Fee: $8.

Climate/When to Go: This area has four distinct seasons. Although the monument is open all year, the best time to visit is during the summer, which is warm, generally dry and very sunny. These are the best conditions for seeing it from a distance as well as close up.

Contact Information: Superintendent, Devils Tower National Monument, PO Box 8, Devils Tower, WY 82714. ☎ (307) 467-5283.

TOURING

In an area this small, you will not be doing a lot of driving. One of the unusual things about Devils Tower is that you will see it as well before you arrive as once you are there. As you approach, the tower just keeps growing until you have to strain your neck to glimpse the top.

About a half-mile inside the entrance station you will come to a **prairie dog colony**, one of the largest of the few remaining in

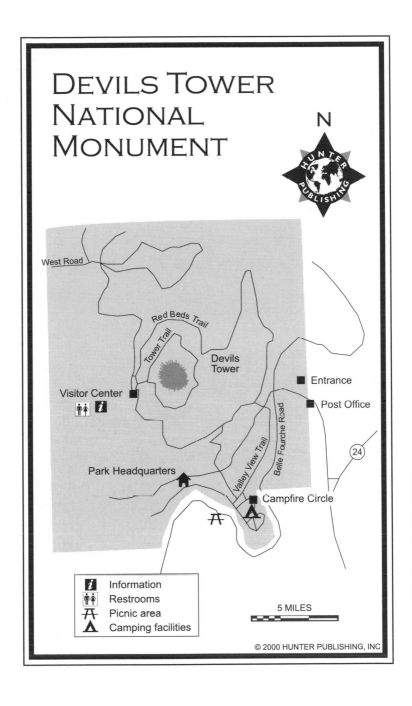

DEVILS TOWER
NATIONAL
MONUMENT

N

West Road

Red Beds Trail

Tower Trail

Devils
Tower

Visitor Center

Entrance

Post Office

Belle Fourche Road

Valley View Trail

24

Park Headquarters

Campfire Circle

i	Information
🚹🚺	Restrooms
🎋	Picnic area
⛺	Camping facilities

5 MILES

© 2000 HUNTER PUBLISHING, INC

THE MIDWEST

the country. These animals live in underground burrows, and you can see the entrances to their homes, which look almost like small volcanic cinder cones. It's likely that you will see quite a few of these cute, squirrel-like animals scampering about.

> NOTE: *Don't feed them or try to touch prairie dogs. They will generally run away, but will bite if cornered.*

Another 2½ miles along the road will bring you to the **visitor center**, where there are exhibits about pioneers as well as information on the history of Devils Tower. From here begins the **Tower Trail** that encircles this monumental rock. The mile-long route is resplendent with its many varieties of plants and flowers, but your eyes will constantly be drawn to the tower, which stands like a sentinel above you.

Your visit to Devils Tower should take under 2½ hours, with the walk around it included.

Devils Tower is visible from miles around.

SPECIAL ACTIVITIES

You should make every effort to attend an especially interesting Park Ranger talk here, one that demonstrates how to climb Devils Tower. The demos are given frequently, especially in summer, and yes, you can simply watch and not be forced to scale the giant beast!

ACCOMMODATIONS

There are no places to stay inside the monument.

❖ HOTELS & MOTELS

NEARBY COMMUNITIES

BEST WESTERN INN AT SUNDANCE ($-$$), 26 State Highway 585, Sundance, a half-mile north of I-90, Exit 187. ☎ (307) 283-2800 or (800) 238-0965. 40 rooms. Attractive and comfortable motel that's a good value. Facilities include sauna and whirlpool as well as heated indoor swimming pool. Restaurants nearby. About 30 miles from Devils Tower.

SUNDANCE INN ($$), 2719 E. Cleveland Avenue, Sundance; on I-90 business loop northwest of Exit 189. ☎ (307) 283-1100 or (888) 399-3639. 44 rooms. Only two years old, this inn is the newest in the vicinity of Devils Tower (also around 30 miles distant). All of the rooms are oversized and nicely decorated. Many have excellent views of the Black Hills. The inn has many recreational facilities and restaurants are within a short distance.

❖ CAMPING

The BELLE FOURCHE RIVER CAMPGROUND is open on a first-come, first-served basis. 50 sites. 14-day limit. $7 per day. RVs allowed. The campground is just inside the monument entrance. You can't miss it!

THE MIDWEST

DINING

There are no eating establishments within the monument's boundaries.

NEARBY COMMUNITIES

ARO RESTAURANT ($-$$), 205 Cleveland Avenue, Sundance; in town on I-90 business loop/US 14. ☎ (307) 283-2000. American food. Friendly, family-style restaurant with good food and ample portions at an attractive price. You won't find fancy dining in this area, so you might as well go for the best of the casual places and this is it.

WHERE DO WE GO FROM HERE?

Devils Tower is very close to the **Black Hills**. Therefore, consider *Suggested Trip 2*, described in the last section of the book. Also, the trip across Wyoming via US 14/16 to **Yellowstone** on the opposite side of the state is one of the most scenic rides in the nation. You may want to compose a trip that takes in the Black Hills and all of northern Wyoming as well. Some of the cities of southern Montana can serve as alternative gateways for such an adventure.

GRAND TETON
NATIONAL PARK

No matter how many national parks you have seen, Grand Teton will rank up there with the most beautiful. It simply offers some of the best mountain scenery anywhere in the world. It is quite different from most of the other mountain-dominated national parks in this country, such as Glacier,

Grand Teton offers some of the best mountain scenery in the States.

Mount Rainier or Rocky Mountain, featuring sharp, jagged peaks that resemble a bit of Switzerland in North America.

The highest mountain in the park is Grand Teton itself at 13,770 feet, but there are 10 other peaks that reach the impressive height of more than 11,000 feet. These mountains appear even larger than the numbers indicate because all rise abruptly from the otherwise flat terrain of the Jackson Hole Valley.

Grand Teton is much more than just mountains. With several major lakes, glaciers, forests and the beautiful valley of Jackson Hole, along with the famous Snake River, it is an outdoor enthusiast's playground and a delight to all who visit.

FACTS & FIGURES

Location/Gateways/Getting There: In northwestern Wyoming (almost immediately south of Yellowstone National Park), Grand Teton is accessible from the south via US 191/189, from the north by US 191/287/89 (the Rockefeller Parkway, which connects it with Yellowstone), and from the east by US 26/287.

67

THE MIDWEST

The town of Jackson is a few miles south of the park and is the hub for all activity in this area. There is air service into Jackson from a number of larger western cities, but the nearest major one is Salt Lake City. From there, I-15, US 26 and US 189 will take you to Grand Teton, a distance of about 300 miles on good roads that pass through scenic countryside.

Year Established: Grand Teton was photographed as early as 1872. It became a national park in 1929.

Size: 310,528 acres (485 square miles).

Admission Fee: $20 for a seven-day period that also entitles you to admission at Yellowstone.

Climate/When to Go: The park is open all year, but winter brings heavy snow and bitter cold. (There is good skiing at nearby resorts.) Summer is generally delightful. A light jacket or sweater is in order for the very cool mornings and evenings, even during the middle of the summer. Rain is rare during this time.

Contact Information: Superintendent, Grand Teton National Park, PO Drawer 170, Moose, WY 83012. ☎ (307) 739-3300.

AUTO TOUR/SHORT STOPS

As big as the Grand Teton peaks are, the best way to see the park is not by car. Other methods will be described below, but here is a brief discussion of what can be seen from your car and with a little walking. We describe attractions from south to north, as most arrive from the Jackson area.

Before actually entering Grand Teton, you should make a short side trip (16 miles, round-trip) to the **Gros Ventre Slide** area, following directional signs. Although technically within the confines of the Bridger-Teton National Forest, this attraction is more commonly associated with Grand Teton. In 1925 a water, mud and rock slide destroyed the town of Kelly. There is still visible evidence of the slide today on the mountain slope, where a section of the forested slope appears to be missing. Debris is scattered along the short trail that leads from the parking area.

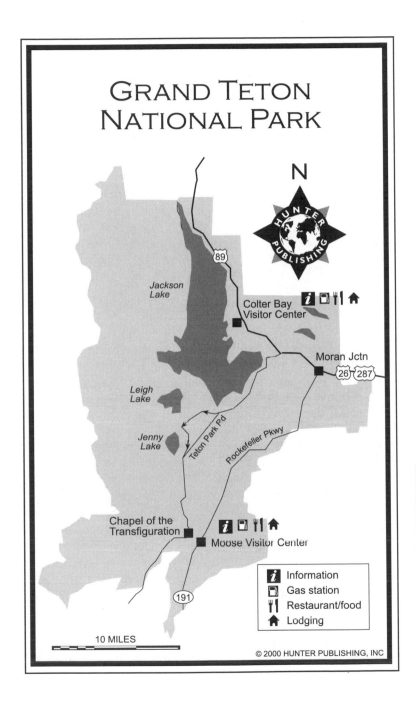

GRAND TETON NATIONAL PARK

N

Jackson Lake

Colter Bay Visitor Center

Moran Jctn

Leigh Lake

Jenny Lake

Teton Park Rd

Rockefeller Pkwy

Chapel of the Transfiguration

Moose Visitor Center

	Information
	Gas station
	Restaurant/food
	Lodging

10 MILES

© 2000 HUNTER PUBLISHING, INC

THE MIDWEST

Shortly after entering Grand Teton National Park itself you will reach the **Moose Visitor Center**, with exhibits on the park and information on the various activities available. Take the time to schedule some of the activities that will be described later on. From the center two roads head north – the **Teton Park Road**, which is nearer to the mountain range, and the **Rockefeller Parkway**, which more or less parallels the Snake River. The two link up at the Jackson Lake Lodge.

> ### ❖ TIP
>
> *While both roads afford truly magnificent views, with numerous turnouts where you can park your car and admire the mountains, the Teton Park Road is the more scenic.*

Both roads are very flat and easy to drive, since they run through the valley. Most likely you will be returning to the Jackson town site for some sightseeing there, so you may have the opportunity to drive both routes, as the distances are not great.

One of the most popular sights along the Teton Park Road is the **Chapel of the Transfiguration**. This small log structure was built in 1925 and has a large picture window behind the altar framing a breathtaking mountain view of God's country at its very best. The road passes numerous mountain and glacier views, and also goes by **Jenny** and **Jackson Lakes**. Finally, there is a five-mile unpaved spur road to the top of 7,730-foot **Signal Mountain**, which provides an unparalleled view of the entire Teton range, 40 miles long and 20 miles wide.

Driving time up and back in the park, including view stops, should be under four hours.

GETTING OUT/LONGER STOPS

Although the scenery from the car and turnouts is extraordinarily beautiful, the real opportunities for enjoying what Grand Teton has to offer are not from behind the driver's seat.

❖ MOUNTAIN CLIMBING

Mountain climbing is especially popular in Grand Teton. Many of the trails in the park lead up towards the peaks and take from two hours to a full day in walking or hiking time.

❖ BOAT TRIPS

At South Jenny Lake Junction take the boat launch to the west shore of Jenny Lake. Not only will you be in the middle of this beautiful lake and mountain setting but, once on the west side, you will find there is a relatively easy trail leading to **Hidden Falls**. As the trail winds through lush forest and rock coves at the base of precipitous peaks, you will hear the thunder of the falls grow louder, but you won't see the falls until you are practically on top of them. The round-trip walk is just over a half-hour. The Park Service launch operates frequently.

> ### ❖ TIP
>
> *The walk can be extended beyond the falls to majestic Inspiration Point if you have a couple of hours to spare. It is not a difficult hike and can be done on your own or with park rangers as guides.*

❖ HIKING

The **Colter Bay Nature Trail** is a pleasant two-mile stroll through a sub-alpine flower meadow with a magnificent mountain backdrop. **Jackson Lake Lodge** is worth a visit even if you are not going to be staying there. This beautiful timber structure has giant picture windows in its large lobby and lounge, which provide a luxurious and comfortable place to ponder the mountains.

Experienced hikers, adventure travelers and those with more time on their hands can choose from a number of spectacular trails that cover many miles and require six to eight hours to complete, round-trip.

THE MIDWEST

The first is the **Amphitheater Lake Trail**, which ascends Disappointment Peak. You definitely won't be disappointed with the view after your 3,000-foot climb to a gorgeous glacial cirque.

Cascade Canyon and **Death Canyon Trails** allow for exploration of the many deep gorges within the Tetons.

SPECIAL ACTIVITIES

One of the most popular ways to see the park is to take a **float trip** on the Snake River. Various concessionaires offer trips from five to 20 miles in length (one to four hours) from several different locations within the park. No matter which one you take, the scenery will be spectacular and the stillness on the river a stark contrast to the constant hum of activity on the roadways. These are not whitewater trips (although other portions of the Snake River are among the wildest in the country). But they use the same type of inflatable rafts as the more adventurous whitewater trips. Among the numerous operators are:

Baker-Ewing . . . . ☎ (800) 365-1800
Grand Teton Lodge Company . . . ☎ (307) 543-3100
Osprey Snake River . . . . ☎ (307) 733-5500
Trianle X Ranch . . . . ☎ (307) 733-6445

The float season generally runs from mid-May through the end of September, depending upon water levels. Prices are about $25-45 for adults. Another possibility is the 1½-hour **boat cruise** on Jackson Lake. Advance reservations are highly recommended, especially during the peak of the summer season.

> ### ❖ TIP
>
> *If time is precious, we would choose the Snake River float trip and the Jenny Lake launch, rather than the Jackson Lake cruise. If you have plenty of time, all are worthwhile.*

Horse and wagon rides ranging from two hours to a half-day are also available; inquire at the visitor center for further information.

The **Colter Bay Visitor Center** in the northern portion of the park offers exhibits on the culture of the native Indian tribes in the area. If you happen to be here on a Friday evening, consider watching the **Laubin Ancient Indian Dances**, performed at Jackson Lake Lodge at 8:30 pm. No tickets needed.

ACCOMMODATIONS

❖ HOTELS & MOTELS

INSIDE THE PARK

COLTER BAY VILLAGE ($-$$$), US Highways 89 and 287, 10 miles north of Moran Junction. ☎ (307) 543-2855 or (800) 628-9988. 208 rooms. Open late May through September. Cabin-style accommodations with minimal amenities (a few units have shared baths). While this place isn't fancy, it does provide a convenient location amid magnificent surroundings, offering a touch of the great outdoors without actually camping. Restaurant and coffee shop on premises. (Part of Grand Teton Lodge Company, which operates all lodging inside Grand Teton and is the park's official concessionaire.)

COWBOY VILLAGE RESORT AT TOGWOTEE ($$$$), on US Highways 26 and 287, about 16 miles east of Moran Junction. ☎ (307) 543-2847 or (800) 543-2847. 89 rooms. Peaceful and secluded location surrounded by thick forest. Lodge units are quite comfortable, or you can opt to stay in one of the attractive cabins with a fireplace. There's a good restaurant.

JACKSON LAKE LODGE ($$$-$$$$), on US Highways 89 and 287, five miles north of Moran Junction. ☎ (307) 543-2811 or (800) 628-9988. 385 rooms. Open mid-May through mid-September. Full-service resort with a breathtaking view from many rooms as well as from the famous lounge with its over-sized picture window. Hotel staff can arrange many in-park

THE MIDWEST

tours and activities. The restaurant, described below, is outstanding. (Part of Grand Teton Lodge Company.)

JENNY LAKE LODGE ($$$$), off Teton Park Road, north of Jenny Lake. ☎ (307) 733-4647 or (800) 628-9988. Rate includes breakfast and dinner. 37 rooms. Open June through September. Luxury level lodge and private cabins in a private location that's close to all of the park's sights and activities. Renowned facilities and services. This is definitely not "roughing it" in the wilderness! (Part of Grand Teton Lodge Company.)

SIGNAL MOUNTAIN LODGE ($$-$$$), Teton Park Road, two miles south of US 89 and 287. ☎ (307) 543-2831. 79 rooms. Open mid-May through early October. Approximately half the rooms are motel style; the remainder are individual cabins. Outstanding views and many services available. Not quite up to the level of the preceding two places, but quite nice.

NEARBY COMMUNITIES

BUCKRAIL LODGE ($$), 110 E. Karns Avenue, Jackson; a quarter-mile from town square via King Street to Karns. ☎ (307) 733-2079. 12 rooms. Open May through mid-October. Motel-style exterior, but individual cabin units have cedar construction and cathedral ceilings. Accommodations are comfortable, spacious and one of the better values in Jackson, where bargains are hard to find. Small restaurant on premises (many more within walking distance).

PARKWAY INN ($$$), 125 N. Jackson Avenue, Jackson; a quarter-mile west of town square at junction of Broadway. ☎ (307) 733-3143 or (800) 247-8390. 50 rooms. Attractive Victorian decor and charm. Entire place was nicely remodeled several years ago. Varied recreational facilities include a spa and swimming pool. Near many restaurants.

QUALITY 49-ER INN & SUITES ($$-$$$), 330 W. Pearl Street, Jackson; just off town square. ☎ (307) 733-7550 or (800) 451-2980. 145 rooms. Rustic wooden exterior gives way to modern, well-appointed rooms and suites. The latter have working fireplaces. Convenient to restaurants and all in-town activities.

SNOW KING RESORT ($$$-$$$$), 400 Snow King Avenue, Jackson; just off town square. ☎ (307) 733-5200 or (800) 522-5464. 254 rooms. Full-service resort covering nearly 500 acres at the base of Snow King Mountain. Considering the lavish facilities, the rooms are a little on the disappointing side, although certainly adequate. Restaurant on premises.

WAGON WHEEL VILLAGE ($$-$$$), 435 N. Cache Street, Jackson; a half-mile north of town on US Highways 26/89/191. ☎ (307) 733-2357 or (800) 323-9279. 79 rooms. Open May to early October and December through February. Log cabin units on spacious and attractive grounds. The cabins are fairly large and nicely decorated. Some have fireplaces and/or whirlpools. Near many restaurants.

❖ CAMPING

No reservations are accepted at these sites. There's a 14-day maximum stay at all campgrounds except Jenny Lake, which has a seven-day limit. RVs are allowed except at Signal Mountain.

CAMPGROUNDS AT A GLANCE			
NAME	LOCATION	SITES	COST
Colter Bay	A mile southwest of Rockefeller Parkway at Colter Bay.	350	$12 per day
Gros Ventre	Along the river between Rockefeller Parkway & Kelly.	360	$12 per day
Jenny Lake	South shore of Jenny Lake off Teton Park Road.	49	$12 per day
Lizard Creek	North end of park off Rockefeller Parkway.	60	$12 per day
Signal Mtn	Jackson Lake, south of Moran via Teton park Road.	86	$12 per day

THE MIDWEST

DINING

INSIDE THE PARK

ASPENS RESTAURANT ($$), in the Signal Mountain Lodge (see listing above). ☎ (307) 543-2831. American food. Casual dining on the lake with spectacular mountain views. Excellent seafood is the specialty of the house.

DINING ROOM AT JENNY LAKE LODGE ($$$$), see listing above. ☎ (307) 733-4647. American/continental cuisine. Fancy decor and service in a magnificent wilderness setting. Superbly prepared meat (including fresh wild game dishes), fish and other delights.

THE MURAL ROOM ($$$), in Jackson Lake Lodge (see listing above). ☎ (307) 543-2811. American food. Another eatery with great mountain views. The casual room is decorated with paintings depicting area history. The nightly outdoor barbeque is a great alternative to the indoor dining.

NEARBY COMMUNITIES

BAR-T FIVE COVERED WAGON COOKOUT ($$-$$$), Cache Creek Road, Jackson; 1½ miles from town via Broadway east and Redmond Avenue south. ☎ (307) 733-5386. American food. Board a covered wagon for a trip into a picturesque canyon where you'll dine on simple wholesome food and be entertained by cowboys and Indians. Great fun for children as well as adults.

CADILLAC GRILLE ($$), 55 N. Cache Street, Jackson; on US 26/89/187. ☎ (307) 733-3279. American food. Attractive restaurant featuring a diverse menu of fresh seafood, wild game and excellent pasta dishes.

THE RANGE ($$-$$$), 225 N. Cache Street, Jackson; on Highways 26/89 north of Gill Avenue. ☎ (307) 733-5481. American food. This place sets the trend for imaginative cooking in Jackson. Exhibition kitchen and excellent service add to the enjoyment. Very popular.

STRUTTING GROUSE RESTAURANT ($$-$$$), at the Jackson Hole Golf Course, seven miles north of Jackson via US 26/89/191 and then west at Gros Ventre Junction. ☎ (307) 733-7788. Continental cuisine. Look out the window at the finely manicured golf course with the Tetons as a backdrop. Then turn your attention to the beautifully presented meals. Good selection, but the limited fresh game dishes are the best.

VISTA GRANDE ($-$$), Teton Village Road, Teton Village; 1½ miles north of State Highway 22. ☎ (307) 733-6964. Mexican food. Cheerful and friendly place with good food and ample portions at very attractive prices (not easy to find in this area).

WHERE DO WE GO FROM HERE?

Suggested Trip 5 includes Grand Teton National Park. Regardless of whether you follow that itinerary, no first visit to Grand Teton should exclude **Yellowstone National Park**, a half-hour to the north. Together, they provide much to see and do, and each of them is a major vacation trip all by itself.

Other possibilities include heading west from Grand Teton or Yellowstone into Idaho and visiting **Craters of the Moon**, or going east through the scenic northern portion of Wyoming over to **Devils Tower** and beyond into the **Black Hills** of South Dakota. The latter option is a long trip, covering many miles.

MOUNT RUSHMORE NATIONAL MEMORIAL

Mount Rushmore National Memorial is part of the highly scenic Black Hills region. It is a symbol of America every bit as much as the Statue of Liberty. And it's worth every effort to see because it is an experience you will never forget. The concept of the memorial was born in 1923, but actual construction did not begin until four years after that and its completion took another 14 years. The sculptor, Gutzon Borglum, selected the site because the 6,000-foot mountain dominated the surrounding terrain and because it faced the sun for most of the day. The heads of George Washington, Thomas Jefferson, Abraham Lincoln and Theodore Roosevelt are each 60 feet high and carved in such intricate detail that the emotions of the subjects are clearly evident to the observer. The colossal carvings are 1,400 feet above the visitor center and the adjacent viewing areas.

FACTS & FIGURES

Location/Gateways/Getting There: In the middle of the Black Hills of southwestern South Dakota, Mount Rushmore is near Rapid City on SR 244 and is accessible from that city by US 16 and 16A. There aren't any large cities within 350 miles of the memorial, but there is regularly scheduled air service into Rapid City.

Year Established: Mount Rushmore was dedicated as a National Memorial in August, 1927.

Size: 1,278 acres (two square miles). Tiny, but there is much to see.

Admission Fee: There is no charge for entering the memorial; however, a nominal fee for parking is assessed.

Climate/When to Go: The site is open all year, with extended visiting hours and some activities available only from Memorial Day through Labor Day. The beginning and end of this main season is marked by cool days and chilly nights. During the summer it is quite warm during the day and comfortably cool at night. Sun is the rule in summer, except for heavy and frequent afternoon thunderstorms. Bring a jacket for activities in the evening.

Contact Information: Superintendent, Mount Rushmore National Memorial, PO Box 268, Keystone, SD 57751. ☎ (605) 574-2523.

TOURING

There is no road system within the memorial nor any extended walks. The Presidential Trail requires about 45 minutes and will bring you closer to the mountain than the viewing areas. Do note, however, that some of the access roads to the memorial are narrow and have tunnels.

> ### ❖ TIP
>
> *Trailers are not allowed in the memorial, so if you have one, leave it in the town of Keystone. Actually, you will be far better off without a trailer when traveling throughout the Black Hills.*

One short drive outside the memorial itself that provides a fantastic distant view of the carving. This is available from the **Norbeck Overlook** on Iron Mountain Road (US 16), about five miles south of the Mount Rushmore. Don't miss it! Not only is the view great, but the road, an engineering marvel, is an exciting drive as it twists its way up to the overlook in a series of spirals.

The famous presidential faces of Mount Rushmore.

SPECIAL ACTIVITIES

The activities here all have to do with viewing the sculpture. The presidents are best seen from special terraces and marked observation points near the visitor center. A paved path, flanked by the flags of the states, leads through the entire area. The **visitor center** has numerous exhibits and films on the lives of the presidents and the carving process used to create the masterpiece. From Memorial Day to Labor Day a talk is given by Rangers at 9 pm every evening in the amphitheater directly beneath the carving. Then, from 9:30 until 10:30 (from 8 to 8:30 during the remainder of the year), the heads are illuminated.

> ### ❖ TIP
> *You will be seated on rather cold benches, so you might want to bring along a cushion or blanket to keep your bottom warm.*

The **sculptor's studio** is on the grounds and displays tools actually used in the carving process. It is only open during the summer season.

> NOTE: *Climbing on Mount Rushmore istelf is strictly prohibited.*

ACCOMMODATIONS

❖ HOTELS & MOTELS

There are no accommodations inside the memorial.

NEARBY COMMUNITIES

The largest number of hotels can be found in Rapid City. However, Hill City (15 miles from Mt. Rushmore) and Keystone (about five miles away), are much closer.

> NOTE: *Area prices tend towards the high side because of the numerous attractions of the Black Hills.*

BEST WESTERN GOLDEN SPIKE INN ($$$-$$$$), 106 Main Street, Hill City; on US Highways 16/385; northwest of Mt. Rushmore via US 16/385 and State Highway 244. ☎ (605) 574-2577 or (800) 528-1234. 62 rooms. Very high quality rooms and attractive grounds (especially the pool area). Restaurant on premises.

FIRST LADY INN ($$-$$$), 702 Highway 16A, Keystone; in center of town on main highway, northeast of Mt. Rushmore via 16A south to State Highway 244. ☎ (605) 666-4990 or (800) 252-2119. 41 rooms. Small but attractive guest rooms that have recently been remodeled. Very convenient to Mt. Rushmore. Indoor pool and spa. Restaurants close by.

THE LODGE AT PALMER GULCH ($$$), 12620 State Highway 244, Hill City; five miles west of Mt. Rushmore. ☎ (605) 574-2525 or (800) 562-8503. 62 rooms. Beautiful Old West-style facility with attractively furnished rooms. Public areas are comfortable and feature a rustic fireplace. Extensive recreational facilities. Quiet location on top of wooded hillside. Shuttle service to Mt. Rushmore. Restaurant adjacent.

POWDER HOUSE LODGE ($$-$$$$), US 16A, Keystone; one mile north of town and northeast of Mt. Rushmore via US 16A south to State Highway 244. ☎ (605) 666-4646 or (800) 321-0692. 37 rooms. Quiet and secluded setting off the road on tree-shaded hillside. Variety of accommodations ranging from simple motel units to rustic cottages to duplex lodges. Friendly atmosphere. Swimming pool. Very nice restaurant on premises.

❖ CAMPING

No camping is permitted within the memorial. For campgrounds in the surrounding Black Hills National Forest, contact the Forest Supervisor in Custer or ☎ (605) 673-2251.

THE MIDWEST

DINING

INSIDE THE MEMORIAL

BUFFALO DINING ROOM ($-$$), adjacent to memorial's visitor center. ☎ (605) 574-2515. American food. Self-serve cafeteria. The selection and food quality is better than you might expect. Eating here will save a trip back to town for a meal. The best part is the fabulous view of the four presidents, who look as though they're eyeing your meal while you eat! Huge gift shop is great for souvenir hunters.

NEARBY COMMUNITIES

ALPINE INN ($), 225 Main Street, Hill City; in town on US Highways 16/385. ☎ (605) 574-2749. American food. Popular place for good food, pleasant service and low prices. You can expect to encounter significant crowds during the height of the visitor season. Worth it, if you're on a tight budget.

RUBY HOUSE RESTAURANT ($$), 126 Winter Street, Keystone; town center. ☎ (605) 666-4404. American food. Good variety of entrées to choose from (including children's menu) in a pleasantly casual 1890s atmosphere. Friendly service.

WHERE DO WE GO FROM HERE?

Suggested Trip 2 is the logical way to see the memorial. Your entire visit here will take no more than a couple of hours (plus the evening program), so at a minimum you should see the rest of the **Black Hills** and **Badlands National Park** in the same trip. A longer journey might include many of Wyoming's sights.

SCOTTS BLUFF NATIONAL MONUMENT

Named for a local fur trapper, Scotts Bluff National Monument was established primarily for its historic importance as a prominent landmark along the Oregon Trail for westward-bound pioneers. The escarpment, which rises 800 feet above the valley of the North Platte River (elevation above sea level is 4,649 feet), provides the most dramatic scenery in all of Nebraska. The hard sandstone, of which the escarpment is composed, has prevented it from eroding to the level of the surrounding plain. No matter which direction you approach it from, Scotts Bluff rises majestically above the land around it and is both beautiful and impressive. Few people know about Scotts Bluff and expectations are usually exceeded.

FACTS & FIGURES

Location/Gateways/Getting There: In the extreme western portion of Nebraska, Scotts Bluff is five miles southwest of the town of Scottsbluff via SR 92. US 26 runs through Scottsbluff and is the primary route into the area. It takes about four hours to travel from Denver via I-25, I-80 and SR 71 to the vicinity of the monument.

Year Established: The area became a national monument in 1919.

Size: 3,084 acres (five square miles).

Admission Fee: $4, which includes the toll road to the summit.

Climate/When to Go: The monument is open all year. The area has four distinct seasons ranging from cold winters to very hot summers, with pleasant spring and fall weather. The summit road may be closed during inclement weather (mainly snow, but sometimes during summer storms, as well), so you should

THE MIDWEST

not plan on coming here during the winter. Any other time is appropriate for a visit.

Contact Information: Superintendent, Scotts National Monument, PO Box 27, Gehring, NE 69341. ☎ (308) 436-4340.

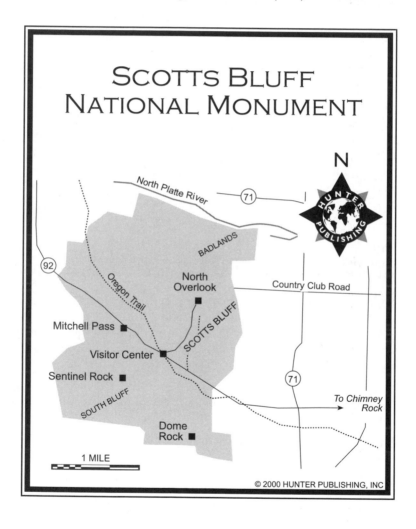

AUTO TOUR/SHORT STOPS

The monument is very small in comparison to most others in this book and there is only a single, short road to take. The road to the summit is only 1½ miles long, but it is quite a ride! Winding its way around the bluff, it passes through three tunnels and has breathtaking views on its journey to the top.

> NOTE: *No trailers are allowed on this road.*

Once on the summit, there are views of the fertile North Platte Valley, the town of Scottsbluff and distant geologic features, such as **Chimney Rock** (23 miles away) and **Laramie Peak** (120 miles away). From the summit parking area there are two short trails (only six-tenths of a mile) leading to the north and south ends of the escarpment. The trails are paved, level and can be taken by everyone, including the handicapped.

Before or after your ride to the top you should make a brief stop at the **visitor center**, which describes both the geologic and human history of the area. Nearby you can walk along a portion of the original Oregon Trail where some wagon ruts are still quite visible. A wagon typical of those that passed through here is on display.

Allow between one hour and 90 minutes for your visit to Scotts Bluff as described here.

GETTING OUT/LONGER STOPS

❖ HIKING

A 1½-mile trail leads from the visitor center to the top of the escarpment. It follows a different route than the road (you cannot walk along the road) and doesn't rise as sharply. Although it isn't terribly difficult, it still requires several hours to make the round-trip. If you want to hike it, the best time is in spring or fall. You should be in reasonably good shape to attempt this route.

THE MIDWEST

> ### ❖ TIP
> *Consider driving to the top and having one person in your party drive back down while the rest of you walk.*

ACCOMMODATIONS

❖ HOTELS & MOTELS

There are no places to stay inside the monument.

NEARBY COMMUNITIES

CANDLELIGHT INN ($$), 1822 E. 20th Place, Scottsbluff; 1½ miles east of the center of town on US 26 and about seven miles north of the monument via US 71 south and State Highway 92. ☎ (308) 635-3751. Rate includes continental breakfast. 56 rooms. Unusually attractive inn with rooms that have been decorated to resemble a "home." Swimming pool. Restaurants within a short distance.

SCOTTSBLUFF INN ($$), 1901 21st Avenue, Scottsbluff; two miles east of downtown on US 26 and eight miles from Scotts Bluff via Highways US 71 and State 92. ☎ (308) 635-3111 or (800) 597-3111. 138 rooms. The nicely decorated rooms here are of a generous size and well kept. Attractive public areas include a swimming pool, exercise room and other recreational facilities. Restaurant on the premises features steak; others are nearby.

SUPER 8 MOTEL ($), 2202 Delta Drive, Scottsbluff; two miles east of the town center on US 26 and about eight miles from the national monument via US 71 and State Highway 92. ☎ (308) 635-1600 or (800) 800-8000. 55 rooms. Basic accommodations. Some of the rooms are quite small, but should suffice after a busy day. Bargain rates. Small pool. Restaurants are close by.

❖ CAMPING

There is no camping inside the national monument. Commercial campgrounds are available in the town of Scott's Bluff and Behring.

DINING

There are no eating establishments inside the monument.

NEARBY COMMUNITIES

BUSH'S GASLIGHT RESTAURANT ($$), 3315 N. 10th, Scottsbluff; two miles south of town center on US 71 Business. ☎ (308) 632-7315. American food. An interesting and varied selection of menu items, all tastefully prepared and nicely served. Some selections are served family-style.

ROSITA'S ($), 1205 E. Overland Avenue, Scottsbluff; one mile east of downtown. ☎ (308) 632-2429. Mexican food. Very casual and friendly place with a lively atmosphere. Well-prepared authentic Mexican cuisine. Not too spicy.

WHERE DO WE GO FROM HERE?

Scotts Bluff is included as a part of *Suggested Trip 2* in the last section of the book. Also, if your trip includes southern Wyoming or northeast Colorado, then Scotts Bluff is not overly out of the way. Although this is certainly not one of America's most visited national monuments (no doubt because of its location) it is a beautiful sight and would be a worthwhile addition to any of your travels.

THE MIDWEST

YELLOWSTONE NATIONAL PARK

Established in 1872, Yellowstone is America's first national park.

America's first national park is also one of its largest, the most extensive in the 48 contiguous states and the only one that extends over three states. Although parts of the park are in Montana and Idaho, most of the park's area and all of its major attractions are in Wyoming. Yellowstone Park is a broad volcanic plateau that generally lies between 7,000 and 8,500 feet above sea level, with peaks that rise 2,000-4,000 feet above the plateau. That dry geologic description hardly begins to do the park justice, but no words really can.

Probably the most famous single feature of Yellowstone is Old Faithful. As beautiful as it is, by the time you have finished seeing Yellowstone you will rank it as one of the lesser attractions. Yellowstone is a microcosm of America's natural beauty, its variety is unsurpassed by any other national park. Besides the geysers, geothermal activity has produced gurgling mudpots and colorful algae-containing waters that simply defy description. Then, too, there are elegant mountains, deep canyons, high rushing waterfalls and rivers, forests and lakes.

FACTS & FIGURES

Location/Gateways/Getting There: There are five entrances to Yellowstone National Park, which is in the northwestern corner of Wyoming, with narrow strips extending across the border into neighboring states. From the south (and Grand Teton National Park), US 89/191/287 is the only approach. The two access routes from the east are US 14/16/20 from Cody, Wyoming and US 212 from Red Lodge, Montana. The northern access is via US 89 from Livingston, Montana and the western approach is US 20 from Idaho Falls.

The nearest significant commercial airports are three hours away in Billings or Bozeman, Montana; Salt Lake City is seven hours away. You can also fly into Jackson, Wyoming if you don't want to drive too far to reach the park.

Year Established: America's original national park, Yellowstone was given this designation by Congress in 1872.

Size: Three times as large as Rhode Island, Yellowstone covers 2,211,823 acres (3,468 square miles).

Admission Fee: $20. Passes from Yellowstone, good for seven days, are also valid at Grand Teton National Park.

Climate/When to Go: Most roads are open from the beginning of May until the end of October, but there are limited facilities after the early part of September. Since the summer is dry and pleasant (mornings are often quite chilly), June, July and August are the best times to see the park, especially for an initial visit. Yellowstone, however, has special wonders reserved for every season of the year.

Contact Information: Superintendent, Yellowstone National Park, PO Box 168, Yellowstone Park, WY 82190. ☎ (307) 344-7381.

> ❖ **TIP**
>
> *When driving in the park, you can get up-to-the-minute information by tuning your AM car radio to 1606 Khz.*

THE MIDWEST

AUTO TOUR/SHORT STOPS

Considering the immensity of this state-sized park, Yellowstone is remarkably easy to see by car. The **Grand Loop Road**, which circles the central plateau area, touches or comes very near to almost every major attraction. This road covers nearly 150 miles and with access roads to and from your entrance and exit points, plan on covering close to 250 total miles within the park itself. We recommend that you allow close to seven hours for travel time alone. You can't go fast on these roads, and you'll want to take in the scenery.

> NOTE: *Traffic in the summer months is often very heavy, sometimes causing considerable delays.*

As the road is a complete loop it doesn't matter which park entrance you use or where you start the tour. For purposes of this discussion, we will begin from the park headquarters at Mammoth Hot Springs. **Mammoth Hot Springs** features the administrative offices of the park and the **Mammoth Visitor Center**, which can provide information on the natural and human history of the park. There are six other visitor centers and/or museums in Yellowstone, all of which are noted as we follow this tour.

The main features of Mammoth Hot Springs are the multicolored terraces – limestone formations being acted upon by geothermal forces. The effect is both stunning and eerie. Easy walking is provided by way of boardwalks.

> ❖ **TIP**
>
> *Stay on boardwalks in the park; the surrounding terrain is often hot and the crust may be very soft.*

You can see everything worth seeing from the designated routes. Some of the major formations in the terrace area are the Liberty Cap, Devil's Thumb, Cleopatra's Terrace and Minerva

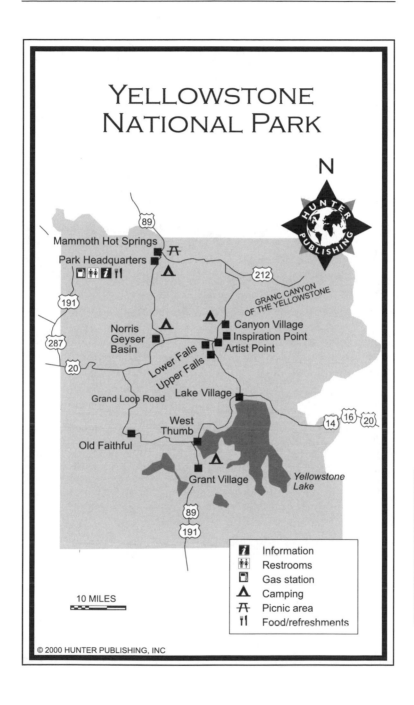

YELLOWSTONE NATIONAL PARK

N

Mammoth Hot Springs
Park Headquarters

89

212

GRANC CANYON
OF THE YELLOWSTONE

191

Norris
Geyser
Basin

287

20

Canyon Village
Inspiration Point
Artist Point

Lower Falls
Upper Falls

Grand Loop Road

Lake Village

West
Thumb

14 16 20

Old Faithful

Grant Village

Yellowstone
Lake

89

191

	Information
	Restrooms
	Gas station
	Camping
	Picnic area
	Food/refreshments

10 MILES

THE MIDWEST

Terrace. After you complete the trail, a short one-way auto loop covers the **Upper** or **White Elephant Back Terrace**. Allow at least an hour to visit the Mammoth Hot Springs area.

Proceeding south now on the Grand Loop Road past the glass-like Obsidian Cliffs, your next stop along this other-worldly journey is the **Norris Geyser Basin**. Just a few steps from the parking area is the **Norris Museum**, which explains the geology of the area. To the left of the museum is the **Back Basin Trail**. You will pass some 27 geysers and, unless you are very unlucky, one or more of them will be erupting during your visit.

> ❖ **TIP**
>
> *The predicted eruption times can be found posted at the museum. There are benches or logs to sit on at most of the larger geysers while you're waiting.*

Return to the museum and begin the boardwalk trail to the right of the building. This is the **Porcelain Basin Trail** and it contains many other beautiful examples of the more than 10,000 geysers in the park. But more important here are the exquisite colors seen on the ground. They are caused by algae growing in the warm water that combines with soft minerals on the surface. It looks as if a giant artist spilled his palette. Allow about 1½-2 hours for the two basins and the museum, excluding any time you have to spend waiting for a geyser to put on its show.

Continuing our Grand Loop tour, the next stop is in Madison, where the **Madison Explorers Museum** has interesting exhibits on the park's earliest visitors. You will then pass by the Firehole Falls and continue your drive next to the Firehole River before arriving at the **Lower** and **Midway Geyser Basins**. The key features here are the colorful paintpots and mud volcanoes, where strange gurgling sounds emanate from the earth and strong aromas as well. Both children and adults will delight in them all.

❖ DID YOU KNOW?

Firehole River was named after the places where steaming hot water runs into the river itself, steaming as it hits the cold water. You will see some of these "fireholes" as you explore.

The Grand Prismatic Spring (Midway Basin) is exceptionally beautiful. Thirty to 45 minutes should be adequate for this area.

Just a few miles farther ahead is **Old Faithful Village**. There is a major visitor center here and just outside the building is the best area for viewing eruptions of **Old Faithful** (which occur approximately every hour and last from two to five minutes). The next predicted eruption will be posted at the visitor center.

❖ TIP

Get here early, as a huge crowd gathers for each eruption and late arrivals will not get good viewing spots.

A trail in this area leads to the **Giant Geyser** (whose eruption schedule will also be on display). Allow one hour minimum for this trail.

About 15 miles past Old Faithful on the Grand Loop Road, you'll reach the Rockefeller Parkway and your route goes to the north.

❖ DID YOU KNOW?

Between Old Faithful and a point on the Rockefeller Parkway just south of the West Thumb Junction, the road crosses the Continental Divide no less than three times.

If you continuing along the Grand Loop, however, you'll now be riding along the edge of huge **Yellowstone Lake**. Just before getting to Lake Junction there is a short spur road leading to **Natural Bridge**, a 10-minute walk. It is worth the time to see this huge

THE MIDWEST

formation in its forested canyon. At **Lake Village** are magnificent views of the blue lake with mountain backdrops. There is another short trail that leads through more thermal areas. The lake provides an interesting backdrop to these features. A visitor center with information about the lake is also here. Allow 30 minutes for exploring the lake area.

Sixteen miles north of Fishing Bridge Junction, the Grand Loop Road will bring you to the remarkable **Canyon Area**. A spur road leads along the south rim of the Grand Canyon of the Yellowstone River. The spectacular coloring, especially the golden and yellowish hues of the rock, combined with the deepness of the canyon and the rushing waterfalls make this one of the most beautiful sights in all the world.

❖ TIP

Be sure to use the short walks from the south rim road to see the views from **Artist Point.**

Just over the bridge that connects the two sides of the canyon is **Canyon Village**. After stopping at the **Canyon Visitor Center,** take the one-way road leading along the north rim. **Red Rock, Lookout Point**, **Grand View Point** and **Inspiration Point** are the must-see features here. From Lookout Point the views of the over 300-foot Lower Falls (twice as high as Niagara) and the 109-foot Upper Falls are fantastic. You've probably seen this famous view in many pictures, but there's nothing quite like experiencing it first hand. At least 1½ hours should be allowed for the Canyon Area.

Continuing north, the terrain becomes more mountainous as you pass Mount Washburn (10,324 feet). At Tower Junction, head westward for the final leg of the Grand Loop back to Mammoth Hot Springs. Although there are no unusual features along this stretch, the overall scenery is quite beautiful; this is especially true once Mammoth Hot Springs comes into view as the road descends.

GETTING OUT/LONGER STOPS

Our Auto Tour included somewhat more walking than is usually the case. More serious hikers might want to walk along the Grand Canyon of the Yellowstone's north and south rims instead of taking their car from one observation point to another. This will add about one hour for each rim.

❖ HIKING

Yellowstone, of course, is much more than just the Grand Loop and the relatively short and easy trails that are part of it. The total length of back-country trails in the park is 1,200 miles – enough to take you from Yellowstone all the way to San Diego, California. Many of the trails are quite easy, although some climb into the mountains.

> **❖ TIP**
>
> *Hikers are advised to secure trail information at any visitor center.*

SPECIAL ACTIVITIES

Many of the sights of Yellowstone can be seen on **horseback**. On Yellowstone Lake you can rent **motorboats, launches** or **rowboats** for a leisurely afternoon on the water. TW Recreational Services has offices at Mammoth Hot Springs, Tower-Roosevelt and Canyon Village, where you can sign up for **guided horse trips**. Boat rentals are available from the same company at the Bridge Marina. The same organization also provides "snowcoach" tours of Yellowstone during the winter months. All of the above activities are offered through **TW Services**, ☎ (307) 344-7311.

THE MIDWEST

> ## ❖ WINTER TRAVEL
>
> *While the landscape is magically beautiful when snow-covered, we suggest that a winter trip be reserved for a return visit as many of the sights that first-timers will want to see cannot be viewed as well during the colder months.*

ACCOMMODATIONS

❖ HOTELS & MOTELS

INSIDE THE PARK

All accommodations within the park are operated by Yellowstone National Park Lodges. Their central reservation number is ☎ (307) 344-7311. Despite the relatively large number of rooms within the park, Yellowstone's popularity requires that reservations be made well in advance. The operating season varies from one facility to another, but is generally between May and October.

> ## ❖ TIP
>
> *Despite the large number of rooms in the park, we always try to stay in one of the nearby communities. Generally, these offer higher standards.*

CASCADE LODGE AT CANYON VILLAGE ($$-$$$), on the Grand Loop Road in the Canyon Village area. 588 rooms. The main lodge (consisting of 35 units) is fairly nice and has been updated. The remainder of the facilities at Cascade Lodge are sub-par and are mentioned for the convenience of those desiring to stay in the park. Many units do not have private bath facilities. Restaurant in the village.

GRANT VILLAGE ($$), located below the West Thumb of Yellowstone Lake in Grant Village, about a mile off the southern access road. 296 rooms. Adequate lodging facilities in a nice area that has a less hectic atmosphere than some of the other establishments in the park. Restaurant on premises.

LAKE LODGE & CABINS ($$), Lake Village, two miles southwest of Fishing Bridge Junction. 186 rooms. Mostly sub-par rooms that I would avoid unless they were the only rooms remaining in the park. Not all have private facilities. Restaurants nearby.

LAKE YELLOWSTONE HOTEL & CABINS ($$), on the shore of Lake Yellowstone west of Fishing Bridge. 292 rooms. Stately old place that, despite some modernization (needs more), still retains an old-time flavor. Nice views from many of the upper floors. Biggest problem is the small, almost claustrophobic size of many of the rooms. Restaurant on premises.

MAMMOTH HOT SPRINGS HOTEL ($$$), in the park headquarters area of Mammoth Hot Springs. 226 rooms. A variety of accommodations ranging from not so good (no private baths) to some of the nicest rooms in the park. Considering the relatively narrow range of prices, you should definitely opt for the better rooms. Restaurant on premises.

OLD FAITHFUL INN ($$$), Old Faithful Village opposite Old Faithful Geyser. 325 rooms. About two-thirds of the units have private baths and those are okay by me. The others, well – they'll do if you don't have high lodging standards. Restaurant on premises.

NEARBY COMMUNITIES

Accommodations within Grand Teton National Park are also within a reasonable distance of the southern portion of Yellowstone (see pages 73-75).

ABSAROKA MOUNTAIN LODGE ($$$), 1231 E. Yellowstone Highway, Wapiti, WY; 19 miles west of Wapiti on US Highways 14/16/20 and about 32 miles from the park's eastern entrance (61 miles from Grand Loop Road at Fishing Bridge Junction). ☎ (307) 587-3963. 16 rooms. Built in 1910, this historic lodge is situated on one of the most beautiful stretches of highway in the world (so said Teddy Roosevelt, and I concur). Accommodations are quite good, although a little overpriced. Extensive recreational facilities include horseback riding. There is a decent restaurant on the premises, which is important considering that there aren't any others close by.

BIG WESTERN PINE MOTEL ($$), 234 Firehole Avenue, W. Yellowstone, MT; on US Highways 20 and 191, immediately west of Yellowstone Park's west entrance and about 14 miles from the Grand Loop Road at Madison Junction. ☎ (406) 646-7622. Rate includes continental breakfast. 45 rooms. Nondescript exterior houses attractive, comfortable rooms. Some efficiency units. Pool and whirlpool. Good restaurant on premises and many more within walking distance.

GRAY WOLF INN ($$-$$$), 250 S. Canyon Street, W. Yellowstone, MT; at the west entrance to the park, 14 miles from Madison Junction and the Grand Loop Road. ☎ (406) 646-0000 or (800) 852-8602. Rate includes continental breakfast. 102 rooms. One of the newest places in town (opened in 1998), it's also one of the nicest, with spacious rooms as well as two-room suites and efficiencies. The decor is well above average and the public areas are pretty. Indoor pool, Jacuzzi and sauna. Restaurants nearby.

MAIDEN BASIN INN ($$-$$$), 4 Maiden Basin Drive, Gardiner, MT; five miles north of town and the northwest park entrance on US Highway 89, about 10 miles from Mammoth Hot Springs area. ☎ (406) 848-7080 or (800) 624-3364. Rate includes continental breakfast. Eight rooms. Beautiful ranch-style facility in a wonderful setting and offering spacious, comfortable accommodations in a warm and inviting atmosphere. Restaurants within a short drive.

SODA BUTTE LODGE ($$), 209 US 212, Cooke City, MT; in the center of town, about four miles from Yellowstone's northeast entrance and 34 miles from Tower Junction and the Grand Loop Road. ☎ (406) 838-2251. 32 rooms. Not quite up to the standards of places in West Yellowstone, but the choices are much slimmer on this side of the park. The rustic lodge is clean and comfortable. Restaurant nearby.

STAGE COACH INN ($$-$$$), 209 Madison Avenue, W. Yellowstone, MT; off US 191 at Dunraven Ave., near the west park entrance and 14 miles from Grand Loop Road/Madison Junction. ☎ (406) 646-7381 or (800) 842-2882. 84 rooms. Old

Western look and feel both in public areas and guest rooms; however, this is a modern and extra-comfy place with friendly service and a nice family atmosphere. Some recreational facilities. Restaurants are close by.

❖ CAMPING

All sites have 14-day limits and allow RVs. Reservations may be accepted at some; call the park Superintendent's office for details.

CAMPGROUNDS AT A GLANCE			
NAME	LOCATION	SITES	COST
Bridge Bay	2 miles south of Lake Village.	429	$14 per day
Canyon	.25 miles east of Canyon Jctn.	271	$14 per day
Grant Village	2 miles south of West Thumb Jctn.	425	$14 per day
Indian Creek	7½ miles south of Mammoth Hot Springs.	75	$8 per day
Lewis Lake	10 miles south of West Thumb Jctn.	85	$8 per day
Madison	14 miles east of West Yellowstone.	280	$14 per day
Mammoth	Mammoth Hot Springs area.	85	$10 per day
Norris	1 mile north of Norris Jctn.	116	$10 per day
Pebble Creek	7 miles south of park's northeast entrance.	36	$8 per day
Slough Creek	10 miles northeast of Lower Falls Jctn.	29	$8 per day
Tower Fall	3 miles southeast of Tower Jctn.	32	$8 per day

THE MIDWEST

DINING

INSIDE THE PARK

All of the hotels inside the park either have their own restaurant or one is close by in the various villages throughout the park. Some have a full-service restaurant as well as a coffee shop or snack bar. The only restaurant, however, that merits a special mention is the LAKE YELLOWSTONE DINING ROOM (in the Lake Yellowstone Hotel). Overlooking the lake, this moderately priced establishment ($$) has well-prepared entrées and live music. Old-world atmosphere and good service.

NEARBY COMMUNITIES

CHINATOWN RESTAURANT ($-$$), 124 Madison Avenue, W. Yellowstone, MT; immediately west of the park entrance. ☎ (406) 646-7296. Chinese cuisine. Well-prepared entrées that run the gamut from Cantonese to Szechuan to Hunan.

RUSTLER'S ROOST ($-$$), in the Big Western Pine Motel (see listing above). ☎ (406) 646-7622. American food. Good variety of tasty food served in ample portions. Try the elk and buffalo specialties of the house for a true Wyoming culinary experience. Nice family atmosphere and friendly service.

THREE BEAR RESTAURANT ($$-$$$), 205 Yellowstone Avenue, W. Yellowstone, MT; in the Three Bear Motor Lodge, just west of the park entrance. ☎ (406) 646-7811. American food. Serving a good variety of food, this is a wise choice for family dining. Historic decor makes for attractive surroundings. Their homebaked desserts are excellent.

YELLOWSTONE MINE RESTAURANT ($$), US 89, Gardiner, MT; about a mile north of the northwest entrance to the park, in the Best Western by Mammoth Hot Springs. ☎ (406) 848-7336. American food. Dine in an atmosphere surrounded by authentic-looking mining items. True spirit of the west. Features well prepared steaks and seafood.

WHERE DO WE GO FROM HERE?

Yellowstone is included in *Suggested Trip 5*. It is logical to visit the adjacent **Grand Teton** at the same time. Rather than heading north to **Glacier** (as outlined in *Suggested Trip 5*), you can make a loop through the state of **Wyoming**. The approach roads from Yellowstone all the way to Cody provide some spectacular scenery, as do major portions of the entire state. It can even be extended to go beyond the Wyoming line into the **Black Hills**.

THE MIDWEST

THE
SOUTHWEST

ARCHES
NATIONAL PARK

Within this arid landscape is the world's greatest concentration of natural stone arches. There are approximately 90 of these formations that geologists consider true natural arches, including famous Landscape Arch, although more than 2,000 smaller ones have been catalogued. All are products of weathering and erosion, created over a period of several million years, in a process that continues to this day.

> ### ❖ DID YOU KNOW?
>
> *Landscape Arch is the world's longest natural arch with a span of 306 feet.*

The landscape is quite harsh to the eye at first glance: hot and dry. Yet it is also a land of exquisite beauty, with the many arches, canyons, spires and balanced rock formations set against a brilliant blue sky. The primary colors are varying shades of reddish brown.

> ### ❖ TIP
>
> *These colors are especially photogenic in the early morning or late afternoon sunlight, and there is plenty of sunshine in this part of the country.*

It is appropriate that Arches is in a rather isolated part of the country, because the landscape evokes visions of another world from some science fiction movie.

FACTS & FIGURES

Location/Gateways/Getting There: In southeastern Utah just five miles north of the town of Moab on US 191 and 30 miles south of I-70. There are no large cities nearby, but a number of logical gateways present themselves. Las Vegas (via I-15 north to I-70 east) is almost 500 miles away. Yet, with the many attractions between these two points, it must be considered a convenient gateway to Arches. Salt Lake City is quite a bit closer (about 300 miles) via I-15 southbound to I-70 eastbound. Denver is approximately the same distance, all via I-70 westbound, and can be an easy alternative gateway if you are going to combine some of the sights in Colorado with those in Utah.

Year Established: Previously a national monument, Arches became a national park in 1971.

Size: 73,379 acres (115 square miles).

Parade of Elephants, Arches National Park.

Admission Fees: $10. The entrance permit is also accepted at nearby Canyonlands National Park if presented within seven days.

Climate/When to Go: Spring and fall are the best times to see the park as the weather is warm and bright. Winter isn't too cold to enjoy walking the trails either. The summer is exceedingly hot, often over 100°F, and the sun can be relentless.

> ### ❖ TIP
>
> *If you do visit in the summer you should time your trip so that most of the touring can be completed in the morning hours before it really heats up. Carry water for yourself and your car and always wear a hat in the sun.*

Contact Information: Superintendent, Arches National Park, PO Box 907, Moab, UT 84532. ☎ (435) 259-8161.

AUTO TOUR/SHORT STOPS

While a great many of the park's arches and other features are visible from the road or are just a short walk away, you might be disappointed with Arches if you don't hit the trails too. We'll begin with the suggested auto route, which covers about 55 miles on paved roadway. On this route you will see only about a quarter of the approximately 90 major arch formations in the park.

Just inside the entrance to the park, after the road quickly winds its way up several hundred feet, is the **visitor center**. You should stop here to view the interesting exhibits explaining how Arches was formed. Here, too, is a short trail that will introduce you to the desert flora found in this region. A short distance past here is the southern terminus of the **Park Avenue Trail**. More will be said about this in the next section, but even if you don't walk down Park Avenue, do at least get out to view it. The narrow, steeply rising rock formations are reminiscent of New York's Park Avenue – a broad thoroughfare flanked by columns of graceful skyscrapers. Among the best features of this area is the formation known as the **Three Gossips**. When viewed from certain angles, these giant stone monoliths resemble three very tall women standing in a circle. It appears as though they are having a pleasant chat about the neighbors (maybe their conversation is about visitors to the park who keep gawking at them!).

Over the next several miles the road passes the **Tower of Babel**, then an area called the **Rock Pinnacles**, before finally reaching the amazing **Balanced Rock**. It is difficult to understand how this huge boulder stays in place on its slim perch. A short trail circles the rock. At Balanced Rock the road branches in two. Go first to the right, a spur road that is approximately 2½ miles long, each way. This leads to the **Windows Section** of the park.

❖ DID YOU KNOW?

The name comes from the many small arches that look like the windows of a house when seen from a distance.

While numerous windows can be seen from the road, you might want to take the trail here (see below).

Rejoining the main road, you then pass **Panorama Point,** which offers a view of the park's arid but colorful landscape. Head down a short spur road for almost four miles to the **Delicate**

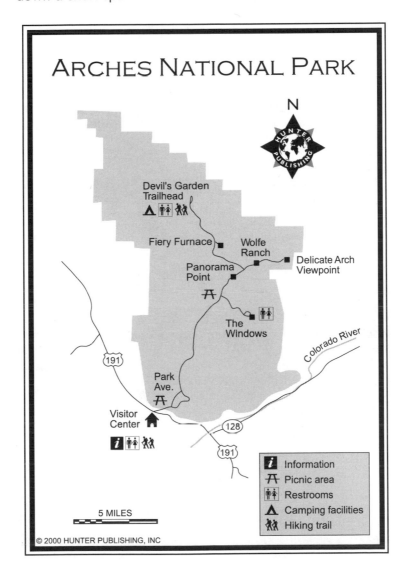

ARCHES NATIONAL PARK

N

Devil's Garden Trailhead

Fiery Furnace

Wolfe Ranch

Delicate Arch Viewpoint

Panorama Point

The Windows

Colorado River

191

Park Ave.

Visitor Center

128

191

5 MILES

© 2000 HUNTER PUBLISHING, INC

i Information

🛆 Picnic area

🚻 Restrooms

⛺ Camping facilities

🥾 Hiking trail

Arch Viewpoint. This is one of the most graceful formations in the park. It can be seen from the viewpoint but, because of the distance to the arch, appears rather small. Check the next section for information on the trail that leads closer to the arch.

Return to the main road, turn right, and continue, stopping to admire the surrounding canyon terrain, first at the **Salt Valley Overlook** and, less than a mile later, the **Fiery Furnace Viewpoint**. Shortly after passing the Skyline Arch, you will come to the end of the road in the area known as the **Devil's Garden**. This is the trailhead for some major park landmarks (described in the next section). After completing your visit here, turn around and drive the 20 miles back to the park's exit. This driving portion of the tour will take approximately three hours, including short walks.

GETTING OUT/LONGER STOPS

As mentioned previously, many of the park's most famous and beautiful sights cannot be readily seen from the road, so some trail activity is a must. A lot of the trails aren't overly difficult.

❖ HIKING

We previously cited **Park Avenue** as a worthy stop, and you can get a good overview of the entire area from the roadside parking area and trailhead. Try to make time for the easy one-mile walk to the northern end, which will get you up-close to these huge formations. Allow about 90 minutes for the round-trip.

> ### ❖ TIP
>
> *If one person in your party is willing to skip the walk, you can cut the time in half by having him or her take the car and meet you at the other end.*

To properly see the arches in the **Windows Section** you should take the mile-long loop trail that passes through the North and

South Windows area. You can climb right up to the base of a number of arches and take a break sitting in the arch's shade and gazing out over the unbelievable landscape. A portion of the route is sandy, as are many of the park's trails. On some of them you will sink into the sand up to your ankles, so wear appropriate shoes. The trail can be completed in an hour or so and is well worth the time and trouble.

> NOTE: *Don't go barefoot, especially during the summer – the sun can make the sand blistering hot!*

The trail to **Delicate Arch** traverses three miles of moderately difficult terrain. Those who have taken the trek, however, will attest that it is worth the effort. This is especially true if you view the arch in the early morning or late afternoon light. At those times it takes on an even more beautiful appearance.

Landscape Arch requires more effort to reach. It is a little over 1½ miles from the Devil's Garden parking area. The difficult trail is hilly and should take about 1½ hours. You will be rewarded with a bird's-eye view of this magnificent arch, which dwarfs all others in the park. Several other arches are also visible from this trail. (The Devil's Garden Trail continues past Landscape Arch for several more miles.)

SPECIAL ACTIVITIES

There is an extensive network of unpaved 4WD negotiable roads in Arches' back-country. Although these routes don't pass by too many important arches, the terrain and scenery is, nonetheless, outstanding. Get a detailed map of these roads at the visitor center.

> NOTE: *Do not attempt these trails in rainy weather or if it has rained heavily within the past 24 hours.*

ACCOMMODATIONS

❖ HOTELS & MOTELS

There are no lodgings inside the park.

NEARBY COMMUNITIES

AARCHWAYS INN ($$$), 1551 N. Highway 191, Moab, UT; north end of town. ☎ (435) 259-2599 or (800) 341-9359. Continental breakfast included. 96 rooms. Spacious and nicely decorated units in an older but well-maintained facility. Some luxury rooms have whirlpools. Not far from several restaurants.

MOAB VALLEY INN ($$), 711 S. Main Street, Moab, UT; US 191, about a mile south of town center. ☎ (435) 259-5556 or (800) 441-6147. Continental breakfast included in rate. 127 rooms. Clean, well-kept rooms at an attractive price, although many are on the small side. Restaurants close by.

RAMADA INN MOAB ($$), 182 S. Main Street, Moab, UT; US 191 in center of town. ☎ (435) 259-6299 or (800) 228-2828. 84 rooms. Lodging in Moab tends toward the plain, but if there is anything approaching "luxury," then this is probably it. Large rooms.

RED STONE INN ($-$$), 535 S. Main Street, Moab, UT; US 191 just south of town center. ☎ (435) 259-2717 or (800) 772-1972. 50 rooms. Nothing fancy here, but this is one of the newest places in town. The comfortable, attractive rooms represent one of the better buys around.

SUNFLOWER HILL BED & BREAKFAST INN ($$$$), 185 N. 300 East, Moab, UT; a quarter-mile northeast of the town center. ☎ (435) 259-2974. Full breakfast included in rate. 11 rooms. Delightful old-fashioned B&B with large, antique-filled rooms in a many-gabled house. Very attractive grounds. Friendly hosts.

❖ CAMPING

DEVILS GLEN CAMPGROUND, near end of the park road (18 miles from park entrance) at Skyline Arch. No reservations accepted. 55 sites. Seven-day limit. $10 per day. RVs allowed.

DINING

There is no place to eat inside the park itself.

NEARBY COMMUNITIES

ARCHES DINING ROOM ($$), 196 S. Main Street, Moab, UT; in the Ramada Inn (see listing above). ☎ (435) 259-7141. American food. Good variety of well-prepared but simple cuisine served in an attractive dining room with large pictures of the nearby national park. Friendly service.

CENTER CAFÉ ($$), 92 E. Center Street, Moab, UT; in middle of town, just off US 191. ☎ (435) 259-4295. American/continental cuisine. Possibly the best place to eat in town. Large selection of excellent entrées prepared with fresh ingredients. Bread and pastries baked on premises.

SUNSET GRILL ($$), 900 N. Highway 191, Moab, UT; north side of town. ☎ (435) 259-7146. Steak/seafood. Fine view from hilltop location in this former house of a local mining baron. The food is excellent and the service is first rate. Some pasta dishes also on the menu.

WHERE DO WE GO FROM HERE?

Arches National Park is best seen as a component of *Suggested Trip 8*, which brings together many of the fascinating and unusual natural wonders of southern Utah. If you're looking for a shorter jaunt, the town of Moab can be used as a base from which to explore many beautiful sights. In addition to Arches, day trips from Moab will enable you to take in **Canyonlands National Park, Dead Horse Point State Park** (☎ 435-259-2614), the **Colorado River Scenic Byway** (SR 128) and the **Manti-La Sal National Forest** (☎ 435-637-2817), as well as other sights.

BANDELIER
NATIONAL MONUMENT

Situated in a narrow canyon in the Pajarito Plateau, this region of northern New Mexico is high mesa country. Beautiful mountains surround deep valleys and thick forests are interspersed with arid rocky areas. Bandelier National Monument was established to preserve the remains of an Ancestral Puebloan community over eight centuries old.

> NOTE: *The term "Ancestral Puebloan" has recently replaced "Anasazi," which meant the ancient ones. The old term has somewhat negative connotation to some Native Americans.*

Although the remains of surface pueblos and the cave dwellings that were carved out of the soft tufa rock of the canyon walls are worthy and interesting sights in and of themselves, we've chosen Bandelier for inclusion in this book because of the outstanding scenery. From the moment you turn off the main highway into the monument, you'll be confronted with awesome panoramas of the deep canyon and the mountains in the distance. Once down at the canyon's bottom, the view up is equally impressive. Bandelier offers a double bonus. Not only will you leave with a sense of nature's wonder, but you'll receive an education in the ancient inhabitants of the region as well.

FACTS & FIGURES

Location/Gateways/Getting There: In northcentral New Mexico, Bandelier is conveniently linked with major urban centers via Interstates. It can be reached in less than two hours from Albuquerque via I-25 and SRs 44 and 4 (the more scenic approach route), or via I-25 to Santa Fe and then north on US 285 to SR

502 west to SR 4. The town of Los Alamos is the nearest community of significance.

Year Established: 1916.

Size: 32,737 acres (51 square miles).

Admission Fee: $5 per vehicle.

Climate/When to Go: The monument is open all year, but there are heavy snows and cold weather in winter. In summer, this mountainous region has comfortable temperatures.

Contact Information: Superintendent, Bandelier National Monument, HCR 1, Box 1, Los Alamos, NM 87544. ☎ (505) 672-0343.

TOURING

There aren't many miles of roads within Bandelier, so you'll have to get out of your car to really see this place. The best of the scenery comes as soon as you leave SR 4 and enter the monument. By way of one long switchback, the road descends from the forested Pajarito Plateau into the narrow canyon where the Anasazi (or Ancestral Puebloans) settled around 1150 A.D. As

Pictographs in the Painted Cave.

113

the road drops, the views of the canyon walls as well as of the canyon itself get better and better. The road soon ends at the **visitor center**. Exhibits there explain the history of the canyon's inhabitants over the past eight centuries.

Beginning directly to the rear of the visitor center is the **Main Ruins Loop**. This covers a round-trip of about 1½ miles on a paved walkway. Along the way you'll see the remains of a surface community as well as the many small caves that were carved into the relatively soft rock and served as home to hundreds of people. You can climb into most of the caves. Some require using a small ladder while others are reached more easily. Children will find this an amusing activity, but even grown-ups seem to like crawling around inside. The natural scenery of the canyon from the walkway along these caves is also quite a sight. The Main Loop (along with the entry road) can be accomplished in under two hours. But there's lots more to see if you have the time.

Another trail continuing from the Main Loop leads an additional mile to the **Ceremonial Cave**. If you want to go inside and see the reconstructed ceremonial kiva chamber, you must ascend (and then descend) 140 feet of stairs, including four rather steep ladders.

> **❖ TIP**
>
> *If you have a fear of ladders or heights, don't even think about attempting this.*

The **Falls Trail** is somewhat easier. This begins at the visitor center and heads in the opposite direction towards the Rio Grande. It is 1½ miles to the Upper Falls (altitude change of 300 feet); another quarter-mile to the Lower Falls (additional 200 feet); and, finally, another three-quarters of a mile to the Rio Grande. The view from the end is spectacular and the falls are enjoyable.

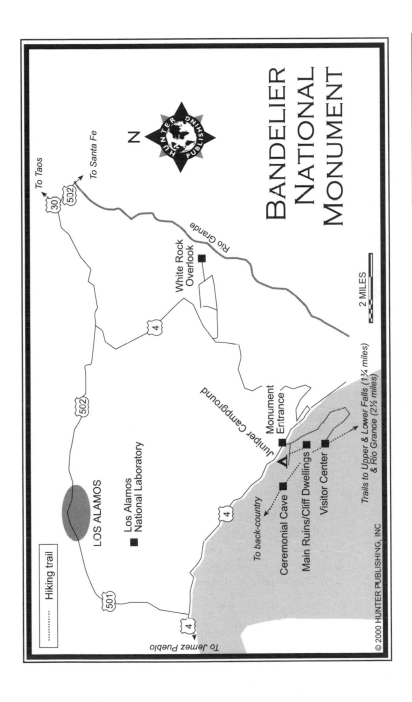

BANDELIER NATIONAL MONUMENT

N

To Taos

To Santa Fe

30
502

502

Rio Grande

White Rock Overlook

4

LOS ALAMOS

■ Los Alamos National Laboratory

502

Juniper Campground

Monument Entrance

To back-country

Ceremonial Cave

Main Ruins/Cliff Dwellings

Visitor Center

Trails to Upper & Lower Falls (1¾ miles) & Rio Grande (2½ miles)

4

501

4

To Jemez Pueblo

.... Hiking trail

2 MILES

© 2000 HUNTER PUBLISHING, INC

SPECIAL ACTIVITIES

If you don't want to hike to the Rio Grande, you can get a similarly great view from the **White Rock Overlook and Park**. This is not within Bandelier National Monument, but is on the way back to Alamosa via SR 4 in an easterly direction. Take Grand Canyon Road off SR 4 and follow the signs to the park.

ACCOMMODATIONS

❖ HOTELS & MOTELS

There are no lodgings inside the monument.

NEARBY COMMUNITIES

BANDELIER INN ($$), 132 State Route 4, White Rock; between Bandelier National Monument and Los Alamos. ☎ (505) 672-3838 or (800) 321-3923. Continental breakfast included in rate. 50 rooms. These good accommodations are the closest to be found near the monument. Nothing fancy, but it's clean and comfortable. Several restaurants nearby.

HILLTOP HOUSE HOTEL ($$), 400 Trinity Drive, Los Alamos; just east of downtown at the intersection with Central Avenue. ☎ (505) 662-2441 or (800) 462-0936. Continental breakfast included in rate. 19 rooms. Attractive wooden A-frame construction and good views from hillside setting. Spacious, nicely decorated rooms. Good restaurant on premises.

LOS ALAMOS INN ($$), 2201 Trinity Drive, Los Alamos; downtown. ☎ (505) 662-7211 or (800) 279-9279. 116 rooms. The best lodging in town and not a bad price either. The large rooms are well furnished and equipped. Some units have hot tubs and refrigerators. There is a restaurant on the premises and several other eating places within a short distance.

❖ CAMPING

JUNIPER CAMPGROUND is situated off the access road near the monument's entrance station. No reservations accepted. 94 sites. 14-day limit. $8 per day. RVs allowed. Contact park headquarters for more details.

DINING

No food is served inside the park.

NEARBY COMMUNITIES

DE COLORES ($$), 820 Trinity Drive, Los Alamos; east of downtown. ☎ (505) 662-6285. Southwestern cuisine. A delightful place for its food, decor and atmosphere.

KATHERINE'S RESTAURANT ($$), 121 Longview Drive, White Rock; just off SR 4. ☎ (505) 672-9661. Continental cuisine. Casually elegant atmosphere and fine service. Varied menu with seafood and veal dishes always a highlight. Excellent homemade desserts.

WHERE DO WE GO FROM HERE?

The **Southwest Sojourn** (*Suggested Trip 4*) includes a visit to Bandelier. Besides the sights of New Mexico that are a part of that trip, you could opt to include some of the attractions in southern Colorado. **Mesa Verde** and the **Great Sand Dunes** are two possibilities.

THE SOUTHWEST

Big Bend National Park

Encompassing a vast tract of wilderness on the north side of a very big bend in the Rio Grande River bordering Mexico, the park combines both desert and mountain terrain. It also contains many striking geologic structures, notably the several deep, sharp-walled canyons.

Because of variations in elevations from less than 3,000 to almost 8,000 feet, Big Bend, although in desert country, has many climatic zones and a wide variety of wildlife and vegetation. The many barren and rocky areas are a sharp contrast to both the desert flowers and cactus that bloom a brilliant white and the heavily forested mountain slopes just a few miles away.

There is a little of everything at Big Bend, but you'll probably be most impressed by the beauty of the rugged Chisos Mountains and their precipitous canyons.

Facts & Figures

Location/Gateways/Getting There: This is one of the more difficult places to reach of all the parks in this book. Big Bend is about 300 miles from El Paso via I-10, US 90 and SR 118. From the east, it can be reached from San Antonio via US 90 and US 385, a distance of about 360 miles. The park is tucked into a small corner of southwestern Texas.

Year Established: The park was established in 1935 and remains one of the lesser-known major units of the National Park System.

Size: 741,118 acres (1,158 square miles), an area just about the same size as the state of Rhode Island.

Admission Fee: $10.

Climate/When to Go: The weather varies widely from the desert areas to the mountain heights and back to the canyons. There is also great variation within a single day in many sections. It is not advisable, however, to visit in the heat of the summer, because daytime temperatures, although relatively comfortable in the mountains, can be well over 100°F in the lower desert areas. Probably the best time to visit is between March and May. Not only is the temperature more comfortable, but this is also the time (especially during March) when the desert cactus is in bloom and there are beautiful white flowers almost everywhere you look.

Contact Information: Superintendent, Big Bend National Park, PO Box 129, Big Bend National Park, TX 79834. ☎ (915) 477-2251.

AUTO TOUR/SHORT STOPS

Your visit to Big Bend National Park will be in the form of a long loop from either Alpine (via SR 118) or Marathon (via US 385). From one point to the other, it is a circuit of 187 miles, of which not quite one-fifth is within the park itself. This does not include close to another 100 miles of side roads leading to the park's main features along the Rio Grande. It does not matter from which end you begin.

> NOTE: *For the purposes of this book, we will work our way through the park from the SR 118 entrance.*

As you pass by the Maverick Ranger Station at the park's entrance, the road starts to climb dramatically, offering views of **Tule Mountain** on your right and, a bit later, **Croton Peak** to your left. Approximately 10 miles into the park, turn off the main route at the Santa Elena Junction and follow the **Ross Maxwell Scenic Drive** to its end, about 25 miles distant. En route are mountain views and the canyon of the Blue Creek. View stops should be made at the **Sotol Vista, Burro Mesa Pouroff** and **Mule Ears Viewpoint**, most of which are reached via very short spurs from the scenic drive. The last eight miles from Castolon to the end are alongside the majestic **Santa Elena Canyon**. There are several vantage points from which you can walk to the rim and see the Rio Grande, more than 1,000 feet below.

❖ DID YOU KNOW?

As you stare across the canyon with the Rio Grande way below, the opposite rim of the canyon is actually in Mexico.

Reverse your route back to the main park road as it continues to wind its way alongside mountain peaks. In about 12 miles another turnoff leads six miles down a spur route to the Basin Campground area and a **ranger information station**. From here there are excellent views of 7,835-foot **Emory Peak**, highest in the park, and 7,535-foot **Lost Mine Peak**. (Several trails begin here; see the following section.)

❖ TIP

This road is narrow and has steep grades, so trailers and RVs are not recommended.

Rejoining the main road once again you will soon come to Panther Junction. Bear right to the **park headquarters**, where you can get information and see exhibits on the park. Then continue your journey along this road to **Boquillas Canyon**. This trip is over 35 miles and just before the end it divides into two short spurs that lead to observation points with excellent canyon vistas. Boquillas Canyon is quite different from Santa Elena, as the Rio Grande in this area has significantly more turns. Note that the angle of the sun will have changed since you last looked at the river, offering a completely different perspective.

Return to the main park route where the road will now begin to drop, but not nearly as steeply as you rose at the very beginning of the journey. Shortly, you will reach a roadside exhibit area of fossilized bones, all of which were found within the park. Continuing, the park ends at Persimmon Gap.

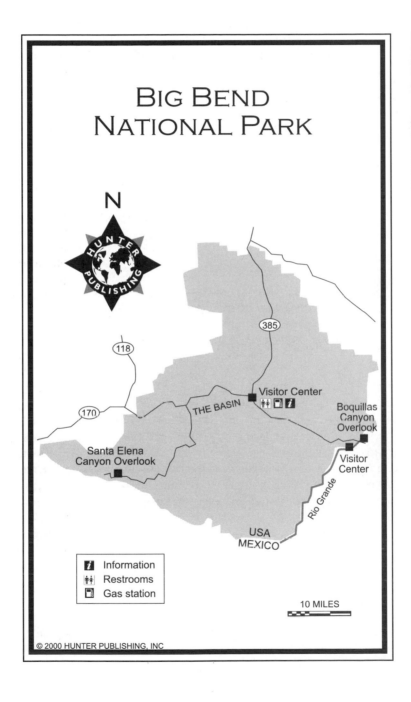

BIG BEND NATIONAL PARK

N

385

118

170

THE BASIN

Visitor Center

Boquillas Canyon Overlook

Visitor Center

Santa Elena Canyon Overlook

Rio Grande

USA
MEXICO

	Information
	Restrooms
	Gas station

10 MILES

© 2000 HUNTER PUBLISHING, INC

You cover a lot of miles and many beautiful sights on the Auto Tour. Allow between seven and eight hours to complete it all.

GETTING OUT/LONGER STOPS

❖ HIKING

A picturesque nature trail leads to **Lost Mine Peak**. The way is not particularly difficult, but it is long, requiring three hours for the round-trip. (You can do only part of it if that's too long.)

Shorter walks lead to formations known as the **South Rim** and the **Window**, but they are more strenuous and require one to 1½ hours apiece.

> NOTE: *The canyon bottoms are also accessible by trail, but these are extremely difficult and should NOT be attempted by anyone without experience in such activities, especially during hot weather.*

❖ 4WD TRIPS

If you have a 4WD vehicle with high clearance you can explore an extensive network of primitive roads that lead through the mountains as well as along the canyon of the Rio Grande. These roads connect Castolon and Rio Grande Village at Boquillas Canyon. They can also be accessed from the road between Panther Junction and Dugout Wells. Obtain maps of these routes from any park visitor center before setting out.

SPECIAL ACTIVITIES

❖ RIVER RUNNING & WHITEWATER RAFTING

The Rio Grande offers everything from slow, quiet areas to fairly wild whitewater. River access is at Study Butte, where you can rent equipment for self-guided river trips. Operators that offer trips include:

Texas River Expeditions . . . . ☎ (800) 839-7238
(Study Butte)
Far Flung Adventures . . . . ☎ (800) 359-4138
(four miles west of Study Butte)
Big Bend River Tours . . . . ☎ (800) 545-4240
(Lajitas)

Call for schedules, prices and reservations.

❖ HORSEBACK RIDING

You can also explore Big Bend via horseback trips into the park interior that last from 2½ hours to a full day.

Big Bend Stables . . . . ☎ (800) 887-4331
(Butte)
Lajitas Stables . . . . ☎ (915) 424-3238
(Lajitas)

ACCOMMODATIONS

❖ HOTELS & MOTELS

INSIDE THE PARK

CHISOS MOUNTAIN LODGE ($$), Chisos Basin section of the park, west of Panther Junction, then south on spur road. ☎ (915) 477-2291. 72 rooms. The lodge has a variety of accommodations in four different facilities in close proximity to one another within the Chisos Basin. These include a motor lodge, motel, lodge and cottages. Prices don't vary much from one type to another, nor does the comfort level, which is adequate.

NEARBY COMMUNITIES

BIG BEND MOTOR INN ($), State Highway 118, Study Butte; 27 miles west of the park entrance. ☎ (915) 371-2218 or (800) 848-BEND. 85 rooms. Decent accommodations at a very affordable price. Nothing to write home about, but you won't find anything on that order in these parts.

LAJITAS ON THE RIO GRANDE ($$-$$$$), State Highway 70, Terlingua; west of the park entrance. ☎ (915) 424-3471. 89 rooms. A full-service resort with swimming, tennis and more. Built on the site of General Pershing's headquarters for his foray into Mexico. Varied accommodations, thus they range in price, from the old officer's quarters and cavalry post to recent additions with mission or village-style architecture.

❖ CAMPING

All campgrounds operate on a first-come, first-served basis – no reservations accepted. There's a 14-day limit. $7 per day. RVs allowed only at Rio Grande Village.

CAMPGROUNDS AT A GLANCE			
NAME	LOCATION	SITES	COST
Rio Grande Village	In the village.	100	$7 per day
Chisos Basin	In the basin.	64	$7 per day
Cottonwood	Cottonwood.	31	$7 per day

DINING

INSIDE THE PARK

CHISOS MOUNTAIN LODGE (see above) has several dining options, none of which are that great, but will do nicely for those staying inside the park. ($-$$)

NEARBY COMMUNITIES

BADLANDS RESTAURANT ($$), in the Lajitas on the Rio Grande resort (see listing above). Mexican/American food. Nicely prepared Tex-Mex, southwestern and other dishes served in a pleasant atmosphere.

BIG BEND MOTOR INN RESTAURANT ($$), Big Bend Motor Inn (see listing above). ☎ (915) 371-2485. American food. Good selection of well-prepared American favorites along with a sprinkling of Tex-Mex.

LONG DRAW SALOON ($), State Highway 170; seven miles west of Study Butte. ☎ (915) 371-2608. Best pizza in this corner of the state. Also ribs, chicken, and the like.

WHERE DO WE GO FROM HERE?

Suggested Trip 4 has an extension that includes Big Bend on its list of attractions. However, you might consider the extra mileage somewhat prohibitive unless time is not a problem. Big Bend's remote location makes it difficult to include a lot of other parks in the same trip.

A manageable itinerary of scenic attractions can be arranged in a loop from El Paso. Also included would be **Guadalupe Mountains** (☎ 915-828-3251) and **Carlsbad Caverns National Parks** (☎ 505-785-2232) as well as the **White Sands National Monument** (☎ 505-479-6124).

BLACK CANYON OF THE GUNNISON NATIONAL MONUMENT

Incorporating 12 miles along the deepest portion of the Gunnison River gorge, this is one of the most amazing sights in the country. Although there are other canyons that may be deeper, longer, or even a bit narrower, none combines so many extraordinary features in such a small area.

The product of more than two million years of cutting action by the river, the canyon reaches a maximum depth of almost 2,700 feet below the rim. At the top it measures as little as 1,200 feet from one rim to the other in some places, making it seem as though you can reach out and touch the opposite side. At one point on the bottom the canyon narrows to only 40 feet wide.

❖ DID YOU KNOW?

There are only a few places where the width exceeds the depth in Black Canyon, which is very unusual.

The canyon's name comes from two factors: much of the canyon is in shadow because sunlight cannot penetrate its narrow opening; secondly, the rock itself is a dark color. Its walls really are sheer drops. Two of the most spectacular are Painted Wall and Chasm Wall, which drop 2,250 and 1,180 feet, respectively. Black Canyon will leave a lasting impression.

FACTS & FIGURES

Location/Gateways/Getting There: The monument is just off US 50 east of Montrose in west-central Colorado. It is 65 miles from the Grand Junction exit of I-70 and about 250 miles from Denver via US 50 and US 285. Allow six hours for the latter drive. This gateway description applies to the South Rim; see the special discussion on the North Rim at the end of this chapter.

Year Established: The Black Canyon of the Gunnison became a national monument in 1933.

Size: 20,763 acres (32 square miles).

Admission Fee: $4.

Climate/When to Go: The South Rim is open all year, but only the beginning of the road may be open when there has been heavy snow. The main travel season is May through October. Summers are quite warm, but usually not uncomfortable.

Contact Information: Superintendent, Black Canyon of the Gunnison National Monument, 2233 East Main, Montrose, CO 81402. ☎ (970) 249-7036.

AUTO TOUR/SHORT STOPS

The **South Rim Road** extends approximately five miles from its beginning at the monument entrance, providing easy access via short trails to more than a dozen overlooks with spectacular views. The contrast between the often sun-drenched overlook areas and the dark, gloomy recesses of the canyon's interior are profound, as is the immensity of the sheer canyon walls. At several of the overlooks the opposite rim is so close that you'll almost be tempted to reach out and touch it.

As the road is short, you should plan to stop at all of the overlooks; but the very best views are at **Gunnison Point** (which is behind the small visitor center), **Chasm View, Painted Wall View** (similar view at Dragon Point), **Sunset View** and **High Point**. Many of these are good places to see the dark, streaked patterns in the sheer rock walls. It looks almost as if the canyon was a canvas for a giant artist, and the Painted Wall certainly got its name from this.

*A staggering view looking down into the Black Canyon
from the North Rim.*

Look east or west and you will see the length of the canyon between the great walls of the gorge and more fully appreciate just how narrow it is. This is also one of the best ways to peer down to the bottom and see the winding Gunnison River as it cuts its way through the channel bottom.

> NOTE: *All of the walks to the overlooks can be completed in a matter of a few minutes. The Devils Lookout and Rock Point are the longest, but even these take less than 15 minutes, round-trip.*

The trails are relatively flat and almost all of them can be accessed by the physically challenged. It will take only about 90 minutes to drive the Monument's South Rim, stop at the visitor center, and do most of the overlooks. Allow an additional hour if you are going to drive the **East Portal Road**, which begins just inside the monument entrance and twists and turns its way down about 1,700 feet to the Gunnison Diversion Dam at East Portal. The canyon itself is not nearly as deep at this point and, although still beautiful, is less spectacular than along the rim. The ride to this point and back will add a little thrill to your day.

GETTING OUT/LONGER STOPS

❖ ROCK CLIMBING

Descents into the canyon are allowed as long as you notify a Park Ranger of your trip. All such trips are arduous and should only be attempted by experienced rock climbers.

❖ HIKING

As the monument is relatively small and mostly confined to the canyon rim, there are few long hikes that can be suggested for the more casual visitor. You can, however, walk along portions of the rim (the **Rim Rock Trail**, which begins at the visitor center, is recommended). A longer trail – 1½-mile **Warner Point Nature Trail** – leads along the rim. Its trailhead is at the road's end.

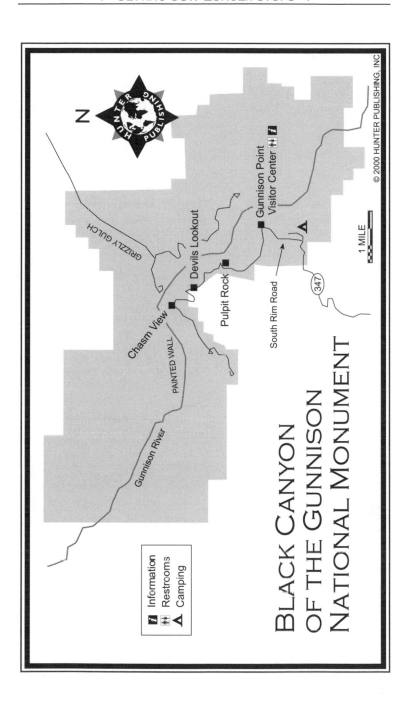

© 2000 HUNTER PUBLISHING, INC

BLACK CANYON
OF THE GUNNISON
NATIONAL MONUMENT

Information
Restrooms
Camping

1 MILE

129

❖ THE NORTH RIM

The North Rim provides vistas just as fantastic as those from the South Rim, but it is much harder to reach. It is accessible by a 14-mile graded road, the last two miles of which are along the canyon's rim, and is open only from May to October. There are no visitor facilities. If you are interested, you can acces this rim via SR 92 from either Delta (between Grand Junction and Montrose if coming from the west) or from just past the town of Sapinero in the Curecanti Recreation Area if coming from the east. The spur road leaves SR 92 at Crawford. Additional mileage from the entrance road on the South Rim to the North Rim is about 75 miles one way, regardless of which route you take.

> NOTE: *Timid drivers should be aware that the roads to and along the North Rim do not have guardrails to provide an emotional security blanket.*

ACCOMMODATIONS

❖ HOTELS & MOTELS

There are to places to stay inside the monument.

NEARBY COMMUNITIES

HOLIDAY INN EXPRESS ($$$), 1391 S. Townsend Avenue, Montrose; one mile south of town center on US 550. ☎ (970) 240-1800 or (800) HOLIDAY. Continental breakfast included in rate. 122 rooms. New and attractive rooms and mini-suites, many with such amenities as microwave/refrigerator, Jacuzzi, wet bar and fireplace. There's also a communal swimming pool. Several restaurants in vicinity.

RED ARROW MOTOR INN ($$$), 1702 E. Main Street, Montrose; one mile east of town center on US 50. ☎ (970) 249-9641 or (800) 468-9323. 60 rooms. Spacious, nicely furnished rooms, some with patio or balcony (not that the view is anything to note). Restaurants are nearby.

WESTERN MOTEL ($), 1200 E. Main Street, Montrose; a half-mile east of town center on US 50. ☎ (970) 249-3481 or (800) 445-7301. 28 rooms. Definitely not as nice as the preceding two options, but at almost half the price, this is a good value for the thrifty traveler. Several restaurants in the vicinity.

❖ CAMPING

No reservations are accepted for either campground. Two-week maximum stay. Call the park headquarters for details.

CAMPGROUNDS AT A GLANCE			
NAME	LOCATION	SITES	COST
South Rim	Off the main road immediately after the entrance station	102	$8 per day
North Rim	Opposite Chasm View	13	$8 per day

DINING

There are no eating establishments within the monument boundary.

NEARBY COMMUNITIES

GLENN EYRIE ($$-$$$), 2351 S. Townsend Avenue, Montrose; two miles south of town center on US 550. ☎ (970) 249-9263. American food. Attractive dining room in a Colonial-style home. Excellently prepared meals featuring beef and wild game as well as seafood. The service is friendly and professional.

JIM'S TEXAS STYLE BBQ ($-$$), 1201 S. Townsend Avenue, Montrose; one mile south of town center on US 550. ☎ (970) 249-4809. American food. Cafeteria style, although the food quality is much higher than you'd normally associate with such an establishment. Popular with the locals. Features mesquite-grilled meats and fowl, as well as a nice salad bar.

WHERE DO WE GO FROM HERE?

Suggested Trip 3, a scenic loop through Colorado, includes the Black Canyon. It is an ideal trip for spectacular scenery, and can be condensed if you need a shorter trip. Regardless of how much or how little of Colorado you plan to visit, any trip to the Black Canyon should be combined with the adjacent **Curecanti National Recreation Area**. Stretching for about 30 miles alongside the Gunnison River and easily traversed by US 50, the Curecanti contains several dams (some can be visited), manmade lakes (boating and fishing are popular), and beautiful mountain scenery. For further information you should contact the recreation area supervisor at ☎ (970) 641-2337.

BRYCE CANYON NATIONAL PARK

Although young in geological terms compared to some of its famous neighbors, Bryce Canyon is one of the most remarkable examples of nature in the world. It is one of the main reasons why this section of southern Utah is called "Color Country." This land is filled with unusually shaped pinnacles, spires, arches and other rock formations that come in a staggering array of colors, including pink, red and rust. Patches of green (which are actually the tops of trees in the canyon) also dot the landscape. The shapes are a result of erosion; the colors come from a combination of mineral deposits in the stone and the play of sunlight. Despite its name, according to geologists the park is not a canyon at all. It is, rather, a series of amphitheaters in the shape of a horseshoe. The name given to it by native Indians translates roughly as "Red rocks standing like men in a bowl-shaped canyon." Indeed, no words in the English language could describe it more succinctly than that.

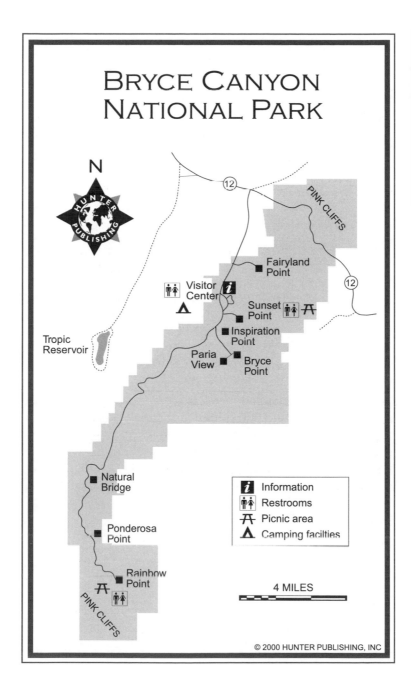

BRYCE CANYON NATIONAL PARK

N

Fairyland Point

Visitor Center

Sunset Point

Inspiration Point

Paria View

Bryce Point

Tropic Reservoir

Natural Bridge

Ponderosa Point

Rainbow Point

PINK CLIFFS

i Information
👫 Restrooms
🏓 Picnic area
🔺 Camping facilties

4 MILES

© 2000 HUNTER PUBLISHING, INC

THE SOUTHWEST

A government surveyor in 1876 said of Bryce that it is the "wildest and most wonderful scene that the eye of man ever beheld," although an early Mormon settler named Ebaneezer Bryce considered it a "hell of a place to lose a cow." No doubt! In reality, Bryce is a land where seeing is not believing. It is not uncommon for visitors to stand and stare at a particular view or formation as if in a trance, then come back and look again later. Travelers who have been to many of our national parks usually rank Bryce high on their list of favorites.

FACTS & FIGURES

Location/Gateways/Getting There: In the southwestern portion of Utah, Bryce is reached from I-15 via SR 14, US 89 and SR 12 from Cedar City if you are coming from the south. From the north, exit at I-15 via SR 20 and take that to US 89, then SR 12. It is about a 4½-hour drive from Las Vegas, and a 5½-6-hour trip from Salt Lake City. Those are the nearest commercial airports. On both routes the roads are excellent and the scenery during the second half of the journey is superb – so much so that you won't mind how long it takes to get there.

Year Established: Mormon settlers were the first white men to come upon this area, one of whom the park is named after. It was surveyed in the 1870s and was given the status of a National Park in 1924.

Size: 36,010 acres (56 square miles). It is not one of the biggest of our national parks but, acre for acre, it packs a wallop that can hardly be equaled.

Admission Fee: $5.

Climate/When to Go: Although the park is beautiful when it is snow-covered, the first-time visitor will probably enjoy it more without a blanket of white. Because of the high elevation (most of the canyon rim is between 8,000 and 9,000 feet above sea level), the summer is quite pleasant. The main touring season, when most facilities are open, is from May 1st through the end of October. Brief afternoon thunderstorms in summer provide most of the precipitation in this generally arid area.

> NOTE: *Be advised that during these storms lightning frequently strikes the rim; so be prepared to seek shelter when the skies open up.*

Contact Information: Superintendent, Bryce Canyon National Park, Bryce Canyon, UT 84717. ☎ (435) 834-5322.

AUTO TOUR/SHORT STOPS

As a casual visitor, you can see Bryce Canyon quite easily from your car and with relatively short, easy walks. The main road extends from the park entrance almost directly south to **Rainbow Point**, a distance of just over 20 miles. The road comes to a dead end, and you must retrace the same route to return. The round-trip, including allowance for a few short spur roads, will still be under 50 miles.

Although relatively small, the park contains an enormous amount to see, including views from 13 roadside overlooks. The best approach is to plan your trip so that there are stops in both directions. This has the additional advantage of letting you see some of the best features at different times, so that the changing light will probably make you wonder if you had previously been at that spot at all.

> NOTE: *This narrative will describe all attractions from north to south (that is, from the park entrance to the end of the road).*

Almost immediately after you pass through the entrance station, a spur road on your left leads to **Fairyland View**. The name tells all. While this view is certainly not atypical of what you will see throughout Bryce, it may well be the most dramatic. Here, like all the other stops to be mentioned on the Auto Tour, the canyon rim overlooks are just a few yards from the parking areas, so touring is extremely easy.

Rejoining the main road, in less than a mile you will reach the **Bryce Canyon Visitor Center**, which has excellent exhibits on the geological history of the park and information on activities.

> NOTE: *All trailers must be unhitched and remain here since they are not permitted south of the visitor center.*

A loop road leaves the main route and gets closer to the canyon edge, providing excellent access to two brilliant vistas: **Sunrise Point** and **Sunset Point**.

> ❖ **TIP**
>
> *It is an awesome feeling to stand on the rim between these two points and see both at once (see next section).*

The two points face each other around the largest of the natural amphitheaters that comprise Bryce. This one is two miles wide, three miles long and reaches depths of nearly 600 feet.

The short loop road meets up with the main road again, and very soon thereafter you will be at **Inspiration Point**, another of the park's most outstanding and popular viewing areas.

From here, a T-shaped spur leads to two more majestic overlooks: **Bryce Point** and **Paria View**. Return to the main road. It's about 10 miles to your next stop, with highly pleasing scenery en route Besides more distant views of the colorful, soldier-like spires, this portion of the road passes through terrain that is partially forested. The elevation in the southern half of the park is higher and it is during this part of your journey that the road rises in a series of gentle switchbacks and turns.

> ❖ **TIP**
>
> *You are more likely to see wildlife during this time than at any other point on the rim.*

Now you come to **Farview Point,** and soon after that is **Natural Bridge**, the largest such structure in the park and one of the most famous. From many of the frequent overlooks in this area you will be able to see other natural bridges and several arches as well as the much more common pinnacles and spires.

Yovimpo Point is the next view stop and it comes just before the end of the road at **Rainbow Point**. Looking north from this last viewpoint you will see an amazing panorama of rock-filled amphitheaters, many of which you passed on the way down (or actually, up) and looking quite different from this vantage point.

> ❖ **DID YOU KNOW?**
>
> *At 9,102 feet, Rainbow Point is the highest elevation of any viewpoint on the Canyon Rim Road.*

You will certainly regret that the road goes no farther, but the consolation is that you can, if you wish, do it all over again on the way back! And that is one of the greatest pleasures of Bryce because even a small change in the angle of sunlight (or the angle at which you view it) has an enormous effect on the coloring in the canyon; thus, the same spot will look very different if seen even a short time later or earlier. It makes for endless variety and is truly a sightseeing bonanza.

Including driving time and stops at the visitor center and the observation points suggested, it should take you less than four hours to complete the Auto Tour of Bryce Canyon.

GETTING OUT/LONGER STOPS

❖ HIKING

Although the high elevation helps keep summers cool, it can also make even relatively short walks a bit tiring for some, so do consider this before attempting anything in this section.

Routes that lead down below the canyon rim are difficult, but everyone we have spoken to who has walked along even a small portion of the 22-mile **Under the Rim Trail** enthusiastically reports that the views of the imaginatively named formations are a worthy reward for the effort.

> NOTE: *When you are on the rim's edge you will frequently see people moving about in the narrow, tunnel-like passages beneath the rim. Do not throw anything in, as you may cause injury to hikers.*

An easy but still exhilarating walk is between **Sunrise and Sunset Points**. The distance is less than three-quarters of a mile (one way). The trail is quite level and you will have views of the canyon that are generally not available from the overlooks alone. Allow more than an hour for this activity, or half that time if one member of your party skips the walk and meets the rest of you with the car at the other end. This trail is actually a portion of the 5½-mile **Rim Trail**, which extends all the way from Fairyland to Bryce Point. You can access this trail at many points along the Rim Drive. The trail is almost always level or nearly level.

Hikers tackle the rugged trails in Bryce Canyon.

> NOTE: *While there are railings at the overlooks by most parking areas, the Rim Trail itself has no such protective barriers and goes right along the edge. It presents no danger so long as you don't do anything foolhardy, but parents should keep a very close watch over small children.*

The Navajo Loop, Fairyland and Tower Bridge Trails all descend into the canyon. While going down may seem easy enough, remember that the return trip involves an ascent out of the canyon ranging up to 750 feet, making these trails of 1½ to eight miles very strenuous. Time required for these trails varies from about two hours for the shortest (the Navajo Loop) to five hours or more for the longest. Be sure to carry plenty of drinking water.

The **Navajo Loop** descends a bit over 500 feet. Among the formations you will pass are: Wall Street, the Camel and Wise Man and Thor's Hammer. You can literally spend the entire day beneath the rim as many of the trails interconnect with one another.

For those of you who want to go into the canyon with less effort, the **Queens Garden Trail** at Sunrise Point is the easiest below-the-rim excursion. The 1½-mile, two-hour hike visits one of the park's most scenic areas. The return climb of 320 feet can be handled by most people – just take it slow. All in all, a below-rim walk will be a worthwhile part of any visit to Bryce.

SPECIAL ACTIVITIES

❖ HORSEBACK RIDING

If you are not up to the rigors of exploring the canyon on foot, consider a horseback ride instead. **Canyon Trail Rides** (☎ 435-679-8665) offers trips of varying lengths. Information can be obtained at the visitor center. Other operators are located at **Ruby's Inn** (☎ 435-834-5341), just north of the park entrance.

> NOTE: *Although not as hard on your legs, horseback riding too can be strenuous.*

❖ HELICOPTER FLIGHTS

Helicopter flights are available from private operators. They, too, can be found north of the park entrance. Contact the Tour Desk at Ruby's Inn, above, for information.

ACCOMMODATIONS

❖ HOTELS & MOTELS

INSIDE THE PARK

BRYCE CANYON LODGE ($$), just off the main park road. ☎ (435) 834-5361. For reservations contact AMFAC/TW Services at ☎ (303) 297-2757. Open April through October. 114 rooms. An historic complex consisting of a main lodge and rustic cabins. Wooded setting within walking distance of Bryce Canyon rim. Comfortable place to stay with lots of atmosphere. Restaurant.

NEARBY COMMUNITIES

BEST WESTERN RUBY'S INN ($$-$$$), Bryce; SR 63, a mile south of SR 12 and a mile north of park entrance. ☎ (435) 834-5341 or (800) 528-1234. 369 rooms. A sprawling motor inn complex with lots of facilities and nicely decorated rooms. The building goes back to the early days of the national park and has grown and been rebuilt since then. A huge general store here has just about anything. Good restaurant on premises (see below).

BRYCE CANYON PINES ($$), Highway 12, Bryce; six miles west of Bryce Canyon National Park entrance. ☎ (435) 834-5441 or (800) 892-7923. 50 rooms. Basic motel accommodations at a good price. Convenient location for park visitors. Some rooms have fireplaces. Restaurant.

BRYCE CANYON WESTERN TOWN ($$), 3800 South Highway 89, Panguitch; seven miles south of town on US 89 and 20 miles from entrance to Bryce via US 89 and State Highway 12. ☎ (435) 676-8770. 56 rooms. Newest motel in the vicinity of the park. Clean and comfortable rooms that are nicely maintained. Restaurant on premises.

❖ CAMPING

No reservations accepted. 14-day limit. RVs allowed.

CAMPGROUNDS AT A GLANCE			
NAME	LOCATION	SITES	COST
North	Just south of visitor center.	111	$12 per day
Sunset	Opposite Sunset Point.	115	$12 per day

DINING

INSIDE THE PARK

BRYCE CANYON LODGE DINING ROOM ($$-$$$), Bryce Canyon Lodge (see listing above). ☎ (435) 834-5361. American/continental cuisine. Nicely prepared entrées that include American and southwestern dishes as well as some European touches. Refined atmosphere and good service.

> ❖ **TIP**
>
> *The Bryce Canyon Lodge and Ruby's Inn (below) will prepare box lunches for guests spending the afternoon in the park.*

NEARBY COMMUNITIES

COWBOY'S SMOKEHOUSE ($$), 95 N. Main Street, Panguitch; downtown on US 89. ☎ (435) 676-8030. American food. Specializing in mesquite-style barbecued beef, pork ribs and chicken as well as steaks. Excellent food and friendly service in a delightful old west atmosphere that the whole family will get a kick out of.

RUBY'S INN RESTAURANT AND STEAKHOUSE ($$), Best Western Ruby's Inn (see listing above). ☎ (435) 834-5341. American food. Wide selection of entrées with steak and seafood being the specialties of the house. Buffet option. Salad bar. Box lunches to go.

WHERE DO WE GO FROM HERE?

Bryce Canyon can be seen in conjunction with *Suggested Trip 8*, **Unique Utah**. However, it is also a very common practice to make a mini-trip of **Bryce, Zion National Park** and the north rim of the **Grand Canyon**. This is often done in a loop from Las Vegas rather than from more distant Salt Lake City. You can also visit a nearby miniature version of Bryce called **Cedar Breaks National Monument** (☎ 435-586-9451). If your route to or from Bryce is passing through Cedar City, then you should definitely include it on your schedule. It won't take long, and is very worthwhile. Even better, organize your trip so you see Cedar Breaks on your way to Bryce – it's an excellent appetizer!

CANYON DE CHELLY NATIONAL MONUMENT

Like Bandelier National Monument, Canyon de Chelly is a dual-purpose facility. It preserves both Native American civilization as well as scenery that is among the most dramatic in the never-lacking-for-wonders American Southwest. First, a few words about the human aspects of Canyon de Chelly. Its history covers five different eras in Native American culture going back to around 2,500 B.C. This begins with the Archaic period, through the Basketmakers and Ancestral Puebloans, to the Hopi, and finally, the Navajo. Some members of the Navajo tribe still reside in the canyon. Several impressive ruins are open to visitors.

From a scenic standpoint, Canyon de Chelly is hard to beat. The 26-mile-long Canyon de Chelly and the 25-mile long Canyon del Muerto converge to form a V-shape that is clearly evident from several vantage points. Other canyons lead into the main canyons in several impressive junctions. The sheer red sandstone walls are only about 30 feet high where the two main canyons meet. They quickly rise, however, to heights of as much as a thousand feet, providing great views from above and below. The smooth surface of the walls is especially surprising, almost as if it were sanded down by human hands. While the red is quite vivid, the dark streaks of natural phenomena known as desert varnish make it look as if it has been painted in some areas. Add to that the huge rock formations in many parts of the canyon and you have a natural wonderland par excellence.

FACTS & FIGURES

Location/Gateways/Getting There: Situated in a remote section of extreme northeastern Arizona, Canyon de Chelly is on the vast expanse of Navajo Indian land. Phoenix is one possible gateway city for those who will be flying into the area. From there, take I-17 north to I-40 east, then US 191 north to the town of Chinle and the entrance to the monument. It is a six-hour trip. The driving time from Albuquerque is about two hours shorter.

Year Established: 1931.

Size: 83,840 acres (131 square miles).

Admission Fee: Admission is free, but see the *Special Activities* section for rates on tours that lead into the canyon.

Climate/When to Go: Summer temperatures are warm to hot. The winter can bring snow and cold weather. Spring and fall are delightful.

Contact Information: Superintendent, Canyon de Chelly National Monument, PO Box 588, Chinle, AZ 86503. ☎ (520) 674-5500.

> NOTE: *Many of the sites are sacred to the Navajo and the entire monument is located on the Navajo Indian Reservation.*

AUTO TOUR/SHORT STOPS

Although the ruins and other aspects of past and present Native American culture are interesting, it is the awe-inspiring scenery that is likely to leave the most lasting impression on you. The Auto Tour is a great way to see that scenery and it's almost too easy. There are two separate drives, each roughly 20 miles one way, that begin at the junction near the monument entrance. This spot is just north of the monument's small visitor center. Allow about two hours for each rim drive and the many overlooks. Besides having good vantage points from which to see many Ancestral Puebloan ruins in the canyon, the overlooks allow you to take in the great scenery. Sheer walls drop about a thousand feet in some places. Reddish hues dominate, but there are amazing streaks of black, dark blue and other colors. These are called desert varnish.

❖ DID YOU KNOW?

Desert varnish is actually living, microscopic organisms that attach themselves to the cliffs.

There are also some astounding views of beautiful rock formations, but more about that later.

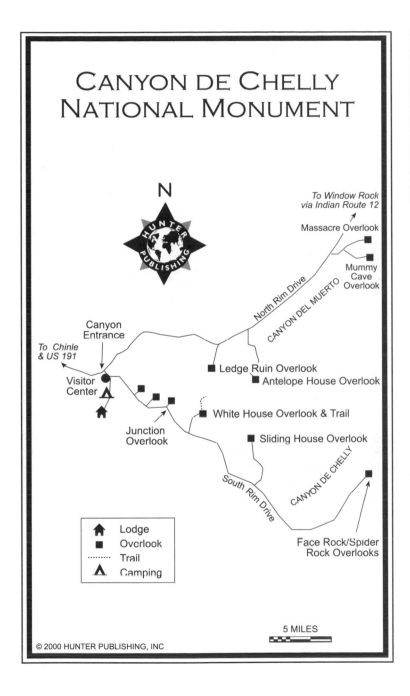

Canyon de Chelly National Monument

N

To Window Rock
via Indian Route 12

Massacre Overlook

Mummy
Cave
Overlook

North Rim Drive

CANYON DEL MUERTO

Canyon
Entrance

To Chinle
& US 191

Visitor
Center

Ledge Ruin Overlook

Antelope House Overlook

White House Overlook & Trail

Junction
Overlook

Sliding House Overlook

CANYON DE CHELLY

South Rim Drive

Face Rock/Spider
Rock Overlooks

Lodge
Overlook
Trail
Camping

5 MILES

© 2000 HUNTER PUBLISHING, INC

> ❖ **TIP**
>
> *The North Rim Drive is lovely, but not as memorable as the South Rim Drive. If your time is limited, go for the latter.*

We'll begin with the **North Rim Drive**. All of the overlooks on this rim (and most on the south) are reached by very short spurs from the main rim road. The **Ledge Ruin, Antelope House, Mummy Cave** and **Massacre Cave Overlooks** all peer into the Canyon del Muerto. Mummified remains of prehistoric inhabitants have been found at Mummy Cave.

> ❖ **DID YOU KNOW?**
>
> *Translated as the Canyon of Death, Canyon del Muerto is so named because of a massacre of the inhabitants by the cavalry in the vicinity of Massacre Cave.*

The **South Rim Drive** faces Canyon de Chelly, the second of the two canyons in the monument that converge to form a giant V. The first stop on this rim is the **Tsegi Canyon Overlook**. Following soon after is the amazing **Junction Overlook**. From this vantage point you have a splendid view of the two canyons converging. **White House Overlook** comes up next and offers a look at one of the best preserved ruins in the monument. Then comes **Sliding House Overlook**, the final ruin on this rim. After a sharp turn in the rim road you'll soon reach the end of the line. Here, in close proximity to one another, are **Face Rock** and **Spider Rock Overlooks,** the most beautiful area in Canyon de Chelly. Two smaller side canyons divert from Canyon de Chelly at this point. The view is even more dramatic here because the canyon is much deeper at this point. Face Rock and Spider Rock are two monumental natural formations that sit in Canyon de Chelly near its convergence with the side canyons. It is an unforgettable sight whether you look down into the beautiful canyon, or towards the horizon, with its distant mountains towering above the landscape.

Getting Out/Longer Stops

❖ Hiking

There aren't that many opportunities to really stretch your legs, and the walks from the overlook parking areas to the rim are quite short.

One opportunity for the more serious walker or hiker is the **White House Trail**, which descends 600 feet from the White House Overlook to the ruins of the same name on the canyon floor.

NOTE: *This is the only place in Canyon de Chelly National Monument where visitors are allowed into the canyon without an official Navajo guide.*

A view from the bottom of Canyon de Chelly.

THE SOUTHWEST

147

Despite the big drop in altitude and the return climb, the well-maintained trail isn't difficult and the grade is not too steep. If you're in decent shape it won't present that much of a challenge, although you do have to be prepared to wade across the Chinle Wash. How much water is in the wash depends on the amount of recent rainfall.

The 2½-mile round-trip requires two hours to complete.

SPECIAL ACTIVITIES

Touring the interior of Canyon de Chelly and Canyon del Muerto is a highlight of any visit to this monument. All options other than the White House Trail will require the services of a Navajo guide. If you have your own four-wheel-drive vehicle, you can use it as long as you are accompanied by a guide. Guides can be hired for $10 an hour with a three-hour minimum.

❖ TRUCK TOURS

The most popular tour is via four- or six-wheel-drive truck. Guides narrate the human and natural history of the canyon and there are frequent stops at ruins and other points of interest. The half-day tour costs $35 for adults, while the full-day trip is $56. Reservations are strongly advised and can be made by calling the folks at **Thunderbird Lodge**, ☎ (800) 679-2473.

❖ HORSEBACK RIDING

Trips range from two hours to a full day. Information on horseback tour operators is available at the visitor center.

ACCOMMODATIONS

❖ HOTELS & MOTELS

INSIDE THE MONUMENT

THUNDERBIRD LODGE ($$), adjacent to visitor center. ☎ (520) 674-5841. 72 rooms. Situated in a pretty grove of trees (you can't see into the canyon from here, though), this Native American-owned and -operated property has Southwestern-style rooms in a new wing as well as in an older stone building. The new ones are bigger, but the older rooms have more charm. Restaurant on premises (see below).

NEARBY COMMUNITIES

BEST WESTERN CANYON DE CHELLY INN ($$), 100 Main Street, Chinle; just east of US 191 on Indian Route 7. ☎ (520) 674-5874 or (800) 528-1234. 99 rooms. Pleasantly furnished modern rooms. Few amenities, but just right for a good night's sleep after a long day of touring. Good-size rooms.

HOLIDAY INN ($$-$$$), Indian Route 7, Chinle; two miles east of US 191 and a half-mile from Canyon de Chelly. ☎ (520) 674-8264 or (800) HOLIDAY. 110 rooms. Nice rooms in typical older style two-story roadside Holiday Inn. The place has been redecorated. Native American jewelry and pottery store on the premises. Restaurant (see below).

❖ CAMPING

COTTONWOOD CAMPGROUND is a half-mile from the visitor center. No reservations accepted. 99 sites. Five-day limit. No fee is charged. RVs allowed. Call the park headquarters for details.

DINING

INSIDE THE MONUMENT

THUNDERBIRD LODGE DINING ROOM ($), Thunderbird Lodge (see listing above). ☎ (520) 674-5841. American food. Although the food is served cafeteria-style, the quality is well above what you would expect from this type of facility and from the prices charged. Besides American, there are Southwestern and Native American dishes.

NEARBY COMMUNITIES

GARCIA'S RESTAURANT ($$), in the Holiday Inn, Chinle (see listing above). ☎ (520) 674-8264. If you have ever wondered what authentic Native American cuisine is like, here's your chance to find out. The popularity of Southwestern cuisine can be traced in large measure to Indian cooking and if you like Southwest, you'll find this just right.

WHERE DO WE GO FROM HERE?

Suggested Trip 7 is a good way to partake of the sights at Canyon de Chelly. However, you can also combine it with a trip that includes southern Utah. **Glen Canyon National Recreation Area** and **Monument Valley** are among the possibilities. The sights of northwest New Mexico are another option. **Chaco Culture National Historical Park** (☎ 505-786-7014) and **Bisti Badlands** are among the attractions that combine scenery with more Native American history.

CANYONLANDS NATIONAL PARK

Canyonlands, as the name implies, is an area of deep, colorful canyons. It is a land filled with natural arches, spires and mesas of all shapes and sizes, a fantasy land where nature has gone wild. While some portions of the park are easily reached, others are among the most remote regions in the United States and are visited only by a handful of hearty adventure travelers. A seemingly endless stretch of almost flat plateaus, broken by a seemingly uncountable number of deep canyons carrying rushing rivers, stretches as far as the eye can see. There actually are only two rivers, but they have numerous turns and hairpin bends. The unusual scenery so common throughout southern Utah can also be found in Canyonlands. Strange formations are numerous and so are the varying shades of color that change with the passing of the day.

*Standing Rock Basin, one of Canyonlands'
prominent features.*

FACTS & FIGURES

Location/Gateways/Getting There: Located in the canyon country of southeastern Utah, Canyonlands is within a short drive of Moab and Arches National Park. Salt Lake City and Denver are the two best gateway cities. From the former, take I-15 south to US 6 and follow that route east to the junction of I-70. Follow the interstate east to US 191 south and the access road into Canyonlands, which is SR 313. It's about 300 miles and will take five to six hours. From Denver, follow I-70 west to US 191 and proceed as above. This route is about 50 miles longer, but since the majority is on the Interstate, the traveling time is about the same.

Year Established: 1964.

Size: 337,570 acres (527 square miles).

Admission Fee: $10. This also allows entrance to Arches National Park within seven days from the purchase date.

Climate/When to Go: Spring and fall are the most delightful times to visit Canyonlands. The very hot summer sun can be rather relentless at times. However, if your summer touring is done mostly in the morning, the low humidity will make the temperature much more tolerable. Winters are chilly and snow is not unknown.

Contact Information: Superintendent, Canyonlands National Park, W. Reserve Blvd., Moab, UT 84532. ☎ (435) 259-7164.

AUTO TOUR/SHORT STOPS

Canyonlands National Park is separated into three areas (or districts) by natural river barriers. There is no in-park connection between the sections. The most heavily visited district is called the Island in the Sky. This is the only one with an extensive road system. Fortunately, it contains some of the best scenery in the park. The Auto Tour, as well as the next section, will be devoted only to this district. The *Special Activities* section will offer tips on visiting the other two districts – The Needles and The Maze.

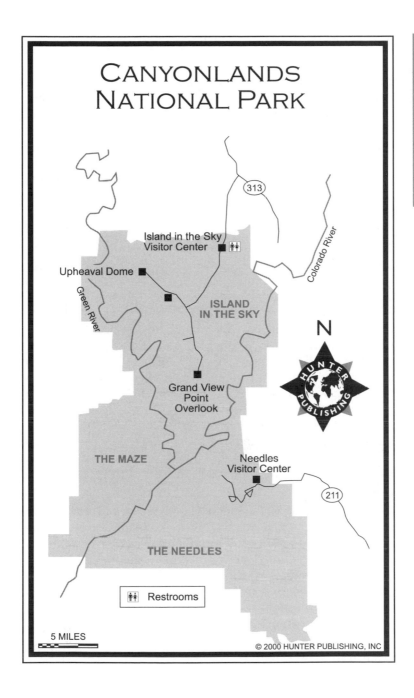

CANYONLANDS NATIONAL PARK

313

Island in the Sky Visitor Center

Colorado River

Upheaval Dome

Green River

ISLAND IN THE SKY

N

HUNTER PUBLISHING

Grand View Point Overlook

THE MAZE

Needles Visitor Center

211

THE NEEDLES

Restrooms

5 MILES

© 2000 HUNTER PUBLISHING, INC

❖ ISLAND IN THE SKY

The short approach road from US 191 into the park via SR 313 is a highly scenic drive. You'll rise in a series of gentle switchbacks through a series of colorful canyons until you reach the top of the plateau that comprises the better portion of the Island in the Sky. A small and not particularly interesting visitor center sits just inside the entrance. A ranger is on duty in case you have any questions or need assistance. Just south of the center is **Shaefer Canyon Overlook**, where you can peer down into the colorful gorge. You'll also see the rough **Shaefer Trail Road** that leads down into the canyon. (See the *Special Activities* section for more details.)

The road continues to gently rise higher onto the plateau and, about four miles farther along, splits. In order to save the best for last, we'll first head toward the right, stopping at the **Holeman Springs Canyon Overlook** before reaching the end of the road at **White Rock**. From here, a relatively short trail leads to one of the park's outstanding features, the **Upheaval Dome**. Scientists continue to argue about its origins. The 1,500-foot-deep dome is either the product of a meteor or the result of slow-moving underground salt deposits pushing up the soft sandstone rock. It is quite a sight. The trail, although not long, is over uneven terrain and is not recommended for those with physical disabilities. Head back toward the main road but, before you reach the original split, take the short unpaved spur road to the fantastic view at the **Green River Overlook**. Here you'll get a good look at some of the many sharp bends in the river as it winds through Stillwater Canyon.

Continue straight past the junction you previously turned at and proceed towards the next dead end in the road. Stop at the **Candlestick Tower** and **Buck Canyon Overlooks**. The formations at the first one will immediately explain its name to you. The **Orange Cliffs Overlook**, just before road's end, is an extremely colorful area. Here, as well as at the previous vista, you'll be amazed by the variety of colors and unusual rock formations. Some of the rocks look like gigantic pieces of furniture strewn about in an immense room.

Finally, at the end of the road, is the **Grand View Point Over-look**. This is a place of unbelievable beauty and a spot that you aren't ever likely to forget. Perched high above the river valleys, you'll gaze out on many of the park's geological wonders. Row after row of canyons can be seen as they drop down from the relatively flat mesa. The colorful spectacle, at an elevation of 6,090 feet, is sure to leave you breathless.

From Grand View Point, simply reverse your route, turning right at the road junction to leave the park. The time needed to do the Auto Tour of the Island in the Sky section of Canyonlands is three to four hours.

GETTING OUT/LONGER STOPS

❖ HIKING

The Island in the Sky has numerous trails that lead to other amazing vistas as well as unusual rock formations. Among these are several that begin in the vicinity of **Upheaval Dome** and **Trail Canyon**, which leads to a formation known as Moses and Zeus. These trails are long and rather difficult. Some easier ones are the trail to **Aztec Butte** and a portion of the **Hogback Trail** (just north of the Buck Canyon Overlook), which leads to a beautiful panorama point.

SPECIAL ACTIVITIES

❖ ISLAND IN THE SKY

INDEPENDENT 4WD TRIPS

This section of the park has many miles of unpaved roads to explore beneath the plateau. Some are short, some are long, but they all require 4WD and high-clearance vehicles. None should be attempted in wet weather or without detailed maps available from the visitor center. Among the more popular routes are the **Shaefer Trail Road**, which leads into Shaefer Canyon as well as to the Gooseneck Overlook Trail and Musselman Arch; and the notorious **White Rim Road**, a long hair-raising journey above both the Colorado and Green Rivers that circumnavigates beneath almost two-thirds of the Island in the Sky. Exploration of the 100-mile-long White Rim Road requires at least a full day.

ORGANIZED JEEP, MOUNTAIN BIKE & HORSEBACK RIDING TOURS

For those who are willing to rough it, but don't want to drive on their own, there are a variety of 4WD jeep tours and mountain bike tours, as well as horseback trips. Most are full-day affairs, but half-day trips (as well as overnight journeys) are available. All of them leave from Moab and you can find numerous operators throughout town. (Lists of authorized concessionairs are also available from the park's visitor centers.) A few to try are:

Cowboy Trails (horseback rides) . . ☎ (435) 259-8053
Kaibab Mountain Bike Tours . . . . ☎ (800) 451-1133
Farabee Adventures (off-roading) . ☎ (800) 806-5337

Prices start as low as $25 and rise to several hundred dollars, depending upon length of tour, distance traveled and mode of transportation.

RAFTING

River trips are also popular and provide a completely different perspective of Canyonlands – you're looking up instead of down. Much of the Colorado and Green Rivers within Canyonlands are whitewater, but you can also take milder float trips. Again, departures are mostly from Moab, but trips are also available from the town of Green River.

Adventure River Expeditions . . . . . ☎ (800) 331-3324
Tag-A-Long Expeditions . . . . ☎ (800) 453-3292

❖ THE NEEDLES

TOURING BY CAR & HIKING

The Needles section of the park is characterized by sharp, pointed rock formations of red and white nestled in rugged canyons. Numerous other formations, including arches, can be found in this diverse landscape. There are many trails that can be explored in the Needles by the adventurous hiker. It can also be seen by road. 40 miles south of Moab via US 191, turn onto **SR 211** for the 48-mile paved ride into the Needles District. There's a small visitor center and several spur roads lead to excellent overlooks, the best being the **Big Spring Canyon Overlook**.

RIVER RUNNING

The Needles section can also be explored on a raft. Operators are based in Moab (see above).

❖ THE MAZE

4WD TRIPS

There are no paved roads within the Maze District, one of the most rugged areas in the world. It can be reached by driving east from SR 24, midway between Hanksville and I-70. After Hans Flat, all of the roads are unpaved and extremely difficult, even with 4WD, high-clearance vehicles. Never attempt them in bad weather.

RIVER RUNNING

The Maze, like major portions of the Needles, can also be explored by river. Refer to the Island in the Sky section above for operators based in Moab.

ACCOMMODATIONS

❖ HOTELS & MOTELS

There are no overnight facilities within the park. Nearby communities offer a number of options. See the listings under Arches National Park, page 110.

❖ CAMPING

Reservations are not accepted at either site. Both campgrounds have a seven-day limit.

CAMPGROUNDS AT A GLANCE			
NAME	LOCATION	SITES	COST
Willow Flat	On spur road leading to Green River Overlook, Island in the Sky.	12	$10 per day
Squaw Flat	On State Hwy 211, past the Needles Visitor Center.	26	$12 per day

DINING

There are no dining facilities within the park. For places to eat in nearby communities, refer to the Arches National Park section, page 111.

WHERE DO WE GO FROM HERE?

Canyonlands is part of the **Unique Utah** itinerary (see *Suggested Trip 8*). Because of its proximity to Arches National Park, the suggestions mentioned in the Arches chapter also apply when visiting Canyonlands. A trip that combines this part of Utah with adjacent Colorado (including the **Colorado National Monument**) is also a good possibility.

Regardless of your overall itinerary, we must emphasize that any visit to Canyonlands' Island in the Sky should definitely include a stop at the adjacent **Dead Horse Point State Park**. This park can be reached from Canyonlands via a short paved road that branches off SR 313 about three miles north of the Island in the Sky entrance. The park is much smaller than Canyonlands, but offers what is perhaps the most gorgeous view in Utah – and that is saying an awful lot! From a vantage point at the end of the road and along a short, paved trail, you will see an amazing gooseneck bend in the Colorado River. The view is made all the more splendid by the fact that you are perched high above the mesa and you can see the mesa, river and the panorama in one fell swoop.

CAPITOL REEF NATIONAL PARK

Capitol Reef's dominant features are its wall-like cliffs, nearly 1,000 feet high, that run like an ocean reef for a distance of 90 miles. The tops of these cliffs are a white sandstone that many people say resembles the United States Capitol – hence the name. This land of the sleeping rainbow, as the Navajo called it, is also a place of many beautiful hues. The towering rock formations take many strange shapes. Some look as if they were built by man. The park also has many interesting narrow canyons cut by the action of water and you can see the water collecting in basins within the rock strata.

Capitol Reef, named after the United States Capitol.

> **❖ DID YOU KNOW?**
>
> *These water "pockets" give rise to the name of the Waterpocket Fold, the chief natural feature in the region of which Capitol Reef is a part.*

This rugged terrain is full of surprises. Perhaps most unusual among them are the fruit orchards in the northern part of the park.

Man has left his mark on the region and, although development is now restricted, the human history of Capitol Reef can also be explored during the time you spend here.

FACTS & FIGURES

Location/Gateways/Getting There: The park sits in southcentral Utah, where Color Country meets the Canyon Country. It is about 230 miles from Salt Lake City via I-15 south to US 50 east, and then SR 24 (just west of Salina) east to the park. Alternatively, you can reach the park from Las Vegas via I-15 north to the junction of I-70 and then east on the interstate to SR 24 near Salina, then proceeding as above. The 350-mile trip takes about 6½ hours.

Year Established: A mostly obscure national monument since its establishment in 1937, Capitol Reef was upgraded to National Park status in 1971. It still remains a largely unknown area to most Americans.

Size: 241,904 acres (378 square miles).

Admission Fee: $4.

Climate/When to Go: Late spring or early fall are the nicest times of the year, but even mid-summer is tolerable because of the generally low humidity. The winter months aren't bitterly cold, but there can be snow.

Contact Information: Superintendent, Capitol Reef National Park, HC 70, Box 15, Torrey, UT 84795. ☎ (435) 425-3791.

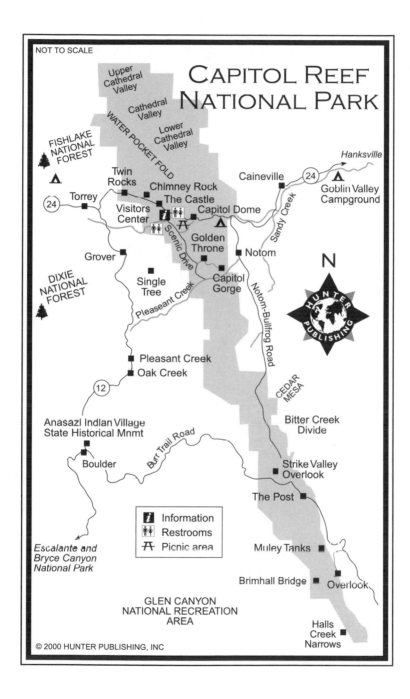

NOT TO SCALE

CAPITOL REEF NATIONAL PARK

Upper Cathedral Valley

Cathedral Valley

Lower Cathedral Valley

WATER POCKET FOLD

FISHLAKE NATIONAL FOREST

Twin Rocks

Chimney Rock

The Castle

Caineville

24

Hanksville

Goblin Valley Campground

24 Torrey

Visitors Center

Capitol Dome

Scenic Drive

Golden Throne

Notom

Sandy Creek

N

Grover

Single Tree

Capitol Gorge

Pleaseant Creek

DIXIE NATIONAL FOREST

Notom-Bullfrog Road

HUNTER PUBLISHING

Pleasant Creek

Oak Creek

12

CEDAR MESA

Anasazl Indian Village State Historical Mnmt

Burr Trail Road

Bitter Creek Divide

Boulder

Strike Valley Overlook

The Post

i Information

👫 Restrooms

🍴 Picnic area

Escalante and Bryce Canyon National Park

Muley Tanks

Brimhall Bridge

Overlook

GLEN CANYON NATIONAL RECREATION AREA

Halls Creek Narrows

© 2000 HUNTER PUBLISHING, INC

THE SOUTHWEST

AUTO TOUR/SHORT STOPS

Capitol Reef has a good system of paved roads in addition to many difficult and rather primitive routes. The paved portions consist of a 17-mile stretch along **SR 24**, which runs from east to west through the northern part of the park; and the seven-mile **Scenic Drive** that extends south from SR 24. We'll first take a look at the sights along SR 24.

❖ STATE ROUTE 24

This is a main through-route in this part of Utah and a drive along it offers some spectacular sights. Beginning at the western entrance to the park, the first thing you'll encounter are the **Twin Rocks**. These two monolithic formations are among many that line the north side of the highway. These colorful formations are huge, towering hundreds of feet above the valley. Red sandstone is the predominant color, but there are plenty of browns, yellows and white too. After passing by massive Chimney Rock you'll see a turn-off for the quarter-mile spur road to **Panorama Point**. The overlook offers excellent views of Sulphur Creek Canyon, but superior vistas are available if you take the very short trail to the **Goosenecks Overlook**. **Sunset Point**, where the warm light at the day's end is spectacular, is also reached by a short trail (about a third of a mile) from the Panorama Point parking area.

Continuing on SR 24, you'll soon pass **The Castle**, one of the park's most striking features. Among the biggest formations in Capitol Reef, the creviced sides of the rocky precipice look as though they were sculpted by hand. There are even many turrets at the top! Soon after is the visitor center and the beginning of Scenic Drive. Skipping that for the moment, farther along the state highway is the beginning of a short trail that leads to ancient **Native American petroglyphs**, and views of massive **Capitol Dome**, the natural feature that gives the park its name.

❖ SCENIC DRIVE

Scenic Drive heads south into the park's heartland along a geologic formation known as the **Waterpocket Fold**. It is this formation which gives the "Reef" part of the name to the park. The drive is easy and the multicolored rock walls are impressive.

At the end of the paved part of the road is an unusual formation called the **Egyptian Temple**. Most of the trails along this route are quite long and are described in the next section.

You should allow approximately 2½ hours for the Auto Tour. Many unpaved roads continue farther into the park's interior. Some are quite difficult. Inquire at the visitor center before setting out on any of them.

GETTING OUT/LONGER STOPS

❖ HIKING

A couple of trails lead off from SR 24.

The easiest is the mile-long **Hickman Bridge Trail**, which leads to a picturesque natural bridge. Scenic Drive also has several popular trails.

The 2¼-mile **Grand Wash Trail** is a mostly level walk through a narrow canyon with sheer rock walls on either side.

The trail to **Cassidy Arch**, a strenuous 1¾-mile hike, branches off from the Grand Wash Trail.

Finally, the **Capitol Gorge Trail** is another mostly level trail that is about a mile long. This one is especially interesting because it will lead you to a number of water pockets, or "tanks."

❖ DID YOU KNOW?

Rainwater that collected in these natural depressions was used by area inhabitants as sources of water for thousands of years.

Capitol Reef has more than a half-dozen other beautiful trails that range in length from little more than a mile to more than four miles. All involve considerable changes in altitude and are quite difficult. Some climb to the top of the rim along SR 24, another goes up closer to Chimney Rock, and others explore more remote areas along Scenic Drive.

> NOTE: *All of these trails are more suited to the experienced hiker.*

SPECIAL ACTIVITIES

A good way to add fun to your visit during the summer is to **pick fruit** that grows in the Fruita area (near the visitor center). From June through October you'll find (depending upon which month you visit) cherries, apricots, peaches, pears and apples. There's no charge for the fruit you pick as long as you consume it within the park. Fees apply if you take fruit out of the park.

ACCOMMODATIONS

❖ HOTELS & MOTELS

There are no overnight facilities within the park boundaries.

NEARBY COMMUNITIES

AQUARIUS MOTEL ($), 240 W. Main Street, Bicknell; on SR 24 about nine miles west of the park. ☎ (435) 425-3835 or (800) 833-5379. 26 rooms. Good places are hard to find in this sparsely populated and not heavily visited region. The Aquarius offers big rooms that are quite comfortable. Restaurant on premises.

WONDERLAND INN ($-$$), junction of state highways 12 and 24, Torrey; three miles west of Capitol Reef. ☎ (435) 425-3775 or (800) 458-0216. 50 rooms. Nice setting overlooking surrounding area. Quite a few guest services and facilities. Better-than-average rooms. Restaurant.

FERN'S PLACE MOTEL ($), 900 E. 100 North, Hanksville; on SR 24, 30 miles east of Capitol Reef. ☎ (435) 542-3251. 18 rooms. If the pickings are slim to the west of the park, they're even more so for those who wish to stay on the east side. Fern's offers very basic accommodations A few so-so places to eat can be found in the vicinity of the motel.

❖ CAMPING

The FRUITA CAMPGROUND (71 sites) is on Scenic Drive, just south of the visitor center. 14-day limit. $6 per day. RVs allowed. No reservations. Call park headquarters for information.

DINING

There are no dining establishments within the park itself.

NEARBY COMMUNITIES

CAFÉ DIABLO ($$), 599 W. Main Street, Torrey; on the west end of town along SR 24. ☎ (435) 425-3070. Southwestern cuisine. While there are restaurants in some motels in Torrey and Bicknell that will do in a pinch, this is the only place in the area we can recommend. Good food and service in pleasant surroundings with patio dining in season. The specials are usually good.

WHERE DO WE GO FROM HERE?

Capitol Reef is an integral part of *Suggested Trip 8*, which visits six of Utah's major natural wonders covered in this book. In addition, many other fascinating sights are included. Because Capitol Reef is in the middle of a rather remote region, it requires a fairly substantial trip from any major city. If Trip 8 is too ambitious, you can always take a shortened version of that itinerary. The **Grand Staircase-Escalante National Monument** and **Bryce and Zion National Parks** could be included on a mini-Unique Utah trip.

CARLSBAD CAVERNS NATIONAL PARK

Although Carlsbad Caverns does not quite have the same extensive network of passageways and sub-caverns found in Mammoth Cave, it is justly noted for its enormous chambers and unusual beauty.

> ❖ **DID YOU KNOW?**
>
> *The 21 miles of known caverns in Carlsbad make it one of the largest underground networks in the world.*

You enter the caverns through a massive archway that reaches 90 feet across and 40 feet high at its greatest point. Inside, you will enter another world, one of beautiful and sometimes delicate formations. Often, these features are surprisingly alive with color. Some 200 million years of earth's history are contained within the cavern.

Some people who visit put the wonders of the cave itself in a position of only secondary importance. They come to visit the cave's famous residents – a huge population of bats. These strange creatures emerge from the cave on summer evenings in a spectacular display that defies description.

The bats and the caves combine to makes Carlsbad Caverns a unique destination.

FACTS AND FIGURES

Location/Gateways/Getting There: Carlsbad is situated at the town of Whites City in the southeastern portion of New Mexico, not far from the Texas state line. You can reach the park from El Paso via US 180, a 160-mile, three-hour trip. It can also be accessed via I-40, US 285 and US 180 from Albuquerque. This is about a six-hour trip.

Year Established: The caverns were made a National Monument in 1923 and received a promotion to National Park just seven years later in 1930.

Size: 46,755 acres (73 square miles).

Admission Fee: No entrance fee is charged. Cave tour prices are given separately under each tour description.

Climate/When to Go: This desert country has mild winters. In summer, days are very hot and evenings are pleasant. However, since the majority of your activities are inside, the outside weather conditions are not terribly important. The cave is always 56°F, a temperature that makes a sweater or light jacket appropriate at all times. Try to visit here between May and October, when the bats make their appearance. To visit at any other time would be to miss half the fun.

Contact Information: Superintendent, Carlsbad Caverns National Park, 3225 National Parks Highway, Carlsbad, NM 88220. ☎ (505) 785-2232.

TOURING

This park is an underground experience and outdoor walks and vistas from your car are not common. However, the seven-mile drive from the entrance to the visitor center rises dramatically through a dark canyon. Other good views can be seen from the 10-mile **Walnut Canyon Desert Drive**, a well-maintained gravel road.

At the **visitor center** itself you'll find excellent displays on the park's natural and human history, as well as that of the surrounding area. Access points to back-country trails can be found on Walnut Canyon Drive and on the road to Slaughter Canyon Cave (via County Route 418). These trails are all long, difficult and primitive.

THE SOUTHWEST

SPECIAL ACTIVITIES

Hall of Giants in the Big Room.

The main cave can be visited on one or more of three different tours. These are called the **Natural Entrance Route**, the **Big Room Route** and the **Kings Palace Guided Tour**. Access to both the Big Room and the Kings Palace is via an elevator. The first route follows a twisting one-mile course and is moderately difficult to strenuous. Note that this tour has no facilities for handicapped individuals. The Big Room Route is also about a mile long, but is relatively flat and even has sections that are accessible to the handicapped.

Finally, the Kings Palace Guided Tour is easier than the Natural Entrance Route but more difficult than the Big Room. It lasts about 1¼ hours. You should allow at least an hour for the Big Room and about 90 minutes for the Natural Entrance Route. All three tours converge at a point near the cave's elevators adjacent to the cafeteria. You can rent an audio commentary for each of the self-guided tours. Each tour costs $5.

❖ NATURAL ENTRANCE ROUTE

You enter through the natural archway, the same one that the famous bats of Carlsbad use to enter and exit the cave. Descent is by a series of switchbacks along a paved path. As you approach the bottom, look up and see the opening to the sky getting smaller and smaller before it disappears completely at the bottom of this twisting and dizzying drop. The path continues to drop as you pass through the Main Corridor. The total drop from the entrance is about 750 feet to the Green Lake Room, so-called because of a small pond there. Soon after, you'll reach the junction where the other tours commence. Return is by elevator.

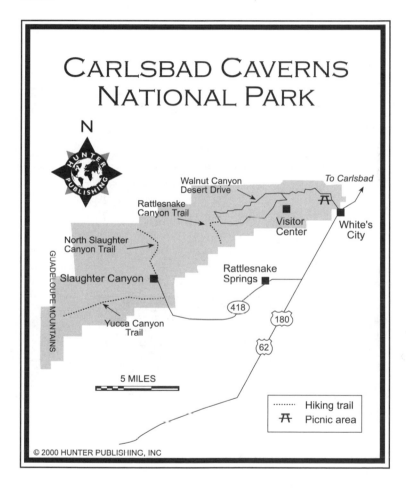

© 2000 HUNTER PUBLISHING, INC

❖ BIG ROOM ROUTE

This tour starts with an elevator ride down into the cavern. As you exit the elevator, you'll walk into the immense Big Room, cross-shaped and measuring 1,800 by 1,100 feet at its greatest point.

The room contains many odd formations, including one that is reminiscent of a totem pole. You exit the cave by elevator.

❖ KING'S PALACE GUIDED TOUR

This is the only tour option for the main cave, and it is done this way to ensure that the delicate formations in this portion of the cave aren't damaged by visitors, either accidentally or deliberately. On this tour, you'll explore four (although it's really three, with two that adjoin) rooms containing some of the most beautiful formations in the entire cave system. These include the **King's Chamber**, a large, almost circular room, and the adjacent **Queen's Chamber**. Here, the fantastic formations are mainly in the form of elephant ears or draperies. The room is also known for its delicate pink and rose colored hues when illuminated. Next, you move on to the **Papoose Room** before returning to the cavern lunchroom.

❖ OTHER TOURS

There are four other tours to less-visited portions of the main cave, as well as one in a separate cavern.

- ❖ The **Hall Of The White Giant** is a strenuous trip that requires crawling and squeezing through long passages. Protective clothing (long pants, knee pads, gloves) should be worn. Groups depart on Saturdays at 1 pm. The cost is $20 and children under age 12 are not admitted.

- ❖ The **Left Hand Tunnel** is not strenuous and covers only about half a mile. You have to carry a lantern as you walk past pretty pools. Tours depart daily at 9 am. The cost is $7 and children under age six are not permitted.

- ❖ The fairly strenuous **Lower Cave** tour visits some beautiful sections of Carlsbad. It leaves weekday afternoons at 1 and costs $20. Children under age 12 are not permitted.

- ❖ The most difficult main cave tour is the one to **Spider Cave**. Protective clothing is recommended as you have to navigate some tight passages. This option takes you to some of the most unusual formations in all of Carlsbad Caverns. It leaves on Sunday afternoons at 1 and costs $20. Children under age 12 are not permitted.

- ❖ Finally, the **Slaughter Canyon Cave** is a difficult tour along undeveloped routes. The cave is 25 miles southwest of the main cave area via US Highways 62/180 and then 11 miles via signed county roads. The last mile is not paved. Reservations are required. Cost: $15. Children under age six are not permitted.

The last trips depart at about 4:30 pm in the summer and earlier during the off-season. Sign up for the guided tour at the visitor center. At a minimum, we suggest you do the Big Room and Kings Palace routes and also highly recommend the Natural Entrance Route as long as you're physically able to do so. Reservations for cave tours can be made in advance by calling ☎ (800) 967-CAVE (2283).

❖ THE BATS

And now... about those bats. These harmless, useful and misunderstood animals thrill many a visitor. The cave is home to about 14 different bat species, but the majority are Mexican freetails – no vampire bats here (and they don't deserve their reputation either). Every night from May to October, people gather in the amphitheater outside the cave. At sundown a park ranger gives an interesting talk about the bats and what you are going to see. At dusk the spectacle begins. All is quiet; soon you will begin to hear the fluttering of wings as the first bats emerge from the cave. At first there are only a few, but then they come out at the rate of up to 300 per second, filling the sky completely with their black silhouettes. Some come so close that you can actually feel a breeze from their wings. (Don't worry, they won't get in your hair, although this doesn't stop folks from shrieking. It's all part of the fun.)

In all, a million or more bats may emerge in a procession that can last as long as an hour, especially during the height of the season (August and September). They will return at dawn after an evening of dining on insects. This is one of the few places in the world where you will have a chance to admire this awesome spectacle, and it's sure to be one that you remember.

> NOTE: *The portion of the cave where the bats reside during the day is off-limits to all visitors.*

ACCOMMODATIONS

❖ HOTELS & MOTELS

There are no places to stay inside the park.

NEARBY COMMUNITIES

BEST WESTERN CAVERN INN/GUADALUPE INN ($$), 17 Carlsbad Caverns Highway, Whites City; immediately off US 62 & 180 at the entrance to the park. ☎ (505) 785-2291 or (800) CAVERNS. 105 rooms. It's a good thing that these two motels are nice, because they're the only places in town. They sit on either side of the road across from one another and they share the same registration area and lobby. Comfortable, attractive rooms; restaurants and other facilities on premises.

There is additional lodging available in the city of Carlsbad, but that's an additional 20 miles.

❖ CAMPING

There is no developed campground within the national park. However, commercial establishments can be found immediately outside the park at Whites City. Additional sites available in the town of Carlsbad. Try CARLSBAD CAMPGROUNDS, ☎ (505) 885-6333 or WINDMILL RV PARK, ☎ (505) 885-9761.

DINING

INSIDE THE PARK

The only place to get food within the park is the cafeteria-style lunchroom (boxed sandwiches, snacks, beverages) within the cave.

NEARBY COMMUNITIES

VELVET GARTER SALOON & RESTAURANT ($$), adjacent to the two inns listed above. ☎ (505) 785-2291. American food.

Varied selection of entrées, including steak and other American favorites, along with a number of Mexican dishes. Friendly, Old West-style and atmosphere with nice stained glass depictions of the caverns decorating some walls.

WHERE DO WE GO FROM HERE?

Although fairly distant from most of the other scenic areas of New Mexico, Carlsbad Caverns is included in *Suggested Trip 4*, which covers many of the beautiful places in the Land of Enchantment. A shorter trip from El Paso can include just the **Guadalupe Mountains National Park** in addition to Carlsbad.

COLORADO NATIONAL MONUMENT

Here is a place that is virtually unknown to most people, even those who have done quite a bit of traveling. This is a most perplexing state of affairs for me, because the Colorado National Monument is easily accessible and, more important, is one of the most beautiful sights in America. Perhaps because of its relative obscurity, the visitor comes away even more impressed by its awe-inspiring vistas.

The monument is an impressive example of the effects of erosion from wind and rain on the landscape. A masterpiece of nature, the immense monolithic formations have such fanciful names as the Coke Ovens and the Pipe Organ. They rise from a flat canyon over 1,000 feet deep and often reach above the plateau rim, from which you will be viewing them.

FACTS & FIGURES

Location/Gateways/Getting There: In the extreme west-central part of Colorado, the monument is conveniently located just three miles south of the Fruita exit of I-70 or by the Monument Road exit in the larger town of Grand Junction. The logical gateway is Denver, which is 260 miles east on I-70, an easy and wonderfully scenic drive of about five hours.

Year Established: 1911.

Size: 20,454 acres (32 square miles).

Admission Fee: $4.

Climate/When to Go: The area has a dry, sunny climate in summer, with daytime highs usually in the high 80s or low 90s. The monument is open all year, but the winters are cold and snowy. Because of the high altitude, spring and fall, though usually pleasant, can become unexpectedly cold. Summer season is the best time to visit.

Contact Information: Superintendent, Colorado National Monument, Fruita, CO 81521. ☎ (970) 858-3617.

AUTO TOUR/SHORT STOPS

One of the monument's best features is how easy it is to tour from the comfort of your car. The area is long and narrow, and is traversed by the 23-mile **Rim Rock Drive**, a two-way thoroughfare. Although it doesn't really matter which way you proceed, this description will follow a west-to-east route, simply because the visitor center is nearer to the western entrance.

Once you reach the canyon rim the route is mostly level, but it does contain a significant number of turns. It is easy going, even for the motorist who isn't used to driving near the edge of a canyon. The canyon rim ranges in elevation from about 5,700 feet near the visitor center to over 6,600 feet. The west and east entrances are at elevations of, respectively, 4,674 and 5,058 feet. Getting to and from the canyon rim is achieved by a long series of relatively easy switchbacks. They are not so hair-raising as to prevent you from admiring the fantastic scenery as you climb to the rim or come down. Just take it easy and you'll be fine!

Most of the best sights in the monument are from overlooks set right off the road or a walk of less than a hundred yards from the many roadside parking areas. There are also three easy trails that are less than a mile long. So let's take a look at Rim Rock Drive in more detail.

❖ RIM ROCK DRIVE

Rising sharply to the canyon rim, you will first reach the **Redlands View** and **Balanced Rock**. Proceed through two tunnels and past Fruita Canyon, and you will come upon **Distant View**. The first of the short trails is at **Window Rock**. With a one-way length of only about a third of a mile, it is easy to do and will give you a fine view of the Window formation, Monument Canyon and the Grand Valley.

Continuing along the road brings you to the **visitor center**, which has some interesting exhibits and information on the monument's development, geology and activities. Directly behind the center is the **Canyon Rim Trail**. This level, half-mile trail leads to a sheltered overlook from which there is the most magnificent view of Monument Canyon.

Leaving the visitor center, the view stops will continue to come upon you one after the other. **Independence View, Grand View** and **Monument Canyon View** are in quick succession, followed by the **Coke Ovens**. The first three of the above provide expansive views of the broad canyon with many large, eroded red rock formations scattered below. The Coke Ovens, grouped together like some metal-working furnace of Paul Bunyon, are easily viewed from the overlook. (There is a longer trail here as well; see the next section.)

Next comes **Artist Point, Highland View** and **Upper Ute Canyon**, then **Fallen Rock** and **Ute Canyon**. At this point, you will have traveled almost two-thirds of the way along Rim Rock Drive and the view stops are spaced farther apart.

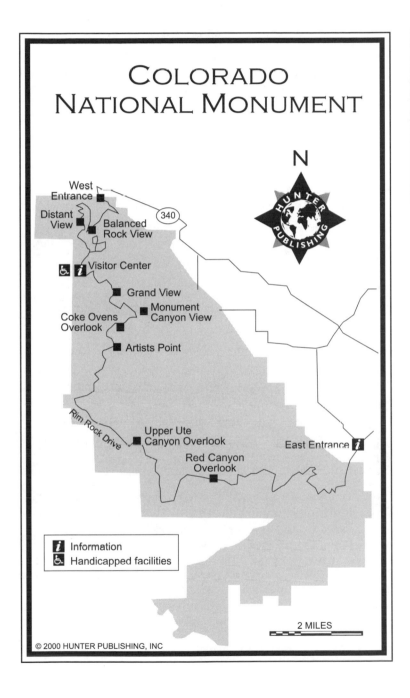

COLORADO
NATIONAL MONUMENT

N

West
Entrance

Distant
View

340

Balanced
Rock View

Visitor Center

Grand View

Monument
Canyon View

Coke Ovens
Overlook

Artists Point

Rim Rock Drive

Upper Ute
Canyon Overlook

East Entrance

Red Canyon
Overlook

i Information
Handicapped facilities

2 MILES

© 2000 HUNTER PUBLISHING, INC

THE SOUTHWEST

> ❖ **TIP**
>
> *No two viewpoints are alike, and even ones that look out upon the same formation from different vantage points tend to appear entirely different. Furthermore, light shadings depending upon where you are standing will have a tremendous affect on what you see.*

Red Canyon and **Cold Shivers Point** are the last two overlooks before the road begins its descent to the east entrance station.

To drive the length of Rim Rock Drive, including time for stopping at the mentioned overlooks and short trails, requires a little over two hours.

GETTING OUT/LONGER STOPS

❖ HIKING

There aren't too many trails other than those on the Auto Tour, but several long ones (up to seven miles) descend into the canyon and are quite strenuous.

> NOTE: *Those who do wish to climb into the canyon should register at the visitor center.*

The **Coke Ovens Trail** is just under a mile, round-trip, and takes about 40 minutes to complete. It will bring you close to the giant, rounded Coke Oven formations and gives you a better perspective of just how large they really are. While they seem big from the distance of the canyon rim, all but the mightiest skyscrapers pale by comparison when you're standing next to them.

ACCOMMODATIONS

❖ HOTELS & MOTELS

There are no overnight facilities within the monument.

NEARBY COMMUNITIES

GRAND JUNCTION COMFORT INN ($$), 750 Horizon Drive, Grand Junction; off I-70, Exit 31. ☎ (970) 245-3335 or (800) 228-5150. Continental breakfast included in rate. 57 rooms. Typical example of this moderately priced chain that is part of the larger Choice family of hotels. Clean, comfortable and no unpleasant surprises. The rooms are a little on the small side.

GRAND JUNCTION HILTON ($$$), 743 Horizon Drive, Grand Junction; off I-70, Exit 31. ☎ (970) 241-8888 or (800) HILTONS. 264 rooms. Grand Junction's most upscale property, this Hilton is an attractive eight-story midrise that affords spectacular views of either the Colorado National Monument or the nearby Grand Mesa. Excellent rooms and extensive guest facilities and services, including two restaurants. Nicely landscaped grounds.

GRAND VISTA HOTEL ($$), 2790 Crossroads Boulevard, Grand Junction; a quarter-mile north of I-70, Exit 31. ☎ (970) 241-8411 or (800) 800-7796. 158 rooms. Almost as nice as the Hilton and with nearly the same amenities, but at a considerably lower price. The best value in town. Many rooms have splendid views of the natural wonders surrounding Grand Junction.

SUPER 8 MOTEL ($$), 399 Jurassic Avenue, Fruita; a half-mile south of I-70, Exit 19. ☎ (970) 858-0808 or (800) 800-8000. 60 rooms. Relatively new member of this decent budget motel chain that provides modern and comfortable surroundings at a reasonable price. Ideal for those who don't want anything fancy. Convenient location on the west side of the monument.

❖ CAMPING

The SADDLEHORN CAMPGROUND is just inside the Fruita (west) monument entrance via State Highway 340. 80 sites. 14-

day limit. $10 per day. No reservations accepted. Call the park's main number for more information.

DINING

There are no dining options inside the monument.

NEARBY COMMUNITIES

OLIVER'S RESTAURANT & BAKERY ($-$$), in the Grand Vista Hotel (see listing above). ☎ (970) 241-8411. American food. Pleasant surroundings and well prepared entrées served by a gracious and friendly staff. The homebaked goods are outstanding, either for dessert or to go (a late night snack in your room, perhaps?).

REDLANDS DOS HOMBRES ($), 421 Brach Drive, Grand Junction; one mile west of town center via Grand Avenue. ☎ (970) 242-8861. Mexican cuisine. Delicious traditional Mexican food served in inviting and pleasant surroundings. Good family dining spot. We especially suggest the fajitas.

THE WINERY ($$-$$$), 642 Main Street, Grand Junction; off I-70 business route. ☎ (970) 242-4100. American food. This is tops in the area for thick, juicy steaks and fresh seafood. The surroundings are casually elegant, making generous use of rich woods. A mature environment, not well suited for family dining. Worth the price if you appreciate fine food and service.

WHERE DO WE GO FROM HERE?

As Denver is the closest major city, you should consider *Suggested Trip 3*, which catches all the scenic and other highlights of Colorado, truly one of America's most beautiful states. If you are pressed for time, the trip to and from Denver along I-70 passes through the heart of the **Rocky Mountains**, with many great sights on or just off the road. And just north of Denver itself is **Rocky Mountain National Park**.

Less than two hours south of the Colorado National Monument is the **Black Canyon of the Gunnison National Monument** and the **Curecanti National Recreation Area.**

DINOSAUR NATIONAL MONUMENT

A trip to Dinosaur National Monument is almost like visiting two parks in one. There's an obvious physical separation caused by the lack of roads from one part of the monument to another. And the two sections also offer completely different experiences. The Utah side of the monument is Dinosaur Country. You'll get to visit a huge sandstone cliff that housed more fossilized remains of prehistoric animals than any other place in the world. On the Colorado side is a beautiful land of deep and narrow gorges, towering cliffs and two wild rivers. The Green and Yampa Rivers, which converge in the monument at Steamboat Rock, have created some of the deepest canyons in America. The Canyon of Lodore, for example, is more than 3,000 feet deep in some places.

For the more adventurous, there are few places in America that have better whitewater rafting than Dinosaur.

FACTS & FIGURES

Location/Gateways/Getting There: Dinosaur occupies a remote corner of extreme northwestern Colorado and an adjacent area in northeastern Utah. Salt Lake City and Denver are the two nearest major cities. From Salt Lake City, take I-80 east to US 40 and then follow the latter east all the way to the town of Jensen near the Colorado line. From there, SR 149 will take you into the Utah section of the park. From Denver, follow I-70 west to the town of Dillon. Then take SR 9 north to the junction with US 40. Follow the latter west to the park entrance road near the town of Dinosaur for access to the Colorado portion of the park, or continue to Jensen and proceed as before for the Utah section. The 300-mile trip from Denver is mostly over good roads (but not Interstates), so it will take about six hours. From Salt Lake, it is 200 miles over mostly slower roads, so allow approximately 4½ hours for the drive.

Year Established: 1915.

Size: 210,844 acres (329 square miles).

Admission Fee: $10 per vehicle.

Climate/When to Go: Winters are cold and even the early spring or late fall can be uncomfortable and see heavy snow. Although the summers can be hot, the atmosphere is dry and fairly comfortable. May through September are good touring months.

Contact Information: Superintendent, Dinosaur National Monument, 4545 US Highway 40, Dinosaur, CO 81610. ☎ (970) 374-2216.

TOURING

Although Dinosaur National Monument lies in one continuous tract of land straddling the Utah-Colorado border, the sections in each state are not connected by a direct road within the monument. A comprehensive visit requires touring each of the two sections. We'll discuss each part separately.

❖ UTAH SECTION

This is the only part of the monument that contains dinosaur bones. Consequently, it is the area most commonly associated with Dinosaur National Monument. A road leads seven miles from US 40 in the Utah town of Jensen to the **Dinosaur Quarry Visitor Center**.

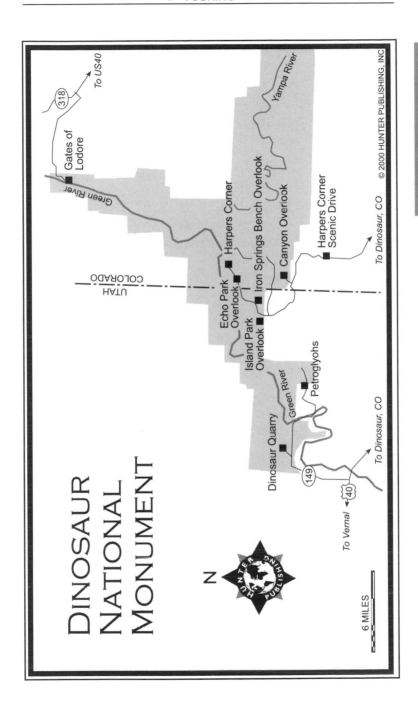

DINOSAUR NATIONAL MONUMENT

To US40

318

Gates of Lodore

Green River

Yampa River

Harpers Corner

Iron Springs Bench Overlook

Canyon Overlook

Harpers Corner Scenic Drive

Echo Park Overlook

Island Park Overlook

UTAH COLORADO

To Dinosaur, CO

© 2000 HUNTER PUBLISHING, INC

Green River

Petroglyohs

Dinosaur Quarry

149

40

To Dinosaur, CO

To Vernal

N

6 MILES

THE SOUTHWEST

> NOTE: *During the summer months you have to take a short shuttle bus ride from the main parking area to the quarry because of limited parking at the site. At other times you can drive all the way to the center.*

All fossilized remains found here are located in a single cliff, making this the most abundant prehistoric fossil site in the world. While many of the bones are now on display in museums all over the world, there are still in excess of 1,600 specimens at the quarry center. These represent not only dinosaur fossils, such as the giant brontosaurus, but more "modern" creatures like turtles, crocodiles and clams.

Another option in the Utah section is to take **Club Creek Road** for 10 miles beyond the quarry (the last mile is unpaved) to a petroglyph site. Here you can see the remains of elaborate drawings carved into the cliffs around 1000 A.D. by the ancient Fremont people. The easy **Red Rock Nature Trail** is also reached via this road. It departs from the Split Mountain campground adjacent to the Green River.

If you are visiting only the quarry, allow about two hours for the Utah Section. Those going on to the petroglyphs and nature trail on Club Creek Road should allow an additional 1½-2 hours.

❖ COLORADO SECTION

The Colorado portion of Dinosaur National Monument is a rugged and remote country of deep canyons and wild rivers. It is 25 miles along US 40 east from Jensen to the town of Dinosaur, Colorado. Just east of the town is the monument headquarters and main visitor center. This also marks the beginning of the outstanding **Harpers Corner Scenic Drive**. The road extends for 31 miles, the first 25 of which are in a narrow strip of land outside the main body of the monument. The route provides good introduction into Canyon Country. The **Escalante and Canyon Overlooks** offer excellent vistas along the way. You'll see many ridges and mountains besides the canyons of the Yampa River. The last six miles include the **Island Park and Harpers Corner**

Overlooks, which face the Green River Canyon, and the **Iron Springs and Echo Park Overlooks**, which face Sand Canyon. The latter overlook can also be reached via **Echo Park Road**. This unpaved road branches off Harpers Corner Drive and stretches for eight miles. A high-clearance, 4WD vehicle is preferable. It ends at Echo Park, a spectacular viewpoint where the Green and Yampa Rivers meet and wind around Steamboat Rock. The drop to the river level is around 2,500 feet.

Allow about two hours to complete the round-trip on the Harpers Corner Scenic Drive. An additional hour should be allowed for the Echo Park Road.

GETTING OUT/LONGER STOPS

❖ HIKING

Most of the interior of Dinosaur National Monument is a remote wilderness, and there are few trails. However, one trail that can be walked in a couple of hours is the **Harpers Corner Trail**. Beginning where the Harpers Corner Scenic Drive ends, the trail is a two-mile (one way) jaunt that drops about 120 feet and provides spectacular views of the aforementioned Steamboat Rock and river junction. It is not overly difficult.

> NOTE: *If you want to explore the monument on foot, a back-country permit is required. You can get the permit and find out about other hiking opportunities from a ranger at the visitor center.*

SPECIAL ACTIVITIES

❖ GATES OF LODORE

One of the most beautiful portions of the monument is visited by few people. This is the Gates of Lodore, one of the deepest and narrowest portions of the Green River Canyon, and worth the little journey it takes to reach. Travel east on US 40 from the monument headquarters to Maybell, then pick up SR 318 to the signed cut-off for the Gates of Lodore. The one-way distance is a hefty 85 miles, the last 10 of which are unpaved. No special vehicle is required to negotiate this portion of the road.

Rafting along the Yampa River.

❖ RIVER RUNNING

The most popular activity at Dinosaur is river running. Some of the best whitewater rafting opportunities in the United States can be had on either the Green or Yampa Rivers within the confines of the monument. Trips last from one to five days. A list of authorized concessionairs is available at the visitor center.

The operating season for river running lasts from around the middle of May through mid-September, depending upon the weather. Among the wildest water in the country, the Yampa River has three sections of rapids, while the Green contains five in the Canyon of Lodore and four in the Split Mountain Canyon, as well as the exciting Whirlpool Canyon.

Adrift Adventures Dinosaur .... ☎ (800) 824-0150
Hatch River Expeditions .... ☎ (800) 342-8243

ACCOMMODATIONS

❖ HOTELS & MOTELS

There are no accommodations inside the monument itself.

NEARBY COMMUNITIES

BEST WESTERN ANTLERS ($$), 423 W. Main Street, Vernal, UT; on US 40 about 19 miles from the monument via US 40 to Jensen and then north on State Highway 149. ☎ (435) 789-1202 or (800) 528-1234. 43 rooms. A wide variety of accommodations that can sleep two to six persons. Modestly furnished but well maintained. Convenient location for restaurants, shopping and local entertainment.

ESCALANTE TRAIL MOTEL ($), 117 S. Grand Street, Rangely, CO; off State Highway 64 (Main Street), 18 miles southeast of Dinosaur town and monument headquarters. ☎ (970) 675-8461. 25 rooms. Clean, well-maintained rooms are the selling points of this basic motel. Decent places to stay near the Colorado portion of the monument are hard to come by.

SPLIT MOUNTAIN MOTEL ($), 1015 East Highway 40, Vernal, UT; 20 miles from from the monument. ☎ (435) 789-9020. 40 rooms. Basic motel-style lodging. Clean, comfortable and a good value for the money. Close to town.

❖ CAMPING

CAMPGROUNDS AT A GLANCE			
NAME	LOCATION	SITES	COST
Split Mountain	Club Creek Road, past the Dinosaur Quary.	35	$8 per day
Green River	Club Creek Road, past the Dinosaur Quary.	100	$8 per day

These are the only developed sites in the monument, and they're both in the Utah section. No reservations accepted.

Contact the Superintendent's office for information. 14-day limit. RVs allowed but no hookups.

DINING

There are no dining options within the monument.

NEARBY COMMUNITIES

CURRY MANOR ($$$), 189 S. Vernal Avenue, Vernal; in town on US 40/191. ☎ (435) 789-2289. American/continental cuisine. Surprisingly sophisticated dining for a remote small town. The attractive surroundings occupy a former two-story home that is listed on the National Register of Historic Places. Well-prepared cuisine. Gracious and efficient staff.

CRACK'D POT RESTAURANT ($$), 1089 East Highway 40, Vernal; one mile from town center. ☎ (435) 781-0133. American/Mexican food. Friendly family-style restaurant with an excellent selection of tasty main courses that includes beef, fish and pasta.

MAGLINO'S FAMILY RESTAURANT ($-$$), 124 W. Main Street, Rangely; State Highway 64. ☎ (970) 675-2321. American food. Varied menu and attractive contemporary decor make this the best place in the area for a good sit-down meal. Pleasant wait staff. Child-friendly.

WHERE DO WE GO FROM HERE?

Dinosaur National Monument is part of the **Colorado Circle** described in *Suggested Trip 3*. It is also possible to redesign either *Unique Utah* (Trip 8) or *Three Crown Jewels* (Trip 5) to include Dinosaur.

GLEN CANYON NATIONAL RECREATION AREA

& RAINBOW BRIDGE NATIONAL MONUMENT

This vast, state-sized recreation area was created upon completion of the Glen Canyon Dam, which backs up manmade Lake Powell for 186 miles. Plenty of water-related recreational opportunities attract thousands of visitors. This is an impressive area of hidden canyons, coves and small inlets, with towering red cliffs enclosing the lake shore.

Rainbow Bridge National Monument, a small enclave surrounded on all four sides by the Glen Canyon Recreation Area, must be included among the greatest of all natural wonders of the world. That it remains standing seems impossible.

This is an area with few roads, but some of the best sights are accessible to drivers. However, a boat trip is necessary to truly appreciate the beauty of this rugged country.

FACTS & FIGURES

Location/Gateways/Getting There: In the southern part of Utah and extending into northern Arizona, Glen Canyon is 285 miles north of Phoenix via I-17 and US 89. It is about 275 miles from Las Vegas in an east/northeasterly direction via I-15, Utah SR 9 and US 89.

Year Established: The Recreation Area was officially established in 1972. Rainbow Bridge has been a National Monument since 1910.

Size: 1,236,880 acres (1,933 square miles), similar in size to the state of Delaware. Rainbow Bridge is only 160 acres, equivalent to a fourth of a square mile.

Admission Fee: There is no charge for entering either area.

Climate/When to Go: This area can be visited during any part of the year. The winters are pleasantly warm, while the spring and fall aren't overbearingly hot. Summer, of course, sees daily high temperature readings of around 100°F, but since much of your time visiting here will be spent on the water, even the summer heat is generally tolerable, especially with the low humidity that is typical of the southwest desert areas.

> ❖ **TIP**
>
> *If you do visit in summer, plan most of your outdoor activities for the morning to avoid the midday heat.*

Contact Information: Information on both areas can be obtained from the Superintendent, Glen Canyon National Recreation Area, Box 1507, Page, AZ 86040. ☎ (520) 645-2511.

Glen Canyon.

TOURING

Your main base will be the town of Page, where US 89 crosses the recreation area. Take a short side-trip on US 89 south for 23 miles and then north on US 89A for 14 miles to Marble Canyon. Here, surrounded by dark red sandstone cliffs, you can walk across the original bridge spanning the Colorado River and peer down into the narrow depths of the canyon.

Besides Marble Canyon and the short stretch of roadway through the recreation area around Page, the only roads that pass through Glen Canyon are SRs 276 and 95. These are in a remote portion of Utah, about 60 and 90 miles, respectively, up-river from Page. The former requires taking a ferry between Bull-frog Basin and Hall's Crossing. SR 95 crosses the river via suspension bridge in a fabulously scenic area at the end of Cataract Canyon. Most visitors to Glen Canyon don't get to see this section of the recreation area. If you're visiting some of the scenic wonders of southeastern Utah, then these routes can be a wonderful way to get to them. Unfortunately, there isn't any direct connection from Page (our *Suggested Itinerary* on Utah, page 471, provides some more details).

SPECIAL ACTIVITIES

❖ GLEN CANYON DAM

The **Carl Hayden Visitor Center** in Page is adjacent to the Glen Canyon Dam and has information and exhibits on the dam, the recreation area and the geology of the surrounding countryside. Guided tours of the dam leave from this point. The power house and other features are quite interesting, but the best part is going down to the dam's base. You will see the sheer, dark red walls of the Colorado River canyon – so steep that the sunlight hardly reaches the bottom, giving the river a dark, almost black appearance. The suspension bridge that carries US 89 over the river and canyon is also an impressive sight from down below. The view looking up gives a better idea of just how deep the canyon is. Canyon viewpoints are also available from near the south side of the bridge.

❖ LAKE POWELL

As beautiful as this area is, the real highlight of your visit will be a boat trip on Lake Powell to Rainbow Bridge National Monument. The monument is accessible only by boat (unless you take a difficult all-day hike through the canyon). There are hour-long, half-day and all-day cruises. The shorter trips are nice, given the great lake scenery, but don't go to Rainbow Bridge, a big shortcoming. The all-day trip goes farther down Lake Powell and visits a few more side canyons.

> ### ❖ TIP
> *Since the scenery beyond Rainbow Bridge is similar to the beginning of the trip, the half-day voyage is the better choice unless you really have a lot of time available.*

The half-day cruises leave from the Wahweap Marina, a few miles north of Page, early in the morning, returning around noon, and at one in the afternoon with return in the early evening. From the boat you will see not only the clean, refreshingly cool-looking blue waters of Lake Powell, but also the towering red cliffs that surround the lake. Your captain will point out some of the more notable landmarks, including Navajo Mountain (which bears a resemblance to Devils Tower) and some odd rock formations that look like an enormous dragon. A side canyon will bring you to the boat dock at Rainbow Bridge National Monument. From the dock it is only a 10-minute walk to the bridge; as you get closer the bridge becomes more dramatic. The largest such natural bridge in the world, Rainbow Bridge is 290 feet above the riverbed and 275 feet across. Be sure to walk directly beneath it and gaze upward. This most unusual view is like nature's version of the Gateway Arch in St. Louis! For information on cruises, ☎ (800) 528-6154. Reservations are suggested.

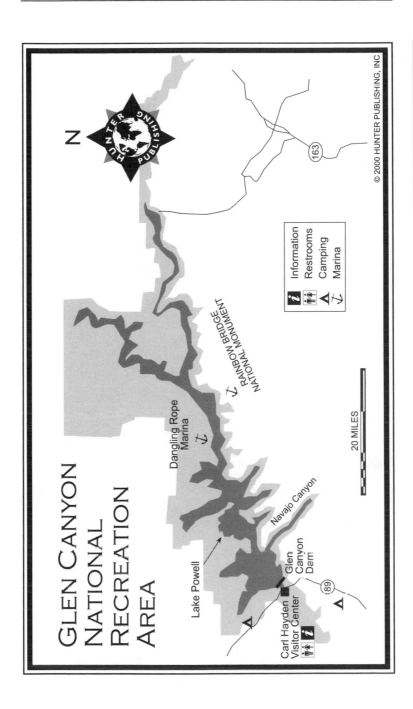

© 2000 HUNTER PUBLISHING, INC

THE SOUTHWEST

GLEN CANYON
NATIONAL
RECREATION
AREA

Information
Restrooms
Camping
Marina

Dangling Rope
Marina

RAINBOW BRIDGE
NATIONAL MONUMENT

Lake Powell

Navajo Canyon

Glen
Canyon
Dam

Carl Hayden
Visitor Center

20 MILES

The lake provides plenty of opportunity for swimming and boating, and there are also some beaches. A very popular way of vacationing here is to rent a houseboat and sail around for a few days or more. Information on this fun and relaxing way to see Lake Powell is available from Lake Powell Resorts & Marinas, ☎ (800) 528-6154.

ACCOMMODATIONS

❖ HOTELS & MOTELS

INSIDE THE RECREATION AREA

LAKE POWELL MOTEL ($$), Wahweap Junction, four miles northwest of Glen Canyon Dam along US 89. ☎ (520) 645-2477 or (800) 528-6154. 24 rooms. Small but comfortable place with a casual feel and nice setting. Many rooms have excellent views. Nearest restaurants are a short drive at the Wahweap Lodge.

WAHWEAP LODGE ($$$), Lake Shore Drive, four miles north of Page. ☎ (520) 645-2433 or (800) 645-1031. 350 rooms. A full-service resort nicely situated along the beautiful Lake Powell shoreline, the lodge is also a good place to arrange for boating and other recreational opportunities on the lake. Good restaurant.

NEARBY COMMUNITIES

BEST WESTERN ARIZONA INN ($$), 716 Rimview Drive, Page; five miles from the recreation area and about three-quarters of a mile off US 89. ☎ (520) 645-2466. 103 rooms. Attractive Southwestern decor along with good views of the lake from its hilltop location make the Arizona Inn one of the nicest places to stay in Page. Restaurant and a good selection of recreational facilities are on the premises.

HOLIDAY INN LAKE POWELL ($$-$$$), 287 North Lake Powell Boulevard, Page; US 89, about one mile from the middle of town. ☎ (520) 645-2523 or (800) 465-4329. 130 rooms. No surprises here from the "no surprises" chain. All of the comfortable rooms feature a host of modern amenities. Some rooms on the upper floors have lake views. Located adjacent to a golf course; tee times can be arranged by the hotel staff. The on-premises restaurant is a little above the usual Holiday Inn fare.

❖ CAMPING

All except one of the campgrounds within the Glen Canyon National Recreation Area are privately operated. Reservations can be made at ☎ (800) 528-6154. Bookings for the government-run campground can be made at ☎ (435) 684-7000.

CAMPGROUNDS AT A GLANCE			
NAME	LOCATION	SITES	COST
Wahweap	Four miles north of Glen Canyon Dam near Wahweap Lodge & Marina.	178	$12 per day
Lees Ferry	At the north end, near Marble Canyon.	54	$7 per day
Bullfrog	Bullfrog Marina, inside the NRA	120	$12-24 per day
Gov't Camping	State Highway 276 on the south shore of the lake at Hall's Crossing	83	$10-22 per day

Wahweap has an adjacent full-service RV park with 123 sites. Charges are from $17-24 per day, depending upon season. RVs are allowed at Lees Ferry and the government campground, which has a 14-day maximum stay.

DINING

❖ INSIDE THE RECREATION AREA

In addition to the main restaurant at the Wahweap Lodge, there are several places for snacks or a quick lunch at the various marinas.

❖ NEARBY COMMUNITIES

KEN'S OLD WEST RESTAURANT ($$), 718 Vista, Page; off US 89. ☎ (520) 645-5160. American food. Limited selection of main courses, but the ribs are an excellent choice. Nice salad bar. Patio dining available. Live country music.

WHERE DO WE GO FROM HERE?

These two areas are both included in *Suggested Trip 7*, which covers most of the major scenic attractions in the state of Arizona. It can also be done as an extension to *Unique Utah* (Trip 8). Alternately, a combination of the two will also work, with Las Vegas as your gateway. Such a trip can include, besides Glen Canyon and Rainbow Bridge, **Bryce and Zion National Parks**, the north rim of the **Grand Canyon**, **Monument Valley** on the Arizona-Utah border, **Natural Bridge Natural Monument** and **Capitol Reef National Park**.

Because of the abundance of national park facilities and state parks in both of these states, the possibilities for a wonderful journey are almost endless.

GRAND CANYON NATIONAL PARK

Grand. As in huge, as in great, as in stupendous. There is no word in our language that better describes the canyon than its very name. It was the noted English author J.B. Priestley who said of the Grand Canyon that "those who have not seen it will not believe any possible description. Those who have seen it know that it cannot be described." Its worldwide fame is attested to by the staggering number of foreign visitors who make it a must-see on their visits to America.

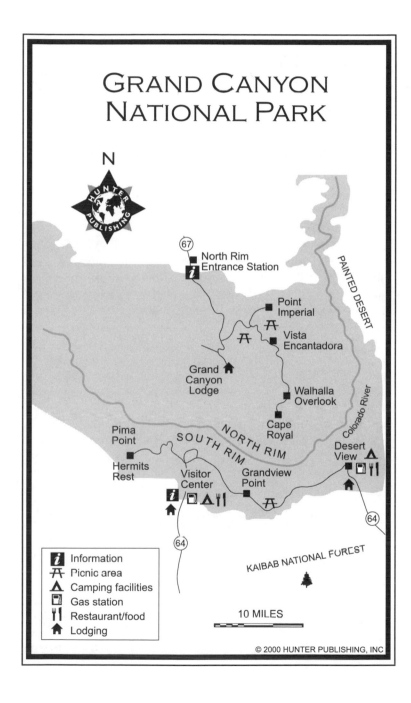

THE SOUTHWEST

GRAND CANYON
NATIONAL PARK

N

67
North Rim
Entrance Station

PAINTED DESERT

Point
Imperial

Vista
Encantadora

Grand
Canyon
Lodge

Walhalla
Overlook

Colorado River

Cape
Royal

Pima
Point

NORTH RIM

SOUTH RIM

Desert
View

Hermits
Rest

Visitor
Center

Grandview
Point

64

64

Information
Picnic area
Camping facilities
Gas station
Restaurant/food
Lodging

KAIBAB NATIONAL FOREST

10 MILES

© 2000 HUNTER PUBLISHING, INC

Just what is it that makes the Grand Canyon one of the most spectacular sights in all the world? Certainly size is one factor. It is 277 miles long and ranges from four to 21 miles wide. From the top of the rim to the canyon floor it is 5,700 feet on the north, and 4,500 feet on the south side. Imagine looking down a drop of a mile or more!

> ### ❖ DID YOU KNOW?
>
> *When you stand on the observation deck of a 100-story building you are only one fourth as high as at the rim of the Grand Canyon.*

Its colors are another factor. Every shade in the color spectrum seems to be represented, but the beautiful purple shading is probably the most impressive. Its geological significance is a final factor. In its uncountable layers are represented the natural history of the earth – a scientific treasure chest.

FACTS & FIGURES

Location/Gateways/Getting There: Grand Canyon National Park, at the South Rim, is a leisurely 4½-hour drive north of Phoenix via I-17 and then US 180 and SR 64. The terrain is relatively flat as you approach the canyon. It is slightly farther from Las Vegas via US 95, I-40 and SR 64. The park covers a significant portion of northcentral Arizona.

> ### ❖ TIP
>
> *If you're going to visit only the North Rim, use Las Vegas as your gateway. It's closer.*

Year Established: European explorers of the Coronado expedition first sighted the canyon in 1540. The 1870 explorations of Major John Powell helped build its reputation and led to creation of the national park in 1919.

Size: 1,218,375 acres (1,904 square miles).

Admission Fee: $20.

Climate/When to Go: Because the canyon rim elevations range from 5,000 to more than 9,000 feet, the summer is not unbearably hot. Spring and fall are delightful and less crowded, but fewer activities are available than in the summer. In winter the South Rim remains open, but it can be cold and even snowy; the North Rim road is open only from the mid-May to mid-October. If you are planning to visit both rims, definitely go in the summer; otherwise any time from April through November will be good.

Contact Information: Superintendent, Grand Canyon National Park, PO Box 129, Grand Canyon, AZ 86023. ☎ (520) 638-7888. There is prerecorded information available at ☎ (520) 638-9304.

The North and South rims are two very different worlds. And although they are clearly visible from one another, getting from one to the other is not easy – even if you are not going to be taking the two-day trek along the Bright Angel Trail, which connects the two. By road, it's over 200 miles from the South Rim to the North via SR 64, US 89 and 89A and, finally, SR 67. The drive takes about five hours. That seems incredible when you realize they are only 10 miles apart as the crow flies! Because of the distance involved and the other differences between them, we will describe each rim in a separate section.

GRAND CANYON'S SOUTH RIM

AUTO TOUR/SHORT STOPS

Approximately 35 miles of good roads on the South Rim provide several excellent vantage points for seeing the Canyon. Soon after passing through the entrance station north of the community of Tusayan, the road will bring you to the Canyon Village area, where most visitor facilities are located. From this point on, the South Rim is further divided between the **East Rim**

Drive and the **West Rim Drive**. We'll start with the West Rim, the most heavily visited portion of Grand Canyon National Park.

❖ WEST RIM DRIVE

Most of the West Rim Drive is closed to private automobile traffic during the summer season, but a free shuttle bus travels along its entire length. You can get on and off at any of numerous designated stops. Using the shuttle allows you to take your eyes off the road and concentrate on the scenery, as well as avoiding monumental traffic tie-ups. Service is frequent and stops are closely spaced. The West Rim shuttle runs from the West Rim Interchange at Kolb Studio to Hermit's Rest. Another shuttle serves primarily the village area and runs from the Interchange to Yavapai Point.

Almost immediately upon beginning the West Rim Drive you'll come upon **Mather Point**, the first of numerous overlooks along the canyon rim. Although this is by no means the most beautiful spot in the park, it will be your first look at the canyon – and its sheer immensity – and is likely to be overwhelming and unforgettable. Soon after Mather comes a short spur leading to **Yavapai Point**, one of the nicest views on this rim. You should then make a stop at the visitor center, which features excellent exhibits on the park; you can also pick up information on activities that are taking place there and in the nearby amphitheater. A half-mile trail leads from behind the visitor center to the canyon rim.

The **Kolb Studio**, where you'll generally have to transfer from your car to the shuttle, is so called because of an early commercial photographer who set up shop and helped to make the Grand Canyon famous throughout the world. Excellent views of the canyon are available from the studio windows that look out over the abyss, as well as from trails that run along the edge in this area.

The eight miles from Kolb Studio to Hermits Rest are filled with great sights that can be seen from overlooks reached by short walks from the shuttle stops. They're also connected by a rim trail (see the *Getting Out* section for details).

> ### ❖ TIP
>
> *Although there are major similarities in the view from each overlook, no two are exactly alike. We recommend that you stop at as many of them as your schedule permits.*

West Rim overlooks include **Trailview Overlook, Maricopa Point, Powell Memorial Point** (where there is a monument to explorer John Powell), **Hopi Point, Mojave Point, The Abyss, Pima Point** and **Hermits Rest** at the western terminus of the road.

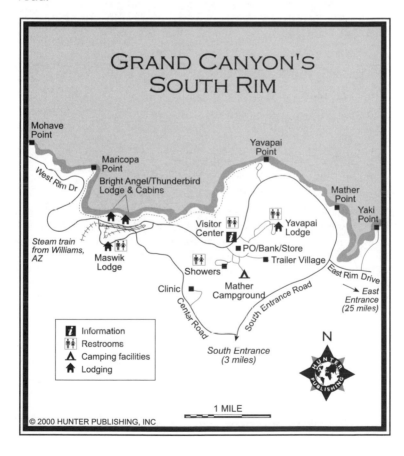

GRAND CANYON'S SOUTH RIM

The views from any and all points will encompass breathtaking vistas of the broad canyon and the many layers of colored rock within the upper reaches of the canyon. You'll also be able to see across to the North Rim.

WHERE'S THE RIVER?

Many first-time visitors are surprised that they don't get a good view of the Colorado River from the West Rim. In fact, there is only one place along this rim where you can see the river – from the spectacular Abyss. This overlook is our favorite on the West Rim because, not only can you see the thin line of the 400-foot-wide river, but you get a look at the canyons within the Grand Canyon. The river is actually within the Tonto Platform, itself a major canyon.

❖ EAST RIM DRIVE

Upon finishing the West Rim and returning to Canyon Village, you'll be ready to set out for the East Rim Drive (also designated as SR 64). While the East Rim sees many more visitors than the North Rim, it may seem almost empty compared to the amount of people you'll have encountered along the always busy West Rim and Village area. The East Rim Drive stretches 22 miles from the village area to Desert View, not counting a few short spur roads that lead to the rim. The spurs lead to **Yaki** and **Grandview Points**, while **Moran Point, Lipan Point** and **Desert View** are set alongside the rim drive. Any of the overlooks on the East Rim Drive will rival or exceed those on the West Rim. Moran and Lipan, especially, are quite different. From these overlooks you'll be looking back directly *into* the canyon, rather than across it, which makes it even easier to appreciate its magnitude. The East Rim overlooks also allow viewing the Colorado River and the canyons within the Grand Canyon from several different places.

Desert View, the final stop, offers views that include everything just mentioned as well as the more distant Vermilion Cliffs and San Francisco Peaks. **The Watchtower** at Desert View, a recreation of an Anasazi tower, was built here early in this century, although it has the appearance of being hundreds of years old.

You can climb up to the top for a more unobstructed view of the canyon. Here, too, you will face an outstanding vista of the Painted Desert, the park's eastern neighbor.

From Desert View, continue on out of the park if you are heading for the North Rim or other points east. Otherwise, turn around and head back to Canyon Village.

You can travel the West Rim in about three hours. The East Rim takes slightly less than that. We suggest allowing a full day for touring the South Rim.

COPING WITH THE CROWDS

Despite the shuttle bus system, the more than five million annual visitors to the South Rim have created a serious traffic problem. The Park Service, in cooperation with private enterprises, have now embarked on a major upgrading of facilities, especially on the West Rim, that will help to relieve congestion and provide a better experience. The biggest project is the building of a major transportation hub at Tusayan. From there, a light rail system will take visitors to the canyon rim at Mather Point. Groundbreaking for the Mather Point facility occurred in April of 1999. Visitor centers and museums, now often in small buildings that are badly in need of repair, will also be upgraded and expanded. Construction is a multi-year task scheduled to be completed by 2002.

GETTING OUT/LONGER STOPS

❖ HIKING

Several trails descend into the canyon, the most popular of which is the famous **Bright Angel Trail**, which actually crosses the canyon floor and then scoots back up onto the North Rim. (Most hikers go only as far as Phantom Ranch on the Colorado River before returning to the same rim from which they departed.) The hike to Phantom Ranch and back (or to the opposite rim) is an overnight affair. If you don't want to spend the night in the canyon, a whole day trek can take you as far as the area called Indian Garden.

> NOTE: *Be aware that the climb back up is difficult and should not be attempted unless you are in the best of condition.*

Grand Canyon's South Rim.

The **South Kaibab Trail** and **Grandview Trail** (both beginning on the East Rim) also descend into the canyon. As difficult as the Bright Angel (and maybe more so in the case of the unmaintained Grandview), each requires from a half to a full day.

> ❖ TIP
>
> *Many visitors walk just a short way along the Bright Angel Trail, which is enough to sample "life beneath the rim."*

A much easier, although less thrilling, alternative is to walk along the canyon rim. This is especially rewarding along the West Rim during summer, because you won't have to walk back to the same place you started from to reach your car – the shuttle bus will pick you up.

The 16-mile-long **West Rim Trail** can be done in its entirety or in little sections. The roughly two-mile section between the Kolb Studio and Hopi Point is especially popular. The first three-quarters of a mile to Maricopa Point is paved and mostly level.

SPECIAL ACTIVITIES

Grand Canyon National Park probably offers more ranger-conducted walks and talks than any other park in the system. Inquire at the visitor center for schedules, or pick up a copy of the park newspaper upon entry.

DAYBREAK & DAY'S END

Watching sunrise or sunset from the canyon rim is a special experience that you should make every attempt to include as part of your visit. For sunrise, try Lipan, Mather, Yaki or Yavapai Points. Sunset is best at Desert View, Hopi, Lipan, Mojave and Pima Points.

❖ FLIGHTSEEING & SIGHTSEEING TOURS

Numerous sightseeing tours by bus cover the east and west rims. Inquire at any of the South Rim hotels for schedules, itineraries and prices.

Helicopter and airplane tours of the canyon are available from Tusayan. Safety and environmental considerations have put an end to the practice of flying into the canyon itself, but this is still a very rewarding way to see the Grand Canyon. It is not, in our opinion, a substitute for actually visiting the park on the ground. Among the many operators are:

Air Grand Canyon . . . . ☎ (800) AIR-GRAND
Grand Canyon Airlines. . . . . ☎ (800) 528-2414
Papillon Helicopters . . . . ☎ (800) 247-6259

THE SOUTHWEST

Most trips last between 30 minutes and an hour. Prices begin at $60 for adults and can go beyond $100, depending upon the features offered. (Grand Canyon flights are also available from many other locations, including Phoenix, Flagstaff and Williams in Arizona, and from Las Vegas.)

❖ HORSEBACK RIDING & MULE TRIPS

Horseback rides can be arranged at the **Apache Stables**, ☎ (520) 638-2891, in Tusayan. Trip lengths range from one hour to half a day. Call for further information and rates. These trips do not enter the canyon. For that, you'll have to take one of the famous Mule Train trips that have safely been transporting visitors into the canyon for decades. Contact **Grand Canyon National Park Lodges** for reservations, ☎ (303) 397-2757.

> NOTE: *This strenuous excursion should not be attempted by those who are in frail condition. Minimum height for riders is 4'7" tall and maximum weight, 200 pounds.*

Full-day and overnight trips are offered. Prices are approximately $110 for the former and $265 for the overnighter.

❖ RAFTING

There are no raft trips on the Colorado River that depart from within Grand Canyon National Park. However, many trips by operators in other communities do venture into the canyon. Call Rivers & Oceans (a reservation service) at ☎ (800) 473-4576 for further information.

❖ IMAX

A large-screen **IMAX** film presentation about the Grand Canyon can be seen just south of the park's entrance station. This is not run by the Park Service or official concessionaire but it is, nevertheless, a worthwhile attraction, especially if you are staying overnight. ☎ (520) 638-2468; admission is $7.50 for adults.

There is a less expensive film of a similar nature in the Village at the **Over The Edge Theater**. ☎ (520) 638-7888.

❖ GRAND CANYON RAILWAY

A final alternative way to see the South Rim is via the **Grand Canyon Railway**, ☎ (800) 843-8724, based in the town of Williams. You board a refurbished early 20th-century steam train for the 110-mile round-trip from the depot to the park. The train leaves at 9:30 am and returns at 5:30 pm.

> ### ❖ TIP
>
> *The train ride is designed so that you spend 4½ hours on the train passing through so-so scenery and only 3½ hours at the South Rim. For a fee in excess of $50, we don't consider it very worthwhile.*

ACCOMMODATIONS

❖ HOTELS & MOTELS

THE SOUTH RIM

All lodging within the South Rim section of the park is operated by the Grand Canyon National Park Lodges, a division of the well-known resort operator, Amfac. You can get information and make reservations at all of their facilities by calling ☎ (303) 297-2757. These are indicated in the listings below by an asterisk next to the local phone number (*), which should not be used for making reservations.

BRIGHT ANGEL LODGE ($$-$$$), Grand Canyon Village, on the rim. ☎ (520) 638-2631; reservations, ☎ (303) 297-2757. 89 rooms. Older establishment with lodge units and some cabins. Rustic and not quite up to the standards of the other village accommodations, but it does cost less. Some units do not have a private bath. Better units have fireplace. Restaurant on premises, more nearby.

EL TOVAR HOTEL ($$$$), Grand Canyon Village, on the rim. ☎ (520) 638-2631; reservations, ☎ (303) 297-2757. 66 rooms. An historic treasure dating from 1905 and one of the nicest places to stay on the South Rim. Variety of accommodations ranging from small to large. Service-oriented. Excellent restaurant on the premises.

KACHINA LODGE ($$$), Grand Canyon Village, on the rim. ☎ (520) 638-2631; reservations, ☎ (303) 297-2757. 49 rooms. This is a more modern and more affordable version of the El Tovar. Many of the attractive rooms face the canyon.

MASWIK LODGE ($$-$$$), Grand Canyon Village, away from the rim. ☎ (520) 638-2631; reservations, ☎ (303) 297-2757. 278 rooms. Motor inn-style facility with comfortable rooms as well as some cabins. Spacious, attractive grounds. Large gift shop and cafeteria.

THUNDERBIRD LODGE ($$$), Grand Canyon Village, on the rim. ☎ (520) 638-2631; reservations, ☎ (303) 297-2757. 55 rooms. Quite a few of the rooms here also face the canyon. This is a comfortable and modern facility, adjacent to Kachina Lodge and the El Tovar. Eating places are nearby.

YAVAPAI LODGE ($$$), opposite the visitor center, about one mile east of Grand Canyon Village. ☎ (303) 297-2757. 358 rooms. Fairly basic clean and comfortable rooms in two sections on spacious wooded grounds. Although there's no canyon view from here, the setting offers a feeling of privacy, despite the large number of units. Cafeteria.

WITHIN THE CANYON

PHANTOM RANCH ($$$, including breakfast and dinner), along Bright Angel Trail. ☎ (303) 297-2757 for reservations. No local incoming phone service to guests. A rustic, basic hostel-type establishment designed for those who are hiking into the canyon. It is reached only by one of the arduous trails or by overnight mule train trips.

NEARBY COMMUNITIES

BEST WESTERN GRAND CANYON SQUIRE INN ($$$-$$$$), State Highway 64, Tusayan; nine miles south of Grand Canyon Village. ☎ (520) 638-2681 or (800) 662-6966. 250 rooms. Very large and attractively decorated rooms and suites. Numerous recreational facilities and several places to eat.

GRAND CANYON SUITES ($$$$), State Highway 64, Tusayan; a few miles south of the park entrance. ☎ (520) 638-3100 or (888) 538-5353. Rate includes continental breakfast. 32 rooms. Modern but rustic exterior houses spacious, well-equipped one- and two-bedroom suites. Decor is Arizona/Southwest style. This is a good choice for families. Restaurants are within a short drive.

HOLIDAY INN EXPRESS ($$$), State Highway 64, Tusayan; eight miles south of Grand Canyon Village. ☎ (520) 638-3000 or (800) HOLIDAY. Rate includes continental breakfast. 166 rooms. Nicely decorated rooms and excellent level of maintenance in a modern motor inn. Restaurants within a short distance.

MOQUI LODGE ($$), State Highway 64, Tusayan; less than a mile from park entrance. ☎ (520) 638-2631; reservations, ☎ (303) 297-2757. 136 rooms. Complex of rustic-style buildings with decent accommodations. Convenient to park and to restaurants (besides the one on the premises). Wide variety of recreational facilities and services available.

❖ CAMPING

CAMPGROUNDS AT A GLANCE			
NAME	LOCATION	SITES	COST
Mather	Grand Canyon Village area.	320	$15 per day
Desert View	Near eastern entrance to South Rim.	50	$10 per day

For reservations at Mather, ☎ (800) 365-2267 or write to PO Box 1600, Cumberland, MD 21502. You can reserve online at http://reservations.nps.gov. Desert View operates on a first-come, first-served basis. Contact park headquarters for more details. Mather allows RVs ($18 day). There is a seven-day limit at both campgrounds.

DINING

ON THE SOUTH RIM

ARIZONA STEAKHOUSE ($$), Grand Canyon Village, between the Bright Angel and Thunderbird Lodges. ☎ (520) 638-2631. American/steakhouse. Gaze out on the canyon while you feast on sumptuous, tender steaks or chicken and seafood.

BRIGHT ANGEL DINING ROOM ($$), Grand Canyon Village in the Bright Angel Lodge (see listing above). ☎ (520) 638-2631. American food. Good variety of entrées, including some vegetarian items. Attractive surroundings. Casual and friendly.

EL TOVAR DINING ROOM ($$$), Grand Canyon Village in the El Tovar Hotel (see listing above). ☎ (520) 638-2631. Continental. The most formal dining at the canyon, this fine establishment features well-prepared dishes and an extensive wine list to accompany the view of the canyon through picture windows.

NEARBY COMMUNITIES

CORONADO ROOM ($$), State Highway 64, Tusayan; in the Grand Canyon Squire Inn. ☎ (520) 638-2681. American food. Good selection of well-prepared dishes. Attractive surroundings. There are always some pasta and Mexican selections on the menu.

MOQUI LODGE DINING ROOM ($$), State Highway 64, Tusayan; in Moqui Lodge (see listing above). ☎ (520) 638-2631. American/Mexican food. Simple but tasty food. Ample portions at attractive prices. Good service. Friendly atmosphere is well suited for families with smaller children.

WHERE DO WE GO FROM HERE?

The South Rim of the Grand Canyon is included among the **Marvels of Arizona** in *Suggested Trip 7*. If you include the North Rim, it's almost enough for a vacation in itself. Some of southern Utah's national parks (including Bryce and Zion) aren't that far away, especially if you're visiting the North Rim. **Petrified Forest National Park** is only a few hours to the east, and **Glen Canyon National Recreation Area** is even closer. More adventurous travelers might consider the largely unknown far western wilderness regions of Grand Canyon National Park. There are few facilities and the trip isn't convenient, but these areas offer fantastic views of the canyon. The **Havasupai Indian Reservation** (west via I-40, then SR 66 and Indian Route 18) is such a possibility.

GRAND CANYON'S NORTH RIM

AUTO TOUR/SHORT STOPS

The North Rim is often considered to be more spectacular than the South Rim. This isn't only because it is more natural (i.e., fewer visitor amenities) and less crowded, but also because the scenery and terrain is better, due to the greater variation and higher elevation. About 22 miles of paved road lead out from the visitor center on the North Rim. The main road takes you from the North Rim Entrance Station to the Grand Canyon Lodge, site of all North Rim services. The main building of he lodge is a venerable gem designed by noted architect Stanley Underwood. The veranda in the back has some of the most fantastic views of anywhere in the park. An absolute must in this area is the short (half-mile) **Bright Angel Point Trail**. Not to be confused with the Bright Angel Trail that descends into the canyon, this paved trail follows the top of a narrow ridge with sheer dropoffs into side canyons on either side. **Bright Angel Point** sits on the edge of a precipice surrounded by canyon walls on three sides. It's a dramatic and beautiful spot.

> NOTE: *Those who are nervous about heights or prone to vertigo may wish to take in the view from the Lodge, rather than the trail.*

Now you can once again set out in your car. Just north of the village area bear right on **Fuller Canyon Road**. In a few miles the road will split. Go left to **Point Imperial**. A truly spectacular sight, the view from this point faces eastward, away from the main canyon, and is a vista of colorful rock formations speckled with the green of distant trees. Make your way back down to the junction and continue on the Cape Royal Road. Two great views are available from roadside pullouts at **Vista Encantadora** and the **Painted Desert Overlook**. Shortly before the end of the road is the **Walhalla Overlook**. But the best part comes at the end of the road when you take the half-mile **Cape Royal Trail**. Along this flat and easy walk are views of the canyon in all its glory, the South Rim, and the Colorado River. You'll have trouble pulling yourself away from what may well be the most beautiful spot in all of the Grand Canyon. Also along this trail is the **Angel's Window,** an unusual natural rock formation. The more adventurous can climb to the top of the window for a spectacular view.

Head back to the Grand Canyon Lodge, or exit from the North Rim upon reaching the main road. Allow about four hours for all of the activities in this section.

GETTING OUT/LONGER STOPS

❖ HIKING

The **Bright Angel** and **Kaibab Trails** can be accessed from the North Rim. There are several trails of varying lengths beginning in the lodge area that skirt the rim. Longer trails venture into the more heavily forested terrain of the North Rim's Kaibab Plateau.

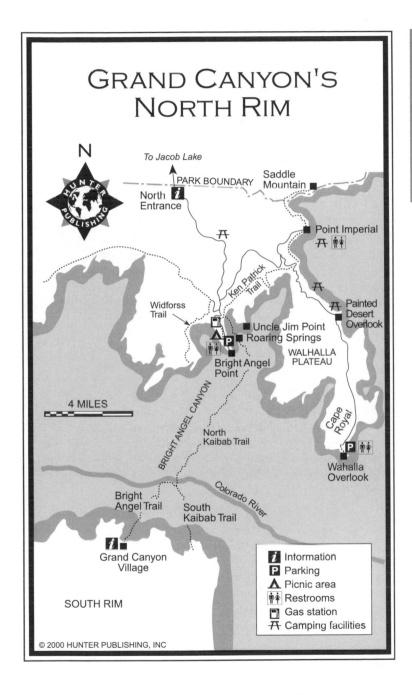

GRAND CANYON'S NORTH RIM

N

To Jacob Lake

PARK BOUNDARY

North Entrance

Saddle Mountain

Point Imperial

Ken Patrick Trail

Widforss Trail

Uncle Jim Point

Roaring Springs

Painted Desert Overlook

WALHALLA PLATEAU

Bright Angel Point

4 MILES

BRIGHT ANGEL CANYON

North Kaibab Trail

Cape Royal

Wahalla Overlook

Bright Angel Trail

South Kaibab Trail

Colorado River

Grand Canyon Village

SOUTH RIM

𝒊	Information
P	Parking
▲	Picnic area
🚻	Restrooms
⛽	Gas station
🏕	Camping facilities

© 2000 HUNTER PUBLISHING, INC

HUNTER PUBLISHING

> NOTE: *Be aware that the climb back up is difficult and should not be attempted unless you are in the best of condition.*

SPECIAL ACTIVITIES

There are ranger-led walks and talks, bus tours and many other activities on the North Rim, including a mule train, which is operated by **North Rim Trail Rides**, ☎ (803) 679-8663. A schedule of available ranger-led walks is posted at the Information Station by the Grand Canyon Lodge. However, you won't find as much in the way of museums and other visitor facilities.

ACCOMMODATIONS

❖ HOTELS & MOTELS

ON THE NORTH RIM

GRAND CANYON LODGE ($$), at the end of the park road at the North Rim. ☎ (303) 297-2757 for reservations; (520) 638-2611 to reach hotel. 201 rooms. Consists of modern motel-style units as well as stone cabin clusters along the rim. Choose the latter; they're a delightful part of the canyon experience. Restaurant and snack facilities.

WITHIN THE CANYON

PHANTOM RANCH ($$$, including breakfast and dinner), along Bright Angel Trail. ☎ (303) 297-2757 for reservations. No local incoming phone service to guests. A rustic, basic hostel-type establishment designed for those who are hiking into the canyon. It is reached only by one of the arduous trails or by overnight mule train trips.

NEARBY COMMUNITIES

There aren't any good accommodations within 50 miles of the North Rim, although if you get desperate you might find something acceptable in **Jacob Lake** (44 miles north). **Kanab** has a better selection, but it's about 80 miles from the North Rim. See the chapter on Grand Staircase-Escalante National Monument for Kanab listings.

❖ CAMPING

There's only one camping option: **North Rim Campground**. It has 83 sites. Seven-day limit. $15 per day. RVs allowed. Reservations can be made through the National Park Reservation Service, ☎ (800) 365-2267. The offices are open daily from 10 am to 10 pm, eastern time. You can write in for reservations at PO Box 1600, Cumberland, MD 21502. Or, you can reserve online at http://reservations.nps.gov.

DINING

ON THE NORTH RIM

GRAND CANYON LODGE DINING ROOM ($$), Grand Canyon Lodge (see listing above). American food. Large restaurant with high timber ceiling and huge picture windows affording spectacular canyon vistas. The food is quite good, although selection is limited. Friendly service. Casual.

WHERE DO WE GO FROM HERE?

The North Rim is part of *Suggested Trip 7*. Everything mentioned under the South Rim's *Where Do We Go From Here?* section also applies here. See page 211.

GRAND STAIRCASE-ESCALANTE NATIONAL MONUMENT

The unusual name of this monument comes from the series of colorful cliffs and mesas that rise like a giant's staircase. They extend from Bryce Canyon all the way to the Grand Canyon and cover a vast tract of mostly rugged, remote and undeveloped land. Many canyons have been created by the cutting action of the Escalante and Paria Rivers, as have a variety of unusual geological formations that are so typical of southern Utah. The Grand Staircase has few visitor facilities, which makes it popular among the adventure travel set. Trips into the interior are via rough, unpaved roads, but more developed roads run along the northern and southern edge. There's much to be seen everywhere in the Grand Staircase, and you'll find that one portion of the monument is totally unlike another, which makes it all that much more fascinating to visit.

FACTS & FIGURES

Location/Gateways/Getting There: Covering the Kaiparowits Plateau of southcentral Utah, the Grand Staircase-Escalante has few paved roads and the northern and southern sections are not connected at all. SR 12 skirts the northern border of the monument, while US 89 does likewise along the southern edge. Both can be reached from Las Vegas, Salt Lake City or Phoenix. From Las Vegas take I-15 north to St. George, Utah and then follow SR 9 to Mt. Carmel Junction and US 89. Follow US 89 south to reach the southern portion of the monument or take it north to the junction of SR 12 and then travel east for the northern section. From Salt Lake City, take I-15 south to Exit 188, then US 50 to UT 24. At Torrey, just before reaching Capitol Reef, take SR 12 to the Grand Staircase area. From Phoenix, take I-17 north to

THE SOUTHWEST

Flagstaff and then pick up US 89 north. Once you pass the Glen Canyon National Recreation Area, you'll be in the southern portion of the Grand Staircase. To reach the northern part, continue on US 89 to SR 12. Phoenix is the closest gateway to the southern section. The best gateway for the SR 12 portion depends upon the rest of your itinerary.

Year Established: The monument was established in 1996.

DISPUTE IN MANAGEMENT

There was a great deal of controversy surrounding the creation of the Grand Staircase because of much opposition within Utah and the fact that the majority of the area was already under other federal controls. In fact, although it is part of the National Park Service, jurisdiction remains with the Bureau of Land Management, just as it did prior to its being made a national monument.

Size: Approximately 1,700,000 acres (2,656 square miles), since the final borders are still the subject of some discussion and adjustment. In any event, it is larger than Delaware.

Admission Fee: There is no charge for entering the monument.

Climate/When to Go: The weather varies quite a bit from one portion of the monument to another. The northern section along SR 12 has warm summers and cold winters, while the southern portion along US 89 sees hot summers and mild winters. If you plan to cover the entire region, spring and fall offer a good compromise in climates.

Contact Information: Bureau of Land Management, Escalante Field Office, PO Box 225; Escalante, UT 84726. ☎ (435) 826-4291.

TOURING

Because of the remoteness of most of the Grand Staircase, the nature of your visit will depend solely on how much adventure you want. This touring section is designed for those who don't like things too rough. The monument covers an incredibly large area. There are few paved roads (none in the interior) and just as few visitor facilities. In fact, future development is still up in the air and the monument isn't even administered by the Park Service. The Bureau of Land Management has responsibility for that and all BLM areas are characterized by a more remote atmosphere. Both sections can be seen along the fringes by car. Let's start with the more spectacular north side.

❖ THE NORTH SIDE

Utah **State Highway 12** (also known as the Utah 12 Scenic Byway or the Boulder-Escalante Scenic Highway) skirts the northern edge of the monument from the town of Boulder on the east to Cannonville on the west. The monument sits between Capitol Reef National Park and Glen Canyon National Recreation Area on the east, and Bryce Canyon National Park on the west. This stretch of the road covers about 60 miles through the monument and is one of the most spectacularly scenic rides in America. With every twist and turn, rise and fall, there are new and more splendid panoramas. It's not a difficult drive and there are many areas where you can pull out and stop to admire the scenery. You'll see an amazing variety of different color rock strata and unusual formations. The **Kaiparowits Plateau** and many smaller mesas and plateaus are the most dominant landform, although distant mountains and several canyons are also visible. The diversity of the terrain is extraordinary and the sheer beauty is staggering. The picturesque **Escalante Canyons** are just off SR 12 by the Escalante River and that road provides access via a two-mile trail to the **Escalante Natural Bridge**.

❖ DID YOU KNOW?

The bridge is a hundred feet across and 130 feet high.

Two state-run natural areas situated along the drive aren't within the monument's borders. They should, however, also be seen. These are **Escalante State Park** (near the town of the same name), which has many petrified remains, and the fabulous

Kodachrome Basin State Park, a colorful world of eroded rocks and canyons that serve as a fitting introduction to Bryce if you're headed in that direction.

The drive along SR 12 can be completed in a little over 1½ hours, but you should allow at least three hours, which will give you ample time to stop and admire the sights as well as visit the two state units.

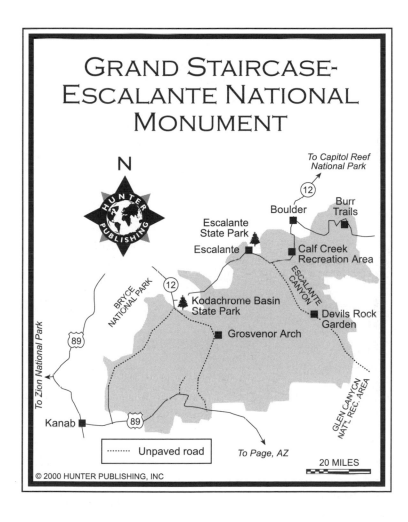

GRAND STAIRCASE-ESCALANTE NATIONAL MONUMENT

N

To Capitol Reef
National Park

12

Burr
Trails

Boulder

Escalante
State Park

Escalante

Calf Creek
Recreation Area

ESCALANTE
CANYON

BRYCE
NATIONAL PARK

12

Kodachrome Basin
State Park

Devils Rock
Garden

To Zion National Park

89

Grosvenor Arch

GLEN CANYON
NATL. REC. AREA

Kanab

89

········· Unpaved road

To Page, AZ

20 MILES

© 2000 HUNTER PUBLISHING, INC

❖ THE SOUTHERN SIDE

The southern stretch of the Grand Staircase can be reached by continuing west on SR 12 to US 89. From Kanab, a 75-mile stretch of US 89 connects the town with the Glen Canyon National Recreation Area at Page, Arizona. About a third of this mileage is within the southern edge of the Grand Staircase-Escalante National Monument. The primary sights in this part of the monument are the colorful mountains, rocks and ridges that make up the **Vermillion Cliffs**.

SPECIAL ACTIVITIES

❖ 4WD TRIPS

The adventure traveler with a high-clearance 4WD vehicle will have a field day in the remote interior portions of the monument.

> NOTE: *There are few emergency services available in Grand Staircase, so be fully prepared for unexpected situations. Weather is one of them. Flash floods are quite common in the many narrow canyons of the Grand Staircase, even after what seems like only moderate rainfall. Do not attempt exploring the interior during or immediately after bad weather, or when it seems especially threatening. And be prepared to get out fast if there is a sudden turn in the weather.*

Several dirt, gravel or graded roads can be used to reach the many interesting and beautiful geological features. We'll briefly describe them, running from the Boulder side of the monument and heading towards Cannonville. The first is the **Burr Trail**. This covers 66 miles (one way) through the extreme northwestern corner of the monument and onto the Waterpocket Fold Cliffs in the southern and largely unvisited portion of Capitol Reef National Park. It ends at the Bullfrog Basin Marina of the Glen Canyon National Recreation Area.

East of Escalante is the Hole In The Rock Road. This one travels along the Kaiparowits Plateau to a remote corner of the Colorado River in Glen Canyon National Recreation Area.

Also, closer to SR 12 is the attractive **Calf Creek Falls**, located in a state recreation area of the same name.

A couple of other rough roads are in the vicinity of Cannonville and the Kodachrome Basin. One unnamed option begins just before Kodachrome and travels along the western edge of the monument. It offers good views of the Pink Cliffs and White Cliffs. The other road – Cottonwood Canyon Road – is reached by continuing beyond Kodachrome. This is the only route, such as it is, that connects with US 89 on the southern side of the monument. It is unpaved and not recommended for regular cars.

Beautiful Grosvenor Arch is about halfway along. If you're continuing to US 89 via this route, then you'll also pass through Cottonwood Canyon farther down the road.

ACCOMMODATIONS

❖ HOTELS & MOTELS

There are no overnight facilities within the monument itself.

NEARBY COMMUNITIES

BEST WESTERN RED HILLS ($$), 125 West Center Street, Kanab; in town center on US 89. ☎ (435) 644-2675 or (800) 830-2675. Rate includes continental breakfast. 75 rooms. Typical small town motel. Nice, comfortable rooms, but certainly nothing to get excited about. Plenty of eating places within short distance.

HOLIDAY INN EXPRESS ($$), 815 East Highway 89, Kanab; on the east edge of town. ☎ (435) 644-8888 or (800) 574-4061. Rate includes continental breakfast. 67 rooms. One of the newest facilities in the area. Attractive, comfortable rooms. Close to restaurants.

PROSPECTOR INN ($), 380 West Main Street, Escalante; State Highway 12 at the west end of town. ☎ (435) 826-4653. 50 rooms. Basic accommodations at low rates. Friendly and helpful staff. Restaurant on premises.

SHILO INN ($$), 296 West 100 North, Kanab; US 89 in town. ☎ (435) 644-2562 or (800) 222-2244. Rate includes continental breakfast. 119 Rooms. This small Western chain offers slightly better than average motel facilities at a reasonable price. Restaurants nearby.

> NOTE: *See the listings for Bryce and Capitol Reef National Parks and the Glen Canyon National Recreation Area for additional possibilities.*

❖ CAMPING

CAMPGROUNDS AT A GLANCE			
NAME	LOCATION	SITES	COST
Calf Creek	State Hwy 12, 15 miles east of Escalante.	13	$6 per day
Ponderosa	14 miles northwest of Kanab via US Hwy 89 and Hancock Road (south side of the monument).	10	Free

RVs are accepted at both campgrounds and there are stay limits.Other campgrounds on the north side of the monument can be found in several Utah state parks that border on or are surrounded by the national monument. Information and reservations are available at ☎ (800) 322-3770.

DINING

There are no dining options inside the monument.

NEARBY COMMUNITIES

FERNANDO'S HIDEAWAY ($), 332 W. 300 North, Kanab; off US 89 on the north side of town. ☎ (435) 644-3222. Mexican food. Reasonably priced fare served in pleasant surroundings.

HOUSTON'S TRAIL'S END RESTAURANT ($$), 32 East Center Street, Kanab; US 89 in the heart of town. ☎ (435) 644-2488. American food. Excellent steaks are the specialty of the house. There's also a good selection of other entrées, including some Mexican dishes. Well-stocked salad bar and a homey Western atmosphere. Friendly and efficient service.

PONDEROSA RESTAURANT ($$), 45 N. 400 West, Escalante; off Utah 12 in town. ☎ (435) 826-4658. American food. Nice family-style restaurant offering a good selection of well-prepared food in a hospitable atmosphere.

WHERE DO WE GO FROM HERE?

Suggested Trip 8 includes the Grand Staircase-Escalante National Monument along with many other natural wonders of Utah. Another option is to combine this park with **Bryce, Zion, Capitol Reef** and **Glen Canyon National Recreation Area** and include some of the sights of northern Arizona. The latter include the **North Rim of the Grand Canyon, Monument Valley** and **Canyon de Chelly National Monument**.

GREAT BASIN NATIONAL PARK

The Great Basin is the name geographers have given to a vast expanse of land that covers much of Nevada and the neighboring portion of Utah. But don't expect to see wide open country in this national park. Rising rather abruptly more than 1½ miles above the desert floor, the mountains of Great Basin National Park cover several different life zones. There is much wildlife and great variations in vegetation. Among the most famous life forms in the park is the bristlecone pine forest.

> ### ❖ DID YOU KNOW?
> *Some of the trees in this forest are more than 4,000 years old.*

Besides mountains, Great Basin has beautiful meadows with splashes of colorful flowers, pristine lakes and even a small glacier. But the most famous feature of the park is Lehman Caves, an underground natural art gallery that's sure to please.

FACTS & FIGURES

Location/Gateways/Getting There: In northcentral Nevada, Great Basin lies just to the west of the Utah state line. The two best gateways are Salt Lake City (250 miles away) and Las Vegas (300 miles). From the former, take I-15 south to US 6 and follow that road west to Baker and the access road into the park (SR 488). From Vegas, take I-15 to US 93 north to the junction of US 6/50. Go east on the latter to Baker and proceed as above. The distance to Great Basin from Reno is a little bit more than from Las Vegas. Take I-80 east to US 50 east and proceed to Baker.

Year Established: Originally encompassing only the immediate area around Lehman Caves, the park was established as a national monument in 1922. It was greatly expanded in 1986 and the current name was given to it at that time.

Size: 77,180 acres (121 square miles).

Admission Fee: There is no charge for entering the park, but a per-person fee is levied for cave tours. See the *Special Activities* section.

Climate/When to Go: The winter months see bitter cold temperatures and plenty of snow. Access to some portions of the park is restricted. Because of the high altitude even spring and fall can be chilly and snow still lingers. The mild summers are the best time to visit, with the period from April to October being the busiest.

Contact Information: Superintendent, Great Basin National Park, Baker, NV 89311. ☎ (775) 234-7331.

AUTO TOUR/SHORT STOPS

The entrance to the park is about five miles west of the tiny community of Baker, Nevada via SR 488. The park's **visitor center** is a mile inside the park. Just beyond the entrance is the cut-off for the paved **Wheeler Peak Scenic Drive** to the base of **Wheeler Peak**. The road rises from an altitude of under 7,000 feet at the start, and 12 miles later, ends at a lofty 9,886 feet. (Wheeler Peak itself soars to 13,063 feet).

> NOTE: *Although Wheeler Peak Scenic Drive is fully paved and not difficult to negotiate, the novice mountain driver should take extra care because of the numerous turns and five switchbacks.*

Along the way are several overlooks (the Mather and Wheeler Peak Overlooks provide the best views of the mountain). In addition to Wheeler Peak and other mountains, you'll have excellent views of several ridges, creeks and the varied terrain of the Great Basin that lies below. With the exception of the overlooks, you'll find that most out-of-car activities in Great Basin are fairly strenuous. However, there is a short **nature trail** (less than a half-mile) in the vicinity of the visitor center.

Allow between 1½ and two hours for this driving trip.

GETTING OUT/LONGER STOPS

❖ HIKING

Check at the visitor center to see if your schedule coincides with one of the many ranger-guided hikes that are conducted throughout the summer season. There are eight popular trails in the park that range from about three miles to more than 16. They vary from moderate to very strenuous. Four of these trails originate near the end of the auto road and several interconnect with one another.

The **Wheeler Peak Summit Trail** ascends almost a mile along its eight-mile length and is the most difficult of all trails in the park. Experienced hikers who can take the altitude boast that they've climbed to the top of this mountain. It's an all-day trip.

The three-mile **Alpine Lakes Loop Trail** is fairly easy. You'll see pretty Stella and Teresa Lakes as well as dazzling fields of wild-flowers. Allow about 90 minutes.

The four-mile **Lehman Creek Trail** has an altitude gain of about 2,000 feet, passing through several different life zones.

Finally, one of the most popular long trails is the **Bristlecone and Glacier Trail.** This five-mile (roughly three-hour) trek climbs at a gentle rate. You'll see the amazing 150-acre bristlecone pine forest, one of nature's marvels. These large trees can live for up to 4,000 years in a harsh environment 9-11,000 feet in altitude. The trail ends at a relatively small glacier that fronts a spectacular view of Wheeler Peak.

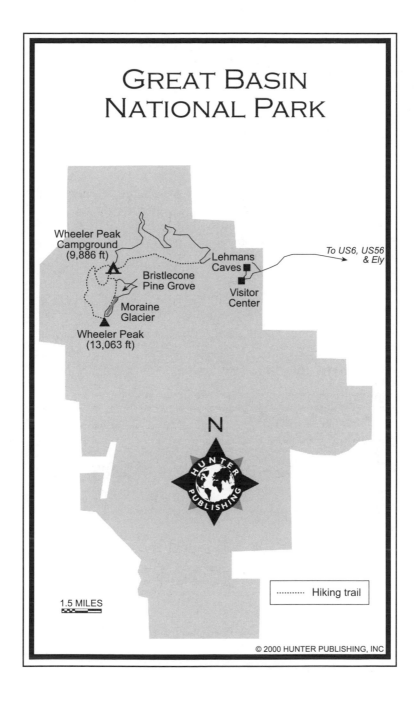

GREAT BASIN
NATIONAL PARK

Wheeler Peak
Campground
(9,886 ft)

Lehmans
Caves

To US6, US56
& Ely

Bristlecone
Pine Grove

Visitor
Center

Moraine
Glacier

Wheeler Peak
(13,063 ft)

N

1.5 MILES

·········· Hiking trail

© 2000 HUNTER PUBLISHING, INC

THE SOUTHWEST

SPECIAL ACTIVITIES

❖ LEHMAN CAVES

While all of the features of Great Basin that have been described up to now make it a worthwhile place to visit, there's little doubt that most people come to the park to see the marvelous Lehman Caves. These beautifully illuminated natural galleries consist of passages of marble and limestone and contain numerous oddly shaped formations. It is a single cavern (despite the plural name) and covers only about a quarter-mile-long. While certainly not one of the country's bigger caves, it makes up for its lack of size with mind-boggling displays of strange cave structures, including:

- ❖ **Shields**, which are two circular pieces flattened like a clam shell. Even geologists can't agree on the processes that have formed them.
- ❖ **Helectites**, which hang down from the cave ceiling.
- ❖ **Cave popcorn**, small, round formations that develop into clusters.

Cave tours are given daily between 9 am and 4 pm. The schedule varies according to number of visitors, but all tours operate on a first-come, first-served basis.

> ### ❖ TIP
> *Weekend tours can fill up early in the day, so allow plenty of time.*

The 1½-hour tour costs $5 for adults and $4 for children ages six through 15. Holders of Golden Age Passports can purchase tickets for $2.50.

ACCOMMODATIONS

❖ HOTELS & MOTELS

There are no facilities inside the park.

NEARBY COMMUNITIES

SILVER JACK MOTEL ($), Baker; town center, near junction of State Highway 480. ☎ (775) 234-7323. Eight rooms. Very basic but clean and comfortable accommodations reasonably close to the park. In addition to seven motel-style units there is also a multi-room house available ($$). There are several places to eat in Baker.

RAMADA INN COPPER QUEEN ($-$$), 815 7th Street, Ely; just south of US Highways 6/50/93. ☎ (775) 289-4884 or (800) 228-2828. 65 rooms. Nice hotel rooms in main building (which has a casino) and motel units across the street. Restaurant on premises. This is about 70 miles from Great Basin, but it's a step above anything you'll find closer to the Basin.

❖ CAMPING

CAMPGROUNDS AT A GLANCE			
NAME	LOCATION	SITES	COST
Lower Lehman	Wheeler Peak Scenic Drive.	11	$8 per day
Upper Lehman	Wheeler Peak Scenic Drive.	24	$8 per day
Baker Creek	At the end of a spur road that begins just before the visitor center.	32	$8 per day
Wheeler Peak	End of Wheeler Peak Scenic Drive.	37	$8 per day

No reservations accepted. No limitations on stay. RVs allowed only at Lower Lehman and at Wheeler Peak, but larger vehicles are not recommended at the other sites. Contact the park for further information.

DINING

INSIDE THE PARK

The LEHMAN CAVES GIFT SHOP & CAFÉ serves breakfast, lunch and snacks from early April through late October.

NEARBY COMMUNITIES

THE OUTLAW ($-$$), on the main road in Baker. ☎ (775) 234-7302. American food. Nice friendly place with decent food as well as take-out service.

WHERE DO WE GO FROM HERE?

Suggested Trip 12 includes a visit to Great Basin National Park. You might consider crossing into northcentral Nevada and combining a park visit with the **Lake Tahoe** area. Or you can head southeast instead, visiting some of Utah's many natural wonders (the entrance to Great Basin National Park lies only about a dozen miles from the state line). In addition, northern Nevada has a number of interesting but little-known scenic areas. Best among these is the **Ruby Mountain Scenic Area**, in the Humboldt National Forest, about 20 miles east of Elko.

GREAT SAND DUNES NATIONAL MONUMENT

If there's one thing that most people don't associate with the forested mountains of Colorado, it's the desert. Well, the Great Sand Dunes isn't exactly a desert, but it might as well be because the dunes, which measure as high as 700 feet, will block the mountains from your view when you're at their base.

HOW THE DUNES DEVELOPED

It's really quite simple. Winds blow sand across the San Luis Valley, but the sand is too heavy to be lifted above the towering peaks of the Sangre de Cristo Range. Instead, it settles at the bottom and, over millions of years, evolved into the golden sand dunes that you see today.

FACTS & FIGURES

Location/Gateways/Getting There: In southcentral Colorado, the Great Sand Dunes can be easily reached from either Denver or Colorado Springs. The fastest way is to take I-25 from either gateway city south to Walsenburg and then follow US 160 west to SR 150, which leads directly into the monument. The distance is under 200 miles from Colorado Springs, and takes about three hours by car. (Add another 1¼ hours from Denver.) A more scenic but slower route is via US 285 south from Denver to Mineral Hot Springs, where you'll pick up SR 17 south into Alamosoa. Then drive east on US 160 to SR 150 and the monument entrance.

Year Established: 1932.

Size: 38,662 acres (60 square miles).

Admission Fee: $3 per vehicle.

Climate/When to Go: Summer is definitely the best time to visit as the temperatures are not too high. Spring and fall are cool but manageable, while the winters are cold.

Contact Information: Superintendent, Great Sand Dunes National Monument, 11500 US Highway 150, Mosca, CO 81146. ☎ (719) 378-2312.

TOURING

There are few roads within the monument. A short road leads from the monument entrance and parallels the face of the dunes, finally leading to the visitor center. From there you can either walk via a nature trail or take the half-mile side road that leads to the base of the dunes. Visitors are actually encouraged to walk and climb on the dunes. Youngsters are especially fond of climbing to the top of a high dune and sliding down. No mechanized vehicles of any type are allowed on the dunes.

> NOTE: *Although the temperature at Great Sand Dunes during the summer is usally comfortable, the sun can raise the sand temperature to as high as 140°F. Therefore, be careful on sunny days and wear clothing/shoes that will protect you from direct contact with the sand.*

In addition to the impressive sight of the 700-foot-high sand masses themselves, you'll be treated to the gorgeous panorama of the dunes fronting the high peaks of the Sangre de Cristo Range. The contrast between the two is awesome and inspiring.

A visit to the dunes can be completed in about an hour, but allow a little longer if you plan to do a lot of dune climbing or take the additional little trip described in the following paragraph.

If you have a vehicle with four-wheel-drive you can continue north for a few miles on an unpaved road to another portion of the dunes. Climbing is also allowed here but, again, you can't take your vehicle onto the sand. There's nothing especially different about the dunes in this section compared with those near the visitor center, but there are fewer people.

ACCOMMODATIONS

❖ HOTELS & MOTELS

There are no overnight facilities within the monument.

NEARBY COMMUNITIES

COMFORT INN ($$), 6301 Road 107 South, Alamosa; 2½ miles west of town on US 160, about 38 miles from the monument. ☎ (719) 587-9000 or (800) 228-5150. Rate includes continental breakfast. 40 rooms. Attractive, modern facility with spacious accommodations and comfortable furnishings. Small spa. Restaurants are within a short distance.

HOLIDAY INN ($$), 333 Santa Fe Avenue, Alamosa; a quarter-mile east of the junction with State Highway 17 on US 160, 35 miles from Great Sand Dunes. ☎ (719) 589-5833 or (800) HOLIDAY. 127 rooms. Slightly above-average motel-style accommodations. The hotel has limited recreational facilities. Decent restaurant and cocktail lounge on the premises.

❖ CAMPING

PINYON FLATS CAMPGROUND has 88 sites and a 14-day limit. Cost is $10 per day. RVs allowed. No reservations accepted.

DINING

There are no eating establishments inside the monument.

❖ NEARBY COMMUNITIES

Alamosa has no restaurants of any particular distinction. The best choices are in the HOLIDAY INN (☎ 719-589-5833) or in the BEST WESTERN ALAMOSA INN (☎ 719-589-2567). Both of these moderately priced, family-style restaurants are adequate.

WHERE DO WE GO FROM HERE?

Great Sand Dunes is an integral part of *Suggested Trip 3*. If you don't have the time or inclination to take this big circle loop through Colorado, a variety of other attractions are nearby.

These include all of the many natural sights in and around **Colorado Springs** (including **Pikes Peak**) as well as the **Royal Gorge** of the Arkansas River in Canon City.

Alternately, take the scenic drive along SR 12 through the Cordova Pass and the San Isabel National Forest. (SR 12 is less than an hour's drive from the monument.) A 120-mile loop from the city of Walsenburg covers the latter sights. Walsenburg is situated on I-25, a major route. The loop is primarily SR12, but also includes sections on I-25 and US 160.

LAKE MEAD NATIONAL RECREATION AREA

The completion of Hoover Dam resulted in the creation of Lake Mead and Lake Mojave in the 1930s. Lake Mead National Recreation Area suddenly existed in what had previously been a large area of mostly barren desert surrounding the Colorado River, with its intermittent flooding and dry periods. Although the primary purpose behind establishment of the recreation area was to provide watersports enthusiasts with myriad opportunities for recreation, the area contains enough beautiful scenery to merit inclusion in this guide.

❖ DID YOU KNOW?

Water comprises only about 15% of the recreation area's total acreage.

Extending for over 115 miles along both sides of the Colorado River on the Arizona and Nevada borders, the area includes Lake Mead, one of the largest man-made lakes in North America, and the smaller Lake Mojave. Surrounding both lakes are colorful mountains, canyons and ravines. The elevation ranges from 517 feet to as much as 6,990 feet, providing a dramatic topographic setting.

FACTS & FIGURES

Location/Gateways/Getting There: In the southern corner of Nevada and northeastern Arizona, the recreation area is under an hour's drive from Las Vegas (the primary gateway) via US 93 and is adjacent to the town of Boulder City. It is also accessible via US 93 from Kingman, Arizona and several other points.

Year Established: The recreation area was created in 1964.

Size: 1,496,601 acres (2,338 square miles), half the size of the state of Connecticut.

Admission Fee: There is no charge for entering the area.

Climate/When to Go: Don't let all the water in those vast lakes fool you – this is still the desert, and summertime temperatures reach 100°F and higher under a relentless sun.

> ❖ **TIP**
>
> *Although it may feel cooler when you are out on the water, be aware that sunburn is still a threat.*

Winters can be surprisingly chilly, so the best time to visit is either spring or fall.

Contact Information: Headquarters, Lake Mead National Recreation Area, 601 Nevada Highway, Boulder City, NV 89005. ☎ (702) 293-8907.

AUTO TOUR/SHORT STOPS

An extensive road system makes the area easy to tour. Arriving from Las Vegas, stop at the **Alan Bible Visitor Center** at the junction of US 93 and Lakeshore Drive to gather additional park information and see the exhibits. Outside the center is a **botanical garden**, which has samples of the flora to be found in the surrounding desert. An overlook to the rear of the center has an excellent view of the lake and surrounding mountains.

Head south on **US 93** from the visitor center. Soon, the road will start to twist and climb through the forbidding, dark red mountains and the narrow canyons until you suddenly reach Hoover Dam. The sight of the huge structure tucked into this strange landscape is staggering – a perfect blend of man's building achievements with beautiful natural surroundings.

Continue down the road, which actually crosses the crest of the dam. The visitor center has information about the dam's construction and functions. You'll have impressive views of Lake Mead on one side and the canyon of the Colorado River on the other. These can be seen from observation points at each end and from along the walkway that runs the entire width of the dam. The Arizona/Nevada border is marked halfway across the dam's crest. (See the *Special Activities* section for other interesting things to do while at the dam.)

You should then continue on US 93 into Arizona to see the beautiful scenery in the **Black Mountains**. The first couple of miles is an exciting winding road that is still easy to drive (except for the abundance of big rigs attempting to make the steep climb). Go a total of 12 miles from the dam to a colorful viewpoint of cliffs and mountains. (If you reach the cut-off for Willow Beach you went too far.) As you make your way back the opposite way you came, you'll come to an unpaved side road to Kingman Wash. This route offers a spectacular view of Lake Mead.

Back at the Alan Bible Visitor Center, turn onto Lakeshore Drive and then **Northshore Drive**. It is 53 miles from the visitor center to **Overton Beach**. Along the way there are several excellent views of the Black Mountains, Lake Mead and various canyons and coves. At Overton Beach you can avoid back-tracking and return to Las Vegas via the beautiful **Valley of Fire State Park**. Adjacent to but not part of the recreation area, this area of desolate beauty and vividly colored strange rock formations is a must-see.

The Auto Tour of the Hoover Dam, visitor center, crossing into Arizona and the north shore route should take four to five hours (without the special activities to be described in the next paragraph).

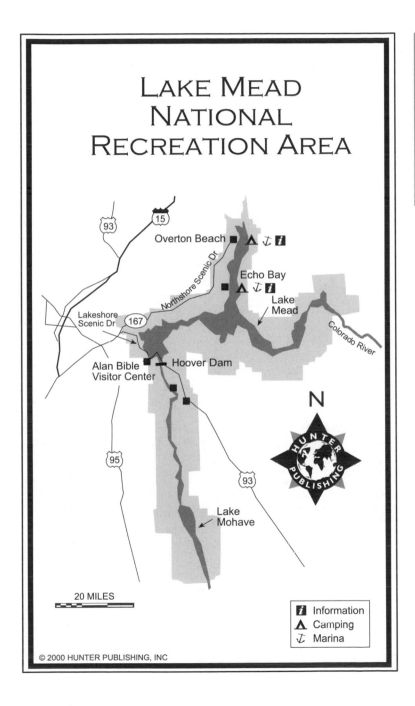

LAKE MEAD NATIONAL RECREATION AREA

Overton Beach ▲ ⚓ ℹ

Echo Bay ▲ ⚓ ℹ

Lake Mead

Northshore Scenic Dr

Colorado River

Lakeshore Scenic Dr

Alan Bible Visitor Center

Hoover Dam

N

Lake Mohave

20 MILES

ℹ Information
▲ Camping
⚓ Marina

© 2000 HUNTER PUBLISHING, INC

There is a huge tract of the recreation area south of Hoover Dam, reached by US 95, that we haven't even touched on yet. Several side roads from US 95 south of Boulder City go into remote areas along the Colorado River. SR 163 winds its way from US 95 to Laughlin and Lake Mojave and the smaller Davis Dam. Although this area is quite picturesque (especially Lake Mojave), it involves a lot of mileage and isn't as impressive as the Auto Tour. It requires at least a half-day to complete and we suggest it only if you have time available.

GETTING OUT/LONGER STOPS

❖ HIKING

Many hiking trails lead from just off the road through the mountains to vistas of the lake and small canyons. However, most are difficult and none should be attempted in the heat of the summer. Inquire at the visitor center for details.

SPECIAL ACTIVITIES

Many watersports are available, including fishing, boating, swimming, water-skiing and diving. There are launching ramps if you bring your own boat, or you can rent one at Lake Mead Marina.

Two of the most popular activities are tours of Hoover Dam and cruises on Lake Mead. The Hoover Dam tour takes about 35 minutes and goes down to the bottom of the dam. Guides inform you of the dam's operation. Although this boat trip isn't especially scenic, it is an integral part of any visit to Lake Mead. The cost for adults is $6 for the basic tour.

> ### ❖ TIP
> There is often a long line waiting for the tour, so try to arrive early in the day.

There are also "hard hat" tours available.

The Lake Mead cruise on the *Desert Princess* lasts about 1½ hours and leaves from just north of the Lake Mead Marina on Lakeshore Drive. It provides a view of the dam from the lake side, which is entirely different from what you see on the road or atop the dam itself. In addition, the mountains and canyons as seen from the lake are quite beautiful and certainly much more colorful than the Black Mountains seen on the Auto Tour. The waters of Lake Mead are an exquisite blue, adding to the beauty of the scene. The fare is $16.

Reservations are suggested during peak season; ☎ (702) 293-6180 for information and schedules for all cruises. Dinner cruises are also available.

You can also take a river rafting trip (no whitewater) on the lower Colorado River with **Black Canyon River Raft Tours**, ☎ (702) 293-3776. The trips last 3½ hours and cost $65 per person.

ACCOMMODATIONS - NORTH SECTION

❖ HOTELS & MOTELS

IN THE RECREATION AREA

ECHO BAY RESORT ($$), Echo Bay; on the lake four miles east of State Highway 167, 45 miles from the Recreation Area Headquarters via scenic North Shore Drive. ☎ (702) 394-4000 or (800) 752-9669. 52 rooms. Pleasant accommodations, but not on the luxury level. Many units have good lake views. The grounds are attractive. Full range of Lake Mead recreational facilities at Echo Bay or a few minutes away. Houseboats and other watercraft rentals are available. Restaurant on the premises.

HACIENDA HOTEL & CASINO ($), US 93, Boulder City; a half-mile south of the Alan Bible Visitor Center on a private parcel of land within the NRA. ☎ (702) 293-5000 or (800) 245-6387. 378 rooms. Formerly the Gold Strike Inn, this highrise reopened with its new name in September, 1999 after a fire burned their casino to the ground. (The room tower was undamaged.) Good accommodations at budget prices. Rooms on the upper stories have excellent views of either the lake or mountains. Several dining options to choose from on the premises. Friendly atmosphere.

NEARBY COMMUNITIES

The northern section of the recreation area is where the great majority of visitors will stay. Las Vegas (about 30 miles away) has over 200 places to stay and selecting some from such an inventory is beyond the scope of this book. Therefore, this listing limits itself to Henderson and Boulder City, both of which are closer to Lake Mead.

BEST WESTERN LAKE MEAD MOTEL ($-$$), 85 W. Lake Mead Drive (State Highway 146), Henderson; one mile east of I-515 and US 93/95, just east of Boulder Highway. ☎ (702) 564-1712 or (800) 528-1234. Rate includes continental breakfast. 59 rooms. Basic motel accommodations, nothing more, nothing less. Clean and comfortable. It's within a few short blocks of downtown Henderson (although "downtown" is not the main commercial hub of the city). You'll find a choice of eating places there and far more within a short drive.

BEST WESTERN LIGHTHOUSE INN ($$), 110 Ville Drive, Boulder City; one mile east of US 93. ☎ (702) 293-6444 or (800) 528-1234. Rate includes continental breakfast. 70 rooms. Pleasant facility in a quiet location. Some units have views of nearby Lake Mead. Minutes from Hoover Dam. Restaurants within a short distance.

EL RANCHO BOULDER MOTEL ($$), 725 Nevada Highway, Boulder City; US 93 in the center of town. ☎ (702) 293-1085. 39 rooms. Decent accommodations at affordable rates. Convenient location for Hoover Dam, Lake Mead Marina and all activities within the recreation area. Attractive Spanish-style architecture. Restaurants are nearby.

THE RESERVE ($-$$), 777 Lake Mead Drive, Henderson; on State Highway 167 at Exit 61 of I-515/US 93/95 and 10 miles from Lake Mead. ☎ (702) 558-7000 or (888) 899-7770. 224

rooms. Pleasant casino hotel with a whimsical African safari theme throughout. Better-than-average accommodations at bargain prices. Several reasonably priced restaurants. Swimming pool. Entertainment.

SUNSET STATION HOTEL ($$-$$$), 1301 W. Sunset Road, Henderson; just west of I-515, Exit 64, 12 miles from Lake Mead. ☎ (702) 547-7744 or (800) 634-3101. 448 rooms. A beautiful casino hotel. While smaller than those on the famous Strip, this one is just as good. Mediterranean theme; stunning Gaudi bar. Excellent rooms. Recreation and entertainment facilities. Huge selection of great restaurants, several of which are among the best in town.

ACCOMMODATIONS - SOUTH SECTION

❖ HOTELS & MOTELS

INSIDE THE RECREATION AREA

COTTONWOOD COVE MOTEL ($$), 1000 Cottonwood Cove Road; at Lake Mojave, 14 miles east of US 95 at Searchlight. ☎ (702) 297-1464. 24 rooms. An attractive facility in a pretty location that offers decent accommodations. Good choice if you want to stay in an isolated area of Lake Mojave without having to drive far. Houseboats and other watercraft rentals are available. Coffee shop on the premises.

NEARBY COMMUNITIES

The resort town of Laughlin is situated on the Colorado River just below Davis Dam at the recreation area's southern edge. There are about a dozen casino hotels (all in the $ price category, although some may go to $$ on weekends and during holiday periods). These include: COLORADO BELLE, ☎ (800) 458-9500; EDGEWATER, ☎ (800) 67-RIVER; FLAMINGO HILTON LAUGHLIN, ☎ (800) FLAMINGO; GOLDEN NUGGET, ☎ (800) 237-1739; HARRAH'S, ☎ (800) 447-8700; RAMADA EXPRESS, ☎ (800) 272-6232; and RIVERSIDE, ☎ (800) 227-3849. All are full-service hotels.

❖ CAMPING

All camping is on a first-come, first-served basis. Maximum stays vary from 30 days to as long as 90 days. There are no RVs allowed at Las Vegas Wash. In all other areas RVs must use the separate trailer villages at an additional cost.

CAMPGROUNDS AT A GLANCE			
NAME	LOCATION	SITES	COST
LAKE MEAD CAMPING			
Boulder Beach	Lakeshore Drive.	146	$6 per day
Las Vegas Wash	Lakeshore Drive.	89	$6 per day
Callville Bay	North Shore Drive.	80	$6 per day
Echo Bay	North Shore Drive.	153	$6 per day
Temple Bar	Remote area on the south shore, 28 miles from US 93 near Willow Beach, AZ.	172	$6 per day
LAKE MOHAVE CAMPING			
Cottonwood Cove	14 miles east of Searchlight.	145	$6 per day
Katherine	Just north of Bullhead City, AZ or Laughlin, NV.	153	$6 per day

DINING

❖ NORTHERN AREA

INSIDE THE RECREATION AREA

You can find several places for snacks and light meals at Hoover Dam, as well as at the Lake Mead Marina. There's a full-service restaurant at the ECHO BAY RESORT, ☎ (702) 394-4000.

NEARBY COMMUNITIES

In addition to the places listed here, almost all of the major national restaurant chains can be found in Henderson.

COSTA DEL SOL ($$), Sunset Station Hotel (see listing above), Henderson. ☎ (702) 547-7744. Seafood. Excellent choice for fresh seafood served in a delightful setting reminiscent of a Mediterranean fishing village. Adjacent Oyster Bar is more casual and has a grotto decor. Efficient and friendly service in both.

FEAST AROUND THE WORLD BUFFET ($), Sunset Station Hotel (see listing above), Henderson. ☎ (702) 547-7744. International cuisine. Good food and tremendous selection at this all-you-can-eat extravaganza. Price includes beverage as well as sumptuous desserts. Attractive dining area.

GRAND SAFARI BUFFET ($), Reserve Hotel (see listing above), Henderson. ☎ (702) 558-7000. International food. Another all-you-can-eat option with good food. The selection is even larger here. African safari theme.

MUSTANG SALLY'S DINER ($-$$), 280 N. Gibson Road, Henderson; a half-mile south of the Sunset Road exit of I-515/US93/US 95. ☎ (702) 566-1965. American food. Don't let the location (inside a Ford dealer in the Valley Auto Mall) deter you – this is a great little place. American favorites in an attractive 50s themed setting.

RENATA'S ($$), 4451 E. Sunset Road, Henderson; between Green Valley Parkway and Mountain Vista. ☎ (702) 435-4000. Continental cuisine, plus a good selection of Chinese dishes and steaks. Fine dining in a semi-casual atmosphere. The more casual Bistro Room is good for lighter meals.

❖ SOUTHERN AREA

INSIDE THE RECREATION AREA

The only option inside the recreation area itself is the coffee shop at the Cottonwood Cove Motel.

NEARBY COMMUNITIES

Laughlin has dozens of restaurants, mostly in the inexpensive to moderate price ranges, inside the casino hotels (see above). They offer all kinds of food, from American to continental to ethnic. For a quick meal at a low price, try one of the major hotels, which all have buffets. They're not as extravagant as those in the Las Vegas area, but they're almost ridiculously low priced and more than adequate.

WHERE DO WE GO FROM HERE?

Lake Mead is part of *Suggested Trip 12*. It also can be done in conjunction with a visit to the national parks of southwestern Utah or the Grand Canyon.

There is some beautiful scenery within minutes of Las Vegas – something that many people aren't aware of. The sights include the colorful **Red Rock Canyon National Conservation Area**, ☎ (702) 363-1921, and the Mount Charleston area of the **Toiyabe National Forest**, ☎ (775) 331-6444.

MESA VERDE NATIONAL PARK

Mesa Verde was established primarily because it is one of the nation's most important archaeological preserves, but it also happens to be an area of outstanding natural beauty. Mesa Verde means Green Table, and that is exactly what it looks like from a distance: a huge flat-topped plateau covered with forest. The plateau is some 2,000 feet above the level of the surrounding valley. On the top of the mesa are many small, deep canyons. In these canyons are found the large and well-preserved remains of cliff dwellings.

The area was inhabited as early as 500 A.D., but the remains that are visible today date from around the 13th century. It is fascinating to see how the so-called primitive cultures that lived here adapted their homes to the difficult environment and terrain. A visit to Mesa Verde is one that will leave a deep impression on you for its beauty as well as its history.

FACTS & FIGURES

Location/Gateways/Getting There: Mesa Verde is 10 miles east of Cortez or 36 miles west of Durango on US 160 in extreme southwestern Colorado. From Denver it is about 380 miles via I-25 and US 160.

Year Established: One of the nation's oldest national parks, Mesa Verde's value was realized early on and it received its status in 1906.

Admission Fee: $10.

Climate/When to Go: The park is open all year, but the facilities operate on a very limited basis in winter when it is cold and there is sometimes heavy snow. Many of the ruins can be seen by guided tours during the spring and fall when the park is less crowded, but are on a self-guiding basis during the busy summer season. Summer temperatures are comfortable because of the high elevation (over 8,000 feet), so it is a good idea to visit during this period, as it may often be chilly in spring and fall.

Contact Information: Superintendent, Mesa Verde National Park, PO Box 8, Mesa Verde, CO 81330. ☎ (970) 529-4465.

AUTO TOUR / SHORT STOPS

Virtually all of the ruins and the best of the park's scenery can easily be seen on a driving tour. How much you want to explore the various ruins on foot is up to you.

From the entrance off US 160, the park road travels 20 miles before reaching the top of the mesa. During this journey the road rises sharply and the curves become increasingly frequent and pronounced. After passing through a long tunnel there begins a series of dramatic switchbacks that provide panoramic vistas of the route you have traveled and what lies ahead, but keep your eyes on the road. The best views are at the **Montezuma Valley Overlook** and, shortly after that, via a short spur road leading to **Park Point**, perhaps the best view in the park. The **North Rim Overlook** is a short distance farther along. At an elevation of 8,572 feet, this spot offers a fantastic view extending into four different states.

Soon afterwards you reach the top of the mesa in an area known as **Far View**. The park's large, modern **visitor center** is here and contains an excellent exhibit on the culture of the cliff dwellers. This will be especially interesting to first-time visitors. Back on the road, after passing the nearby Far View Ruins, the road reaches the **Chapin Mesa**. A fine museum here details the development of the Anasazi Indian culture. A short walk from the museum takes you to the **Spruce Tree Ruin**.

> NOTE: *Although the walk to Spruce Tree takes only a few minutes, the climb back up is quite steep.*

Spruce Tree Ruin is one of the best preserved cliff dwellings in the park – and one of the more accessible. If you decide not to visit it, you can at least get an excellent view of the ruin from the mesa's rim.

Immediately south from Spruce Tree, the road divides into two loops, each about six miles long. These loops lead to excellent vantage points into the dwellings from a series of canyon rim lookouts.

> ❖ **TIP**
>
> *If you bring along a pair of binoculars you can see details of the dwelling interiors without actually going into them. (Some are not open to visitors so it is a good idea to have those binoculars handy in any case.)*

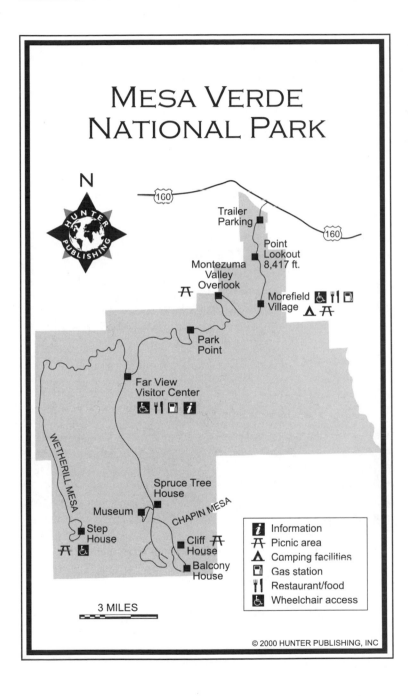

Mesa Verde National Park

N

160

Trailer Parking

Point Lookout 8,417 ft.

Montezuma Valley Overlook

Morefield Village

160

Park Point

Far View Visitor Center

WETHERILL MESA

Spruce Tree House

Museum

CHAPIN MESA

Step House

Cliff House

Balcony House

3 MILES

i	Information
⊼	Picnic area
▲	Camping facilities
▯	Gas station
¶	Restaurant/food
♿	Wheelchair access

© 2000 HUNTER PUBLISHING, INC

THE SOUTHWEST

In the order that you will approach them, your stops should include the **Square Tower House** (viewed from the canyon rim only); a short walk through a series of **pithouses and pueblos** on the mesa's surface; a fabulous view of the **Cliff Palace**, the park's largest and most famous dwelling (best seen from Sun Point) and, finally, the **Sun Temple**. The second loop passes along Cliff Palace and Balcony House (see the next section for details on these) as well as the Fewkes Canyon ruins.

Including the access road drive, the two loops, view stops and the short walk to Spruce Tree House, the Auto Tour will require three to four well-spent hours.

GETTING OUT/LONGER STOPS

Even though Mesa Verde is a large park, it has fewer lengthy trails than most others. The short walks described under the Auto Tour comprise most of the major things to see. While the preceding tour is a relaxing and excellent introduction to Mesa Verde, its major shortcoming is that entry into only one of the major dwellings was included.

❖ RANGER-GUIDED TOURS

For the more adventurous, and those with more time to explore, the **Cliff Palace** and **Balcony House** can be visited via ranger-guided tours. Cliff Palace is the easier of the two to reach, requiring that you ascend and descend several long ladders to reach the interior. In allocating time for your visit, figure about one hour for each structure that you will be touring. Trips depart every 30 minutes from 9 am until 5 pm, mid-May through mid-October. Hourly trips are scheduled (weather permitting) until mid-November. There is a nominal charge for each tour and tickets can be purchased at the Far View Visitor Center.

> **❖ TIP**
>
> *Arrive early; tours can fill up quickly during the middle of summer.*

Ranger-led tours take you to ruins such as these.

❖ HIKING

The **Petroglyph Point Trail** covers three miles and follows the edge of a canyon cliff to the point before returning on the top of the mesa. It is quite strenuous and involves a considerable change in altitude. The journey requires at least two hours and you must register at the ranger office near the museum. The trail is only open during the summer season, with exact dates depending upon the weather.

SPECIAL ACTIVITIES

❖ WETHERILL MESA

A side trip available only during the summer between 8 am and 4:30 pm is the ride to adjacent Wetherill Mesa. The trip encompasses beautiful scenery and cliff dwellings not visible from Chapin Mesa's main loop roads. The 12-mile road is steep, with many curves. No trailers are allowed. Although the sights are similar to those at Chapin Mesa, Wetherill is far less crowded. If you have the time (three hours at a minimum) and feel like seeing ruins in an isolated setting, then the trip will prove worthwhile.

❖ ORGANIZED EVENTS

Visitors wishing to learn more about the Ancestral Puebloans (Anasazi) will want to spend more time in the museum at Far View. In addition, if you plan to spend the evening in the park, there is an excellent multi-media presentation at Far View Lodge that will greatly increase your understanding of this early Native American culture. It is available at 6:30 to 9:30 nightly from April to the middle of October and costs $3 for adults.

ACCOMMODATIONS

❖ HOTELS & MOTELS

INSIDE THE PARK

FAR VIEW LODGE ($$), near the visitor center. ☎ (970) 529-4421. 150 rooms. Open late April to mid-October only. Beautifully furnished in Southwestern style, the lodge offers large, comfortable rooms with patios and picture windows so you can take in the fantastic view. One of the better lodgings (at a moderate price) to be found inside a major national park. Good restaurant.

NEARBY COMMUNITIES

BEST WESTERN TURQUOISE INN ($$), 535 E. Main Street, Cortez; on US 160 near town center, 10 miles west of park entrance. ☎ (970) 565-3778 or (800) 547-3376. Rate includes continental breakfast. 77 rooms. Very attractive and well-kept motel that has regular rooms as well as 31 two-room suites with microwave, refrigerator and more. Some have fireplaces. Seasonal pool; Jacuzzi. Several restaurants nearby.

DAYS INN ($$), junction of US 160 and State Highway 145, Cortez; 1½ miles east of town and nine miles from Mesa Verde entrance road. ☎ (970) 565-8577 or (800) 628-2183. 77 rooms.

Spacious accommodations, nicely furnished. There are some two-room family units. Swimming pool and Jacuzzi. Restaurant on premises.

IRON HORSE INN ($$$), 5800 N. Main Avenue, Durango; five miles north of US 160/550 junction, adjacent to narrow gauge railroad station and 40 miles east of Mesa Verde park entrance. ☎ (970) 259-1010. 142 rooms. Excellent accommodations. Each unit is a spacious, nicely decorated bi-level loft. Many restaurants nearby. Although Durango is a lot farther from the park (and much higher priced than towns nearer to Mesa Verde), a lot of visitors stay in Durango because it offers the Silverton Railroad, a popular attraction.

MESA VERDE MOTEL ($-$$), 191 W. Railroad Avenue, Mancos; on US 160, seven miles east of the national park entrance. ☎ (970) 533-7741 or (800) 825-6372. 16 rooms. A small place. Basic accommodations that are nicely maintained. This is the closest place to Mesa Verde without actually staying in the park itself. Excellent views. Restaurant nearby.

TOMAHAWK LODGE ($), 728 South Broadway, Cortez; 1½ miles from downtown on US Highways 160/666, 11 miles west of the park entrance. ☎ (970) 565-8521 or (800) 643-7705. 39 rooms. Small, comfortable units in a basic roadside motel that will certainly meet the expectations of budget travelers. Swimming pool. Many restaurants to suit all price categories and tastes can be found nearby on Main Street.

❖ CAMPING

The only in-park camping is at the huge **Morefield Village** (450 sites), four miles from the park entrance. Reservations are not required, but will be accepted. Call ☎ (970) 529-4421 or (800) 449-2288. No stay limit. $14 per day basic charge. Some sites can range up to $23. RVs allowed.

DINING

INSIDE THE PARK

METATE ROOM ($$), Far View Lodge (see listing above). ☎ (970) 529-4421. Southwestern cuisine. Excellent regional cuisine that is well prepared and presented. Attentive staff. Outstanding views of Chapin Mesa from the dining room. For more casual dining, especially a quick lunch during a busy touring day, you can opt for the cafeteria that's a part of the Far View Lodge complex ($).

NEARBY COMMUNITIES

DRY DOCK LOUNGE & RESTAURANT ($$), 200 W. Main Street, Cortez; downtown. ☎ (970) 564-9404. American food. Attractive dining room with good service. Features a varied menu that includes several excellent Southwestern regional entrées. Patio dining during the warmer months.

MAIN STREET BREWERY ($-$$), 21 E. Main Street, Cortez; town center. ☎ (970) 564-9112. American food. Large, popular place that offers five of its own brewed beers. Varied menu, including pizza and other favorites. Especially good are the Rocky Mountain oysters. Although it's a brew pub, this is appropriate for family dining – they even have a children's menu.

NERO'S ITALIAN RESTAURANT ($$), 303 W. Main Street, Cortez; just west of downtown on US 160 at the junction of US Highway 666. ☎ (970) 565-7366. Italian food. Pleasant and casual fine dining with a good selection of pastas as well as veal, seafood and chicken. Patio dining in season.

WHERE DO WE GO FROM HERE?

As you will probably be using fairly distant Denver as your gateway for visiting Mesa Verde, you should try to do all of *Suggested Trip 3*. At a minimum, a visit to southern Colorado, in addition to Mesa Verde, should include **Durango** and the **Silverton Railroad** (and/or the Million Dollar Highway), **Black Can-**

THE SOUTHWEST

yon of the Gunnison and Curecanti National Recreation Area, as well as Colorado Springs and Canon City.

Alternatively, Mesa Verde can be combined with some of the attractions in southeastern Utah, such as Arches and Canyonlands National Parks. Those who are especially interested in the Anasazi may also want to consider Hovenweep National Monument, which consists of several scattered ruins in both Colorado and Utah.

PETRIFIED FOREST NATIONAL PARK

It is hard to imagine that 200 million years ago this arid desert landscape was covered by a thick forest of tall coniferous trees. The passing of eons has changed all of this remarkably. It is now a multicolored desert with petrified logs in an array of brilliant colors. The petrified trees are mostly lying on their sides rather than standing, and more often than not are broken into smaller fragments. Petrified Forest National Park is a land of exquisite and delicate beauty. Its two main features are the thousands of petrified logs that give it its name, as well as a large

Petrified wood.

area of Arizona's fantastic Painted Desert. Each is an unforgettable sight on its own.

FACTS & FIGURES

Location/Gateways/Getting There: In east-central Arizona, Petrified Forest is immediately off I-40; in fact, there is an exit on the interstate highway right in the northern part of the park. It is less than a five-hour ride from Phoenix via I-17 and then I-40. Going westbound from the city of Albuquerque, it is only 4½ hours away, also by I-40.

Year Established: Originally a national monument, the Petrified Forest was designated a national park in 1962.

Size: 93,493 acres (146 square miles).

Admission Fee: $5.

Climate/When to Go: The dry, hot desert climate makes summer the least desirable time to visit, although the dryness makes it tolerable. Spring and fall are delightful; winters are quite mild. The park is open throughout the year, and you will find it well-visited at all times.

Contact Information: Superintendent, Petrified Forest National Park, PO Box 2217, Petrified Forest National Park, AZ 86028. ☎ (520) 524-6228.

AUTO TOUR/SHORT STOPS

The park is narrow, and almost all of it is easily accessible from the 27-mile road that runs from north to south. Many of the major attractions are just a short walk from the paved road. You can enter the park from two points. If traveling westbound, exit from I-40 at the park and work your way south, getting back to I-40 by going west on US 180 at the southern end of the park to Holbrook. If you are heading east, then exit at Holbrook onto US 180 and see the park going northbound, finally reaching I-40 again after completing the park.

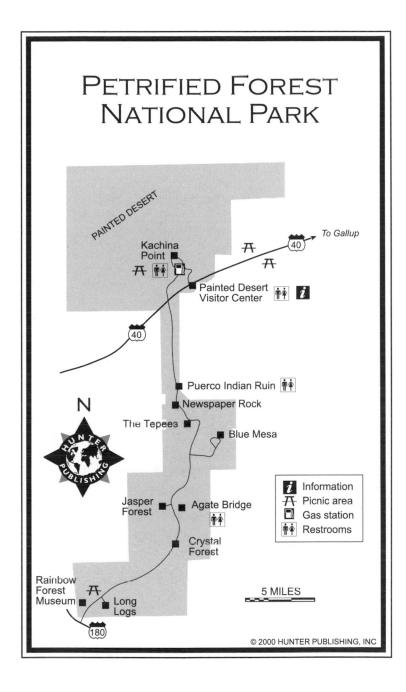

PETRIFIED FOREST NATIONAL PARK

PAINTED DESERT

To Gallup

Kachina Point

Painted Desert Visitor Center

Puerco Indian Ruin

Newspaper Rock

The Tepees

Blue Mesa

N

Jasper Forest

Agate Bridge

Crystal Forest

Rainbow Forest Museum

Long Logs

i	Information
Picnic area	
Gas station	
Restrooms	

5 MILES

© 2000 HUNTER PUBLISHING, INC

> NOTE: *We will work our way from north to south, but you can reverse the route if you wish.*

Right off the interstate is the excellent **Painted Desert Visitor Center**, which describes in detail the geologic processes that have occurred over the various periods in the earth's history and that have contributed to the formation of today's Petrified Forest. Leaving the visitor center, the road twists its way downward for a short time via a series of dramatic hairpin bends. Just as you turn southward and catch your breath from the dizzying descent, an extraordinary vista appears – the magical colors of the Painted Desert. Within a very short space there are eight overlooks with outstanding views of the Painted Desert. The best are **Kachina Point, Chinde Point, Pintado Point** and **Lacey Point**. Continuing south, the Painted Desert fades away. Before you reach the petrified logs, you'll come across the remains of an 800-year-old **Puerco Indian settlement**, which has been partially restored. Less than a mile farther along is Newspaper Rock (see next section for trail description).

At this point you come face to face with one of the most amazing of all the sights in the park, an area known as **The Tepees**. Their shape and coloration – various layers of red, white and gray – will definitely remind you of Indian tepees. These are, in fact, large and mostly eroded mountains of clay.

Now, finally, begins the main area of petrified formations. The **Blue Mesa** area is at the end of a three-mile spur off the main route. Here, you'll enjoy excellent views of various petrified objects, many having a distinct blue color. Back on the main road is **Agate Bridge**. At over 100 feet in length, it is one of the largest unbroken petrified trees in the park, and the largest visible from near the road. It is now supported by a concrete column to prevent it from breaking. This "bridge" spans a 40-foot ravine. The **Jasper Forest** and **Crystal Forest** viewpoints are next and then you will enter a portion of the park known as the **Rainbow Forest**. The **Long Logs** section contains the most colorful petrified logs in the entire park. Finally, at the southern entrance station area is a small **museum** and additional exhibits about the park and local Indian cultures.

Since all of the areas above are either right on the road or reached via short walks, the entire Auto Tour should take you no more than 2½ hours.

GETTING OUT/LONGER STOPS

Newspaper Rock, an Indian petroglyph, is near the road. To reach it, you must descend about 120 steps. Coming back up, especially in summer, can be tiring, so take it very slow. Because of the need to protect the petroglyph, the Park Service has been considering restricting visitors to the overlook.

> ❖ **TIP**
>
> *Newspaper Rock can be seen from an overlook if you don't want to make the climb.*

❖ HIKING

There is only one major trail in the park. It leads to Giant Logs in the Rainbow Forest area. The trip covers more than three miles and takes several hours. It does not have any unusually steep grades or other difficulties, but be careful about attempting it on a hot summer day unless you are in excellent shape.

> NOTE: *Make sure that you are protected from the sun and carry plenty of drinking water. All off-road hikers are required to register with park rangers, a useful precaution in this harsh land.*

THE SOUTHWEST

SOUVENIRS

Many of the petrified logs are small, light and easy to pick up. While we all like souvenirs, remember that it is against the law to remove any petrified rocks or logs from the park. Please leave everything just as you found it so tomorrow's visitor will enjoy the park as much as you did.

ACCOMMODATIONS

❖ HOTELS & MOTELS

There are no facilities inside the park.

NEARBY COMMUNITIES

BEST WESTERN CHIEFTAIN ($-$$), US 191, Chambers; Exit 333 of I-40, 22 miles east of the park entrance. ☎ (520) 688-2754 or (800) 528-1234. 52 rooms. Typical off-the-interstate motel facility that should satisfy most travelers. Swimming pool. The on-premises restaurant is just okay, and might well be the best choice in Chambers.

COMFORT INN ($$), 2602 E. Navajo Blvd., Holbrook; off I-40, Exit 289, 22 miles west of northern entrance to national park via I-40 or 22 miles from southern entrance via US 180. ☎ (520) 524-6131 or (800) 228-5150. Rate includes continental breakfast. 60 rooms. One of several chain properties right along the highway and (except for the slightly better Holiday Inn listed below), you could easily substitute any of the others and not know which one you're in! Swimming pool. Restaurants within short distance.

HOLIDAY INN EXPRESS ($$), 1308 Navajo Blvd., Holbrook; just north of Exit 286 of I-40, 25 miles west of park's northern entrance and 23 miles from southern entrance. ☎ (520) 524-1466 or (800) HOLIDAY. Rate includes continental breakfast. 59 rooms. Newer facility with good-sized rooms and very pleasant decor. Swimming pool. Restaurant within walking distance.

RAINBOW INN ($), 2211 E. Navajo Blvd., Holbrook; one mile
west of I-40, Exit 289, 22 miles west of northern park entrance
and 22 miles from southern entrance via US 180. ☎ (520) 524-
2654 or (800) 551-1923. 40 rooms. Average-sized rooms with
decent decor. Well-maintained. A good value. Restaurants
nearby.

❖ CAMPING

There are no in-park camping facilities. There are some commercial RV parks in the neighboring towns of Holbrook or Chambers. The nearest government-operated campgrounds are
about 100 miles away in northern Arizona's national forests.

DINING

There are no dining options inside the park itself.

NEARBY COMMUNITIES

MESA ITALIANA RESTAURANT ($-$$), 2318 E. Navajo Blvd.,
Holbrook; 1¼ miles east of I-40, Exit 286. ☎ (520) 524-6696.
Italian cuisine. Not as fancy a place as the prices may indicate.
Lots of traditional Italian entrées like pasta, veal and fish. They
also serve a few Southwestern dishes. Very casual and friendly.

WHERE DO WE GO FROM HERE?

Suggested Trip 7 includes the Petrified Forest. It is a long way
from major cities, so we recommend that you include several of
the other attractions in that trip. If you're short on time, shorten
the trip by just taking in the sights of northern Arizona. You can
also combine portions of southern Utah with northern Arizona.

ROCKY MOUNTAIN NATIONAL PARK

Rocky Mountain National Park epitomizes the grandeur of classic mountain scenery. The park contains a large segment of the Rockies Front Range one of the most impressive collections of jagged peaks, valleys, glaciers and alpine lakes anywhere in the United States. The western face of the park has thickly forested slopes and expansive meadows, while the eastern face rises precipitously into rugged, snow-covered peaks.

> ❖ **DID YOU KNOW?**
>
> *The lowlands of this park are 8,000 feet above sea level, while the highest point (Longs Peak) soars to 14,255 feet. There are some 70 peaks higher than 12,000 feet.*

Nowhere else in America (save for Alaska) is there such a concentration of towering peaks in so small an area. A visit to Rocky Mountain National Park is an unforgettable journey into rarefied air and breathtaking vistas.

FACTS & FIGURES

Location/Gateways/Getting There: It requires only an hour's drive from Denver to reach Estes Park in northcentral Colorado, the resort community at the park's front door. US 36 is the direct route to Estes Park, although a somewhat longer detour via SR 7 is more scenic. After exiting the park at Grand Lake, a return trip to Denver via US 40 and I-70 will complete a loop of 250 miles. It is rare for such magnificent scenery to be found so close to a major metropolis.

Year Established: Rocky Mountain National Park was established in 1915.

Size: 265,229 acres (414 square miles).

Admission Fee: $10.

Climate/When to Go: The park's major road network is open from late May to late October, depending upon the amount of snowfall. Although the park is beautiful in autumn, you take a chance that early snows will interfere with your visit. Summer offers the best weather. At these altitudes the temperature is cool. Sunshine is the rule, but take along a sweater or light jacket for the morning.

Contact Information: Superintendent, Rocky Mountain National Park, Estes Park, Co 80517. ☎ (970) 586-1206. 24-hour recorded information is available at ☎ (970) 586-1333.

AUTO TOUR/SHORT STOPS

Even though there are over 300 miles of trails in the park, it is remarkably accessible and amenable to touring by car. The primary feature of any visit is the drive along magnificent **Trail Ridge Road** (US 34). Covering about 45 miles in total, the road features one three-mile section at an elevation over 12,000 feet, 11 miles above the timberline.

> ❖ **DID YOU KNOW?**
>
> *The single highest point on the road reaches an incredible 12,183 feet above sea level. It the highest continuous through highway in the country.*

The road contains many sharp curves, switchbacks and steep grades. It is well maintained and not overly difficult to drive, though you may not want to attempt it if you lack mountain driving experience. Start out with some smaller mountains before coming to this part of Colorado!

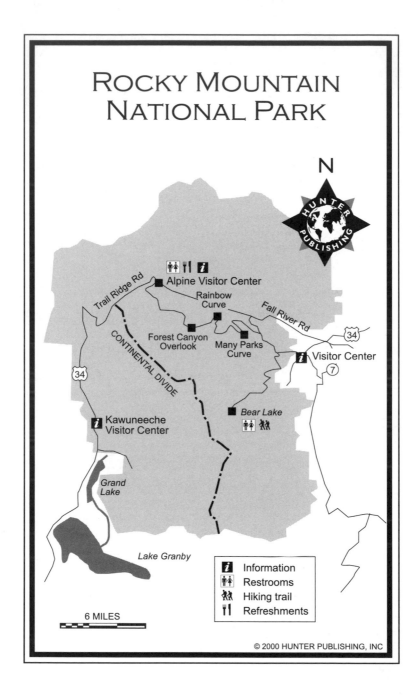

ROCKY MOUNTAIN NATIONAL PARK

N

Trail Ridge Rd

Alpine Visitor Center

Rainbow Curve

Fall River Rd

Forest Canyon Overlook

Many Parks Curve

CONTINENTAL DIVIDE

34

Visitor Center

7

Kawuneeche Visitor Center

Bear Lake

Grand Lake

Lake Granby

6 MILES

	Information
	Restrooms
	Hiking trail
	Refreshments

THE SOUTHWEST

> NOTE: *Keep your eye on the road at all times. It may be tempting to look at the scenery, but save your viewing for the overlooks. If you think you're missing something, change drivers periodically at an overlook.*

You can enter the park either through the Estes Park or Grand Lakes sides. We will start our description from Estes Park, as this is the most popular route. Just inside the entrance you will come to the **Morraine Park Visitor Center**, where you will find excellent information about the park's features and facilities. Outside, an easy half-mile nature trail (20 minutes) will introduce you to the park's varied flora. At an elevation of 8,000 feet, this trail will help prepare you for further physical activity in these higher altitudes.

Before embarking on Trail Ridge Road, take the drive down **Bear Lake Road**. En route there is fantastic scenery – high mountain peaks both near and distant, glaciers, cirques and alpine lakes. This mostly level road ends at Bear Lake. In summer you can take the shuttle bus from the road's end to the Glacier Basin campground adjacent to the visitor center. At Bear Lake itself an unforgettable experience is the trail around the lake (see next section for a more complete description). Make your way back to Trail Ridge Road.

> NOTE: *The Fall River Road parallels a portion of Trail Ridge Road and links up with it again later on. This road is unpaved and rather difficult. Although it also provides splendid mountain vistas and access to several waterfalls, you should first do Trail Ridge Road. If this doesn't give you any trouble, you can then backtrack to the beginning of Fall River Road.*

There are numerous overlooks on Trail Ridge Road, many strategically placed at the center of the road's switchbacks. This also helps widen the road at the worst turns and makes you feel less likely to slip off the mountain at any moment! The best ones are listed here in the sequence that you will reach them. First is the **Many Peaks Curve**, followed in quick succession by **Rainbow Curve**, **Forest Canyon Overlook** and **Rock Cut**, where there is a spectacular and dizzying view of the forest-covered canyon floor 2,000 feet below. Opposite Rock Cut is the **Tundra Nature Trail**, a half-mile paved walk through a beautiful alpine environment leading to views of the beautiful Lava Cliffs.

Shortly after that you pass the highest point on the road before coming to the **Gore Range Overlook**. Here, on top of the world, you will see a building ahead of you. This is the **Alpine Visitor Center**, where you can pick up information and take a rest from driving. This area features some of the finest views in the park, either from inside the building or on the outside observation deck. Your eyes will be drawn to the snake-like outline of the road silhouetted against a backdrop of massive mountains. Similar views are available just beyond the visitor center at Fall **River Pass** and **Medicine Bow Curve**.

Continuing your drive, Trail Ridge Road then brings you through **Milner Pass**, where you will cross the Continental Divide. The last important overlook is at **Fairview Curve**. From this point forward the road gradually descends along the western side of the park through Kawuneeche Valley. Another visitor center is here. This heavily wooded section of the road is picturesque, but certainly not nearly as spectacular the preceding portion. It does, however, offer excellent vistas of Grand Lake (near the park's exit).

You should allocate about five hours for the Auto Tour (and another 1½ hours if you decide to add on the Fall River Road).

❖ OUTSIDE THE PARK

The scenery doesn't stop once you leave the park at Grand Lake. **US 40** back towards Denver passes through some spectacular mountain terrain and the drive through the Berthoud Pass is an amazing experience. The so-called "grand loop" from Denver (passing through Boulder and Estes Park on the way to the park and via the Berthoud Pass and Idaho Springs on the way back) covers 240 miles. Although it can theoretically be done in a single day, an overnight trip is likely to make it more enjoyable.

GETTING OUT/LONGER STOPS

❖ HIKING

Most of the trails in Rocky Mountain National Park are long (sometimes 15 miles or more) and involve steep grades. However, in addition to the previously mentioned trails, one that can and should be done by everyone is the half-mile circuit of **Bear Lake**. It is an easy, level walk with views of the mountains reflected in the clear, still waters of the lake – it simply has to be seen. If you are here at a time when there aren't too many other visitors (morning is best), you can literally hear your own heart beating.

> **❖ TIP**
>
> *Although the trail is easy, take it slow if it is your first walk in the park, because the high altitude takes some getting used to.*

SPECIAL ACTIVITIES

❖ ORGANIZED TOURS

An extensive schedule of **nature programs** and **guided hikes** is available during the summer season. A popular way to experience some of the beauties of the park's interior (many parts of which cannot be reached by road) is by guided **horseback ride**. You can make inquiries at the Morraine Park Visitor Center or contact **Hi Country Stables** (in Morraine Park) at ☎ (970) 586-2327. Rates vary depending upon the length of the trip.

ACCOMMODATIONS

❖ HOTELS & MOTELS

There are no overnight facilities within the park.

NEARBY COMMUNITIES

DEER CREST ($$), 1200 Fall River Road, Estes Park; one mile northwest of town center on US 34, about three miles from park entrance. ☎ (970) 586-2324 or (800) 331-2324. 26 rooms. Situated beside a pretty little river, this newly redecorated property is meticulously kept. Western lodge style. Rooms have refrigerator and microwave and either a balcony or patio. Pool and other recreational facilities. Restaurants are nearby.

GRAND LAKE LODGE ($$-$$$), US 34, Grand Lake; a half-mile from the village of Grand Lake, just outside the park's western edge. ☎ (970) 627-3967. 58 rooms. A 1920 wooden lodge consisting of main building and tree-shaded units with a great deal of privacy. Rustic but elegant public facilities. Great views of the mountains surrounding Grand Lake. Plenty of recreational facilities. Restaurant on premises.

SILVER MOON ($$), 175 Spruce Drive, Estes Park; north of town center over bridge off US 34, four miles from park entrance. ☎ (970) 586-6006 or (800) 818-6006. 40 rooms. Very nice facility that has the appearance of a mansion. Basic units, including some suites ($$$). Swimming pool. Restaurants in walking distance.

STANLEY HOTEL ($$$$), 333 Wonderview Avenue, Estes Park; just east of downtown via US 34, four miles from the park's eastern entrance. ☎ (970) 586-3371 or (800) 976-1377. 133 rooms. Historic property dating from 1909 and built by the founder of the Stanley Steamer company. Lavish and ornate – a throwback to the elegance of an earlier era. Pricey, but worth it for those who are looking for a bit of luxury before setting out into nature. Beautiful grounds and magnificent views. Three restaurants. Less expensive dining options available in town.

❖ CAMPING

NPRS handles reservations for Moraine Park and Glacier Basin. ☎ (800) 365-2267. The offices are open daily from 10 am to 10 pm, eastern time. You can write for reservations at PO Box 1600, Cumberland, MD 21502. Or, you can reserve online at http://reservations.nps.gov. For all other campgrounds, contact the park directly.

All campgrounds allow trailers/RVs and have a seven-day limit, with the exception of Longs Peak (three days).

CAMPGROUNDS AT A GLANCE			
NAME	LOCATION	SITES	COST
Moraine Park	Four miles west of Estes Park near the visitor center.	247	$14 per day
Glacier Basin	Eight miles west of Estes Park.	150	$14 per day
Aspenglen	Near the Fall River entrance.	54	$12 per day
Longs Peak	11 miles south of Estes Park via State Highway 7.	26	$12 per day
Timber Creek	10 miles north of Grand Lake.	100	$12 per day

DINING

INSIDE THE PARK

TRAIL RIDGE RESTAURANT ($), Trail Ridge Road; halfway from either Estes Park or Grand Lake entrances. ☎ (970) 881-2142. Open Memorial Day weekend through mid-October. American food. Although it calls itself a "restaurant," this place is more of an oversized snack bar. Good for a late breakfast or for lunch on the go.

NEARBY COMMUNITIES

CAROLINE'S CUISINE ($$), 9921 US 34, Grand Lake; immediately outside the park. ☎ (970) 627-9494. American and continental cuisine. Delightful French decor throughout several small and intimate dining rooms. Their reputation is based on traditional preparation of great Colorado beef. Patio dining available in season.

COWPOKE CAFÉ ($$), 165 Virginia Avenue, Estes Park; in center of town. ☎ (970) 586-0234. American food. Good family dining spot with Western decor and excellent views. Variety of meat, chicken and fish dishes. Daily special is usually an outstanding value. Bountiful salad bar.

GRUMPY GRINGO ($$), 1560 Big Thompson Avenue, Estes Park; on the east side of town. ☎ (970) 586-7705. Mexican food. Well-prepared authentic Mexican cuisine graciously served by a decidedly non-grumpy staff in colorful and attractive surroundings. A fun place for the whole familly. Wonderful views from the outdoor dining patio.

WHERE DO WE GO FROM HERE?

As any trip to Rocky Mountain National Park will likely have originated in Denver, why not take in all the sights included in the **Colorado Circle**, *Suggested Trip 3*? If that is more than you want to undertake on one trip, head south (after returning to Denver) to the many attractions in **Colorado Springs** and just beyond that **Canon City**, where the gorge of the Arkansas River is one of Colorado's most unusual sights.

SAGUARO
NATIONAL PARK

Unlike many of the parks we've visited up to now, Saguaro doesn't overwhelm you with its magnificence. Instead, you'll learn to appreciate the great variety of vegetation and landforms that exist in the desert and see a special sort of beauty that can't be found anywhere else. Divided into two separate sections, Saguaro is a classic Sonoran desert environment. The famous cactus that gives the park its name grows only in southern Arizona and in the neighboring Mexican state of Sonora.

> ### ❖ DID YOU KNOW?
>
> *The Saguaro, a protected species, can live upwards of 200 years and often grows to between 30 and 40 feet in height. Some have actually exceeded 50 feet.*

But you'll see much more than the saguaro, for this relatively small national park has a great variety of desert vegetation as well as some gentle mountain scenery.

FACTS & FIGURES

Location/Gateways/Getting There: Part of the greater Tucson metropolitan area, Saguaro consists of two sections – the Tucson Mountain district to the west, and the Rincon Mountain district to the east. For the Tucson Mountain portion, use Exit 257 off I-10 and take Speedway Boulevard west to the park. For Rincon Mountain, follow the Old Spanish Trail east (reached from downtown Tucson via Broadway). While downtown Tucson is just minutes away from both sections, you might consider Phoenix as a gateway since it offers a better selection of flights.

From Phoenix, use I-10 south to reach the park (a 1½-hour drive).

Year Established: First established as a national monument in 1933, Saguaro was made a national park in 1994.

Size: 91,453 acres (143 square miles).

Admission Fee: $4 per vehicle for the Rincon Mountain district; admisson to the Tucson Mountain district is free.

Climate/When to Go: Tucson experiences hot, dry summers, although not quite as hot as in the Phoenix area. Still, daytime temperatures of 100°F are not uncommon, so the middle of summer is definitely not the most comfortable time to visit. Spring and fall are excellent choices. Winter is usually on the mild side, but there can be some frosty periods.

Contact Information: Superintendent, Saguaro National Park, 3693 Old Spanish Trail, Tucson, AZ 85730. ☎ (520) 296-8576.

*Organ Pipe cacti, a common sight at
Saguaro National Park.*

TOURING

The two sections of Saguaro National Park are separated by a distance of only 30 miles, so it is easy to do both in a single day. The names **Saguaro West** and **Saguaro East** are relatively new monikers.

> NOTE: *You may find that the locals refer to the two portions by their traditional names, namely the Tucson Mountain and Rincon Mountain Districts.*

❖ SAGUARO WEST (TUCSON MOUNTAIN DISTRICT)

Located within minutes of downtown Tucson, this national park is the closest to an urban area of any scenic park in America. Speedway Boulevard changes its name to Gates Pass Road as it enters the Tucson Mountain County Park, which abuts the southern edge of Saguaro West. Turn right onto Kinney Road and you will be led directly into the national treasure.

Before you get to the park's boundary, you will come to the excellent **Arizona-Sonora Desert Museum** (not a part of the national park). You should plan to spend some time here, as it provides an excellent education on the desert environment and its relationship to man. More than a museum, it is part zoological park and part desert park. Most of the exhibits are outdoors, and some are even underground. The museum maintains long visiting hours. The cost is $9 for adults and $2 for children ages six through 12.

Right after you enter Saguaro West you'll come to the **Red Hills Visitor Center**, where you can get information on trails. Exhibits here focus on the environment within the park, but they are not as well done as those at the Arizona-Sonora Desert Museum. The **Cactus Garden Nature Trail** at the center is an easy, paved, level walk through desert flora that is quite interesting.

The main part of your visit to Saguaro West will be via the nine-mile-long **Bajada Loop Drive**.

> NOTE: *About two-thirds of the route is a graded dirt road, but no special vehicle or driving skills are needed.*

The road passes through a thick saguaro forest. Now, don't expect to see every bit of land covered by cactus – "thick" and "forest" are relative terms in the desert. There is considerable spacing between larger cacti because of the small amount of water available. This is true in both "forest" sections of Saguaro National Park. In addition to the tall saguaros, the Bajada Loop Drive will take you past a staggering variety of cacti. The half-mile **Desert Discovery Trail** and the 1½-mile **Valley View Overlook Trail** (both of which begin at the visitor center) will give you more time to explore and see the flora close up. The latter trail also has good views of the surrounding desert and mountain terrain. There are a series of longer intersecting trails in Saguaro West. Inquire at the visitor center before setting out on any of these.

Your visit to Saguaro West will take between one and three hours, depending upon how many of the shorter trails you take. This time does not include any of the longer trails nor time for seeing the Arizona-Sonora Desert Museum.

❖ SAGUARO EAST (RINCON MOUNTAIN DISTRICT)

After you reach the Old Spanish Trail via Broadway Boulevard, you'll soon enter the Rincon Mountain District of Saguaro. A visitor center is located immediately inside the park border. From here you will begin the eight-mile-long paved, one-way road called the **Cactus Forest Drive**. It is along this drive that you will encounter the most stately examples of the noble saguaro cactus.

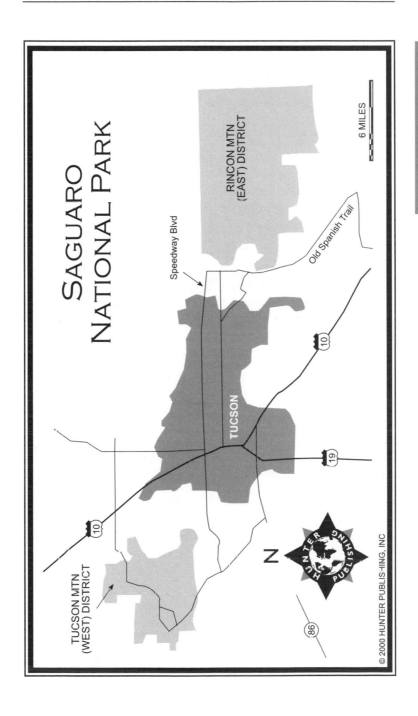

SAGUARO NATIONAL PARK

RINCON MTN (EAST) DISTRICT

Speedway Blvd

Old Spanish Trail

TUCSON

TUCSON MTN (WEST) DISTRICT

6 MILES

N

86

10

10

19

© 2000 HUNTER PUBLISHING, INC

Despite its size, the saguaro is fragile and protected by law. Do not touch any saguaro or attempt to remove smaller ones for your backyard. You will be heavily fined. In addition, sharp spines on most varieties of cacti can make touching them a painful experience. Be especially careful when hiking.

The quarter-mile **Desert Ecology Trail** is just off Cactus Forest Drive, as is the mile-long **Freeman Homestead Nature Trail**.

About an hour is required for the Auto Tour of Saguaro East.

GETTING OUT/LONGER STOPS

❖ HIKING

There are more than 40 miles of trails in Saguaro East, many of which are quite long and climb through the desert into the surrounding mountains. Some of the elevations in Saguaro East reach 8,000 feet. But there is one trail that can be done by all and is very worthwhile if you have an extra hour. The **Cactus Forest Trail** runs north-south and roughly bisects the Cactus Forest Drive. It allows you to get more up close and personal with the giant saguaros. It is a little more than two miles long.

SPECIAL ACTIVITIES

❖ HORSEBACK RIDING

Horseback riding is a popular way to see some of the back country and longer trails in Saguaro East. Operators seem to change frequently, so contact the visitor center for a list of reputable stables.

ACCOMMODATIONS

❖ HOTELS & MOTELS

There are no overnight facilities inside the park.

NEARBY COMMUNITIES

Saguaro is just minutes away from a major city with dozens of lodging choices. Besides many independent properties, among the chains you'll find in Tucson are: BEST WESTERN, ☎ (800) 528-1234; CLARION, ☎ (800) CLARION; COMFORT INN, ☎ (800) 228-5150; DAYS INN, ☎ (800) 329-7466; DOUBLETREE, ☎ (800) 222-TREE; EMBASSY SUITES, ☎ (800) EMBASSY; HAMPTON INN, ☎ (800) HAMPTON; HILTON, ☎ (800) HILTONS; HOLIDAY INN, ☎ (800) HOLIDAY; HOWARD JOHNSON, ☎ (800) I-GO-HOJO; LAQUINTA, ☎ (800) 531-5900; MARRIOTT, ☎ (800) 228-9290; RAMADA, ☎ (800) 2-RAMADA and SHERATON, ☎ (800) 325-3535.

Lodging along the I-10 corridor from downtown to the Miracle Mile is convenient to both the east and west sections of Saguaro.

❖ CAMPING

Other than some primitive campgrounds in the eastern section of the park (a hike of several miles from the loop road), there is no camping in Saguaro. You may camp, however, adjacent to the West section at the GILBERT RAY CAMPGROUND, ☎ (520) 883-4200 in Tucson Mountain County Park.

DINING

There are no eateries inside the park.

NEARBY COMMUNITIES

A situation identical to that for lodging. The nearest places for food when visiting the West section of Saguaro are in Tucson

Mountain Park (immediately adjacent) and along Speedway Boulevard going back towards the city. Fast food, national chains and other eateries are abundant. On the road to the East section you'll find varied choices along Broadway and the Old Spanish Trail.

WHERE DO WE GO FROM HERE?

Both parts of Saguaro are on the itinerary in *Suggested Trip 7*. If that's too ambitious, include only those sights in the southern portion of Arizona. If you want to keep the scenery relatively close to the Tucson area as part of a winter getaway, you might visit **Organ Pipe Cactus National Monument**. If you enjoyed Saguaro, you'll find this place equally interesting. It's 125 miles to the west. Along the way you can take in some of the scenery both on this planet and on others by stopping at the **Kitt Peak Observatory**, ☎ (520) 318-8726.

WHITE SANDS
NATIONAL MONUMENT

Nowhere else will you encounter the pure white gypsum sand that is found in this amazing national monument. It is whiter than snow. In fact, combined with the abundant sunshine in this part of New Mexico, it can almost be blinding. Unlike the Great Sand Dunes, the dunes of White Sands are rather low in comparison – only 60 feet high. But you come here for the color and the surreal surroundings, not the size. Although there is some vegetation that has uniquely adapted to this hostile environment, it is the white sands that draws the visitor.

Before we get started with our visit, a few words are in order about how the White Sands got here. About 250 million years ago, gypsum was deposited in a shallow body of water that covered this region in prehistoric times. Over a period of almost

200 million years the gypsum turned to stone. The formation of the Rocky Mountains lifted the basin into a huge dome. This dome began to collapse about 10 million years ago and created what is today known as the **Tularosa Basin**. Water from the nearby mountains flows into the basin. As there is no outlet to drain the area, the water goes into **Lake Lucero**, which is within the confines of the monument. There is a great deal of erosion caused by the dry winds, leaving pulverized gypsum in its wake. The winds blow the remnants northeast across the region and they pile into the widespread dunes.

FACTS & FIGURES

Location/Gateways/Getting There: In the southcentral portion of New Mexico, not far from the city of Alamogordo, the White Sands is easily reached from either El Paso, Texas, or Albuquerque. The Texas city is the closer of the two, about 100 miles distant. The two-hour trip from there is via I-10 west to I-25 north at Las Cruces, and then US 70 east to the monument. From Albuquerque, take I-25 south to US 70 at Las Cruces and proceed as above. The 270-mile drive requires only 4½ hours as most of it is on interstate highway.

Year Established: 1933.

Size: 143,733 acres (225 square miles).

Admission Fee: $4 per vehicle.

Climate/When to Go: The monument is open all year and can be visited at just about any time. The summers are hot and dry, while the winters are crisp (and almost equally dry). At visit here in spring or fall will avoid the temperature extremes.

Contact Information: Superintendent, White Sands National Monument, PO Box 1086, Holloman AFB, NM 88330. ☎ (505) 479-6124.

TOURING

At the entrance to the monument is a small **visitor center**, which has exhibits explaining the formation of the dunes. This is also the point where the eight-mile (one-way) **Dunes Drive** begins. The road affords excellent views of many of the largest dunes as well as pullouts with interesting roadside exhibits.

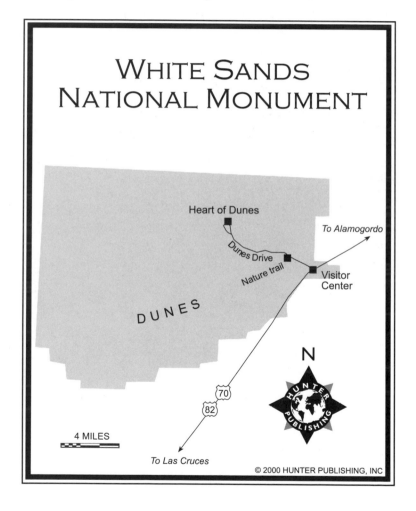

The one-mile **Big Dune Nature Trail** is one of the most popular places at White Sands. It's relatively easy to walk (although you will get sand in your shoes) and is especially interesting because this area contains many more plants and small animals than any other portion of the dunes. The biggest dunes that can be reached by the road are near the end in a section called the **Heart of the Sands**.

> ### ❖ TIP
>
> *Feel free to climb and run around on the dunes (but be careful during the summer because the sand can get quite hot). Don't worry about all the footprints you leave – the winds will soon take care of that by erasing all traces of your recent visit.*

A basic visit to White Sands, including the drive, nature trail and a little time out on the Heart of the Sands, will take 1½-2 hours.

Longer hikes on the dunes are possible, but be sure you have your bearings straight – it is easy to get lost on what is a seemingly simple terrain to negotiate.

Check at the visitor center for a schedule of **ranger-led walks**. There are also some evening programs during times of a full moon, when the dunes take on a special quality.

> NOTE: *The White Sands National Monument is a neighbor of Holloman Air Force Base and is completely surrounded by the* **White Sands Missile Range***. The base and range are active installations and missile tests occur frequently. It is not unusual for the road to the monument to be closed for one or two hours a couple of times each week. If you should be delayed by one of these tests, just be patient – the road closure is for your safety.*

ACCOMMODATIONS

❖ HOTELS & MOTELS

There are no overnight facilities inside the monument.

NEARBY COMMUNITIES

BEST WESTERN DESERT AIRE MOTOR HOTEL ($-$$), 1021 S. White Sands Blvd., Alamogordo; 1½ miles south of downtown on US Highways 54/70/82 and 15 miles northeast of White Sands National Monument. ☎ (505) 437-2110 or (800) 528-1234. Rate includes continental breakfast. 100 rooms. These standard motel units are nothing to rave about, but they are clean and comfortable. A few European spa units ($$$) are much better. Swimming pool. Restaurants within a short distance

DAYS INN ($$), 907 S. White Sands Blvd., Alamogordo; one mile south of town center on US Highways 54/70/82 and about 15 miles from monument entrance via US 70 west. ☎ (505) 437-5090 or (800) 329-7466. Rate includes continental breakfast. 40 rooms. Decent accommodations, a little better than those at the Best Western, but not as good as those in the next listing. Swimming pool. Restaurants nearby.

HOLIDAY INN ($$), 1401 S. White Sands Blvd., Alamogordo; two miles south of town center on US Highways 54/70/82 and 14 miles northeast of White Sands National Monument via US Highway 70. ☎ (505) 437-7100 or (800) HOLIDAY. 106 rooms. No surprises here. Slightly better than average rooms and decent public facilities. Swimming pool. Good restaurant on premises.

❖ CAMPING

There is no overnight camping at White Sands National Monument. Several commercial campgrounds are located in Alamogordo, 16 miles away.

DINING

There are no eateries within the monument itself.

NEARBY COMMUNITIES

MARGO'S ($-$$), 504 1st Street, Alamogordo; off the main US Highway in the center of town. ☎ (505) 434-0689. $-$$. Mexican food. Delicious, authentic dishes served in an attractive atmosphere featuring colorful and casual Southwestern decor.

YESTERDAY'S RESTAURANT ($$), in the Holiday Inn (see listing above). ☎ (505) 437-7100. American food. Alamogordo isn't a small town, but we've always had some trouble finding a good place to eat. Although this attractive dining room isn't anything special, it is one of the best in town.

WHERE DO WE GO FROM HERE?

White Sands is visited in our *Suggested Trip 5*, along with several other wonders of New Mexico. You can also create a nice trip that covers the southern portion of Arizona (**Saguaro National Park** and **Chiracahua National Monument**), along with the **White Sands** and **Carlsbad Caverns**, before heading into Texas to do **Big Bend National Park**. This "South-Southwestern trip" makes for a good journey in spring or fall.

ZION NATIONAL PARK

The rugged, lush and narrow canyon with a sometimes raging river and spectacularly colored rocky promontories characterize Zion Canyon, which has been compared by many to the Valley of Yosemite. The sheer rock walls are indeed similar, but those at Zion have far more color. The canyon road extends eight miles through canyons, past buttes and mesas, interspersed with vegetation.

❖ **DID YOU KNOW?**

The canyon itself narrows from half a mile in width at the beginning to just about 300 feet at the end.

Zion's mountains are famous for their color – brownish-red at the bottom, becoming whiter as they rise toward the sky. Then, too, there are fantastic shades of purple and lilac, all the more brilliant when captured in the sunlight. The fanciful names of many of the park's features probably owe their origin to early Mormon settlers. But when you see the dramatic formations that gave rise to these names, you will fully understand the awe that must have been felt by these early visitors.

FACTS & FIGURES

Location/Gateways/Getting There: In the southwestern corner of Utah's Color Country, the park entrance is on SR 9, which connects to I-15 near St. George on the west and with US 89 (access to Bryce) on the east. SR 9 is referred to as the Zion-Mount Carmel Highway and a portion of it forms an integral part of the park's road network.

Year Established: Seen by white men as early as 1776, the area was more fully explored in the 1870s. Zion became a national park in 1919, but did not take its current form until the completion of the Zion-Mount Carmel Highway in 1930.

Size: 146,551 acres (229 square miles).

Admission Fee: $10.

Climate/When to Go: Zion's summers are very hot, especially on the canyon floor. Spring and fall are better times to visit, when temperatures are moderate. The park is open in winter. It can be quite beautiful when covered with snow, but the snow can sometimes be heavy enough to close portions of the road network, so stick to other times of the year if you can.

Contact Information: Superintendent, Zion National Park, Springdale, UT 84767. ☎ (435) 772-3256.

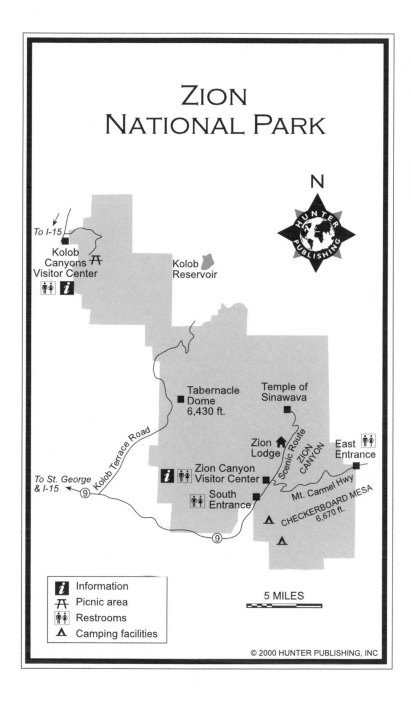

ZION NATIONAL PARK

N

To I-15

Kolob Canyons Visitor Center

Kolob Reservoir

Tabernacle Dome 6,430 ft.

Temple of Sinawava

Zion Lodge

Scenic Route

ZION CANYON

East Entrance

Zion Canyon Visitor Center

Kolob Terrace Road

To St. George & I-15

South Entrance

Mt. Carmel Hwy

CHECKERBOARD MESA 6,670 ft.

i Information
⊼ Picnic area
⚥ Restrooms
⛺ Camping facilities

5 MILES

© 2000 HUNTER PUBLISHING, INC

Auto Tour / Short Stops

While Zion can be reached from the east or west (many people come from St. George and I-15 to the west of Zion), we'll be describing your tour from the east. This is a common approach road because it comes from Bryce Canyon National Park. Total mileage within the park is not great, so you can spend most of your time seeing and doing rather than driving. From US 89 at the town of Mount Carmel Junction, head west on SR 9. This is the famous **Zion-Mount Carmel Highway**, considered an engineering marvel when built and still quite wonderful with its constant zig-zagging and climbing. Despite this, it is fairly easy to drive. The scenery along the way is great, but becomes even better once you enter the park. Shortly past the East Entrance Station is **Checkerboard Mesa**, an unusual sloping, whitish-gray formation with thin lines criss-crossing it like a giant checkerboard. You then pass through a short tunnel and approach the second, and longer, **Zion Tunnel**. There is a great trail that begins here (see the *Getting Out* section for details). The tunnel is well over a mile long. Inside there are several openings, or windows that look out into the canyon. When the road first opened you were allowed to stop and get out to take a better look through the windows. This practice has now been stopped to ensure safety.

> NOTE: *Vehicles exceeding 7'10" in width or 11'4" in height require an escort through the tunnel. This can be arranged by calling ☎ (435) 772-0178. There is a $10 fee for the escort service, which is valid for a round-trip through the tunnel within a seven-day period.*

After emerging from the tunnel, the highway begins a series of six dizzying switchbacks along the mountain slopes of the **Pine Creek Canyon**. You'll find it hard to keep your eyes on the road – the scenery is fantastic as you literally drop into the canyon. We strongly suggest you concentrate on your driving, but do stop at the parking area amid the switchbacks to take in the amazing glory of nature that surrounds you. This portion of the highway ends at the junction with the Zion Canyon Scenic Drive. Just to the south of the junction is the **Zion Canyon Visitor Center**. In addition to the interesting exhibits, this area has a good view of two peaks called the **Towers of the Virgin**, as well as of the canyon itself.

SHUTTLE BUS FOR THE YEAR 2000

The narrowness of Zion Canyon makes it easy to explore with your car, except for the horrendous traffic jams during the summer. In response to this problem, officials at Zion have implemented a plan (effective in 2000) that will require visitors to leave their vehicles at a new transportation center being built in the town of Springfield, just outside the park's main entrance. Use of the shuttle buses will be required from Memorial Day through Labor Day (except for guests registered at Zion Lodge, which is within the canyon). At other times you will still be permitted to drive into the canyon. These new rules do not affect other portions of the park – cars are still allowed there at all times. All in all, the changes should enhance the quality of your visit to Zion (it's not much fun looking for a parking place along the canyon's many pull-outs).

Now you're ready to begin touring Zion Canyon. Visible from the road or roadside pullouts are dozens of beautiful and interesting formations. As the route parallels the North Fork of the Virgin River, you'll first see **The Beehives** and **The Sentinel** to the west; and the **East Temple, Twin Brothers** and **Mountain of the Sun** on the east side. These come upon you in quick succession (the entire canyon road is only seven miles long). A bit farther along is a very short side road leading to a footbridge over the river. From the bridge, you can get a great view of the magnificent Court of the Patriarchs, including the **Three Patriarchs, Lady Mountain** and **Castle Dome.** Then, beyond Zion Lodge are pullouts for **Red Arch Mountain** and **The Grotto**, after which you pass the **Great White Throne**. A bend in the road goes around the **Organ.**

We've been throwing out names at a furious rate, and you're probably asking yourself what is so special about all of them. The formations in Zion Canyon are impressive because of their immense size, but even more so because of their coloration. Consisting of sandstone and shale, the predominant colors are red and grey, although various other shadings are present as well. The tops of many of the cliffs are tinged with the green of trees (from the bottom of the canyon they look like part of the rock). The strange shapes of many of the aforementioned stops enhance the experience all the more. When you see them, their rather fanciful names will have a lot more meaning.

At the **Weeping Rock Trail** it's time to take a little stretch. This easy half-mile-long walk ends at a rocky alcove with dripping springs. During the spring months wildflowers hang from the sides of the rock. This type of formation is quite common along many of the walks within Zion Canyon, but the Weeping Rock is one of the easiest to reach. After leaving the parking area for the Weeping Rock, you'll soon reach the road's end at the **Temple of Sinawana**, a huge natural amphitheater. Two large stone objects in the middle of the amphitheater are called the Altar and the Pulpit. The Temple of Sinawana is the beginning of the Gateway to the Narrows (see *Getting Out/Longer Stops*). When finished here, head back down the canyon. Before leaving the park you will see **The Watchman**, a vast mountain that guards the southern end of the park.

Allow about three hours for the driving portion of your visit.

GETTING OUT/LONGER STOPS

Although the scenery from the car or shuttle bus and from the many overlooks is wonderful, there are several opportunities for easy walks that will add considerably to your enjoyment of the park. Those looking for major hiking treks will also find rewards in Zion.

❖ HIKING

Beginning again with the Zion-Mount Carmel section of the park, the **Canyon Overlook Trail** (at the east entrance of the Zion Tunnel) covers one mile and can be done in an hour. It is an easy walk with spectacular views of Zion Canyon as well as the Pine Creek Canyon. There are long drop-offs from the trail, but most of them are fenced.

Within Zion Canyon itself are several popular longer trails, which will be listed in the order you reach them traveling north on the canyon road. The **Emerald Pools Trail** (1¼ miles) is a moderately difficult route with several drop-offs that ends at the lower pools in a pretty area containing three waterfalls. There is also the more difficult upper pool.

The two-mile **Hidden Canyon Trail** begins at the Weeping Rock parking area and leads to a narrow side canyon. This interesting trail has some steep dropoffs and is fairly strenuous. One of the longer trails is the one to **Angel's Landing**, a strenuous trek that covers five miles (requiring about a half-day) and climbs to a point high above the Zion Canyon. It's certainly not for everyone, but is very worthwhile.

Probably the most popular trail in Zion is the two-mile **Gateway to the Narrows**, originating from the Temple of Sinawana. It ends at the entrance to the Narrows. Also known as the Riverside Walk, the trail goes through a canyon that is only a couple of hundred feet wide. As you walk here, with the Virgin River at your feet,

Hikers take to the trails.

287

you'll see water dripping down the canyon walls which are decorated with sporadic plants. It is worth every minute of the trip.

> NOTE: *Handicapped individuals can make it through this trail with some assistance.*

At the end you can peer into the Narrows, one of the narrowest canyons on earth. The Narrows itself extends more than 10 miles beyond this point and should not be attempted by the casual visitor. It requires wading through several feet of water and scrambling over rocks. However, you will be rewarded with entry into a canyon that is, at one point, less than 20 feet wide and flanked by thousand-foot-high cliffs. Simply spectacular. While the Gateway can be walked in less than two hours, the complete Narrows Trail requires a full day.

> NOTE: *Flash floods are a constant threat in the Narrows. Check with a park ranger before setting out to determine conditions and avoid the area when the weather is threatening. The Gateway, too, can sometimes become hazardous during or immediately after heavy rains.*

❖ THE KOLOB CANYONS AREA

The park's northwestern section is not accessible by road from the main portion of the park. Despite its easily reached location right off I-15, it isn't visited by many people, simply because most don't know about it or because, having visited the main part of the park, they think they've seen "everything." Well, that isn't the case – the Kolob Canyons are worthwhile regardless of what you've seen. To get there from the southern entrance of Zion, travel west on SR 9 for 22 miles to SR 17 and then north on that road for six miles to the Interstate. From there go north one exit (15 miles) to the Kolob Canyons entrance.

A small visitor center is located immediately off the highway. From there, the five-mile **Kolob Canyons Road** will take you on an unforgettable journey as it twists up alongside the spectacular red rock monoliths and mountains. You'll view several "finger canyons" before coming to the end at majestic **Kolob Canyons Viewpoint**. The panorama is awesome, and the rocks here take on a salmon coloration. While you can see the major sights from your car or from the pullouts, the Kolob Canyons section also has several trails, ranging from two to nine miles. All are somewhat difficult.

SPECIAL ACTIVITIES

❖ TRAM TOURS

At Zion Lodge (about halfway through the canyon) you can arrange, during the summer, to take an open-air tram tour of Zion Canyon. While this isn't a bad idea (as it allows you to see the canyon without having to drive and find parking places), it may be less useful once the new shuttle bus system is implemented. Of course, many people do enjoy the informed commentary that these tours provide.

❖ ORGANIZED TOURS & HORSEBACK RIDING

Guided horseback rides are available from spring through fall. They are operated by **Bryce-Zion Trail Rides**, ☎ (435) 772-3967.

Park rangers conduct an extensive program of guided walks talks, except during the winter months. Schedules are posted at all visitor centers.

❖ 4WD TRIPS

Finally, there are some unpaved backcountry roads that penetrate remote areas of the park and lead to some of the most beautiful scenery anywhere. The best known is the **Kolob Terrace Road**, which shouldn't be confused with the Kolob Canyons. This road diverts off of SR 9 at the town of Virgin (west of the park entrance) and travels through the Kolob Plateau. There are several scenic pullouts. The route can be difficult and a 4WD, high-clearance vehicle is strongly suggested.

ACCOMMODATIONS

❖ HOTELS & MOTELS

INSIDE THE PARK

ZION LODGE ($$-$$$), four miles north of the main park entrance along Zion Canyon Drive. ☎ (435) 772-3213. 121 rooms. Built in the 1920s, this is one of the many works of famous architect Gilbert Stanley Underwood (the lodge was reconstructed in 1990 according to the original plan). It consists of about one-third cabin-style units and two-thirds newer motel units. Although the latter are bigger, the former have more atmosphere and charm. Restaurant on premises.

NEARBY COMMUNITIES

CANYON RANCH MOTEL ($), 668 Zion Park Blvd., Springdale; on State Highway 9, a quarter-mile from the park entrance. ☎ (435) 772-3357. 22 rooms. Lodging in nearby Springdale is not terribly expensive, but this is the best choice for the budget traveler. Comfortable individual cabins on nice grounds. Swimming pool. Restaurants are close by.

CLIFFROSE LODGE ($$), 281 Zion Park Blvd., Springdale; on State Highway 9, half a mile from the park entrance. ☎ (435) 772-3234 or (800) 243-8824. 36 rooms. Attractive accommodations set on five acres of nicely landscaped grounds with excellent views of Zion. Swimming pool. Restaurants are within a short distance.

NOVEL HOUSE INN ($$-$$$), 73 Paradise Road, Springdale; just off State Highway 9, one mile from the park entrance. ☎ (435) 772-3650 or (800) 711-8400. Rate includes full breakfast. 10 rooms. Unique and delightful bed and breakfast-style inn with spacious units, each named and decorated in a theme related to a famous author. Modern exterior. Lovely grounds. Great breakfast. Restaurants are within a short distance.

ZION PARK INN RESORT ($$), 1215 Zion Park Blvd., Springdale; on State Highway 9 in town, two miles from the park entrance. ☎ (435) 772-3200 or (800) 934-7275. 120 rooms. A modern structure with rustic style that is suited to its beautiful surroundings. Spacious and nicely decorated. Superb views.

❖ CAMPING

CAMPGROUNDS AT A GLANCE			
NAME	LOCATION	SITES	COST
South Campground	A half-mile north of Springdale.	125	$14 per day
The Watchman	At the south entrance station.	228	$14 per day

No reservations are accepted (call park headquarters for information). There is a 14-day limit. RVs are allowed.

DINING

INSIDE THE PARK

ZION LODGE DINING ROOM ($$), Zion Lodge (see listing above). ☎ (435) 772-3213. American food. Nicely prepared dinners in a casual, attractive atmosphere.

Zion Lodge offers box lunches to go, as well as a fast-food facility for quicker meals at lower cost.

NEARBY COMMUNITIES

MAJESTIC VIEW ($$), 2400 Zion Park Blvd., Springdale; on State Highway 9, 2½ miles from the park entrance. ☎ (435) 772-3000. American food. Pleasant family-style restaurant serving a good variety of dishes. Outdoor patio dining is available. The view from either inside or out can best be summarized by the restaurant's name.

PIONEER FAMILY RESTAURANT ($), 828 Zion Park Blvd., Springdale; State Highway 9. ☎ (435) 772-3009. American food. Very casual place serving decent food in adequate portions. A good value.

SWITCHBACK GRILLE ($$), Zion Park Inn Resort, Springdale (see listing above). ☎ (435) 772-3777. International cuisine. Excellent selection of steak, seafood and Italian dishes. Pleasant surroundings. The service is friendly and efficient.

WHERE DO WE GO FROM HERE?

Zion is included in *Suggested Trip 8*. Shorter trips, ideally planned from Las Vegas, can take you to nearby national parks and monuments like **Bryce, Cedar Breaks** and the **North Rim of the Grand Canyon**.

THE WEST

DEATH VALLEY NATIONAL PARK

Despite the fact that people have lived in this region for more than 9,000 years, the 19th-century stranding of a group of settlers and the loss of some has forever sealed the forbidding Death Valley name on one of the most beautiful places you can imagine. Created over three million years ago, the valley, which measures between four and 46 miles in width, extends for almost 150 miles and is surrounded on either side by towering mountain ranges. In fact, the entire region is a series of alternating valleys and mountains.

Death Valley is a land of stark contrasts. None is more evident than the variation in elevation. Within the park's boundaries are 11,049-foot-high Telescope Peak and Badwater, 282 feet below sea level. Badwater is the lowest point in the United States.

These two points are only 15 miles apart, making the contrast of more than two miles in elevation even more striking. Death Valley also has large sand dunes, colorful sculpted rocks, canyons and even a volcanic crater. They're all here for you to see from a number of outstanding vista points.

FACTS & FIGURES

Location/Gateways/Getting There: Covering a huge area along the central California border with Nevada (and slightly extending into the latter), Death Valley occupies a largely wilderness area. The most logical gateway is Las Vegas, only 100 miles away. Two routes are possible. The first follows SR 160 (reached just south of Las Vegas via I-15) through Pahrump, and then SR 210 west across into California and picking up SR 190 into the southern entrance of the park. Or, take US 95 north from Las Vegas to Beatty, then follow SR 374 west into Death Valley.

Year Established: A National Monument since 1933, Death Valley was made a National Park in 1994.

Size: One of the largest of America's parks, Death Valley covers an area of 3,367,628 acres (5,262 square miles), roughly twice the size of Delaware.

Admission Fee: $10 per vehicle.

Climate/When to Go: Death Valley is usually the hottest spot in the nation during the summer. In fact, the highest temperature ever recorded in the United States was right here, a staggering 134°. The weather is pleasant from around mid-October through April. Summer travel is highly discouraged.

SUMMER IN DEATH VALLEY

If you should decide to visit Death Valley during the hotter months, preparedness is the key to a safe and pleasant trip. Make sure that your car is in top operating condition, and be certain to check the condition of all hoses, the cooling system and, of course, your air-conditioning. Radiator water is available in barrels alongside the park's roads at frequent intervals. This water is NOT for drinking purposes. Be sure you have plenty of drinking water with you as well as clothing that will protect you from the sun. Summer services in the park are limited.

Contact Information: Superintendent, Death Valley National Park, PO Box 579, Death Valley, CA 92328. ☎ (619) 786-2331.

AUTO TOUR/SHORT STOPS

The valley's sights are well suited to automobile touring. Because of the monument's vast size and many entrances, there are several touring routes. We'll begin by approaching the park via Death Valley Junction and California's SR 190. Upon completion, you'll leave from the park's southern entrance near the town of Shoshone.

Tumbleweed blows across dry Death Valley.

Almost immediately inside the park's entrance is a cut-off leading to **Dante's View**. This road (no trailers allowed towards the end of the road) rises steadily upward from around 1,000 feet to almost 5,500 feet at its end, just over 13 miles away. This is the parking area for Dante's View, one of the most impressive scenic panoramas you'll encounter anywhere in your travels. Standing on the Black Mountains of the Amargosa Range, the view takes in a mind-boggling array of altitudes and terrains. Directly beneath you is Death Valley, including an extensive area that is below sea level. The drop of over a mile is quite a sight – even a little scary for those who are afraid of heights. The buzzards that hang around Dante's View make some people uncomfortable

THE WEST

enough to want to make a quick return to the lowlands. Actually, they're harmless and just waiting for a little handout (which you shouldn't give them). Besides seeing the valley, Dante's View affords excellent vistas of the even higher mountains on the far side of the valley. Telescope Peak and a wall of mountains exceeding 9,000 feet is a great backdrop for the valley. Now you can descend back to the entry road and turn left.

Several miles later there is a cut-off for a short one-way loop road that travels through narrow **Twenty Mule Team Canyon**. This road isn't paved, but is easily driven. Beyond the entrance to the canyon is another of the park's highlights – **Zabriskie Point**. A short walk leads to the top of a low rise from which there is an excellent view of the magnificent **Golden Canyon**. The rocks are literally a golden color when glistening in the almost constant sunshine of the valley. Ripples, folds and unusual shapes create a dramatic scene.

After Zabriskie Point you will soon reach a junction. A right turn brings you to **Furnace Creek**, the main area for visitor services in Death Valley. The visitor center and park museum are also here. About 12 miles north is the **Salt Creek Interpretive Trail**, where you can get out for a little stretch. An extensive area of sand dunes is just a few miles farther north. Continue north on the main road for about 30 miles to Grapevine. To the right is a short ride to Scotty's Castle, but more about that under *Special Activities*. For now, drive to the left for about five miles to the road's end at the **Ubehebe Crater**. Formed by volcanic action about 1,000 years ago, the crater measures 2,400 feet across and can be easily viewed from the parking area.

Now retrace your route southbound. Approximately 12 miles south of Furnace Creek is the entrance to the paved one-way scenic route known as **Artist's Drive.** The generally level road traverses some small, narrow canyons and passes rocks that are tinted in many different colors (indicating the presence of various mineral deposits). The array of colors is both beautiful and eerie. Nowhere are the colors more vivid then at one point on the loop called the **Artist's Palette**.

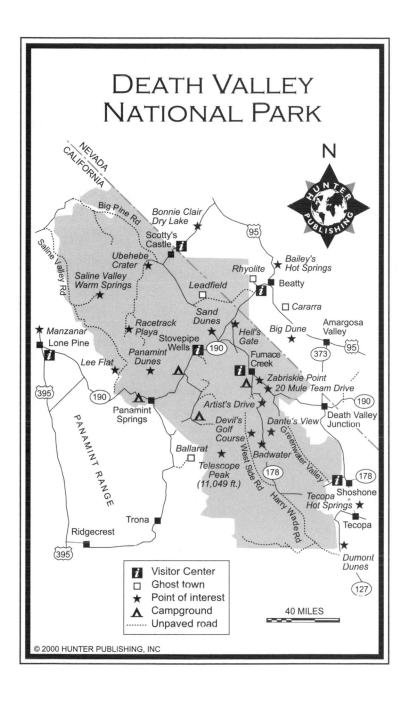

DEATH VALLEY NATIONAL PARK

N

THE WEST

Legend:
- 🅸 Visitor Center
- ☐ Ghost town
- ★ Point of interest
- ⛰ Campground
- ······· Unpaved road

40 MILES

Map labels:

NEVADA
CALIFORNIA

Saline Valley Rd

Big Pine Rd

Bonnie Clair Dry Lake

Scotty's Castle

Ubehebe Crater

Saline Valley Warm Springs

Rhyolite

Leadfield

Beatty

Bailey's Hot Springs

Cararra

95

Racetrack Playa

Sand Dunes

Hell's Gate

Big Dune

Amargosa Valley

373

95

Manzanar

Lone Pine

Lee Flat

Stovepipe Wells

Panamint Dunes

190

Fumace Creek

Zabriskie Point

20 Mule Team Drive

190

395

190

Panamint Springs

Artist's Drive

Dante's View

Death Valley Junction

PANAMINT RANGE

Devil's Golf Course

Greenwater Valley

Ballarat

Telescope Peak (11,049 ft.)

West Side Rd

Badwater

178

178

🅸

178

Shoshone

Tecopa Hot Springs

Harry Wade Rd

Trona

Tecopa

Ridgecrest

395

Dumont Dunes

127

Upon rejoining the main road, turn left. Soon you'll come to an area with several interesting sights that are reached by short unpaved spurs. These include the wild-looking volcanic remains of the **Devil's Golf Course** and **Natural Bridge**. Just beyond this area is **Badwater**, the lowest point in the United States at an altitude of 282 feet below sea level. From this point the road continues south for 40 more miles before exiting the park. The scenery on this final stretch is pleasant, but nothing spectacular compared with the sights you've already seen. You will, however, see many examples of the white salt deposits that are so common throughout the valley floor.

Almost a full day is required for the Auto Tour.

GETTING OUT/LONGER STOPS

❖ HIKING & CLIMBING

There are few formal long trails in Death Valley due to its severe climate, harsh terrain and undeveloped nature, but there are a few.

A 1¼-mile trail leads to the **Harmony Borax Works**, near the Furnace Creek area.

Rugged hikers sometimes trek over the colorful rocks in the **Zabriskie Point** area, and in Mosaic Canyon near Stovepipe Wells. This trail is about 2½ miles long.

There are also many trails up some of the mountains, including one that goes to the summit of Telescope Peak.

❖ JEEPING

This is a popular way to see even more remote portions of Death Valley. Roads are quite primitive and anyone planning to use them should secure additional information from park rangers at the visitor center.

SPECIAL ACTIVITIES

Scotty's Castle, in the northern section of the park, looks quite out of place in this environment. It was built in 1922 for a wealthy midwestern businessman as a winter retreat. The government purchased it in 1970. Tours are offered on the hour from 9 am to 5 pm. The hour-long tours cost $8 for adults and $4 for seniors and children.

Scotty's Castle, once a winter retreat for a wealthy businessman, is now open for tours.

ACCOMMODATIONS

❖ HOTELS & MOTELS

INSIDE THE PARK

FURNACE CREEK INN ($$$$), Highway 190, one mile south of the park visitor center. ☎ (760) 786-2345. 66 rooms. This isn't a bad looking place, but we think the prices are exorbitant (approaching $300 a night), and recommend you stay at one of the other places if possible.

FURNACE CREEK RANCH ($$-$$), at the visitor center; ☎ (760) 786-2345. 224 rooms. The quality of rooms and service here is not much lower than is found at the inn. But the rates are much lower. Motor inn-style facility.

STOVEPIPE WELLS VILLAGE ($$), Highway 94, 25 miles north of the visitor center. ☎ (760) 786-2387. 83 rooms. This place offers the lowest priced and most basic accommodations in Death Valley. More than adequate if you just want a place to sleep.

NEARBY COMMUNITIES

BURRO INN ($), US 95 at Third Street, Beatty; 40 miles northeast of the Furnace Creek area. ☎ (775) 553-2225. 62 rooms. Basic, but it'll do in a pinch. Decent restaurant on the premises.

❖ CAMPING

CAMPGROUNDS AT A GLANCE			
NAME	LOCATION	SITES	COST
Furnace Creek	Opposite visitor center.	136	$16 per day
Stovepipe Wells Village	Stovepipe Wells Village.	200	$10-16 per day
Mesquite Spring	Near Scotty's Castle.	30	$10-16 per day
Panamint Springs	30 miles west of Stovepipe Wells.	52	$10-16 per day
Sunset & Texas Springs	Furnace Creek area.	93	$10-16 per day

Furnace Creek Campground can be booked through **NPRS**, ☎ (800) 365-2267. The offices are open daily from 10 am to 10 pm, eastern time. You can write for reservations at PO Box 1600, Cumberland, MD 21502. Or reserve online at http://reservations.nps.gov. There's a 14-day limit. RVs allowed.

All other sites operate on a first-come, first-served basis. Limitations on stay vary from 14 to 30 days. Additional sites are in remote sections of the park. Contact the Park Superintendent's

Office for information on all sites other than Furnace Creek. (Most of the latter group are open only during the winter season.) Some of these sites are free of charge.

DINING

INSIDE THE PARK

THE INN DINING ROOM ($$), in the Furnace Creek Inn (see above listing). ☎ (760) 786-2345. American food. A very elegant eatery (jackets requested for men) that seems strangely out of place in this harsh environment. Maybe the stark contrast is what attracts people, although there are always plenty of hotel guests as well.

Furnace Creek offers more casual dining in the park in the form of a cafeteria and coffee shop. There's also a restaurant at the **Furnace Creek Ranch** and in **Stovepipe Wells**.

WHERE DO WE GO FROM HERE?

Death Valley is part of *Suggested Trip 12*. Winter visitors can take in **Lake Mead National Recreation Area, Joshua Tree National Monument, East Mojave Natural Preserve**, as well as the Palm Springs area. Summer trips are not recommended in this region because of the intense heat.

LASSEN VOLCANIC NATIONAL PARK

This is the nation's first volcanic national park. It contains not only the dormant 10,457-foot Lassen Peak, but three other major volcanic structures, two shield volcanoes (ranging from 6,000 to 8,000 feet) and a cinder cone. Virtually every other

THE WEST

type of volcanic activity is also represented here, including lava flows, hot springs, mudpots and boiling lakes.

Lassen's last major eruption occurred from 1914-1915, although major steam eruptions continued all the way through 1921 and, even today, still occur periodically. Scientists are convinced that we haven't heard the last from Lassen. However, for the time being you can visit without fear of any dangerous activity from the mountain. Lassen is much more than the remains of a volcanic eruption. It contains many beautiful mountain vistas and dozens of tranquil lakes. Excellent snow skiing is also on offer.

FACTS & FIGURES

Location/Gateways/Getting There: In northcentral California, Lassen Park is 47 miles off I-5 at Redding, via SR 44, or 46 miles via SR 36 from the Red Bluff exit of I-5. It is about 235 miles northeast of San Francisco via I-80, I-505 and I-5 to either of the above access routes.

Year Established: The park was established in 1916, right after the conclusion of the most recent major eruptive period.

Size: 106,372 acres (166 square miles).

Admission Fee: $5.

Climate/When to Go: Even though the park is open all year, winter snows close some roads. From the middle of June through mid- to late October is the primary touring season. At this time, it is very warm, but not nearly so hot as the surrounding valleys because of the park's high elevation.

Contact Information: Superintendent, Lassen Volcanic National Park, 38050 Highway 36 East, Mineral, CA 96063. ☎ (530) 595-4444.

Auto Tour/Short Stops

❖ Lassen Park Road

This route extends for 30 miles from the northwest entrance at Manzanita to the southwest entrance just north of Mineral. Along its route are many of the major points of interest in the park although, unfortunately, most of the largest lakes are in the eastern section, to which there is no road access. Even so, there is much to see on this road. We will begin our trip from the northernmost entrance, but you can easily reverse the entire route.

Just inside the entrance station is a small **visitor center** where you can get information and view exhibits about the park. Farther along the road is **Manzanita Lake**, a beautiful blue jewel nestled in the mountains. Although there is no roadside stopping point you can pull off the main road and into the adjacent campground for a closer look. The road then passes through an area called the **Chaos Crags** (to the driver's left) and **Chaos Jumbles** (to the right). The Crags are large plugs of lava strewn about on the mountainside like toys tossed aside by a boy giant. Also here is the **Dwarf Forest**, so-called because of the small coniferous trees in this area. They are not young trees, as many visitors mistakenly assume, but full-grown specimens, some over 300 years old. Next are **The Jumbles**. In a geological sense, these are same formations as the Crags, but numerous rock slides have scattered them about, mostly at lower elevations than the Crags.

A bit beyond this area is a roadside pullout by a formation known as **Hot Rock**, a large volcanic boulder weighing several hundred tons.

THE WEST

❖ TIP

Hot Rock doesn't look as though it weighs very much. Go ahead and try to move it, as hundreds of thousands of others have, without success.

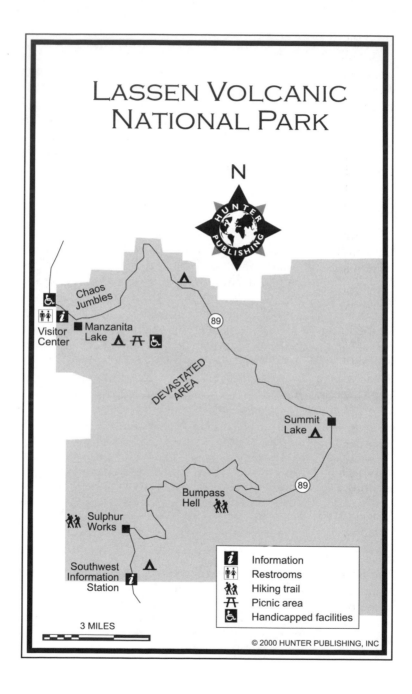

LASSEN VOLCANIC NATIONAL PARK

N

Chaos Jumbles

Visitor Center
Manzanita Lake

DEVASTATED AREA

Summit Lake

Bumpass Hell

Sulphur Works

Southwest Information Station

3 MILES

𝒊	Information
🚻	Restrooms
🥾	Hiking trail
⛱	Picnic area
♿	Handicapped facilities

© 2000 HUNTER PUBLISHING, INC

You will now be entering the **Devastated Area,** a desolate section in which all vegetation was completely erased during the last eruption. The passage of more than 80 years has restored much of the landscape, and the forest has regrown nicely, but there are still piles of rocks and volcanic debris clearly visible from two nearby overlooks at **Emigrant Pass** and **Hat Lake.** The next two scenic panoramas of mountains, both near and distant, are at **Summit Lake** and **Lupine.** Later you will pass **Diamond Peak,** where there is sometimes steam pouring out from vents in the mountainside. There is no place to stop here, but right after Diamond Peak you can park your car at the **Sulphur Works Thermal Area.** Here, a short boardwalk trail leads past a number of thermal spots. The yellowish color and awful aroma of sulphur are evident in this 15-minute loop walk. More thermal activity is in Bumpass Hell (see below).

After you have toured the thermal areas, you will reach the ski chalet which, of course, is mostly inactive during the summer season. Beyond this is the southwest entrance station, where there is another small visitor center.

You should allow a bit more than two hours for the Auto Tour.

GETTING OUT/LONGER STOPS

❖ HIKING

The back-country trails as well as those to the higher summits are long and strenuous. However, there are two easier trails that you should definitely consider. The first is at **Kings Creek Meadows,** where a 1¼-mile trail leads to beautiful Kings Creek Falls. There are some fairly steep grades, but the trail is not terribly difficult. It can be completed in about 1½ hours, round-trip.

The second option is the **Bumpass Hell Trail.** This one-mile route leads to Bumpass Hell, the primary area of thermal activity in the park. While not nearly as large or as spectacular as those found in Yellowstone, the trail will still take you past many boiling pots, mudpots, hot springs and other volcanic activity. Allow two hours for the complete trip.

In the vicinity of Butte Lake (six miles off the park road) is a trail that leads to the **Cinder Cone**. Among the formations that can be seen here are the Fantastic Lava Beds.

❖ DID YOU KNOW?

This was a relatively recent active volcanic area. It is estimated that some of the lava flows in the vicinity are less than 300 years old.

ACCOMMODATIONS

❖ HOTELS & MOTELS

INSIDE THE PARK

DRAKESBAD GUEST RANCH ($$$$), southeastern section of the park via Chester-Warner Valley Road, 23 miles from State Highway 36 in Chester (last three miles are via a dirt road). Call the Susanville operator (503) and ask for Drakesbad 2. Rates include three meals daily. 19 rooms. This is the only lodging in the park, and it is remotely located from the main visitor facilities. However, if you're looking for a guest ranch in an absolutely beautiful natural setting with plenty of recreational activities, this is definitely the place.

NEARBY COMMUNITIES

CHARM MOTEL ($), 37363 Main Street, Burney; one mile east of town on State Highway 299; about 35 miles north of park entrance via State Highway 89. ☎ (530) 335-4500. 42 rooms. Modest-sized units, several with full kitchen facilities. Restaurants are within a short distance.

DOUBLETREE HOTEL ($$-$$$), 1830 Hilltop Drive, Redding; west of I-5 via State Highways 44/299 and 60 miles west of the park entrance via State Highway 44. ☎ (530) 221-8700 or (800) 222-TREE. 193 rooms. Extremely attractive modern motor inn with oversized rooms and comfortable furnishings. Swimming pool and other recreational facilities. Restaurant and lounge on the premises.

GRAND MANOR INN ($$), 850 Mistletoe Lane, Redding; one mile from the Cypress Avenue exit of I-5 and then via Hilltop Drive and about 60 miles west of Lassen via State Highway 44. ☎ (530) 221-4472. Rate includes continental breakfast. 71 rooms. Not quite as nice as the Doubletree, but may well be a better value. Swimming pool. Quite a few dining choices within a short drive.

GREEN GABLES MOTEL ($), 37385 Main Street, Burney; one mile east of town on State Highway 299 and 35 miles north of Lassen via State Highway 89. ☎ (530) 335-2264. 26 rooms. Family-run motel with well-kept and comfortable units that should satisfy most travelers. Swimming pool. Restaurants nearby.

I.M.A. RED BLUFF INN ($), 30 Gilmore Road, Red Bluff; west of I-5 on State Highway 36 and 50 miles from the southern entrance of Lassen via State Highways 36 and 89. ☎ (530) 529-2028 or (800) 341-8000. Rate includes continental breakfast. 60 rooms. A friendly and comfortable place to stay at an affordable rate. Nothing fancy. Swimming pool. Restaurants nearby.

LA QUINTA INN ($-$$), 2180 Hilltop Drive, Redding; half a mile north of Cypress Avenue exit of I-5 and 60 miles west of Lassen via State Highway 44. ☎ (530) 221-8200 or (800) 531-5900. Rate includes continental breakfast. 140 rooms. Nicely decorated rooms that are a good size and represent excellent value. There's a pool and Jacuzzi. Restaurant on premises with several national chain restaurants within a short distance.

TRAVELODGE ($), 38 Antelope Blvd., Red Bluff; a quarter-mile west of I-5 via State Highway 36 and 50 miles from Lassen via State Highways 36 and 89. ☎ (530) 527-6020 or (800) 367-2250. Rate includes continental breakfast. 41 rooms. Attractive, newly redecorated units, many of which have either a patio or a view of the Sacramento River. Some units have refrigerators and/or microwave ovens. A 24-hour Denny's restaurants is adjacent. Other dining options nearby.

THE WEST

❖ CAMPING

Reservations are not accepted at any park campground. Call the park headquarters for more details. There is a 14-day limit at all sites. RVs allowed, but no hookups.

CAMPGROUNDS AT A GLANCE			
NAME	LOCATION	SITES	COST
Warner Valley	Drakesbad.	18	$8-12 daily
Manzanita Lake	Near north entrance, main park road.	79	$8-12 daily
Crags	3½ miles past Manzanita Lake on main park road.	45	$8-12 daily
Summit Lake North & South	Midway along park road.	94	$8-12 daily
Southwest	Near the southern entrance station.	21	$8-12 daily

DINING

INSIDE THE PARK

Excluding some restaurants at the remote Drakesbad Road entrance of the park, the only place to grab a bite is during the winter months at LASSEN CHALET in the ski area at the southern end of the main park road.

NEARBY COMMUNITIES

DE MERCURIO'S RESTAURANT ($$), 1647 Hartnell Avenue, Redding; two miles southeast of Cypress Avenue exit of I-5. ☎ (530) 222-1307. Continental cuisine. Casual elegance at affordable prices. French and Italian entrées as well as a smattering of American dishes. All are well prepared.

HATCH COVER ($$), 202 Hemsted Drive, Redding; west of Cypress Avenue exit of I-5. ☎ (530) 223-5606. American food.

Good variety of steaks, seafood, chicken and pasta entrées nicely served in a casual and attractive setting.

J.C. GREEN BARN RESTAURANT ($-$$), 5 Chestnut Avenue, Red Bluff; State Highway 36 East. ☎ (530) 527-3161. Steak-house. While steaks are the specialty of the house at this popular eatery, there's also a good variety of other selections, including quite a few that will appeal to children.

WHERE DO WE GO FROM HERE?

Suggested Trip 11 includes Lassen among the many marvelous parks and other sights of the High Sierras. Because this is a long trip in terms of mileage, you may wish to see Lassen as part of a smaller geographic area. If so, consider covering the **northern California coastal** region by traveling west from Lassen, or the **Lake Tahoe** area by heading to the southeast.

THE WEST

SEQUOIA & KINGS CANYON NATIONAL PARKS

These two huge parks are adjacent to one another at the edge of California's magnificent Sierra Nevada range. They are jointly administered and are almost always referred to collectively. The parks are home to some of the largest living things on earth – the giant sequoia trees, some of which are as much as 4,000 years old. These trees are not as tall as they might be, since they keep getting trimmed by bolts of lightning! But the area offers far more than these wonderful trees. The highest elevation in the contiguous United States, 14,494-foot Mount Whitney, is also here in the park. There is majestic alpine scenery throughout the park's high country and the lower elevations are graced by large forests of pine, cedar and fir trees. Although the road system, primarily consisting of the Generals Highway (which connects the two parks), does not penetrate into the high country, it does provide wonderful panoramas of the mountains and, of course, access to those huge trees.

FACTS & FIGURES

Location/Gateways/Getting There: Comprising a large chunk of east-central California, the parks are easily reached from SR 99. From the intersection of that road in Fresno it is only 54 miles along SR 180 to the park; from Visalia, less than 40 miles via SR 198. From San Francisco it is just under 300 miles (six hours) and from Los Angeles 225 miles (about 4½ hours).

Year Established: Sequoia became America's second national park in 1890, but neighboring Kings Canyon was not given this status until 1940.

Size: The combined area is 864,124 acres (1,350 square miles). The two parks are roughly the same size.

Admission Fee: $10. Entrance pass good at both parks for up to seven days.

Climate/When to Go: Some of the roads are not open until late June or early July. Also, cooler temperatures in the higher elevations make it wise to visit during the summer or very early in the fall, before the snows set in.

Contact Information: Information on both parks is available from the Superintendent, Sequoia and Kings Canyon National Parks, Three Rivers, CA 93271. ☎ (559) 565-3341.

> ❖ **TIP**
>
> *Call ☎ (559) 565-3351 for 24-hour recorded road and weather information.*

AUTO TOUR/SHORT STOPS

While only long hikes will deliver you into the extraordinary environment of the alpine high country, the sights from along and near the roads are spectacular. There's a lot to see and most of it is easy to reach. The **Generals Highway** is 46 miles long and provides access to the main features of both parks. However, including one other long road and several spur roads, the total mileage in the two parks comes to about 150. You can enter from north or south, but our description will begin from the Big Stump Entrance Station of Kings Canyon National Park. This entrance, in the northern part of the adjoining parks, is reached via SR 180 from Fresno, itself a highly scenic route.

Just inside the entrance is the **Big Stump Basin**, so called because of numerous tree stumps here that date from the days before the park's trees were protected. A short nature trail goes through the basin. Further exploration of this area, however, calls for a much longer trek.

Upon reaching the Generals Highway about a mile further up the entrance road, turn to the left. This will bring you into the **Grant Grove** section of the park. Within Grant Grove are several short trails leading through the quiet carpeted forest, bringing you face to face with several of these awesome giant trees. These specimens are all huge, but there will be no mistaking the **General Grant Tree** itself, which is 267 feet high and almost 108 feet around. Also notable are the **General Lee** and **Tennessee trees**. One felled tree is partially decayed and you can actually walk through the inside of it, allowing you to appreciate its giant size. Keep in mind that this was by no means the biggest of the park's trees. All of the aforementioned examples are along a paved trail measuring only about a third of a mile.

Nearby, still within the Grant Grove area, is a short spur road (2½ miles) leading to **Panoramic Point**. The road is steep and is closed during the winter. From the end of the road is a short trail leading to the viewpoint where you can get an unobstructed vista of the High Sierras.

THE WEST

Once you get back to the main road, continue north. This is an extension of SR 180 and is a dead-end trip of approximately 40 miles that leads to Kings Canyon's **Cedar Grove** section. The longer part of the trip is not within the borders of the park, but in the Sequoia National Forest. Along this road you'll encounter one vista after another of distant mountains, deep canyons and rushing rivers. The road rises and falls steeply in places and has countless turns, but isn't overly difficult to negotiate. The family sedan will do nicely. Nice stops along the way include the furious whitewater of the **South Fork of the Kings River** at Boyden Cave, **Grizzly Falls**, **Canyon Viewpoint**, the **Roaring River Falls** and, near the end of the road, the colorful **Zumwalt Meadow** and **Grand Sentinel Viewpoint**. All of these are either right on the road or reached by short, easy walks. At Road's End you'll find the trailheads for long excursions into the high country (see next section).

Although you have to return to the main portion of the park via the same route, the views look different when you're going in the opposite direction. Once you pass by the Grant Grove, continue on the Generals Highway. Just before leaving Kings Canyon there is a fabulous vista from the **Red Mountain Overlook** before you briefly reenter the Sequoia National Forest. After Stoney Creek, you'll then enter Sequoia National Park.

The Highway makes a major turn in direction at **Lodgepole**, site of a visitor center and some longer trails, and then reaches one of the most famous and beautiful areas in the park – the **Giant Forest**. The trees here are even larger than those in the Grant Grove and there are far more of them. The **General Sherman Tree** is the largest in the park, towering to 275 feet, a few feet less in girth than the Grant. It is reached by a short trail from the parking area. The area has an unreal atmosphere as you stroll down paved walkways in a huge basin filled with these immense and beautifully colored trees. Longer walks in this area are described in the section that follows.

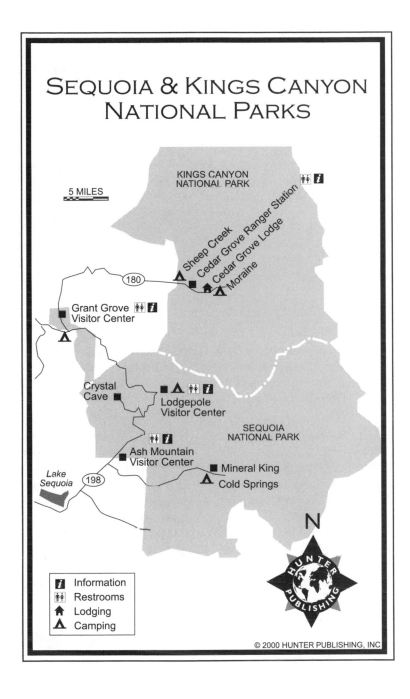

SEQUOIA & KINGS CANYON NATIONAL PARKS

KINGS CANYON
NATIONAL PARK

5 MILES

Sheep Creek
Cedar Grove Ranger Station
Cedar Grove Lodge
Moraine

180

Grant Grove
Visitor Center

Crystal
Cave

Lodgepole
Visitor Center

SEQUOIA
NATIONAL PARK

Ash Mountain
Visitor Center

Lake
Sequoia

198

Mineral King
Cold Springs

N

	Information
	Restrooms
	Lodging
	Camping

© 2000 HUNTER PUBLISHING, INC

THE WEST

❖ TIP

A shuttle bus service operates in the Grant Grove area if you wish to leave your car for awhile. Schedules are posted on bulletin boards at all visitor centers.

Soon after the Giant Forest a short detour off the Generals Highway leads to a couple of interesting attractions. The **Auto Log** is a fallen giant sequoia that has been evened out so you can actually drive your car onto it. This is a great photo opportunity. Nearby is **Tunnel Log**, another fallen giant. This one you can drive through (cars only – a bypass is provided for campers). Another great photo stop.

NOTE: *Traffic is one at a time through the log, so exercise caution before entering.*

This side road is also the way to reach **Morro Rock**, perhaps the best known feature of Sequoia National Park. There is a good view of it from the base, but climbing to the top is definitely a worthwhile activity (see *Getting Out/Longer Stops*).

South of this area, the Generals Highway begins its descent to the southern entrance station. The drive takes you from an elevation of well over 6,000 feet to only 1,700 feet at the Foothills Visitor Center by the entrance. It is a continuous steep downgrade so use a low gear. The turns are endless and often spectacular – long switchbacks provide sweeping panoramas of the mountains as well as the road. There are several pullouts where you can stop to admire the scenery. While all are beautiful, the best is definitely **Amphitheater Point.** From this spot you'll not only have an unobstructed view of many peaks in the High Sierras, but you'll also be able to see Morro Rock in its entirety.

If you look closely (binoculars are helpful), you'll even be able to see tiny specks at the top. These are people who have climbed to the 6,725-foot summit of Morro Rock.

The Auto Tour as described above requires a full day. Thus, if you are going to be doing even a minimal number of activities as described in the *Getting Out* section, you'll probably have to spend a night in the park.

GETTING OUT/LONGER STOPS

❖ HIKING

To make things a little easier, we'll list some of the more popular longer trails section by section.

Grant Grove: The **North Grove Loop** and the **Dead Giant Loop** each cover about 1½ miles. The latter is an extension of the route to the Grant Tree, while the North Grove branches off the other trail. You can do both in about 1½ hours.

Cedar Grove: Zumwalt Meadow was mentioned on the Auto Tour. However, a full exploration of the area requires traversing a longer trail. In the hour or so it takes, you'll see not only the meadows, but sheer high granite walls. From **Road's End** there are several trails leading into the mountains. Another possibility is the eight-mile round-trip to **Mist Falls**, one of the park's largest. There is a 600-foot change in altitude on this trail, which requires four hours to complete.

Lodgepole: The **Tokopah Falls Trail** is slightly under two miles long. It travels through the Kaweah River gorge and provides a stunning close-up of granite cliffs as well as the falls itself. Allow three hours.

Giant Forest: The **Congress Trail** (two miles) is in the vicinity of the General Sherman Tree and is among the most popular trails in the park. Mostly level, the walk can be done in under 1½ hours and passes through the Senate and House Sequoia Groves. Among the bigger sequoias encountered will be the President Tree and the McKinley Tree.

Slightly south of the main Giant Forest area is the easy **Trail for All People** (two-thirds of a mile) that circles the Round Meadow. The sequoia specimens aren't nearly as good here, but during the summer the wildflower meadow is quite pretty. The mile-long **Hazelwood Nature Trail** is also an easy jaunt.

The impressive granite dome known as **Morro Rock** can be climbed without any special skills or equipment. That's because the "trail" is actually a staircase.

> NOTE: *Although only a quarter-mile long, the stairway is very steep and, because of the altitude, requires that you be in good shape to make the ascent.*

Those who make it to the top will be rewarded with an unparalleled view of the Great Western Divide. There are also many other longer trails that begin off the spur road that leads to Morro Rock. The trail to Tharp's Log is one of the better ones in this vicinity.

SPECIAL ACTIVITIES

❖ HORSEBACK RIDING

Sequoia and Kings Canyon contain hundreds of miles of trails suitable for horseback riding. Hourly to all-day trips can be arranged at a number of locations, including the **Cedar Grove Pack Station**, ☎ (559) 565-3464; and **Grant Grove Stables**, ☎ (559) 565-3464. Prices vary depending upon the length of the trip.

❖ CRYSTAL CAVE

Crystal Cave is a beautiful marble rock cavern. Guided tours are available for $5 (tickets must be purchased in advance at either the Lodgepole or Foothills visitor centers). Tours are given daily on the half-hour beginning at 11:30 am through 3:30 pm.

> **❖ TIP**
>
> *Bring a jacket as it can be quite chilly in the cave.*

The tours last about 50 minutes, but allow at least two hours for the entire excursion, including the drive of seven miles off the Generals Highway as well as the steep half-mile-long trail that leads to the cave entrance.

❖ MINERAL KING

Finally, the more adventurous traveler has access via partially paved roads to a wonderfully scenic section in the extreme southern Sequoia. Mineral King can be reached during the summer via a long and steep winding road that begins just south of the Foothills Entrance Station. The sub-alpine valley at the end is a gem. Trails of varying lengths (all are quite long) lead to magnificent mountain lakes. Horseback riding is also available from the stables at Mineral King. Visitors to this area should allow an entire day.

ACCOMMODATIONS

❖ HOTELS & MOTELS

INSIDE THE PARK

In-park accommodations are operated by Kings Canyon Park Services. The central reservations number for all of their properties (indicated by KCPS after the establishment's name) is ☎ (559) 335-5500.

THE WEST

CEDAR GROVE LODGE (KCPS), Cedar Grove Village area, along State Highway 180. ☎ (559) 565-0111. $-$$. 18 rooms. Small roadside motel with basic but clean accommodations. Food service available.

GIANT FOREST LODGE (KCPS), Giant Forest Village area of Sequoia along the Generals Highway. ☎ (559) 565-4035. $$. 245 rooms. Large motel complex with standard rooms in a tree-shaded location. Restaurant.

GRANT GROVE LODGE (KCPS), Grant Grove Village of Kings Canyon, opposite the visitor center. ☎ (559) 335-2135. $$. 52 rooms. Simple, rustic cabins. (New motel-type units were just completed as of press time and have not been reviewed. However, we do not expect them to be fancy.) Restaurant on the premises.

MONTICELLO-SEQUOIA LODGE, Generals Highway, Sequoia National Forest (between the southern entrance of Kings Canyon and northern entrance of Sequoia). ☎ (559) 565-3388 or ☎ (800) 227-9900. $$$$. Rate includes three daily meals. 50 rooms. While not technically in either park, the location offers the same type of scenery and terrain. Most of the lodge's rooms are in a central building, although there are a number of rustic cabins with shared bath. Recreational facilities include a swimming pool and tennis. Restaurant on premises.

STONY CREEK LODGE (KCPS), Generals Highway in the Sequoia National Forest between the two parks. ☎ (209) 565-3650. $$. 11 rooms. While this isn't anything special, it does have a bit more charm than the other KCPS facilities and is well situated for touring both parks. You have to drive a little ways to reach restaurants.

NEARBY COMMUNITIES

BADGER INN MOTEL ($$-$$$$), State Highway 245, Badger; 12 miles south of the Big Stump (west) entrance to Kings Canyon National Park. ☎ (559) 337-0022. 9 rooms. Tranquil location that's convenient to the parks. Fairly basic, although the upper price range is for a nice two-level suite. The nearest restaurants are a 20-minute drive away.

BEST WESTERN HOLIDAY LODGE ($$), 40105 Sierra Drive, Three Rivers; two miles from town center on State Highway 198 and seven miles from the southern entrance of Sequoia National Park via Highway 198. ☎ (559) 561-4119 or (800) 528-1234. 20 rooms. Good-quality rooms in attractive facility along the Keawah River (fishing and hiking trails available). Restaurants within a short distance.

BUCKEYE TREE LODGE ($$), State Highway 198, Three Rivers; a half-mile from the southern entrance of Sequoia National Park. ☎ (559) 561-5900. 12 rooms. Slightly better than basic motel-style units (also one cabin suite, $$$). Recreational facilities. Nice location in river canyon. Restaurant nearby.

COURTYARD BY MARRIOTT ($$), 1551 N. Peach Avenue, Fresno; four miles east of State Highway 41 via McKinley Avenue and about 53 miles west of the Big Stump entrance of Kings Canyon via State Highway 180. ☎ (559) 251-5200 or (800) 321-2211. 116 rooms. Spacious, attractive and comfortable rooms in a modern building with nice grounds. Good value. Restaurants are nearby.

LAZY J RANCH MOTEL ($$-$$$), 39625 Sierra Drive, Three Rivers; 2½ miles from town on State Highway 198 and eight miles from southern entrance of Sequoia. ☎ (559) 561-4449 or (800) 341-8000. 18 rooms. Despite the small number of units, there's a good variety of accommodations from motel to cabins to multi-room facilities. Some have kitchens. Swimming, fishing and hiking. Nice setting. Restaurants within a short drive.

PICCADILLY INN ($$), 5515 McKinley Avenue, Fresno; four miles east of State Highway 41 and 52 miles from Kings Canyon National Park via State Highway 198. ☎ (559) 251-6000. Rate includes continental breakfast. 185 rooms. A beautiful motor inn with large and tastefully decorated rooms. Elegant public areas. A real winner for the price. Swimming pool. Excellent restaurant on the premises as well as lower-priced coffee shop.

❖ CAMPING

NPRS for the Lodgepole and Dorst campgrounds only. ☎ (800) 365-2267. The offices are open daily from 10 am to 10 pm, eastern time. You can write in for reservations at PO Box 1600, Cumberland, MD 21502. Or, you can reserve online at www. reservations.nps.gov. All other campgrounds operate on a first-come, first-served basis.

CAMPGROUNDS AT A GLANCE			
NAME	LOCATION	SITES	COST
KINGS CANYON NATIONAL PARK			
The Azalea	Grant Grove area.	114	$12-16 per day
Crystal Springs	Grant Grove area.	66	$12-16 per day
Sunset	Grant Grove area.	119	$12-16 per day
Sentinel	Cedar Grove area.	83	$12-16 per day
Sheep Creek	Cedar Grove area.	111	$12-16 per day
Canyon View	Cedar Grove area.	37	$12-16 per day
Moraine	Cedar Grove area.	120	$12-16 per day
SEQUOIA NATIONAL PARK			
Potwisha	Foothills area.	44	$12-16 per day
Buckeye Flat	Foothills area.	28	$12-16 per day
Lodgepole	Lodgepole.	250	$12-16 per day
Dorst	Lodgepole.	218	$12-16 per day

RVs are permitted at all of the above sites but there are no hook-ups. There is a 14-day limit at all campgrounds.

DINING

INSIDE THE PARK

MONTICELLO-SEQUOIA LODGE DINING ROOM ($$, Monticello-Sequoia Lodge (see listing above). ☎ (559) 565-3388. American/international cuisine. Attractive dining room offering a lavish buffet of well-prepared foods.

With the exception of the lodge dining room, we can't enthusiastically recommend the other dining options within either park. There are restaurants or coffee shops in the lodging facilities at Grant Grove and Giant Forest, as well as several snack bars in other park village areas. They're better for breakfast or lunch, but will do in a pinch at supper time. The best of the lot is the coffee shop at the Grant Grove Lodge.

NEARBY COMMUNITIES

STEAK AND ANCHOR RESTAURANT ($$-$$$), Piccadilly Inn, Fresno (see listing above). ☎ (559) 251-6000. American food. Excellent steak, seafood and other entrées in a casually elegant dining room with first-rate service.

WHITE HORSE INN ($$), 42975 Sierra Drive, Three Rivers; one mile east of town on State Highway 198. ☎ (559) 561-4185. American food. Good family dining in an attractive setting offering a wide variety of dishes, including many favorites. The duck is especially good.

THE WEST

WHERE DO WE GO FROM HERE?

Sequoia and Kings Canyon are part of *Suggested Trip 10*. That trip also includes Yosemite and the proximity of the three makes it natural to see them as part of a single tour.

If you are coming from Los Angeles you could also combine Sequoia and Kings Canyon with a trip through the **Angeles** and **San Bernardino National Forests**. These beautiful locations include a thrilling ride on the Angeles Crest Highway and the Rim of the World Drive. The latter goes to several mountain lakes that are truly gems.

YOSEMITE NATIONAL PARK

Yosemite is justifiably one of America's most famous and popular parks; its spectacular scenery is sure to impress even those who have seen practically every other park. On the western slopes of the Sierra Nevada mountains, Yosemite encompasses a staggering array of sights – majestic peaks, sheer granite walls, the well-known domes and pinnacles, waterfalls of immense height, rushing rivers, huge trees, forests and more.

To most visitors, Yosemite National Park refers to a small but dramatic area known as Yosemite Valley.

> ### ❖ DID YOU KNOW?
>
> *Yosemite Valley represents only one-half of one percent of the park's total area, an almost unbelievable statistic when one is standing in the valley and pondering its immensity! The other, far bigger portion has enough to make the visit worthwhile even if Yosemite Valley did not exist.*

Only Yellowstone and possibly Olympic National Park have a diversity of sights comparable to what you will find in Yosemite.

FACTS & FIGURES

Location/Gateways/Getting There: Yosemite National Park is in north-central California, only a four-hour drive from San Francisco. The major approach road from the Bay area (and also from Sacramento) is SR 120. SR 140 is another access route from San Francisco or from the central California coastal region. SR 41 from Fresno is the major approach from the south. From Reno, Nevada, the park can be reached via US 395 to SR 120 westbound. The most direct route to SR 120 from San Francisco is I-580 and then I-205 directly to SR 120.

Year Established: Designated a state reserve in 1864, Yosemite became the nation's second national park in 1890.

Size: 761,150 acres (1,189 square miles).

Admission Fee: $20

Climate/When to Go: A summer visitor in Yosemite will find the weather very pleasant. Fall and spring are also nice but, at the higher elevations, can be cold. One of the most important attractions, Yosemite's majestic waterfalls, tend to dry up by late summer. They are at their peak in May and June. Some sections of the park will remain inaccessible if there have been heavy winter snows, usually in May. Though the park will be crowded, I suggest you plan your trip for the second half of June or the first half of July at the very latest.

Contact Information: Superintendent, Yosemite National Park, PO Box 577, Yosemite National Park, CA 95389. ☎ (209) 372-0200.

AUTO TOUR/SHORT STOPS

Because of traffic restrictions, most portions of Yosemite do not lend themselves to the kind of continuous tour by car that served us so well in other parks. Secondly, in some ways Yosemite is almost like three parks in one. Our description, therefore, will be based on seeing the park in four sections. These are (1) Yosemite Valley, (2) Glacier Point, (3) Mariposa Grove and (4) Tioga Pass Road/Tuolumne Meadows. The final section is the least visited. Although many visitors see only the Yosemite Valley, a trip to that portion of the park can easily be combined with the second and third areas. We'll show you how.

❖ YOSEMITE VALLEY

The valley is the most famous section of Yosemite because of its beauty and drama. Another reason for its popularity is that it is quite easy to visit. The millions of visitors who come here, especially during the summer months, creates heavy traffic. Because of that, private vehicles are banned (except for registered hotel guests) beyond the Curry Village area. A shuttle bus service operates throughout the valley. The shuttles operate every 10 minutes from mid-June through mid-September. Frequencies decrease to every 20 minutes in the early morning and evening. There are 19 stops within the valley, including just about every major important point of interest.

The valley is approximately seven miles long and has an average width of only three-quarters of a mile. The **Merced River** flows through the valley's sheer granite walls, and is famous for its many waterfalls. These walls often rise more than 3,000 feet above the valley floor.

Seeing the valley is easy because it is extremely flat – you can walk along it as you would along a street in your home town. Roads are generally one-way (the south side road is eastbound and the north side is westbound).

Yosemite Falls is truly an awesome sight. The Upper Falls drop an incredible 1,430 feet in one fell swoop, while the Lower Falls plunge another 320. Including some smaller intervening cascades, the total drop is 2,425 feet, almost half a mile. (Imagine, if you will, water dropping from the top of two World Trade Centers piled on top of one another – that is roughly the distance involved.). A short and easy trail (a half-mile) leads through a thickly forested area to the base of the falls.

> ❖ **TIP**
>
> *The falls are best from around May through early July when the spring snow run-off is greatest. Unfortunately, late summer visitors will often see only a shadow of the full show, but this, of course, varies from year to year depending upon the amount of winter precipitation.*

The valley has several other major waterfalls ranging in height from 317 feet to 1,612 feet. The ones that you should see close up are **Vernal Falls, Illilouette Falls, Nevada Falls, Bridal Veil Falls** and **Ribbon Falls**. Generally short trails of about a half-mile lead from the road to each of them and, take our word – you won't get tired of seeing so many.

The walls of the valley (domes and pinnacles, to use the proper geological terms) are just as famous as the waterfalls. The best known is, of course, **El Capitan**, whose smooth surface rises 3,600 feet and is so close to the road that you can easily walk up and touch it. (Many people also climb El Capitan!) Other significant similar features are the **Half Dome, North Dome, Cathedral Spires** and the **Three Brothers**. They are all easy to spot and a visit to the valley isn't complete unless you've seen them all.

> ❖ **TIP**
>
> *You don't have to actually go to each one during your visit, and sometimes it is best to just stand in the meadows of Yosemite Valley and slowly turn around – creating your own moving panorama of these marvelously beautiful formations.*

Yosemite is also home to **Mirror Lake** in the easternmost portion of the valley. The shuttle bus ends about one mile before reaching this point, but you can continue on foot. You will not be disappointed with the beautiful image of the nearby mountain peaks reflected in the lake.

Finally, on the more mundane side, you'll find the **Valley Visitor Center**, along with some other facilities. These include the **Ansel Adams Gallery, the Yosemite Museum** and the **LeConte Lodge**, where educational programs are held. The valley is also where many of the park's special activities originate. Allow at least five hours for exploring the valley.

❖ Glacier Point

The road to Glacier Point is usually open from June through October. To reach Glacier Point, go into the valley via Southside Road. Just before Bridal Veil Falls, make a sharp right. The road

THE WEST

will quickly begin to rise above the valley floor, providing spectacular views.

Once you get through the tunnel the road turns sharply towards the south. It's paved all the way and isn't difficult to negotiate, although you will be on the edge heading southbound. The distant vistas are splendid. Several miles down the road, turn onto Glacier Point Road. This road continues to rise but travels through a heavily forested area so you won't see much in the way of scenery for a little while. Of course, if you like forests, then the sights will be great. The last mile or so of the road rises and falls and twists and turns its way to the parking area at the end of the road. From there it is only a short walk to Glacier Point itself, an unforgettable sight.

The spectacular panorama includes many of Yosemite's domes (including Half Dome) as well as countless distant peaks of the Sierra Nevada and many waterfalls. The latter look like thin ribbons of silver from this vantage point. Equally breathtaking is the view looking straight down into Yosemite Valley. Details such as roads and buildings are readily discernible, but they look more like little toys than the real thing. Even though it seems to be at your feet, the distance back to Yosemite Valley by road is 30 miles. The valley is more than 3,200 feet beneath where you'll be standing. There are many different angles to take the view in at Glacier Point as walkways encircle the entire area.

Including the ride on Glacier Point Road, you should allow a minimum of 2½ hours for the Glacier Point excursion. After dragging yourself away from the view, reverse your route back down Glacier Point Road to the main highway, which is SR 41. If you're heading back to the valley (or north to Tuolumne Meadows) turn right. To continue on to Mariposa Grove, turn to the left.

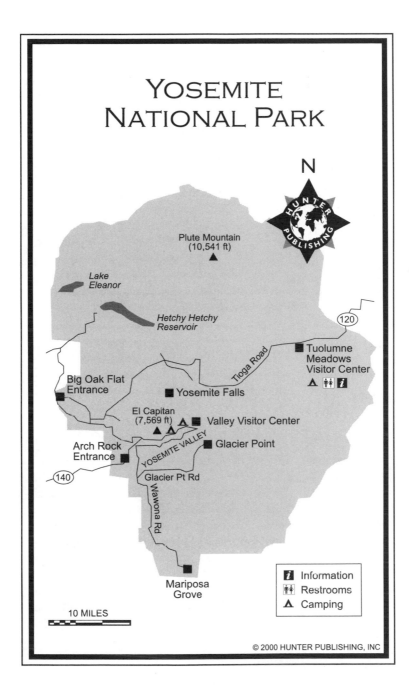

YOSEMITE NATIONAL PARK

N

Plute Mountain
(10,541 ft)
▲

Lake
Eleanor

Hetchy Hetchy
Reservoir

120

Tioga Road

■ Tuolumne
Meadows
Visitor Center
▲ 👫 🛈

Big Oak Flat
Entrance
■

■ Yosemite Falls

El Capitan
(7,569 ft)
▲ ▲ ■ Valley Visitor Center
▲

Arch Rock
Entrance
■

YOSEMITE VALLEY

■ Glacier Point

140

Glacier Pt Rd

Wawona Rd

■
Mariposa
Grove

10 MILES

🛈 Information
👫 Restrooms
▲ Camping

© 2000 HUNTER PUBLISHING, INC

THE WEST

❖ MARIPOSA GROVE

Mariposa is 36 miles from the valley, just beyond the Wawona Village area near the park's southern boundary. The grove offers quite a contrast from the other sights of Yosemite. Although you can drive into the grove itself, there is often a lot of traffic and the roads are very narrow and winding. Consider taking the shuttle bus service from Wawona. There is also a tram ride within the grove itself (see *Special Activities*).

Mariposa Grove contains stands of giant sequoia that rival those in Sequoia National Park. The oldest tree in the grove is the famous **Grizzly Giant**, with a girth of almost 97 feet and a height of 210 feet. There are taller specimens here, but none is as immense overall. There are also two trees within the grove that have had tunnels cut through them, the most famous being the 232-foot **California Tree**. A trail runs through the grove and can be used to discover many other outstanding examples of sequoia.

Give yourself about 1½ hours to visit Mariposa Grove. Total time for this area depends upon where you'll be traveling to next. The one-way trip from the valley should take about an hour under optimal traffic conditions but, during the peak travel season, can take considerably longer.

❖ TIOGA PASS/TUOLUMNE MEADOWS

Only a small percentage of visitors to Yosemite see this part of the park, so there are few traffic problems here. The **Tioga Pass Road** crosses the entire northern portion of the park from east to west. Unless you're headed to Lake Taho/Reno you will have to turn around and come back when you reach the eastern terminus of the park near the town of Lee Vining. That makes for a long drive, so you might want to arrange an overnight in town. There are many steep grades and sharp turns, but the overall journey isn't difficult unless you're a novice to mountain driving. The mountain scenery is rewarding. Pretty and colorful mountain meadows, canyons, lakes and rivers are also in abundance. The Tioga Pass Road is also an access point for those wishing to explore the extensive Yosemite back-country. The road, however, has numerous pullouts for those who simply want to drive through the Tuolumne Meadows and take in the scenery.

To reach this area from the valley, take the Big Oak Flat Road from the valley's north side. The road, like the route to Glacier or Mariposa, begins to rise quickly and steeply, affording some excellent views. Along the way you'll pass through three tunnels and also be able to stop and view a small waterfall and raging river. The Tioga Pass Road is also called SR 120. Take it heading east and you'll be on your way.

The scenery is excellent all the way and there are many convenient pullouts, but the best part is between **Olmsted Point** and the **Tuolumne Meadows**. Olmsted Point looks out over the tops of many famous domes in Yosemite Valley, as well as more distant Sierra peaks. You are actually standing on another dome. The cracks in the rock surface here are interesting and hold a special beauty. The road then swings around **Tenaya Lake** before reaching the visitor center at Tuolumne Meadows. During the summer the meadows are an explosion of wildflowers in every color under the sun.

You can traverse the Tioga Pass Road from end to end (about 50 miles), including the mentioned stops, in about two hours. However, if you're making a round-trip to and from the valley, we suggest allowing the better part of a full day.

GETTING OUT/LONGER STOPS

❖ HIKING

YOSEMITE VALLEY

The valley is the starting point for some long and difficult treks that climb up to the tops of waterfalls or even to Glacier Point (see below). Most of these trails are sections of the **John Muir Trail**, also called the Mist Trail. You can do as little or as much of the trail as time and ability permits. The entire route is 17 miles long and goes to the top of Half Dome. Within three to seven miles you can reach the top of Vernal and Nevada Falls.

One of the best parts about visiting Yosemite Valley is that you are always surrounded by magnificent scenery no matter where you are. So it isn't always necessary to stick to the formal trail system. Just wandering around the valley is a most enjoyable way to spend a day.

GLACIER POINT

The **Glacier Point 4 Mile Trail** (actually closer to five miles) runs between Glacier Point and Yosemite Valley. The trip is a difficult one either up or down. The strenuous route ascends more than 3,000 feet and requires at least three hours for someone in excellent shape.

MARIPOSA GROVE

There are more than three miles of trails within the grove. If you go from the grove trailhead all the way to Wawona Point, it involves an altitude change of about 1,200 feet and is fairly strenuous.

TIOGA PASS ROAD/TUOLUMNE MEADOWS

The longer trails in the northern part of the park lead into the back-country. Inquire at the Tuolumne Meadows ranger station for advice and details.

SPECIAL ACTIVITIES

Yosemite probably has more ranger-conducted naturalist programs, walks and talks than any other national park in America. Schedules are posted in visitor centers and you can also get information in the park's seasonally published newspaper.

> ❖ **TIP**
>
> *One of the nicest places to listen to a ranger talk is in the amphitheater at Glacier Point.*

❖ ORGANIZED BUS/TRAM RIDES

There is a two-hour guided tour of the valley in an open-air tram for those of you who do not want to use the shuttle bus. Departures are frequent. Many people like to take this tour to get an overview of the valley, then decide what else they want to do. Information, schedules and prices are available from the Yosemite Lodge Tour Desk or by calling ☎ (209) 372-1240. This is also the source for information on many other bus trips that cover all parts of Yosemite, including Glacier Point and the Mariposa Grove. (This is particularly appealing if you are a little nervous about the precipitous drop-off at the road's edge.) If you take the bus you can keep your eyes closed until you get to your destination (although we've heard that the bus drivers sometimes keep their eyes closed too!).

❖ HORSEBACK RIDING

Trips of two hours and a half-day are available from stables in the valley, at Wawona and in the Tuolumne Meadows. ☎ (209) 372-8348 for further information and prices.

❖ ROCK CLIMBING

The sheer rock walls of Yosemite's domes make an attractive target for climbers. If this is of interest to you, but you don't know how to climb, why not take a rock climbing class? ☎ (209) 372-8435 for information.

❖ SCENIC DRIVE

Finally, if you have some extra time available (about six hours or so), a lovely side trip can be made on **Big Oak Flat Road**, SR 120 and then a marked road to Yosemite's **Hetch Hetchy** country. At the end of the road is the 312-foot-high dam that impounds the Hetch Hetchy Reservoir from the Tuolumne River.

This rather empty region of the park is quite attractive today. Back-country trails lead from the dam area into the sparsely visited but spectacular **Grand Canyon of the Tuolumne**.

ACCOMMODATIONS

❖ HOTELS & MOTELS

INSIDE THE PARK

All in-park accommodations, except for the Redwoods, are operated by the authorized National Park Service concessionaire, Yosemite Concession Services. The central reservations number is ☎ (559) 252-4848. Because of the popularity of Yosemite, we suggest that reservations be made well in advance.

AHWAHNEE HOTEL ($$$$), Yosemite Valley, one mile past the park headquarters. 123 rooms. An historic property with very elegant public areas that are worth seeing even if you don't stay here. Great views from many rooms. The accommodations aren't worthy of the high price tag. They are very comfortable, although many units (other than the duplex cabins) are quite small. Known for refined service. Restaurant. Many recreational facilities.

CURRY VILLAGE ($-$$), Yosemite Valley near the eastern end at Curry Village. 625 rooms. Only the motel-style units are recommended for those who don't like camping out in the great outdoors; the lower-priced accommodations are little more than glorified tents without private bath. Restaurants nearby.

THE REDWOODS ($$$-$$$$), Wawona area of the park, via State Highway 41 and Chilnualna Falls Road. ☎ (209) 375-6666. 129 units. Options at the Redwoods range from fairly modest rustic cabins to spectacular six-room homes. Most units are multi-room facilities and all have kitchens. Many fireplaces, patios and decks. Wonderful forest setting along the river. Tennis courts. Restaurant within a short drive.

WAWONA HOTEL ($$), State Highway 41 in the Wawona section of the park, eight miles north of the Mariposa Grove. 104 rooms. An old property with barely average guest units but, despite that, a refreshingly charming place with lots of style and atmosphere, not to mention a fantastic natural setting. Golf, tennis and hiking are among the many recreational activities. Restaurant.

YOSEMITE LODGE ($$-$$$), Yosemite Valley, near the park headquarters and Yosemite Falls. 245 rooms. Like most of the in-park lodging, the lodge offers adequate rooms and nothing more. Central location and a host of recreational activities as well as ranger programs. Dining and shopping on premises.

Among the establishments within the park's borders that are not recommended (but included for informational purposes) are the TUOLUMNE MEADOWS LODGE and the WHITE WOLF LODGE. Both of these smaller places ($$) are off State Highway 120 in Yosemite's vast northern section.

NEARBY COMMUNITIES

APPLE TREE INN ($$-$$$$), 1110 State Highway 41, Fish Camp; two miles south of the southern entrance to Yosemite National Park. ☎ (559) 683-5111 or (888) 683-5111. Rate includes full breakfast. 53 rooms. Many two- and three-bedroom units (thus the wide range in prices), as well as regular rooms. High-end rustic cabin-style. Lovely forest setting. Fireplaces, decks or patios are common features. Extensive recreation facilities. Restaurant on the premises.

BEST WESTERN LAKE VIEW LODGE ($$-$$$), 30 Main Street, Lee Vining; US 395 in the center of town, 10 miles from the eastern side of Yosemite (Tioga Pass Entrance) and 75 miles from Yosemite Valley, mostly via Tioga Road. ☎ (760) 647-6543 or (800) 528-1234. 46 rooms. Attractive and comfortable accommodations on nice grounds. Surprisingly good facility in this small (300 people) town. Restaurant is nearby.

CEDAR LODGE ($$$), 9966 State Highway 140, El Portal; seven miles west of Yosemite's west entrance. ☎ (209) 379-2612. 206 rooms. Slightly better than average accommodations. A few multi-room units and upgraded facilities also available. Swimming pool and whirlpool. Restaurant on premises.

TENAYA LODGE AT YOSEMITE ($$$$), 1122 State Highway 41, Fish Camp; two miles south of the park's southern entrance. ☎ (559) 683-6555 or (800) 332-3135. 242 rooms. Face it, lodging around Yosemite carries a hefty price tag. At least at Tenaya, though, you get a first-class, full-service resort facility with outstanding rooms and a host of activities, including children's programs. Varied recreational opportunities. Several restaurants on the premises.

YOSEMITE VIEW LODGE ($$$-$$$$), 11156 State Highway 140, El Portal; less than a mile from the park's west entrance. ☎ (209) 379-2681. 278 rooms. Multi-building facility with attractively decorated, comfortable rooms, some with gas fireplaces and whirlpools. Rooms facing the Merced River are the most desirable. Limited recreational facilities. Restaurant on premises.

> ### ❖ TIP
> *You may find it difficult to get a room either in the park or close by. An alternative is to stay in Mariposa (30 miles farther down State Highway 140 from El Portal). There, in addition to quite a few independent places, you'll find affiliates of Best Western, Comfort and Holiday Inn, among others.*

❖ CAMPING

Reservations can be made only for those campgrounds marked with an asterisk (*). Call the NPRS at ☎ (800) 436-7275. Their offices are open daily from 10 am to 10 pm, eastern time. You can write for reservations at PO Box 1600, Cumberland, MD 21502. Or, you can reserve online at http://reservations.nps.gov.

All other sites listed here operate on a first-come, first-served basis. Campgrounds are listed here by general area.

CAMPGROUNDS AT A GLANCE			
NAME	LOCATION	SITES	COST
North Pines *	Yosemite Valley	85	$15 per day
Upper Pines *	Yosemite Valley	238	$15 per day
Sunnyside	Yosemite Valley	35	$3 per day per person
Wawona *	Mariposa/Wawona/ Glacier Point area	100	$15 per day
Bridal Veil Creek *	Glacier Point Road, Mariposa/Wawona/ Glacier Point area	110	$15 per day
Hodgon Meadow *	Tuolumne Meadows/State Highway 120 area	105	$15 per day
Crane Flat *	Tuolumne Meadows/State Highway 120 area	166	$15 per day
Tamarack Flat	Tuolumne Meadows/State Highway 120 area	52	$6 per day
White Wolf	Tuolumne Meadows/State Highway 120 area	87	$10 per day
Yosemite Creek	Tuolumne Meadows/State Highway 120 area	75	$6 per day
Porcupine Flat	Tuolumne Meadows/State Highway 120 area	52	$6 per day
Tuolumne Meadows	Tuolumne Meadows/State Highway 120 area	314	$15 per day

THE WEST

RVs allowed in: North Pines, Upper Pines, Wawona, Bridal Veil (long trailers not recommended), Hogdon Meadow, Crane Flat, White Wolf, Porcupine Flat, Toulumne Meadows.

There is a seven-day limit on valley campgrounds during the summer. Otherwise, the limit is 30 days.

DINING

INSIDE THE PARK

AHWAHNEE DINING ROOM ($$$), in the Ahwahnee Hotel, Yosemite Valley (see listing above). American/continental cuisine. Fine dining in a magnificent setting with a standard of service you would expect in a cosmopolitan city. Definitely in a class by itself as far as Yosemite dining is concerned, but you pay for it!

None of the other restaurants inside the park are anything special, but you might try the GARDEN TERRACE and the MOUNTAIN ROOM in the Yosemite Lodge.

Valley choices also include a cafeteria in the Yosemite Lodge, the PAVILION (Curry Village), DEGNAN'S (deli, fast food and some dinner items) in the Village and semi-fast food at the VILLAGE GRILL. The Wawona Hotel has a restaurant, as do the Tuolumne Meadows Lodge and White Wolf Lodge.

Snack bars can be found at Happy Isles and Glacier Point.

NEARBY COMMUNITIES

If you're staying in El Portal, there are a couple of eating places in the village-like Yosemite View Lodge. However, the food tends to be overpriced and not terribly good. I'd rather drive a few miles into the valley and get better food at the same cost.

For Fish Camp overnighters, the situation is essentially the same – taking advantage of the location when it comes to price. However, the restaurants at the Apple Tree Inn and Tenaya Lodge at least have good food.

MONO INN RESTAURANT ($$), 55620 US 395, Lee Vining; four miles north of town. ☎ (760) 647-6581. American food. Considering the smallness of Lee Vining, this is a surprisingly nice looking place with good food and excellent service. The view of Mono Lake is alone a reason to eat here, as is the interesting Ansel Adams Gallery.

WHERE DO WE GO FROM HERE?

Suggested Trip 10 incorporates Yosemite National Park along with nearby Sequoia and Kings Canyon. Many visitors to Yosemite like to make a loop from San Francisco that covers the California coast in addition to the park. Or you could head to the north and take in **Lassen Volcanic National Park** as well as the northern **Redwood country**. A final option, especially if you want to do the Tuolumne Meadows section of the park, is to continue to **Lee Vining** and then head towards the **Lake Tahoe** area.

THE WEST

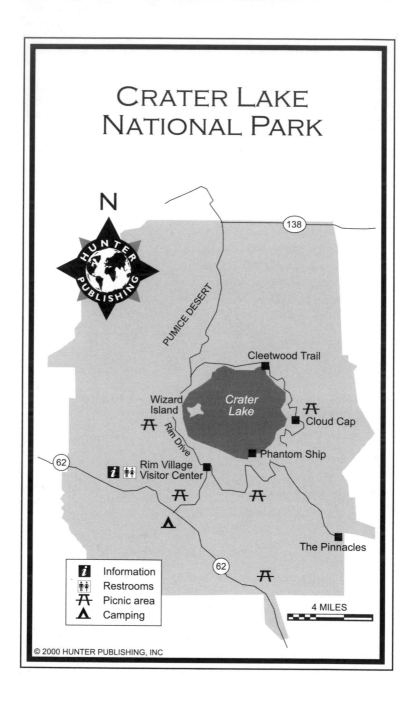

CRATER LAKE NATIONAL PARK

N

PUMICE DESERT

Cleetwood Trail

Wizard
Island

Crater Lake

Cloud Cap

Rim Drive

Phantom Ship

62

i 🚻 Rim Village
Visitor Center

The Pinnacles

62

i	Information
🚻	Restrooms
⛺	Picnic area
▲	Camping

4 MILES

© 2000 HUNTER PUBLISHING, INC

THE NORTHWEST

CRATER LAKE NATIONAL PARK

The deep blue color of Crater Lake has been the objective of many attempted descriptions, but none comes close to the impact you will feel on seeing it for the first time. The first name given to it by non-native Americans was simply Deep Blue Lake. Perhaps that was not such a bad name, because the best description I can offer is to say that it is the bluest blue in all the world. The blue is a result of the lake's great depth – 1,932 feet at its maximum – which makes it one of the world's deepest. It is 4½ miles wide and six miles long, with a 20-mile shoreline. The dimensions and color are enough to attract visitors, but its setting, surrounded by lava cliffs ranging from 500 to 2,000 feet above the lake surface, make it all the more remarkable.

The present mountain, which encompasses Crater Lake, is all that remains of a much larger mountain called Mount Mazama. This former giant reached 12,000 feet, before an ancient volcanic eruption caused the mountaintop to collapse, creating the huge caldera which is now Crater Lake. While the crater is the focal point of the park – people sometimes just come to stare at it for the whole day – there is a lot more to do and see.

FACTS & FIGURES

Location/Gateways/Getting There: Set in the southwestern portion of Oregon, Crater Lake is not close to any large city. It can be reached from I-5 by taking SR 62 at Medford. From US 97 (at the town of Klamath Falls), take SR 62 after it branches off from US 97 just past Modoc Point. Coming from the north via US 97, SR 136 leads to the park's North Entrance. The nearest major city is Portland, and if you are coming directly from there, take I-5 south to Roseburg and pick up scenic SR 138 eastbound to the park. The total driving time from Portland is six hours.

Year Established: First discovered by white explorers in 1853, Crater Lake became a national park in 1902.

Size: 183,227 acres (268 square miles).

Admission Fee: $10.

Climate/When to Go: The park is open all year, but the main attraction, the drive around the crater, is covered by the remains of winter's heavy snows until mid-July. Most other activities in the park are also restricted to the summer season, especially July and August. The park is certainly the most crowded at this time, but it is also at its most beautiful. Fortunately, summer weather is excellent – most days are sunny and mild.

Contact Information: Superintendent, Crater Lake National Park, Box 7, Crater Lake, OR 97604. ☎ (541) 594-2211. If you are planning to come in early July, be sure to call ahead and find out which roads will be open.

AUTO TOUR/SHORT STOPS

Much of Crater Lake can be seen from your car or in short, easy walks. **Crater Rim Drive** does just as its name implies – it completely encircles the crater and its lake. You may pick up Crater Rim Drive from the south and north entrances. This Auto Tour will travel clockwise, beginning where the access road from SR 62 reaches the 33-mile Rim Drive at the Steel Information Center. Just beyond this point is Rim Village, the focal point of activities and site of all park services, including lodging and food.

> NOTE: *Trailers should not be taken on Rim Drive. They can be left at the visitor center or at Rim Village.*

Begin your activities with the **visitor center**, which has excellent exhibits on the formation of Crater Lake. From here it is a short walk via paved path to the **Sinnot Memorial Overlook**, built in two levels upon a parapet overlooking the lake. Your first view of the lake is likely to be the most impressive, no matter where you begin the tour.

❖ TIP

In summer you are almost certain to have ideal viewing conditions, except perhaps during the early morning hours.

Now you can begin your excursion around the lake on the **Rim Drive**. It is mostly level with some easy grades and numerous, mostly gentle turns. One of the major points you pass is **Hillman Peak**, the highest elevation on the rim at 8,156 feet. Shortly after comes **Llao Rock**, a lava flow rising abruptly from the water and reaching a height of 1,850 feet above the lake. Up ahead is **Cleetwood Cove**, from which there is an excellent overall view of the lake and the surrounding mountains. (There will be more about Cleetwood Cove in the next section.) At **Cloudcap** you should take a short spur road that rises for approximately three-quarters of a mile. From this impressive formation, towering 1,775 feet above the surface of the lake, you'll have what is perhaps the single best view of the lake without climbing to the top of a peak. Shortly after Cloudcap comes **Kerr Notch**, with an outstanding view of the rock formation known as the **Phantom Ship**. This huge rock outcropping certainly does have the shape of an ancient sea vessel and the lonely, desolate rock would make you believe that its inhabitants could be ghosts.

Right after Kerr Notch is a side road leading down through **Wheeler Creek Canyon**. This easy round-trip covers 12 miles

THE NORTHWEST

through lesser-known areas of the park, allowing views unlike any others found elsewhere in the park. Towering grey pumice formations known as **The Pinnacles** line the side of the road, many reaching heights of nearly 200 feet. At the far end of the drive they become very numerous. The pinnacles can be observed in more detail from several pullouts along the road.

While the preceding area affords a brief interlude from the lake scene, the dazzling blue waters will quickly reappear as you rejoin Rim Drive. **Sun Notch** provides another excellent, tree-framed view of Crater Lake and the Phantom Ship. Soon you will return to Rim Village, having completed the loop road.

The drive as described with stops for views should take just over two hours.

GETTING OUT/LONGER STOPS

❖ HIKING

If you have more time and are willing to expend a little effort, there is much to see and do. Again, we will work clockwise from the Rim Visitor Center, where a trail leads to **Garfield Peak**. An easy ascent of less than two miles to the 8,060-foot summit provides views that are truly magnificent, encompassing the entire lake and Wizard Island. Allow two hours for the round-trip.

The Watchman is another peak and the trail here is shorter and easier than the one to Garfield Peak, taking only 40 minutes to complete. Among the sights you'll see from either of these trails is Wizard Island. Although it can be seen well from a number of stops along the Rim Drive, at these higher elevations the view is more impressive.

Near the SR 62 entrance is the **Godfrey Glen Trail**, an easy, level one-mile trail that takes 30-40 minutes. It passes through heavily forested areas and numerous small canyons with pinnacle formations. If you did not venture down Wheeler Canyon on the Auto Tour, then this trail is a must. The adjacent **Annie Creek Trail** is slightly longer and traverses a small canyon.

Cleetwood Cove features a trail that leads down to the lake shore itself. It is a bit over a mile long.

> NOTE: *While the Cleetwood Clove Trail is not so bad going down, it can be hard on the return trip. This trail should not be attempted by anyone with physical impairments, including breathing disorders.*

It is nice to see the lake from water level, which is one reason for taking this trail. The other is to gain access to the boat tours of the lake which leave from the dock at the end of the trail (see next section).

SPECIAL ACTIVITIES

❖ BOAT TOURS

Viewing beautiful Crater Lake is an unforgettable experience; sailing on it is an exerience you'll never forget. Boat tours on Crater Lake last about 1¾ hours. These trips stop at **Wizard Island**, the largest island in the lake. (Wizard is another cinder cone.) Trails on the island lead to the top of the cone. If you do this trail you will have to return on a later boat. The daily trips depart hourly from 10 am until 4 pm, late June through early September, weather permitting. The adult fare is $12.50. Children under 12 are charged $7. ☎ (541) 830-8700 for information and reservations.

ACCOMMODATIONS

❖ HOTELS & MOTELS

INSIDE THE PARK

CRATER LAKE LODGE ($$$), Rim Village. ☎ (541) 830-8700. 71 rooms. Open late May through late October. Rustic, four-story wooden lodge with lots of history and atmosphere. Guest rooms are comfortable. Several larger loft units that are good for families are available at a higher price.

Also within the park is the 40-room MAZAMA LODGE ($$); same telephone as the lodge. Mazama offers more basic accommodations than the Crater Lake Lodge and, although we don't particularly recommend it, it's there if you want to stay in the park for less money.

NEARBY COMMUNITIES

There are few towns near the national park and acceptable lodging is scarce. The best selection is in Klamath Falls, about 50 miles south of the Rim Village.

CIMARRON MOTOR INN ($), 3060 S. 6th Street, Klamath Falls; off US 97. ☎ (541) 882-4601 or (800) 742-2648. Rate includes continental breakfast. 163 rooms. Attractive and comfortable alternative to the usual chain establishments. Swimming pool. A decent family restaurant is adjacent.

❖ CAMPING

No stay limit. RVs allowed. No reservations (contact the park headquarters for more information).

CAMPGROUNDS AT A GLANCE			
NAME	LOCATION	SITES	COST
Mazama	Eight miles south of Rim Village.	198	$14 per day
Lost Creek	On spur road leading to the Pinnacles, three miles south of Rim Road.	12	$14 per day

DINING

INSIDE THE PARK

CRATER LAKE LODGE DINING ROOM ($$), Crater Lake Lodge (see listing above). American food. Adequate selection of decent food served in a pleasant environment. You're a captive audience here, so don't expect anything wonderful.

Cafeteria-style food is available at Rim Village if you're in a rush or don't want to spend too much money.

WHERE DO WE GO FROM HERE?

Although we have included Crater Lake as part of the itinerary in *Suggested Trip 11*, it isn't close to any of the other major attractions in this book. In addition, it is far from any major city, and air connections aren't convenient. A shorter round-trip from Portland could include, besides Crater Lake, the **Columbia River Gorge**, the many beautiful sights of the **Cascade Range** within the **Willamette** and **Deschutes National Forests**, and a return to Portland via the spectacular **Oregon coast**.

CRATERS OF THE MOON NATIONAL MONUMENT

Only in Hawaii will you be able to find a greater number of volcanic basalt formations. At Craters of the Moon, volcanic eruptions ages ago and huge rivers of molten lava gushing out from a rift in the earth have created immense fields of hardened lava, dotted with many thousands of cinder cones and deep crater-like depressions.

THE NORTHWEST

DID YOU KNOW?

So much is the surface like that on the moon, that astronauts in the Apollo program were brought here to get a better idea of the type of landscape they would encounter on the moon itself.

The last known eruptions in this area took place over 2,000 years ago. They have left a legacy for all to see. When it was first discovered by explorers, the area was described as a desolate, awful waste. This may be quite true from an agricultural standpoint (even though you will find various shrubs and plants here and there). But the area is not a waste to the human eye, which can, even in these rather eerie surroundings, find a certain beauty in it all. Certainly it is different enough to be called out of this world.

FACTS & FIGURES

Location/Gateways/Getting There: In the southcentral portion of Idaho, the monument is on US 20/26/93, about 80 miles west of Idaho Falls and 180 miles east of Boise via I-84 to US 26. Boise provides the nearest decent scheduled airline service. Salt Lake City is another alternative, although it is more than 200 miles away via I-15 and US 26.

Year Established: First explored as early as 1833, the area was designated a National Monument in 1924.

Size: 53,545 acres (84 square miles).

Admission Fee: $4.

Climate/When to Go: The Monument Road is open from late April to early November, which presents a small problem: the summer is quite hot, but spring and fall are a bit chilly for seeing some of the relatively nearby national parks that will probably be combined with your visit. So, unless you are specifically coming to see this Monument, you'll have to put up with a midsummer sun that brings temperatures well into the 90s and frequently higher. It is, fortunately, a dry climate. Try to visit during the morning hours.

Contact Information: Superintendent, Craters of the Moon National Monument, PO Box 29, Arco, ID 83213. ☎ (208) 527-3257.

AUTO TOUR/SHORT STOPS

Many of the monument's major features are easily accessible via a seven-mile **loop road** that begins from near the Monument entrance station. Most portions of the drive have one-way traffic. Some features are reached by way of short spurs off the main road. However, no visit to Craters of the Moon is complete without some more strenuous activity, which we'll get to later. First, stop into the visitor center for a good orientation about the Monument and a description of its very active geologic past.

Soon after departing the visitor center you'll come to the parking area for the short **North Crater Flow Trail**. The easy, paved trail crosses one of the more recent eruption areas (less than 2,000 years ago) and brings you to a fragmented wall of black volcanic rock. Good examples of both "rough" and "smooth" lava can be seen.

Drive a little more than a mile to the **Devils Orchard Nature Trail**. This level and easy trail is in one of the more colorful sections of the monument, and contains many small lava fragments and other eerie-looking natural features. This trail is handicapped-accessible.

Now the road will enter the **Great Rift Zone**, opening up views of near and distant volcanic formations as well as lava flows. You'll pass the 6,181-foot-high **Inferno Cone**, which can be seen from a viewpoint of the same name. This is the highest cone along the loop (see next section for trail details). At the **Spatter Cones** a trail leads through these fragile volcanic formations. This area is perhaps the most moon-like in its appearance. The other is in the Cave area, which will be described in the next section. After the Spatter Cones you can complete the rest of the Loop Road. The auto portion of your visit can be done in 1-1½ hours.

GETTING OUT/LONGER STOPS

❖ HIKING

There are many longer trails that explore other areas. These vary from relatively easy to extremely strenuous.

> NOTE: *All of the back-country trails are long and difficult and are for experienced hikers only. Inquire at the visitor center for advice.*

Let's take a closer look at several walking/hiking routes that are reached via the Loop Road.

The **North Crater Trail** begins just a few feet past the previously discussed North Crater Flow Trail. The scenery is similar but at the end you can look into an actual volcano vent. This trail connects with another that leaves from the Spatter Cones area. The Big Craters and Snow Cone can be seen on this hike. Allow at least two hours for the combined trails.

The Inferno Cone is one of the most dramatic features at Craters of the Moon. The smooth cone can be climbed along the slope facing the viewpoint parking area. The walk is not long, but it is quite steep, so you have to be in fairly decent shape to reach the top. At the summit is a magnificent volcanic landscape of countless cinder cones spread out along the Great Rift. Allow about 45 minutes for the round-trip.

Perhaps the most popular part of the monument for exploration is in the **Cave Area**. A relatively easy T-shaped trail leads to Dewdrop Cave, Indian Tunnel, Boy Scout Cave, Beauty Cave and Surprise Cave. Along the half-mile route you'll see lava tubes and collapsed caves. Indian Tunnel is easily explored and enough daylight comes in to allow you to walk about without artificial light. The Cave Area can be visited in one to three hours, depending upon how many caves you do.

THE NORTHWEST

> ❖ **TIP**
>
> *It is necessary to carry a flashlight for all caves except Indian Tunnel. These trips involve a significant amount of climbing and sometimes a few contortions to get in and out. Youngsters will enjoy them, but be sure they remain under your control as rock surfaces are often sharp.*

A 1½-mile hike (each way) takes you to the **Tree Molds Area** (trailhead accessed by a mile-long spur about half-way along the Loop Road). The tree molds result from lava that surrounded the trees and then hardened. The round molds remained after the wood eventually rotted away. Allow a minimum of two hours for exploring the Tree Molds Area.

ACCOMMODATIONS

❖ HOTELS & MOTELS

There are no places to stay inside the monument.

NEARBY COMMUNITIES

ARCO INN ($), 540 Grand Avenue West, Arco, ☎ (208) 527-3100. Located on US 93, about 20 miles northeast of Craters of the Moon via US 20/26/93. 12 rooms. To say that Craters of the Moon is remotely situated is an understatement, especially when it comes to lodging and dining. This is the closest place to stay. It's quite basic, but will certainly be adequate for most people.

If your itinerary is taking you in the other direction after the park, the situation is even worse. The nearest accommodations to be found are 50 miles away in Hailey.

> **❖ TIP**
>
> *If you're going as far as Hailey, you might as well go another 20 minutes and choose from a wider selection of places to stay in the Ketchum/Sun Valley resort area.*

❖ CAMPING

The CRATERS OF THE MOON CAMPGROUND is just past the visitor center and is available on a first-come, first-served basis. 52 sites. No limitation on days. $10 per day. RVs allowed, but no hookups are provided. Call the park's main number for details.

DINING

There are no places to eat inside the monument.

NEARBY COMMUNITIES

While there isn't any nearby place that I can heartily endorse, hunger pangs can be quelled at a number of roadside cafés (along the highway) either in **Arco** or in **Carey**. The latter is about 25 miles to the southwest of the monument entrance. These simple places offer simple food. Service and surroundings are acceptable.

WHERE DO WE GO FROM HERE?

The **Idaho Adventure** (*Suggested Trip* 6) includes Craters of the Moon National Monument. It can also be visited in conjunction with Yellowstone and Grand Teton National Parks.

THE NORTHWEST

GLACIER NATIONAL PARK

The worst thing you can say about Glacier is that it doesn't quite have the diversity of features found in, for example, Yellowstone, Yosemite or Olympic National Park. What it does have in abundance is the finest mountain scenery in the country. The mountainous terrain is highlighted by over 50 major glaciers and more than 200 lakes. Top that off with a tremendous variety of trees and all colors of wildflowers in summer, and you have a natural setting par excellence.

The highlight of the park for most visitors is the famous Going to the Sun Road, an engineering marvel that crosses the Continental Divide at 6,680 feet and provides access to some outstanding scenery. This majestic area extends beyond the northern edge of the park into Canada. The United States and Canada have created an international park here. Together, the two parks form Waterton Lakes-Glacier International Peace Park. A special section on Waterton Lakes is found at the end of this chapter.

One of many stunning views in Glacier National Park.

There is a special tranquillity here in the rarefied mountain air. And beauty everywhere. A visit will not soon be forgotten.

FACTS & FIGURES

Location/Gateways/Getting There: In the northwestern part of Montana, the park is accessible from the western side via US 2 to West Glacier and from the east via US 89. It is 170 miles from Great Falls via I-15 and US 2/89, or 275 miles from Spokane, Washington via US 2. Missoula is the closest gateway, 150 miles south of the park via US 93 and US 2. Each has commercial airline service.

Year Established: Glacier became a national park in 1910.

Size: 1,013,595 acres (1,584 square miles).

Admission Fee: $10.

Climate/When to Go: Since the full length of the Going to the Sun Road is open only from mid-June to mid-October, a first-time visitor should plan to come here during that time. The summer weather is excellent: comfortable temperatures with cool mornings and evenings, plenty of sunshine and infrequent rain. A light jacket is advisable, even in mid-summer. In early summer the wildflowers are at their glorious peak.

> NOTE: *Trailers are banned from crossing the park on Going to the Sun Road during July and August.*

Contact Information: Superintendent, Glacier National Park, West Glacier, MT 59936. ☎ (406) 888-5441.

AUTO TOUR/SHORT STOPS

Although many of the park's largest glaciers are in the back-country and are, therefore, accessible only to overnight hikers, even from the road and short trails there's plenty of beauty.

THE NORTHWEST

❖ GOING TO THE SUN ROAD

The major portion of the park is traversed by the Going to the Sun Road. We'll work our way from the West Glacier entrance eastward to the St. Mary's entrance. You can do it the other way as well but, if you do, be sure to work out when you will see the attractions in the other sections of the park (in this routing they are given at the end of the Auto Tour).

The road has 17 scenic overlooks. We'll dispense with the normal practice of noting the best ones and urge you to stop at all of them because each is truly majestic. And, since the course of this wonderful highway will take you a distance of some 50 miles, 17 stops are welcome.

Just inside the west entrance the roadway runs along **Lake Mac-Donald**. At 10 miles long and a mile across, this is the park's largest lake. The heavily forested shoreline is set against a backdrop of lofty 6,000-foot mountains. As soon as you get past the lake, the road begins its dramatic climb toward the Continental Divide.

At the Avalanche Creek parking area you should make a stop to explore the quarter-mile-long **Trail of the Cedars**. This boardwalk trail is very easy, taking no more than 15 minutes. During the course of this walk you will see beautiful trees and a rushing river. Another trail from here goes on to **Avalanche Creek** itself, a deep and narrow gorge with stunning views from the trail. (A continuation of this trail is described in the following section.)

Resume the breathtaking climb around a section of the road called The Loop and head towards the Continental Divide at **Logan Pass**, which is about halfway through the park. At many points en route the road is located on a narrow perch – on one side is a precipitous drop off the edge of the mountain and on the other, a sheer wall of rock. Often you will see water from melting snow cascading down these rock walls and onto the roadway. It is an unusual and beautiful sight. Even during the middle of summer you will see patches of snow. It is also in this area that the road is most dramatic, as switchbacks provide dizzying views of mountain peaks and the road itself.

The park's main **visitor center** is at the Logan Pass. It has interesting exhibits and is the starting point for many guided walks as well as self-guiding trails (to be described later).

Upon leaving Logan Pass, the road will start winding downward and you will soon reach the beginning of **St. Mary's Lake**. At **Sun Point**, after a spectacular whirlwind descent, one of the park's most beautiful vistas will unfold before you. Here, too, is a short trail to majestic **Baring Falls**. Then, when you reach the far end of the lake, you'll be at the St. Mary's Visitor Center and the eastern entrance of the park.

❖ ADDITIONAL TRIPS

Many people feel that, having seen all of this, their visit to Glacier is complete. But there is much more. Ten miles north of St. Mary's on US 89, at the town of Babb, a 13-mile road leads back into the park. This area is known as the **Many Glacier**. At the end of the road is **Swiftcurrent Lake**, one of the most impressive areas in the entire park. There are many trails leading from the end of the road (see next section).

Return to Babb. You can head south, but we strongly suggest heading north, via the **Chief Mountain International Highway**. This detour will not only enable you to pass through the fantastic scenery of Glacier Park's **Belly River Country** (especially popular among backpackers); it also provides direct access to Canada's Waterton Lakes National Park. (Details on Waterton are provided at the end of this chapter.)

Now you can head back south, picking up US 89 once again and taking it to SR 49 and the **Two Medicine** entrance of Glacier in the park's southeastern corner. Here, at the end of a short unnamed road, are a beautiful lake, more majestic mountain peaks and one of the deepest and most impressive valleys in the park. There is a short trail to beautiful **Twin Falls**.

The Going to the Sun Road portion can be accomplished in four hours. Allow another two hours to visit the Many Glacier region. Then, it is over an hour to Two Medicine, and you should allow another half-hour once there. Even without an extension to Waterton Lakes, the complete tour of Glacier will take a full day.

THE NORTHWEST

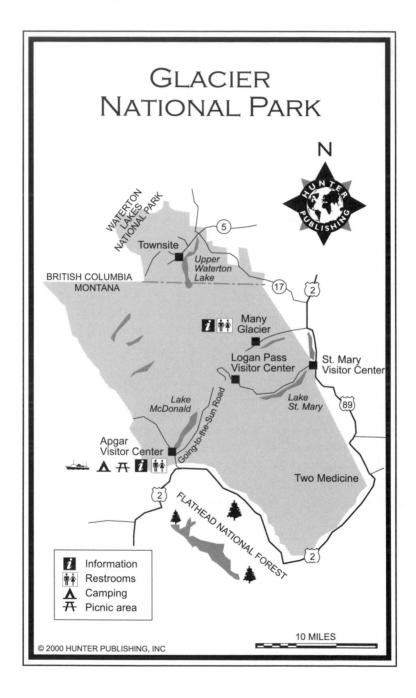

GLACIER NATIONAL PARK

N

WATERTON LAKES NATIONAL PARK

5

Townsite

Upper Waterton Lake

BRITISH COLUMBIA
MONTANA

17

2

i 🛉🛉 Many Glacier

Logan Pass Visitor Center

St. Mary Visitor Center

Lake McDonald

Lake St. Mary

89

Going-to-the-Sun Road

Apgar Visitor Center

🛥 ▲ 🛆 *i* 🛉🛉

2

Two Medicine

FLATHEAD NATIONAL FOREST

2

i	Information
🛉🛉	Restrooms
▲	Camping
🛆	Picnic area

10 MILES

© 2000 HUNTER PUBLISHING, INC

GETTING OUT/LONGER STOPS

❖ HIKING

There are numerous additional trails in Glacier that don't require back-country hiking. The four-mile **Avalanche Lake Trail** starts just past Avalanche Gorge and leads to Avalanche Lake and Basin. This is one of the most beautiful spots in the entire park, where you will stand at the lake shore surrounded by rocky mountains. The hike requires almost three hours to complete, but if you have time to do just one long trail, this should definitely be it. The trail, despite its length, is not at all difficult.

From the Logan Pass Visitor Center the three-mile **Hanging Gardens Trail** extends along a feature known as the **Garden Wall**, a section of the Continental Divide. The views are simply wonderful. The entire route takes two hours. You will be walking on some snow along this trail even in the middle of summer, so dress appropriately.

> ❖ **TIP**
>
> *Those with less time or stamina can walk only a relatively small portion of it before turning back. This will still give you excellent views and a look at the environment.*

There is a long boardwalk behind the visitor center leading towards giant rock formations. This is part of the trail to beautiful **Hidden Lake** (1½ miles each way). Diverse topography, including meadows and a glacial moraine, will be encountered along the way.

Finally, in the Many Glacier area there are numerous trails surrounding **Swiftcurrent Lake**. It is advisable to walk around part of the lakeside trail to see it from various angles with its different backgrounds of gray mountains, icy glaciers and deep green waters.

THE NORTHWEST

357

SPECIAL ACTIVITIES

❖ ORGANIZED TOURS

Day-long **bus tours** depart from various hotels within the park, but we strongly recommend that you complete the Auto Tour above in your own vehicle.

Boat rides are offered on **Lake MacDonald, St. Mary's Lake** and in the **Many Glacier** area. These 1½-hour rides are operated from June through late September by **Scenicruise Boat Tours**, ☎ (406) 888-5727 for Lake MacDonald Lodge departures; ☎ (406) 732-4430 for St. Mary's Lake; and ☎ (406) 732-4480 for Many Glacier. Cost for adults ranges from $8 to $10. Boat rentals are also available.

> ### ❖ TIP
>
> *If you're hiking into the back-country, consider having a boat drop you off and pick you up at the beginning and end of your trip.*

❖ FLOAT & WHITEWATER TRIPS

From the town of West Glacier there are float and whitewater trips on the middle fork of the Flathead River, which forms the southwestern border of the park. These trips, which vary from several hours to all day, go into areas that are not near the park's road system, so people are few and far between. They have a big advantage over the lake boat rides, which stick to the more visited areas. Prices begin at $25. Reservations are strongly suggested. Among the operators are:

Great Northern . . . . ☎ (800) 735-7897
   Whitewater Float Trips
Montana Raft Company . . . . ☎ (800) 521-7238
Wild River Adventures . . . . ☎ (800) 700-7056

❖ SCENIC DRIVES

For those who want more beautiful scenery, one option is to skirt the southern boundary of the park between West Glacier and East Glacier via US 2. The scenery along the Flathead River and by 5,220-foot-high Marias Pass is beautiful, but is not a substitute for the Going to the Sun Road.

> ### ❖ TIP
> *If your itinerary requires backtracking to the same side of the park you originally entered, the US 2 option will allow you to do so without repeating the same scenery.*

ACCOMMODATIONS

❖ HOTELS & MOTELS

INSIDE THE PARK

All of the in-park lodging is operated by Glacier Park, Inc., the official concessioner. Call ☎ (602) 207-6000 for centralized reservation service. All properties are open only from late May through early October. Reserve early!

APGAR VILLAGE LODGE ($$), Going to the Sun Road (Apgar Village), two miles inside park from West Glacier entrance. ☎ (406) 888-5484. 48 rooms. Conveniently located and comfortable for those who want to stay in the park. Slightly lower standard of facilities than the next three offerings, but cheaper, too. Restaurants nearby.

GLACIER PARK LODGE ($$-$$$), east side of the park (East Glacier). ☎ (406) 226-9311. 154 rooms. Built in 1913, this stately lodge features massive 800-year-old timber and cedar logs, displaying the grace and elegance of a time gone by. The rooms are attractive and comfortable. Swimming pool. Golf. Restaurant on premises.

THE NORTHWEST

LAKE McDONALD LODGE ($$), Going to the Sun Road, on Lake McDonald shoreline. ☎ (406) 888-5431. 100 rooms. Lovely setting on the lake with great mountain views. Varied accommodations consist of motel units, private cabins (with and without kitchens) and main lodge units. Mounted animal specimens grace the lobby. Quite a few recreational opportunities. Restaurants on premises.

MANY GLACIER HOTEL ($$-$$$), Many Glacier Road, 12 miles west of Babb at the end of the road into the Many Glacier area, at Swiftcurrent Lake. ☎ (406) 732-4411. 208 rooms. This gracious grand old lady of the park is situated in a majestic spot next to a mountain-rimmed lake. Just sitting by the huge fireplace in the lobby is a delightful experience. The rooms aren't up to the standards of public areas, but are reasonably sized and decorated. Great place if you like hiking. Restaurant on premises.

SWIFTCURRENT HOTEL ($$), end of Many Glacier Road, by the lake. ☎ (406) 732-4411. 88 rooms. A motel facility similar in style to the Apgar Village Inn. This place has less charm than the stately older park hotels, but it does offer clean and comfortable facilities. Restaurant at the Many Glacier Hotel is the nearest eating place.

NEARBY COMMUNITIES

IZAAK WALTON INN ($$), just south of US 2, Essex; 27 miles east of West Glacier and 29 miles west of East Glacier, both via US 2. ☎ (406) 888-5700. 33 rooms. An historic and delightful old country inn that provides a "get-away-from-it-all" atmosphere and fits in nicely with the scenic wonders of Glacier. Restaurant on the premises. Separate cabins available at higher rates (and with a minimum three-night stay).

MOUNTAIN PINE MOTEL ($-$$$), State Highway 49, East Glacier; a half-mile north of the US2 junction. ☎ (406) 226-4403. 27 rooms. Quiet location with varied accommodations ranging from motel units to multi-bedroom facilities and entire houses – thus the big price range. All are clean and comfortable. Near town restaurants.

❖ CAMPING

CAMPGROUNDS AT A GLANCE			
NAME	LOCATION	SITES	COST
St. Mary's	A half-mile west of the St. Mary's entrance.	156	$15 per day
Fish Creek	Four miles northwest of the western entrance at West Glacier.	180	$15 per day
Apgar	Apgar Village.	196	$10 per day
Avalanche Creek	Going to the Sun Road at the Trail of the Cedars.	87	$10 per day
Rising Sun	St. Mary's Lake.	83	$10 per day
Sprague Creek	North end of Lake McDonald.	25	$10 per day
Many Glacier	Swiftcurrent Lake.	112	$10 per day
Two Medicine	Remote location northeast of the East Glacier entrance.	99	$10 per day

Reservations for St. Mary's and Fish Creek can be made through NPRS, ☎ (800) 365-2267. The offices are open daily from 10 am to 10 pm, eastern time. You can write for reservations at PO Box 1600, Cumberland, MD 21502. Or you can reserve online at www.reservations.nps.gov. (Those without reservations are charged only $10 per day.) The rest of the campgrounds operate on a first-come, first-served basis. Contact the park for more details. All campgrounds have a seven-day limit and allow RVs (except Sprague Creek).

DINING

INSIDE THE PARK

I wouldn't describe any of these offerings as culinary delights. Within the park, try the GLACIER PARK LODGE, LAKE MCDONALD LODGE and the MANY GLACIER HOTEL (see

THE NORTHWEST

above). Informal eating places can also be found in the APGAR VILLAGE area as well as at LAKE MCDONALD.

NEARBY COMMUNITIES

VILLAGER DINING ROOM ($$), 304 Highway 2 East, East Glacier; adjacent to East Glacier entrance of park. ☎ (406) 226-4464. American food. The amicable chef-proprietor cooks up a nice variety of well-prepared dishes that aren't too plain or too fancy. All of the excellent desserts are homemade.

WHERE DO WE GO FROM HERE?

Suggested Trip 5, a fabulous scenic adventure, features Glacier as a star of the trio. However, an interesting alternative, especially if you are going to Waterton Lakes, is to head north into Canada and visit the four national parks that comprise the heart of the Canadian Rockies – **Banff, Jasper, Kootenay** and **Yoho**.

A SIDE TRIP TO WATERTON LAKES NATIONAL PARK

You should include Waterton on any visit to Glacier. The parks are so closely associated with one another that if you write to Glacier Park's Superintendent for information, they will include brochures on Waterton... even if you don't ask for them.

After arriving via the **Chief Mountain International Highway**, you will be in Waterton town site. Like many Canadian parks, Waterton has a quaint and picturesque community set in the park itself. These towns are always the focal points for visitor centers, museums, accommodations and services of all kinds. Within the town is a short trail leading to beautiful **Cameron Falls**.

> **NOTE:** *Don't be surprised if you see deer and other animals strolling about the streets. They've become accustomed to people. However, you shouldn't get too close or attempt to feed them. Tame as they may appear, they are still wild.*

The main feature of your visit to the park is **Waterton Lake** itself – a mountain-surrounded jewel. At the northern end is the stately old **Prince of Wales Hotel**. A stroll through it is like taking a walk in 19th-century England, and lake views are gorgeous.

The two-hour **boat ride** on spectacular Waterton Lake is a must. These cruises make a brief stop at **Goat Haunt**, which is actually back in the States. It is in the northern part of Glacier Park and, except for this boat access, can be reached accessible only by an overnight hike.

❖ TIP

If you want to stay awhile at Goat Haunt, let your boat return to the mainland and join another vessel for your return.

Trips leave at 9, 10, 1, 4 and 7 daily from late June through Labour Day and on a more limited schedule during the spring and early fall. The fare is $18 in Canadian dollars. (Admission to the park itself is C$4.)

You should also take the drive through **Red Rock Canyon**, where the narrow valley is flanked by precipitous red spire-like mountains.

A comprehensive visit to Waterton should take at least four hours and, with the travel time there and back to Glacier, will add one day to your Glacier National Park excursion.

There is ample accommodation and dining available in the town of Waterton Lakes. Otherwise, the nearest lodging is in the Many Glacier section of Glacier National Park. Carry proof of US citizenship to avoid border crossing problems.

THE NORTHWEST

HELLS CANYON NATIONAL RECREATION AREA

O ne of the more rugged and least accessible areas in the nation, Hells Canyon incorporates a 71-mile stretch of the fantastic Snake River Canyon. The black basalt walls give a forbidding appearance to North America's deepest gorge – more than 7,900 feet at one point, although some points are much lower. But it is impressive, to say the least. The recreation area is popular with outdoor enthusiasts of all types, from those who just want to take in the view to lovers of great whitewater rafting.

❖ DID YOU KNOW?

Hells Canyon has some of the wildest rapids of any major American river.

The canyon is home to a variety of climatic zones, ranging from the desert-like surroundings of the canyon floor to the alpine atmosphere found at the top. The canyon also sports a diversity of wildlife and vegetation. Recreational opportunities abound.

FACTS & FIGURES

Location/Gateways/Getting There: Beginning at the point where the Idaho, Oregon and Washington borders meet, Hells Canyon continues south along both sides of the Snake River, mostly in Oregon, but also covering a sizable area in Idaho. This is one of the more difficult areas to visit in this book. It can be reached via a number of routes on the Oregon side, but the easiest access routes are on the Idaho side. Boise is the best gateway city. From there, take I-84 west to Payette, on the Snake

River opposite Oregon, and then follow US 95 north to the town of Cambridge. SR 71 will then lead you directly into the southern portion of the recreation area at Hells Canyon Dam. This trip covers 150 miles and will take about 3½ hours to complete.

Other portions of Hells Canyon on the Idaho side can be reached by a number of Forest Service roads that branch off US 95 between the towns of Riggins and White Bird. You can get there from Boise as described before (just stay on US 95 at Cambridge) or from Spokane, Washington. From the latter, take US 195 south to Lewiston and then pick up US 95 south.

Year Established: This U.S. Forest Service-administered area was established in 1975.

Size: 536,648 acres (838 square miles).

Admission Fee: None.

Climate/When to Go: There is a wide temperature variance between the top and bottom of the canyon. Summer is comfortable on the canyon rims, but can often be hot down at the river level. Similarly, winter is cold on the rim and relatively mild within the canyon. Late spring to early fall is the best time to visit.

> NOTE: *Many access roads to the rim are closed during the winter season.*

Contact Information: Supervisor, Hells Canyon National Recreation Area, PO Box 699, Clarkston, WA 99403. ☎ (509) 758-0616.

AUTO TOUR/SHORT STOPS

Views of Hells Canyon can be achieved by a number of different auto routes, some from the Idaho side and some from Oregon.

❖ THE IDAHO SIDE

The first three suggestions are all reached from side roads on the Idaho side of the canyon that leave US 95 between the towns of Riggins and White Bird. The third route is the easiest and is accessible all year, while the first two are open only during the summer.

> NOTE: *All of these are dirt or gravel roads that, in theory, can be traveled in good weather in the family sedan. However, high-clearance and 4WD are certainly helpful.*

Forest Route 517 from just south of Riggins leads to the **Heavens Gate Overlook**. This is one of the most spectacular Hells Canyon views available, situated at a lofty 8,600 feet. A second possibility is **Forest Route 241** from just north of Riggins. This road leads to three close-by overlooks: the **Low Saddle, Sawpit Saddle** and **Iron Phone Junction Overlooks**.

Forest Route 493 (Deer Creek Road) goes from White Bird to the Petersburg Saddle, a 10-mile trip from US 95.

While it isn't necessary to take each of these routes (since the views don't differ that much), those who are inclined to do more than one can use Forest Route 420 to get from one to the other. This avoids having to return all the way to US 95 to pick up another one of the access roads. All of these routes pass through the **Seven Devils Mountains**, a rugged area of beautiful vistas.

❖ THE OREGON SIDE

> NOTE: *All routes on the Oregon side of the canyon are more difficult to navigate than the Idaho routings.*

Hells Canyon Overlook can be reached by a 40-mile trip via **Forest Routes 39 and 3965** from Joseph. The **Buckhorn Lookout** is accessed from Enterprise or Joseph via **Zumwalt Road** (County Route 697/Forest Routes 46 and 780). The third way in

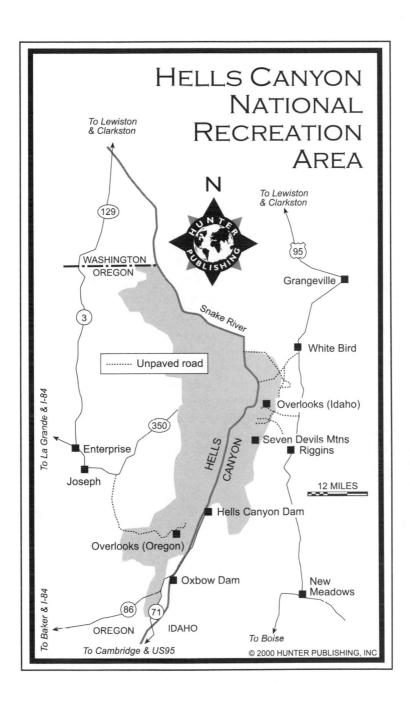

HELLS CANYON
NATIONAL
RECREATION
AREA

N

HUNTER PUBLISHING

To Lewiston & Clarkston

129

To Lewiston & Clarkston

95

WASHINGTON
OREGON

Grangeville

3

Snake River

White Bird

Unpaved road

Overlooks (Idaho)

To La Grande & I-84

350

Seven Devils Mtns

Enterprise

Riggins

Joseph

12 MILES

Hells Canyon Dam

HELLS CANYON

Overlooks (Oregon)

To Baker & I-84

Oxbow Dam

New Meadows

86   71

OREGON   IDAHO

To Boise

To Cambridge & US95

© 2000 HUNTER PUBLISHING, INC

THE NORTHWEST

on this side is by taking **Forest Route 4240**, which travels 24 miles from Imnaha to an overlook at **Hat Point**. At 5,600-foot elevation, Hat Point is the highest overlook on the Oregon side. None of the Oregon access roads are paved.

❖ AT RIVER LEVEL

One thing that all of the above routes have in common is that you see Hells Canyon from the top, looking down. For auto access to the Snake River level, the easiest and most popular route is to take **SR 71** from the junction of US 95 in Cambridge, Idaho. This road goes to the **Oxbow Dam** on the Oregon/Idaho border, where you'll pick up a utility company road to Hells Canyon Dam at road's end. From the point where this route first reaches the Snake River to the end at the dam, it is extremely scenic. You'll cross back and forth between the two states on several occasions and have glorious views of the canyon, although this is not the deepest and most impressive portion of Hells Canyon. (Boat trips on the Snake River depart from the Hells Canyon Dam, another reason to come this way. See the *Special Activities* section for more details.)

It's hard to suggest an appropriate time frame for this Auto Tour because it depends on which route or routes you're going to take. The last one requires about two hours from Cambridge. All of the other Idaho access routes will take at least an hour, one way, while the Oregon trips will take anywhere from two to four hours, one way.

GETTING OUT/LONGER STOPS

❖ HIKING

Hells Canyon National Recreation Area has more than 900 miles of trails, most of which are strenuous. To find a trail that is less than 10 miles long is a challenge. They generally all feature significant changes in altitude.

> NOTE: *If you wish to attempt any of these trails you should get information and maps from the office in Clarkston, Washington; Enterprise, Oregon; or Riggins, Idaho.*

SPECIAL ACTIVITIES

❖ FLOAT & JET BOAT TRIPS

Trips on the Snake River through the deep recesses of Hells Canyon are one of the most popular and rewarding ways to see this remote area. It is only from the river level looking up that you can fully appreciate the awesome proportions of Hells Canyon. Several dozen operators run excursions from the Hells Canyon Dam as well as from Lewiston and Clarkston. The range of trips available is extensive – you can choose from trips lasting two, four, and six hours or one- and two-day excursions. Among the more popular outfitters are:

Beamers Hells Canyon Tours. . . . ☎ (800) 522-6966
Clarkston
Hells Canyon Adventures. . . . . . . ☎ (800) 422-3568
Hells Canyon Dam

For other tour operators, contact the Lewiston or Clarkston Chambers of Commerce (☎ 800-933-2128 and ☎ 800-473-3543, respectively).

ACCOMMODATIONS

❖ HOTELS & MOTELS

There are no overnight facilities inside the recreation area itself.

NEARBY COMMUNITIES

To make things a little less confusing, the accommodations are arranged according to location.

THE NORTHWEST

IDAHO SIDE
(NEW MEADOWS TO GRANGERVILLE)

DOWN TOWNER INN ($), 113 E. North Street, Grangerville; one mile east of US 95 via State Highway 13. The nearest gateway into the recreation area is 17 miles from the hotel at White Bird. ☎ (208) 983-1110. 16 rooms. A small, simple roadside motel that's typical of many in this rather isolated area. Restaurants can be found along the main road in Grangeville.

HARTLAND INN ($-$$), 211 Norris Street, New Meadows; on the main road in town (US 95), 34 miles the recreation area at Riggins. ☎ (208) 347-2114. 14 rooms. Consists of motel-style units as well as three attractive and charming B&B units ($$$). Nice views. Small spa. Restaurants within a short drive.

PINEHURST RESORT ($), 5604 US 95, between Riggins and New Meadows; within 10 miles of several park access routes around Riggins. ☎ (208) 628-3323. 6 rooms. Tranquil and beautiful setting along the Salmon River. Units are rather modest in size and decor, but are well maintained. Several restaurants are in the vicinity.

HELLS CANYON DAM AREA
(IDAHO & OREGON ACCESS)

BEST WESTERN INN ($$), 251 Goodfellow Street, Ontario; just off Exit 376 of I-84, 75 miles from Oxbow Dam. ☎ (541) 889-2600 or (800) 528-1234. 61 units. Attractively decorated rooms, many with coffee makers and microwave ovens. There are also quite a few studio units. Swimming pool and spa. Numerous restaurants in town.

HOLIDAY INN ($$), 1249 Tapadera Avenue, Ontario; US 30, immediately east of I-84, Exit 376 and 75 miles from Oxbow Dam. ☎ (541) 889-8621 or (800) HOLIDAY. 98 rooms. The biggest and best-equipped lodging establishment in Ontario. Nice courtyard area with spa and small pool. There's a decent family-style restaurant on the premises.

INDIANHEAD MOTEL ($), 747 US 95, Weiser; one mile north of town center on the main highway to Hells Canyon Dam, about 58 miles from Oxbow Dam. ☎ (208) 549-0331. 8 rooms.

Basic accommodations. Very clean and comfortable. Homey atmosphere. Restaurant nearby.

OREGON SIDE

BEST WESTERN SUNRIDGE INN ($$), 1 Sunridge Lane, Baker City; Exit 304 of I-84, 52 miles from Halfway (which is 17 miles to Oxbow Dam and nine miles to Forest Route 39, main access road to points on the Oregon side of the canyon). ☎ (541) 523-6444 or (800) 528-1234. 156 rooms. Spacious, well-appointed rooms on nicely kept grounds. Spa, swimming pool and two restaurants on the premises.

SUPER 8 MOTEL ($$), 250 Campbell Street, Baker City; just off I-84 at Exit 304 (see *Facts & Figures*, above, for travel to recreation area). ☎ (541) 523-8282 or (800) 800-8000. Rate includes continental breakfast. 72 rooms. Adequate accommodations typical of this chain. Level of housekeeping is excellent. Several restaurants are within a short distance.

> NOTE: *Other lodging we consider to be below the standards for this book is available in Joseph and Enterprise. These might be better suited for those wishing to stay closer to the Oregon side of the recreation area.*

LEWISTON/CLARKSTON AREA

If you're touring Hells Canyon via jet boat from the Lewiston/Clarkston area, the following accommodations will be of interest:

RED LION HOTEL ($$), 621 21st Street, Lewiston; 1¼ miles south of the junction of US 95 on US 12. ☎ (208) 799-1000 or (800) 547-8010. Rate includes continental breakfast during summer; full breakfast at other times. 134 rooms. Beautiful accommodations at a surprisingly low price for this upscale Western chain of motor hotels. More luxurious suites and other facilities are available at higher prices. Nice setting along river. Considerable recreational facilities available on premises. Restaurant.

SACAJAWEA SELECT INN ($), 1824 Main Street, Lewiston; 1½ miles south of the junction of US 95 on US 12. ☎ (208) 746-1393. Rate includes continental breakfast. 90 Rooms. Very nice accommodations, especially considering the low prices. The inn also has plenty of recreational facilities and a decent restaurant.

❖ CAMPING

Reservations can be made through the US Forest Service centralized system. ☎ (800) 280-CAMP. The recreation area supervisor's office can provide general information on camping within Hells Canyon. Forest Service campgrounds are located as follows:

Oregon side: Dougherty Springs, Buckhorn Overlook, Saddle Creek, Lick Creek, Blackhorse, Ollokot, Coverdale, Evergreen, Hidden and Indian Crossing.

Idaho side: Pittsburg Landing, Windy Saddle, Seven Devils and Black Lake.

DINING

There are no eateries inside the recreation area.

NEARBY COMMUNITIES

Although there are a few towns along US Highway 89, they have no accommodations worthy of a recommendation. A few cafés in Riggins might meet your needs, but a better choice of full-service restaurants can be found in Grangerville along the main road.

IDAHO SIDE
(HELLS CANYON DAM ACCESS)

ALEXANDER'S ON THE RIVER ($$), 1930 SE 5th Avenue, Ontario; via East Lane from Exit 376 of I-84. ☎ (541) 889-8070. American food. Wide variety of well-prepared meals (steak, seafood, chicken and pasta as well as other dishes) in an inviting atmosphere. During good weather you can dine on the patio along the Salmon River.

OREGON SIDE

PHONE COMPANY RESTAURANT ($$), 1926 First Street, Baker City; 1¼ miles southwest of I-84, Exit 304. ☎ (541) 523-7997. American food. Occupying an historic building that once housed the local telephone exchange, this is a nice place for casual dining. Specialties of the house include a variety of Northwestern regional fish and seafood entrées.

SONNY'S BAR & GRILL ($$), Best Western Sunridge Inn (see listing above). ☎ (541) 523-6444. American food. Sophisticated atmosphere and well-prepared dinners. Menu is fairly limited. Outdoor patio dining in season.

LEWISTON

ZANY'S ($-$$), 2006 19th Street, 1¼ miles south of the junction of US 95 via US 12. ☎ (208) 746-8131. American food. Varied selection of family favorites (including plenty that kids will like). The 1950s theme is well done and will leave you in no doubt as to how this unusual eatery got its name.

WHERE DO WE GO FROM HERE?

Suggested Trip 6 includes Hells Canyon. An alternative to that itinerary is to travel north from Hells Canyon into the **Idaho Panhandle**. This region of the state has many recreational opportunities and is home to some of the nation's most beautiful lakes. **Lake Coeur d'Alene** and **Lake Pend Oreille** are the two foremost examples.

THE NORTHWEST

MOUNT RAINIER NATIONAL PARK

Perhaps the most famous peak of the Pacific Northwest's Cascade Range, Mount Rainier is a dormant, but not extinct, ice-clad volcanic mountain. At 14,410 feet, it is a giant. Though it is not the highest of mountains, Mount Rainier's sheer bulk and the fact that it is set apart from its neighboring peaks in the range make it the dominant landmark of the region. So much does it dominate the surrounding landscape, that it is commonly referred to by locals simply as "The Mountain."

> ❖ **DID YOU KNOW?**
>
> *Mount Rainier is visible from over 100 miles away on clear days. It towers more than 8,000 feet above the surrounding terrain.*

Rainier's legendary beauty is as great as its overpowering size. Its 27 glaciers cover more than 34 square miles, making it the largest single-peak glacial system in the lower 48 states. The smooth glacial ice hides what is really an extremely rugged mountain composed of many jagged surfaces. Other scenery in the park is equally impressive and heavily forested up to an altitude of about 5,000 feet. The landscape then becomes covered with absolutely magnificent meadows of wildflowers, a feature second only to the mountain itself in attracting visitors. Then, above the timberline, at about 6,500 feet, there is only rock and ice. Its beauty and awe-inspiring presence must be seen and felt. It is our good fortune that Mount Rainier National Park is highly accessible, so let us begin our journey.

FACTS & FIGURES

Location/Gateways/Getting There: Mount Rainier is in west-central Washington, less than two hours from Seattle. There are approaches from all directions, but the two primary routes (coming from the Seattle-Tacoma metropolitan area) are SR 410 from I-5 via the town of Enumclaw (White River entrance), or SRs 7 and 706 from Tacoma (Nisqually entrance). Coming from the south, US 12 leads into SR 123 (the Ohanapecosh entrance); and SR 410 also approaches the park from the east (the direction of Yakima) at the Chinook Pass entrance.

Year Established: Known to the Indians since prehistoric times, the great mountain was first sighted by European explorers in 1792. Extensive exploration of Mount Rainier did not begin until the 1850s and it became America's fourth national park in 1899.

Size: 235,404 acres (368 square miles).

Admission Fee: $10.

Climate/When to Go: Although open all year, many roads are closed by heavy winter snows until the middle of June. Only the Nisqually entrance is open throughout the year. The comfortably cool summer season lasts from the time that all roads open until August or perhaps early September. This is the only practical time for most visitors, especially first-timers, even though the park is at its most crowded. Very simply, at all other times of the year there will be portions of the park that you cannot get to see and these areas should not be missed. While crowded roads may be a negative, summer is when views are least likely to be obscured by clouds. Despite the Pacific Northwest's reputation for rain and overcast skies, it has surprisingly dry summers.

Contact Information: Superintendent, Mount Rainier National Park, Tahoma Woods-Star Route, Ashford, WA 98304. ☎ (360) 569-2211.

AUTO TOUR / SHORT STOPS

Although the park road system does not climb up Mount Rainier itself, or even surround it on all sides, it is surprisingly easy to see the park's many highlights from your car. The main road network, starting from the Nisqually entrance, runs through the southern part of the park (Nisqually-Paradise and Stevens Canyon Roads) and then along the eastern edge of the park (East Side Road and Mather Memorial Parkway). These, along with one major spur road (Sunrise/White River Road) will be the key to your trip. Other roads in the park are unpaved and difficult to negotiate. It is most logical to begin your tour at either the Nisqually or White River entrances, but for those coming from either the south or east, you can actually begin at any entrance and see everything with a little extra mileage for back-tracking. Frequent overlooks make it possible to see the best scenery no matter which direction you are traveling. We'll follow a south and then westerly route in this description (i.e., beginning from the northeast corner of the park), because this is the way many people will arrive if they start their trip in Seattle.

About four miles after the north entrance is a cutoff for the **White River Road**, which later becomes the **Sunrise Road**.

> NOTE: *You'd better get used to name shifts; it is common for a road to receive a new name as it enters different regions of the park.*

This spur, with an approximate one-way distance of 15 miles, leads to the magnificent **Sunrise** area of the park. It is a detour that is too often missed by visitors simply because it is not on the main road, but the half-hour it takes to drive each way is certainly well worth the time, as you will soon see. About two-thirds of the way to Sunrise, there is a parking area called **Sunrise Point**. Perched in the middle of a long, gentle switchback, it is the first of many unforgettable stops you will make. This is where you will likely first fully appreciate the immensity of Mount Rainier. Amazing views of the snow- and ice-covered mountain, including the very top of Mount Rainier, await you here. Do not fret if there is some cloudiness, especially in the morning, for in summer it will likely clear before the day is out and you will see the top. In fact, if it is still cloud-covered on your way up to Sunrise there is a good chance it will have cleared by the time you pass this spot on your way back to the main road. At the end of the road is **Sunrise Visitor Center** (one of four in

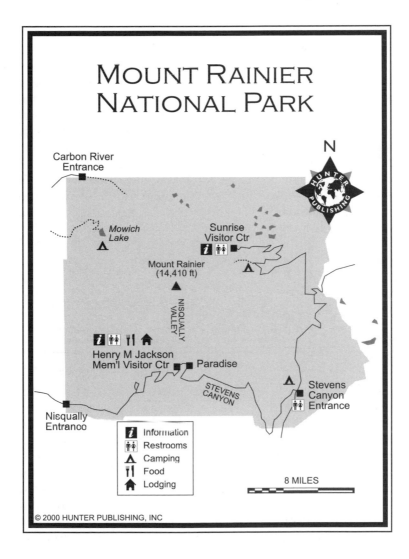

MOUNT RAINIER NATIONAL PARK

N

Carbon River Entrance

Mowich Lake

Sunrise Visitor Ctr

Mount Rainier (14,410 ft)

NISQUALLY VALLEY

Henry M Jackson Mem'l Visitor Ctr

Paradise

STEVENS CANYON

Stevens Canyon Entrance

Nisqually Entrance

i Information
👫 Restrooms
⛺ Camping
🍴 Food
🏠 Lodging

8 MILES

© 2000 HUNTER PUBLISHING, INC

THE NORTHWEST

the park) that has exhibits explaining the topography of the area. You can take a brief walk in the surrounding wildflower meadow, aglow with color in the shadow of the great mountain and its icy blanket.

Sunrise is the closest you can get to the summit by car. At 6,400 feet, Sunrise Visitor Center is more than 1,000 feet higher than the more heavily visited Paradise headquarters area. Take a deep breath, finish here, and reverse your route to the East Side Road, then continue south.

Once you are past the Chinook Pass entrance road, the road changes names again, becoming the **Stevens Canyon Road** as it enters a more scenic section of the park. Stop for the panoramas at **Backbone Ridge** and **Box Canyon**, where there is a dizzying view into the waterfall-filled canyon. **Reflection Lake** is another overlook that shouldn't be missed. These stops are all within a short distance of one another and provide some of the most breathtaking views of Mount Rainier itself while also showcasing the park's other beautiful features – canyons, rivers, lakes and waterfalls. Several other distant peaks of the magnificent Cascade Range are also visible. The road appears as a thin ribbon dwarfed by the surrounding landscape, as the switchbacks place the highway both above and beneath you. It is a dramatic sight.

You will then come upon the junction to **Paradise**. Take the spur road that climbs sharply for a short time to **Paradise Village**, site of the park headquarters and the majority of visitor services.

> NOTE: *Because of the heavy traffic in this area and the steep grades, low gear is highly recommended.*

At Paradise be sure to visit the modernistic **Henry M. Jackson Visitor Center**, perched at the foot of the **Nisqually Glacier**. The circular building provides an awesome 360° panorama. Opportunities for pleasant strolls through the Paradise area's many wildflower meadows are plentiful and you will be rewarded with clear views of quite a few of the 26 glaciers that descend from Mt. Rainier (see the next section for detail).

Leaving Paradise, pick up the **Nisqually-Paradise Road** going westbound. The first stop on this leg of the route will be **Narada Falls**. A brief walk from the parking area descends to the bottom of a ravine and the foot of the very picturesque falls. Just beyond here the road brings you to **Ricksecker Point**, one of the most beautiful of all the viewpoints along the road system. Next you will approach **Longmire**, where there is an historical museum with interesting exhibits about the native population. Shortly before reaching the southwestern (or Nisqually) exit of the park is the site of the **Kautz Mudflow**. A mud slide in the 1920s did extensive damage here. You would be hard-pressed to see true evidence of the damage today for nature has done an outstanding job of rejuvenation. However, within a short walk are exhibits about the mudflow and nice views of streams and wildflowers with Mount Rainier as a backdrop.

This concludes the auto portion of your tour. The drive, with breaks to stop, look and walk, should take six hours.

GETTING OUT/LONGER STOPS

❖ HIKING

There are more than 300 miles of trails in the park, many of which are difficult, long trails that lead upward toward or around the summit and over its glaciers. As such, they are not well suited for the casual visitor. But many other trails are easier. In the Sunrise area, the half-mile **Emmons Vista Trail** provides excellent views of Mount Rainier and the Emmons Glacier. It takes a half-hour to complete. The 1½-mile **Sourdough Ridge Nature Trail** is another walk that does not require any unusual amount of effort. Many varieties of flowers and plants encountered en route are labeled for easy identification. Other trails at Sunrise range from three to six miles and may take up to four hours. These are more extensive versions of the Emmons Vista Trail. The Paradise area provides the greatest number of opportunities for exploration on foot. The **Nisqually Vista Trail** (1½ miles round-trip) is the easiest and one of the best. It provides an excellent view of the Nisqually Glacier, and is well known for the beautiful wildflower meadows that it passes through. Allow one hour. The **Skyline Trail** is a more strenuous, 4½-mile loop requiring about four hours to complete. Boots are advisable as you are likely to encounter snow and ice. Several other trails are spurs off the Skyline Trail or variations of it.

Outdoor enthusiasts can even circumnavigate the base of Mt. Rainier via the 75-mile **Wonderland Trail**. This loop trail is divided into several different sections to make it more manageable to explore. It is accessible from many points, the most popular of which is at Paradise.

Finally, if you have a lot of time to spare (minimum of six hours) you might consider the six-mile round-trip to an area of unusual beauty – an underground palace of ice, the brilliant blue **Ice Caves**. Inquire at the Paradise Visitor Center before embarking: access to the cave is sometimes blocked almost all summer because of heavy snow and ice. There are also several trails of varying length and difficulty departing from the Longmire Visitor Center, but none of these are as popular or as rewarding as those in either Sunrise or Paradise.

❖ 4WD TRIPS

Several roads, varying from improved but unsurfaced to wild and difficult, are available to those with 4WD, high-clearance vehicles. The **Carbon River Road** explores the thick virgin forests of the park's northwestern section and provides access to many trails. The **West Side Road** begins at the Nisqually-Paradise Road just inside the park's entrance and skirts the western edge of the park, also providing access to many backcountry trails.

> NOTE: *Because of varying weather conditions (and frequent closures due to damaging winter storms), it is imperative that you check with a park ranger before setting out on these or other unpaved park roads. Even under ideal conditions, most unimproved roads are only open during the summer.*

ACCOMMODATIONS

❖ HOTELS & MOTELS

INSIDE THE PARK

NATIONAL PARK INN ($$), Longmire; six miles from the Southwest entrance. ☎ (360) 569-2275. 25 rooms. A delightful and historic wood-beamed lodge in one of the most majestic settings you could ever imagine. Units are on the small side, but quite comfortable. Restaurant on premises.

NEARBY COMMUNITIES

Although Seattle is only 70 miles away, we don't recommend staying there and doing Mt. Rainier as a day trip – there just won't be enough time to do it justice. The area accommodations below cover localities on all sides of the park.

BEST WESTERN PARK CENTER HOTEL ($$), 1000 Griffin Avenue, Enumclaw; town center, 30 miles from the northeastern park entrance via State Highway 410. ☎ (360) 825-4490 or (800) 528-1234. 40 rooms. A comfortable roadside motel with slightly better than average accommodations. Whirlpool. Decent restaurant on the premises.

INN OF PACKWOOD ($$), 13032 US 12, Packwood; center of town, 12 miles from the southeast entrance of Mt. Rainier National Park. ☎ (360) 494-5500. Rate includes continental breakfast. 33 rooms. The small town of Packwood serves travelers to both Mt. Rainier and Mt. St. Helens. Despite that, the pickings aren't that good, and this is the best of the lot. It's a clean and comfortable facility with some family units available ($$$$). Swimming pool.

NISQUALLY LODGE ($$), 31609 State Highway 706, Ashford; half a mile east of town and 10 miles west of the southwestern entrance of the park. ☎ (360) 569-8804. Rate includes continental breakfast. 24 rooms. Very nice rooms and well-maintained facilities. Quiet setting. Restaurants within a short drive.

THE NORTHWEST

❖ CAMPING

CAMPGROUNDS AT A GLANCE			
NAME	LOCATION	SITES	COST
Cougar Rock	2½ miles north of Longmire.	200	$14 per day
White River	End of the road to Sunrise.	117	$8 per day
Sunshine Point	Just east of the Nisqually (southwest) entrance.	18	$6 per day

There is a 14-day limit at all sites. Cougar Rock offers walk-in sites for $8 and allows RVs. Reservations ($14) can be made through NPRS, ☎ (800) 365-2267. The offices are open daily from 10 am to 10 pm, eastern time. You can write in for reservations at PO Box 1600, Cumberland, MD 21502. Or, you can reserve online at http://reservations.nps.gov.

White River and Sunshine Point operate on a first-come, first-served basis (call the park for details).

DINING

INSIDE THE PARK

PARADISE INN DINING ROOM ($$), at Paradise. ☎ (360) 569-2413. American food. A charming lodge-style facility with magnificent views of the Nisqually Glacier as well as Mount Rainier itself. Offers a variety of dishes, from simple to almost gourmet. Northwest regional favorites are an especially good choice. Excellent Sunday brunch. The restaurant at the NATIONAL PARK INN ($$) also serves adequate meals.

NEARBY COMMUNITIES

ALEXANDER'S ($$), 37515 State Highway 706, Ashford; Alexander's Country Inn, a mile west of the southwest entrance to the park. ☎ (360) 569-2323. American food. Situated inside a picturesque old country inn, Alexander's features country-style cooking and outstanding fresh-baked products.

Suggested Trip 9 in the final section of this book is an excellent way to see the many scenic parts of Washington state, including Mount Rainier National Park. However, if you are pressed for time, Mount Rainier can be done as part of an overnight trip from Seattle. Depending upon how much time is available to you, additions can then be made to the **Olympic Peninsula, the North Cascades** or possibly even **Mount St. Helens**.

MOUNT ST. HELENS NATIONAL VOLCANIC MONUMENT

Many of us can still vividly remember that fateful morning in May of 1980 when, after several months of rumbling and threatening, Mount St. Helens blew its top, sending over a thousand feet of its peak and much of the north face of the mountain high into the air in an explosion of unimaginable force. Ash and darkened skies blanketed hundreds of square miles downwind as far as Spokane. Everything in the immediate path of the blast was instantaneously destroyed by the combination of intense heat and winds of several hundred miles per hour. It was nature at its most furious. What had before been one of the jewels of the Cascade Range was turned into a barren wasteland. Visiting Mount St. Helens today, the destruction is still clearly evident, though signs of life are rapidly reappearing in the fertile land that the volcano left behind. It is a strange world, with a unique kind of beauty. To truly understand what immense power must have been unleashed that morning, you have to see and feel it in person.

THE NORTHWEST

FACTS & FIGURES

Location/Gateways/Getting There: The monument is northeast of Portland, Oregon, via I-5 and SR 504 (west side) or via I-5 and SR 503 and then Forest Service roads (details later) on the east side. Allow about two hours from Portland to reach the volcanic area. It can also be accessed from Seattle via I-5 south to SR 504 or; on the east side, I-5 to US 12 onto Forest Service roads at the town of Randle.

Year Established: The area became the nation's only National Volcanic Monument in 1982. It is administered by the U.S. Forest Service.

Size: 110,000 acres (172 square miles).

Admission Fee: There is no charge for entering the monument itself; however, access to most facilities (including visitor centers) requires purchasing a Monument Pass ($8 for adults and $4 for seniors/children). Note that this is a per-person charge, not per vehicle. National Park Service passports are honored for admission.

Climate/When to Go: The west side is open all year (except for the final six miles to Johnston Ridge), but the east and south side roads are open only from the middle of June to late October, depending upon the weather. Summer is the best time to visit either side because it is drier and more comfortable than other times of the year.

Contact Information: Mount St. Helens National Volcanic Monument Headquarters, 42218 N.E. Yale Bridge Road, Amboy, WA 98601. ☎ (360) 247-3900.

AUTO TOUR/ SHORT STOPS

The monument is physically divided into three areas – the West, East and South sides. While the east and south are directly connected by road, access to the west requires a long drive from the other sections. A complete loop (e.g., from Castle Rock and back) covers about 325 miles and a minimum of two days is required. Because of this, many visitors will be able to do either the west *or* east/south sides.

Which is better if you're short of time? There is no correct answer. The west is easier to reach and the roads are better. From a scenic standpoint (and from the perspective of getting a "feel" for the eruption), they're different, but equally fascinating. If you're coming through the area and are short of time, we would suggest the west. On the other hand, if you're coming from Mount Rainier, then it is just as easy to see the east and south sides.

The area is still being developed and, while there have been numerous road and facilities improvements, more are likely to occur as time goes by.

❖ WEST SIDE

From the Castle Rock exit (#49) of I-5, **SR 504** (also known as the **Spirit Lake Memorial Highway**) extends 53 miles and leads into the monument before reaching its end at Johnston Ridge. Most of this excellent road follows the course of the Toutle River. There are many sights and interpretive facilities along the way.

> NOTE: *The indicated mileages represent the approximate distance from Castle Rock.*

The **Mount St. Helens Visitor Center** (Mile 5) is picturesquely set near the shore of beautiful **Silver Lake**. A short trail leads to the lake overview from where Mt. St. Helens can also be seen. A highlight of the visitor center is the "walk-in" model of a volcano. At Mile 27 is the **Hoffstadt Bluffs Visitor Center**. Here are fine views of both the Toutle River and the valley that connects it with the mountain. Some of the exhibits are interesting and you can find access here to a **nature trail** through some wetlands. The **Forest Learning Center** (Mile 33) has displays about the eruption and subsequent events. You can take a simulated helicopter ride through the eruption. Outside is an observation deck with views of the now much closer mountain. Up to this point you haven't actually been inside the boundaries of the monument, but that changes at Mile 43 when you reach the **Coldwater Ridge Visitor Center**. From this point Mt. St. Helens is only seven miles away and the views of it, as well as Coldwater Lake, the river and valley, are truly spectacular. In the vicinity of the visitor center are two quarter-mile trails: the **Birth of a Lake Interpretive Trail** and the **Winds of Change Trail**. Both emphasize the recolonization of the area with flora and fauna since the eruption.

The final leg of your trip along the Spirit Lake Memorial Highway comes to an end at the **Johnston Ridge Observatory**. In addition to many interesting exhibits, this facility monitors seismic activity within Mt. St. Helens. It is less than five miles from the mountain and included in the fabulous views from this point are the still-steaming lava dome and the tremendous amount of debris from the landslide that resulted from the eruption. Also visible is the crater itself – its size is overwhelming and will help galvanize your understanding of the tremendous power of nature.

SR 504 is a dead end and you must reverse your route towards the interstate highway. You should allocate between five and six hours for the trip and the sights along the way as described above. (Opportunities for longer walks are discussed later.)

❖ EAST SIDE & SOUTH SIDE

From the town of Randle, take SR 131 south until it runs into **Forest Route (FR) 99**. This road runs parallel to the east side of the monument and, along with **FR 25**, provides access to many points of interest. Among the highlights of the Auto Tour on this side of Mt. St. Helens are **Meta Lake, Harmony Falls Viewpoint, the Blast Edge** and **Independence Pass**. FR 25 ends at **Windy Ridge**. All of these provide excellent views of Mt. St. Helens. At Meta Lake there is an easy quarter-mile trail and an attraction called the **Miner's Car**. This car was in the blast area when the volcano erupted, and it has been fenced off and left as a sample of what nature can do. The heat literally stripped off the paint. There is also a relatively easy trail of one mile at Harmony Falls.

Windy Ridge provides a panorama that is equaled only by that at Johnston Ridge.

> NOTE: *The forest roads are generally narrow and winding, but have been improved to the point where they aren't difficult to negotiate. The sights are worth the small effort.*

You should allow 2½ hours to tour the east side.

The south side connects the interstate at Woodland via SR 503 and FRs 90 and 83 with FR 99. If you're coming from that direction you'll do the south side first and then the east side. This side of the monument is the least rewarding portion of the monument for touring by car., although hikers will find ample opportunity for a great time (see next section). The auto route includes the **Lahar Viewpoint**, 10 miles east of the junction of FR 90 and FR 83. It is a weird landscape that has been sculpted by enormous mudslides following the eruption. Also on the south side is the short **Trail of Two Forests**, which starts at Ape Cave, reached via FR 8303.

GETTING OUT/LONGER STOPS

❖ HIKING

West Side: This side of the monument is the lazy person's way to see Mt. St. Helens. However, those wishing to take a longer stretch can select from a number of lengthy and generally not too difficult trails. Among the more popular ones are the **Elks Bench Trail** (¾ miles) and the **Hummocks Trail** (2½ miles). Elks Bench starts at Coldwater Ridge Visitor Center; Hummocks begins along the Spirit Lake Highway.

East Side: Most of the trails on the east side involve extensive climbing, but there are a few for every skill level. The 1½-mile **Iron Creek Trail** and the 3½-mile **Independence Pass Trail** are excellent. They provide stunning vistas as well as access to areas that show the recovery of nature.

THE NORTHWEST

You can also climb to the summit of **Mt. St. Helens**. Access is limited and you must be given permission to do so by park rangers. Inquire at any visitor center.

South Side: The three-mile **Lava Canyon Trail** is one of the best. Some parts are easy, other stretches are moderately strenuous, and some sections are quite difficult. Located a mile east of the Lahar Viewpoint, this trail passes through mud-scoured terrain as well as a waterfall and several ancient lava flows. At least two hours are required to complete this trail.

Another interesting experience along the southern edge is a visit to **Ape Cave**. Reached via FR 8303 off FR 83, this is a two-mile-long tunnel – or more exactly, a lava tube. It is more than 2,000 years old and was created when lava flowed downhill and, as the outer edge cooled, the hotter lava in the middle continued to flow through it. The result is the cave-like structure that remains today. You must carry your own source of light (lanterns can be rented at the Ape Cave Information Station). The cave is chilly year-round, so wear a jacket. Guided tours of the cave are offered daily from 10:30 am through 3:30 pm during the summer. Allow about an hour.

SPECIAL ACTIVITIES

A large number of **ranger-guided activities** are offered. Check schedules at the various visitor centers or information stations.

You might also consider getting a bird's eye view of the crater by taking a **scenic flight.** These are available from local airports in the vicinity of the monument as well as from the Portland and Seattle areas. (You can get a list of operators at any visitor center.) **Whirl Tours**, at the Hoffstadt Bluffs Visitor Center, is the closest (☎ 800-752-8439), or you can try **Seattle Seaplanes**, ☎ (206) 329-9617. Trips last 1-1½ hours (depending upon how far away they start) and prices start at about $75.

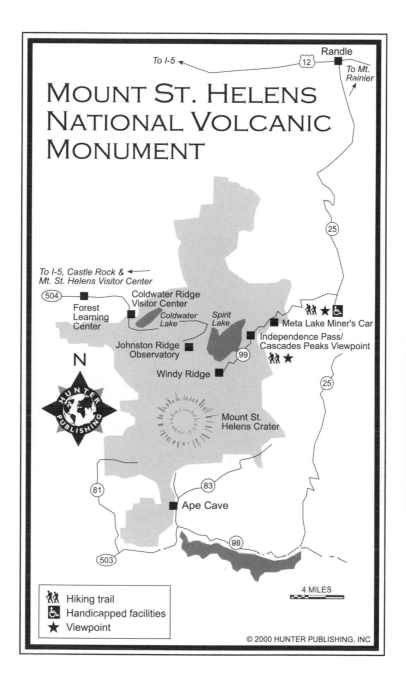

To I-5 ◄

Randle

12

To Mt.
Rainier

MOUNT ST. HELENS
NATIONAL VOLCANIC
MONUMENT

25

To I-5, Castle Rock & ◄
Mt. St. Helens Visitor Center

504

Coldwater Ridge
Visitor Center

Forest
Learning
Center

Coldwater
Lake

Spirit
Lake

Meta Lake Miner's Car

Johnston Ridge
Observatory

Independence Pass/
Cascades Peaks Viewpoint

99

Windy Ridge

N

HUNTER
PUBLISHING

25

Mount St.
Helens Crater

81

83

Ape Cave

98

503

4 MILES

🚶 Hiking trail
♿ Handicapped facilities
★ Viewpoint

© 2000 HUNTER PUBLISHING, INC.

THE NORTHWEST

ACCOMMODATIONS

❖ HOTELS & MOTELS

There are no overnight facilities within the monument.

NEARBY COMMUNITIES

INN OF PACKWOOD ($$), 13032 US 12, Packwood; center of town. Access to east side. ☎ (360) 494-5500. Rate includes continental breakfast. 33 rooms. The small town of Packwood serves travelers to both Mt. Rainier and Mt. St. Helens. Despite that, the pickings aren't that good, and this is the best of the lot. It's a clean and comfortable facility with some family units available ($$$$). Swimming pool.

LONE FIR RESORT ($), 16806 Lewis River Road, Cougar; in the center of town, just east of the south side of the monument via Forest Route 90. ☎ (360) 238-5210. 16 rooms. Basic motel accommodations. About half of the units have kitchens, which might serve you well as there is a distinct lack of good restaurants in this area.

SEASONS MOTEL ($$), 200 Westlake, Morton; at the junction of US 12 and State Highway 7, 17 miles west of Randle (access to east side of monument via Forest Route 25 from Randle). ☎ (360) 496-6835. 50 rooms. One of the nicest motels within hailing distance of the monument's east side, the Seasons offers spacious and well-decorated units. Limited restaurant choices available within a short to moderate drive.

TIMBERLAND INN ($$), 1271 Mt. St. Helens Way, Castle Rock; off I-5, Exit 49. Access to east side of monument via State Highway 504. ☎ (360) 274-6002. 40 rooms. While there are more lodging choices about a dozen miles to the south in Longview, this is the closest good choice to the west side of the monument. Nice rooms and larger family suites available ($$$). Restaurants nearby.

❖ CAMPING

While there isn't any camping within the monument borders, a couple of Forest Service-run sites are nearby. Reservations are required and can be made through the U.S. Forest Service at ☎ (800) 280-2267. Both campgrounds admit RVs. Call for current rates and stay limitations.

CAMPGROUNDS AT A GLANCE		
NAME	LOCATION	SITES
Iron Creek (east side)	Forest Route 25 at the junction of Forest Route 76, 8 miles from the monument.	98
Kalma Horse (south side)	Forest Route 81, six miles north of Cougar and 1 mile west of the monument.	10

DINING

There are no eateries within the monument itself.

NEARBY COMMUNITIES

WALDO'S ($$), 51 Cowlitz Avenue, Castle Rock; one mile west of I-15, Exit 49. ☎ (360) 274-7486. American food. Popular local place with good selection of steak, prime rib, fresh fish and seafood, as well as some pasta dishes. Nice atmosphere and service.

WHERE DO WE GO FROM HERE?

Suggested Trip 9 includes Mount St. Helens along with many other sights in Washington. However, since Mt. St. Helens isn't far from the Oregon border, you can opt to include it in a trip that visits the **Columbia River Gorge** and/or the **Oregon coast** or extend it farther south to **Crater Lake National Park**.

THE NORTHWEST

NORTH CASCADES NATIONAL PARK & ROSS LAKE NRA

These two adjacent areas contain majestic ice-covered mountain peaks and canyons. Ross Lake Recreation Area actually is an L-shaped strip of land that separates the northern and southern portions of North Cascades. There are more than 300 glaciers in North Cascades alone. In addition, rushing rivers and brilliant green glacial lakes add to the breathtaking vistas. Many of the park's peaks are over 8,000 feet and the highest is 9,127-foot Mount Shuksan. These tower above the valley where the North Cascades Highway (SR 20) runs, taking you into this pristine wilderness of unimaginable beauty.

> ### ❖ DID YOU KNOW?
>
> *Many of the lakes in the Ross Lake National Recreation Area are the result of hydroelectric projects that supply power for the city of Seattle.*

FACTS & FIGURES

Location/Gateways/Getting There: It is about 120 miles from the city of Seattle to the heart of the Ross Lake area, an easy drive via I-5 to Burlington and then via the highly scenic North Cascades Highway (SR 20). The trip from Seattle takes less than three hours.

Year Established: North Cascades was created in 1968, as was Ross Lake.

Size: North Cascades is 504,781 acres (789 square miles). Ross Lake is 117,574 acres (184 square miles).

Admission Fee: There is no charge for entering either area.

Climate/When to Go: Summer is the best time to visit as the sun is likely to be out and the temperatures will be comfortable. The park road is open from April through the middle of November, depending upon the amount of snowfall.

Contact Information: Information for both areas can be obtained from the Superintendent, North Cascades National Park, 2105 State Hwy 20, Sedro Wooley, WA 98284. ☎ (360) 856-5700.

AUTO TOUR/ SHORT STOPS

Ross Lake National Recreation Area lies right in the middle of the National Park. Essentially, the two parks can be considered as one. SR 20 provides easy access to what nature has to offer in the vast area of Ross Lake. (We'll describe some ways to see the interior of the North Cascades a bit later.)

About 20 miles before you enter the recreation area, the scenery along **SR 20** becomes quite splendid. There are mountain vistas, rivers and canyons, some of which can be easily seen from roadside rest areas. As the highway cuts through the recreation area itself, the views become even more spectacular. When you reach the **Diablo** area there are several short nature trails and attractive gardens that have been developed in connection with the Skagit Hydroelectric project (see *Special Activities*). Ross Lake itself is visible from observation points just past Diablo.

We suggest that you continue 25 miles past the NRA (still on SR 20) until you reach the **Washington Pass**. Although the pass is not in either North Cascades or Ross Lake (it is in the neighboring Okanogan National Forest), there is a scenic overlook here that faces the peaks of the southern North Cascades and it is one of the most dramatic views we've ever seen. A short trail leads to the overlook at an elevation of 5,500 feet. The scenery along the entire stretch of road in this area justifies the additional mileage. On the way back you will get an excellent view of Liberty Bell Mountain as you reenter the park. This is an area of especially rugged peaks.

Allow 2½ hours for the driving portion of your visit.

GETTING OUT/LONGER STOPS

There are a number of longer trails originating from the Skagit project in Diablo, including some leading to the Diablo Dam. The next section, however, outlines a better way to see these sights.

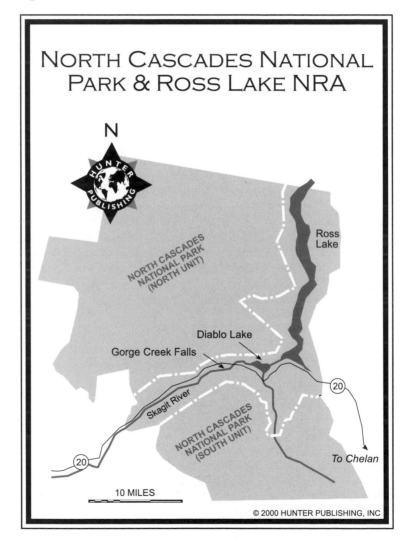

SPECIAL ACTIVITIES

❖ SKAGIT HYDROELECTRIC PROJECT

North Cascades is not a highly developed park, and even better-developed Ross Lake has relatively few ranger-conducted activities. But the Seattle City Light Company, which operates the hydro project, conducts a fantastic four-hour trip that includes a home-style lunch. After a brief orientation film you take a ride to the top of **Sourdough Mountain** on a large open platform that dates from the power project's construction. During your 560-foot ascent you will have great views of mountain peaks, glacial valleys and emerald-colored lakes. At the top a short walk leads to a boat dock and you will take a 20-minute cruise to one of the power houses at Ross Dam in the huge hydroelectric project – all amid wonderful scenery. You return the same way you came.

Very little time is spent in the industrial portion of the project; this is primarily an opportunity to see some great scenery. Short of backpacking into the interior of North Cascades, this is the best way to see the natural beauty of this area. This not-to-be-missed tour operates from the middle of June through the end of August. Departures are Thursday through Monday at 11 and on Saturday and Sunday only during September. Reservations are recommended and can be made by writing to **Skagit Tours**, 500 Newhalem Street, Rockport, WA 98283. The cost is $25, including lunch. You can also take a shorter (1½-hour) trip that tours Diablo Dam and takes a ride up the incline. This tour costs $5 (no lunch) and departs Thursday through Monday at 10 am, 1 pm and 3 pm; and at 1:30 on Saturdays during September. Call ☎ (206) 684-3030 for further information.

❖ LAKE CHELAN

There is one other option that includes marvelous scenery and a pleasant boat journey. It requires almost 200 miles of additional driving and a considerable amount of time. Continue on SR 20 past the Washington Pass Overlook described earlier, then onto SR 153 and US 97 until you arrive at the town of Chelan. All-day steamer trips on Lake Chelan will actually take you into the southernmost portion of North Cascades National Park. The scenery is absolutely beautiful and penetrates a wilderness area that cannot be reached by road. For additional information on the boat trips, contact the **Lake Chelan Boat Company** at ☎ (509) 682-2224. Fares run $40-50 for adults.

ACCOMMODATIONS

❖ HOTELS & MOTELS

INSIDE THE PARK/RECREATION AREA

DIABLO LAKE RESORT ($-$$), just above Diablo Dam. ☎ (360) 386-4429. 18 rooms. Basic housekeeping cottages make this suitable only for those who expect little. Lovely location. There is a restaurant, grocery store and boat rental facility.

NEARBY COMMUNITIES

Choices are rather limited in this remote region. Sedro Wooley, 50 miles to the east, offers the best selection of places if you're heading to or from that direction. For those who plan to explore the interior of North Cascades via boat from Chelan, that community has accommodations as well.

> NOTE: *You won't be able to stay in Chelan and tour the park and/or recreation area by car in one day.*

THREE RIVERS INN ($$), 210 Ball Street, Sedro Wooley; State Highway 20, near the junction of State Highway 9. ☎ (360) 855-2626. Rate includes full breakfast. 40 rooms. Good-sized units that are nicely decorated and extremely comfortable. Many units have patio or balcony. Swimming pool. Good restaurant on the premises.

WESTVIEW RESORT MOTEL ($$$), 2312 Woodin Avenue, Chelan; US 97A on the west side of town. ☎ (509) 682-4396. 25 rooms. Nice property with well-kept rooms and a pleasant setting. Minutes from lakefront and boat trip departures. A quarter of the units are efficiencies.

❖ CAMPING

CAMPGROUNDS AT A GLANCE			
NAME	LOCATION	SITES	COST
Colonial Creek	Ross Lake NRA corridor, State Hwy 20.	163	$10 per day
Goodell Creek	Ross Lake NRA corridor, State Hwy 20.	21	$7 per day
Hozomeen	Ross Lake NRA corridor, State Hwy 20.	122	Free
Newhalem Creek	Ross Lake NRA corridor, State Hwy 20.	128	$10 per day

All campgrounds have a 14-day limit and accept RVs.

DINING

INSIDE THE PARK/RECREATION AREA

Aside from the acceptable DIABLO LAKE RESORT (see above), there are no eating places for walk-in visitors.

> ❖ **TIP**
>
> *If you take the Skagit-Seattle City Light Tour, the admission price includes a family-style country dinner.*

NEARBY COMMUNITIES

Don't expect to find any culinary delights along State Highway 20 anywhere near the park and recreation area. Coming from the west, you will see several roadside cafés in the towns of

THE NORTHWEST

Concrete, Rockport and Marblemount. These are decent for lunch.

WHERE DO WE GO FROM HERE?

Suggested Trip 9 includes both Ross Lake and the North Cascades. However, the region's relative proximity to Seattle means that it can be included in a number of alternative trips using Seattle as a base. Certainly **Mount Rainier, Olympic National Parks** and the **San Juan Islands** can be included. Also, once you get back to the junction of I-5, the Canadian border is very close, so a trip to beautiful **Manning Provincial Park** (located just over the US border and looking back into the States) is also possible.

OLYMPIC NATIONAL PARK

O ccupying the major portion of the Olympic Peninsula, this is one of the wildest areas in the nation. In fact, the road network is deliberately confined to just a few miles near the edge of the park in several places, so that the wilderness will be preserved. The landscape here is some of the most diverse in the National Park System, with 57 miles of rocky beaches to glacier-covered mountain peaks. And, of course, there is the rain forest for which the area is so famous. The centerpiece of the park is 7,965-foot Mount Olympus, a glacial mountain that appears even taller because it rises so abruptly from the nearby shoreline. The park boasts extraordinary meadows of wildflowers and dozens of varieties of trees, including some of America's tallest. This great diversity has made Olympic a treasured national park as well as a World Heritage Park because of its great biological and geological significance. There is something for everyone in Olympic, one of America's largest parks and among its most ravishing beauties!

FACTS & FIGURES

Location/Gateways/Getting There: Encircled by US 101 on northwest Washington's Olympic Peninsula, the headquarters area of the park is at Port Angeles, on the north coast. To this point it is 178 miles from Seattle via I-5 and US 101, a drive of just under four hours. It is less than 100 miles if you take the ferry from Seattle to Bremerton and then take SR 3 and 104 into US 101. The driving time will be cut in half, but the total travel time is not significantly different because of the ferry trip. However, this is certainly a more relaxing and scenic way to get to the park. Ferry service is frequent. **Washington State Ferries**, ☎ (800) 843-3779.

Year Established: The interior was first sighted by European explorers in 1774, but it was not really traversed until the 1890s. The area became a national monument in 1909 and, finally, a national park in 1938.

Size: 914,576 miles (1,429 square miles), three-fourths the size of Delaware.

Admission Fee: $10.

Climate/When to Go: The Olympic Peninsula has mild winters and cool summers. It's one of the wettest areas in the United States, with much of the rain forest receiving over 150 inches of precipitation a year and more than 200 inches usually falling on Mount Olympus itself. However, most of this comes in the form of winter snowfalls and rains in spring and fall. The summer is relatively dry. Combine this with the fact that many roads are closed from October through late June, and it is clear that the best time for a visit is during July, August or early September.

Contact Information: Superintendent, Olympic National Park, 600 East Park Avenue, Port Angeles, WA 98362. ☎ (360) 452-0330.

THE NORTHWEST

AUTO TOUR / SHORT STOPS

The network of paved roads does not penetrate the interior of the park, and even the unpaved roads – which are often very difficult to negotiate – only skirt the edges of this vast domain. (Trailers, by the way, are not recommended for visitors to the park.) Yet, US 101, which surrounds most of the perimeter of the park, has several spurs that provide good access to many of the most significant of Olympic's features. We will describe your *Auto Tour* in a counter-clockwise direction, beginning at Port Angeles.

The park begins right at the city limits with a narrow strip of land that includes the Visitor Center and it is also the starting point for Hurricane Ridge Road. The **visitor center** has excellent exhibits and films on the park, but its best feature is the **Pioneer Memorial Museum**, which documents the lives and artifacts of the area's early settlers.

Now you are ready to begin your drive up to **Hurricane Ridge Road**. The road rises sharply from the low foothills and will eventually reach an elevation of over 5,200 feet in less than 20 miles. It is not a difficult road to drive and there are a few scenic turnouts where you can stop and catch your breath. At **Hurricane Ridge**, the rewards are great. From here you can look southward into the park's interior, with a view of mighty Mount Olympus and scores of other lofty peaks, many perpetually covered with snow and ice. Looking north, you will see the steep ridge you just navigated. If visibility is good you will be able to see beyond Port Angeles to the Strait of Juan de Fuca, which separates the United States from Canada's Vancouver Island. (If it is really clear, the island will actually be visible.) A stroll around the top of Hurricane Ridge during the summer will take you through a delightfully colorful alpine meadow.

> ❖ **TIP**
>
> *Get a bite to eat at Hurricane Lodge and take in the view from the deck.*

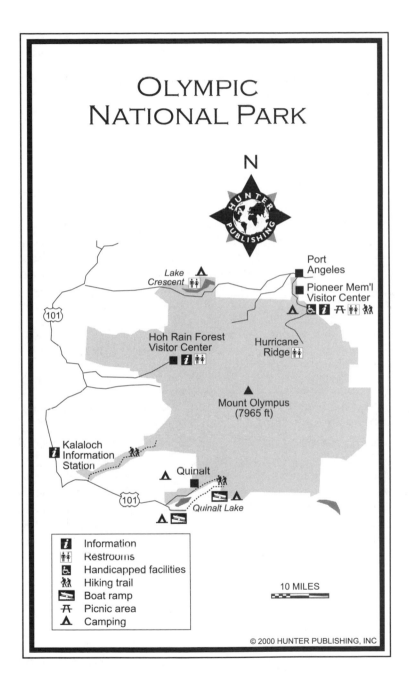

OLYMPIC NATIONAL PARK

N

Lake Crescent

Port Angeles

Pioneer Mem'l Visitor Center

Hoh Rain Forest Visitor Center

Hurricane Ridge

Mount Olympus (7965 ft)

Kalaloch Information Station

Quinalt

Quinalt Lake

i Information
†♦ Restrooms
♿ Handicapped facilities
🏃 Hiking trail
🚤 Boat ramp
π Picnic area
▲ Camping

10 MILES

© 2000 HUNTER PUBLISHING, INC

THE NORTHWEST

More adventurous folks travel from Hurricane Ridge along the crest to **Obstruction Peak** via an eight-mile-long gravel road.

❖ **TIP**

When returning to the lowlands via the Hurricane Ridge Road, second gear is advisable as it is a 7% grade most of the way. You might find lower gear useful on the way up as well.

Another road leading from Port Angeles (five miles east to be more precise) up to the ridge is the 17-mile route Deer Park Road to – you guessed it! – **Deer Park**. Just as spectacular as Hurricane Ridge, if not even more so, this road has sharp turns and steep grades and requires some mountain driving experience. Trailers are discouraged. At the end of the road there is a short trail leading to the summit of **Blue Mountain**. At just over 6,000 feet, it affords a splendid view of the surrounding mountains as well as the Dungeness Valley. This road is generally closed during the winter.

Once back in the lowlands, head out on US 101 to your next stop, **Lake Crescent**. This large lake is 8½ miles long and, because it is over 600 feet deep, is a beautiful deep blue. And it is surrounded by mountains, which make it one of the loveliest lakes to be found anywhere. There are also some trails here (see next section).

It is about 50 miles to the next cutoff from US 101 at Forks. This is the 17-mile drive into the **Hoh Rain Forest**. You've probably seen the Amazon Jungle in many movies, but it doesn't have anything on the Hoh Forest! Everywhere there is green. The trees and vegetation are so thick that even if it rains you won't get too wet because the forest keeps most of the water from hitting the ground. What does reach you is more like a mist. At the road's end there is a visitor center and several trails which are described later. You have to leave by the same route you came in.

After working your way back to the highway, US 101 will now take you down to the coastal section of the park, along **Ruby**

Beach. This is a rugged area of seacoast and there are quite a few offshore rocks and islands to make the landscape all the more beautiful.

> NOTE: *Bathing is an option, but expect both the air and water to be chilly. Also, be aware of dangerous tides, especially near rocks.*

After leaving the coast area, it is less than 30 miles to the **Quinnault Road**. This short side road leads to another lush forest, the **Quinnault Rain Forest** at Queets.

> ❖ **TIP**
>
> *The second half of the road is unpaved, but if that troubles you, you needn't go any farther than the end of the paved portion to get an idea of what it is like.*

Returning to US 101 the road continues south. At US 12, head east and it will take you back to SR 8 and then I-5 to Seattle. The US 101 loop around the park is approximately 100 miles, and the several access roads into the park and back will add on another 100 miles, so there is quite a bit of driving to do, not to mention the other activities. You should allocate an entire day for the portion of the tour just described.

GETTING OUT/LONGER STOPS

❖ HIKING

There are several easy trails of interest in addition to the short ones in the vicinity of the lodge at Hurricane Ridge, some of which can be extended into longer walks if you want. Olympic is a hiker's paradise – it has more than 600 miles of trails. Many are long and lead into true wilderness areas. Those interested in this type of experience should stop at any ranger station or visi-

THE NORTHWEST

tor center for guidance in planning their trek. Following is a brief selection of some of the more popular trails.

At Lake Crescent there is a three-quarter-mile trail leading to beautiful **Marymere Falls**. Allow one hour for the round-trip. At the end of the road in the Hoh Rain Forest there are several trails, the best of which leads to the **Hall of the Mosses**. The dense forest floor is so thick here that you will not even hear your footsteps. This walk will give you a true appreciation of the rain forest. Allow at least one hour. The pretty **Elwha River Valley, Lake Mills** and **Olympic Hot Springs** are all accessible via a two-mile trail that begins at the lake. It is reached by taking a paved road for five miles off US 101, eight miles west of Port Angeles.

SPECIAL ACTIVITIES

In addition to Ruby Beach, the coastal section of Olympic Park has many deserted beaches. Many of these are reached via a detour from US 101 at the town of Forks. Drive 14 miles to the small village of Lapush. The scenery and swimming at these beaches is excellent, but most require a good hike to reach them. Warmer swimming, and we do mean a lot warmer, is available at pools by the **Sol Duc Hot Springs**. The 128° water is piped in from the springs to the pools. It is reached by a spur road leading south from US 101 just past the west side of Lake Crescent.

ACCOMMODATIONS

❖ HOTELS & MOTELS

INSIDE THE PARK

LAKE CRESCENT LODGE ($$-$$$$), 20 miles west of Port Angeles on Star Route 1 at Lake Crescent. ☎ (360) 928-3211. 52 rooms. Varied facilities ranging from lodge units (lowest priced) to cottages to "deluxe" motel units (highest). All are adequate.

The picturesque, quiet setting makes this a nice place to stay. Restaurant adjacent.

LOG CABIN RESORT ($$-$$$), at the Piedmont Recreaton Area (Lake Crescent), 3¼ miles off US 101. ☎ (360) 928-3325. 24 rooms. Basic units with simple decor are not overly big, but the location at the lake is beautiful. Peaceful and relaxing. Adequate restaurant on the premises.

SOL DUC HOT SPRINGS ($$), 30 miles west of Port Angeles and then 12 miles south of US 101. ☎ (360) 327-3583. 32 units. Comprised of 32 one-bedroom cottages, this facility is what remains of what was once intended to be an elegant European-style spa. The accommodations aren't of particularly high level, but you can take advantage of the natural mineral pools as well as a regular swimming pool. Restaurant on the premises.

NEARBY COMMUNITIES

DOUBLETREE HOTEL ($$-$$$), 221 North Lincoln Street, Port Angeles; in town on US 101 at the ferry terminal, about a mile from park entrance road. ☎ (360) 452-9215 or (800) 222-TREE. 187 rooms. First-class accommodations in a modern midrise facility. Some units have balconies. Those facing the Strait of Juan de Fuca have outstanding views – you can watch the ferries come in. Swimming pool; two restaurants.

FORKS MOTEL ($$), 351 Forks Avenue, Forks; south of town on US 101, 30 miles from Olympic's coastal section and 54 miles from the main park entrance to Hurricane Ridge. ☎ (360) 374-6243 or (800) 544-3416. 73 rooms. Variety of accommodations including kitchen units, suite with Jacuzzi and many rooms with refrigerator/microwave. Rooms have nice decor and are a good size. Restaurant within short drive. Convenient location either for national park's beaches and the Hoh Rain Forest.

PORTSIDE INN ($$), 1510 East Front Street, Port Angeles; at the east end of town (US 101), three miles from park entrance road. ☎ (360) 452-4015. 109 rooms. Pretty motor inn with comfortable and tastefully decorated units. Some mini-suites available. Many rooms have refrigerators. Swimming pool and spa. Quite a few good restaurants nearby.

THE NORTHWEST

UPTOWN INN ($$), 101 E. 2nd Street, Port Angeles; in town, one block off US 101 via Laurel Street; about two miles from park entrance road. ☎ (360) 457-9434 or (800) 858-3812.

Situated atop a bluff, many rooms offer outstanding panoramas of the Strait or limited views of Olympic. This older inn was re-modeled several years ago. Good-sized units with coffee makers and refrigerators. Within a short distance of restaurants.

❖ CAMPING

There are almost 20 different campgrounds within Olympic National Park. The ones listed here are not deep into the remote interior and are grouped by approximate location. No reservations are accepted.

Call the park headquarters for full details.

CAMPGROUNDS AT A GLANCE			
NAME	LOCATION	SITES	COST
Access from US 101, along the park's northern edge:			
Elwha	Four miles south of US 101.	41	$8 per day
Boulder Creek	Twelve miles south of US 101.	50	$8 per day
Soleduck	Near the Sol Duc Hot Springs area.	84	$8 per day
Altaire	Four miles from US 101.	29	$8 per day
Lake Crescent/ Fairholm	At the west end of the lake.	87	$8 per day
Heart of the Hills	By Port Angeles at the start of the road to Hurricane Ridge.	105	$8 per day
Along the coast:			
Rialto Beach	US 101.	91	$8 per day
Kalalolch	US 101.	179	$8 per day

CAMPGROUNDS AT A GLANCE			
NAME	LOCATION	SITES	COST
Access from US 101, along the park's western edge:			
Hoh	At the end of road to Hoh Rain Forest.	95	$8 per day
Queets	At the end of the road to Queets.	26	$8 per day
July Creek	By Quinault Lake.	45	$8 per day

There is a 14-day limit at all sites. RVs are allowed at all of the above locations except Queets and July Creek.

DINING

INSIDE THE PARK

There are restaurants, coffee shops and snack bars in or adjacent to all of the accommodations within the park., as well as at Kalaloch along the coastal section. They range from adequate to slightly better and are mostly in the moderate price category.

The HURRICANE RIDGE LODGE ($-$$), at the end of the road to Hurricane Ridge, isn't any better than options in the park from a culinary standpoint, but it affords a magnificent view that can make any hamburger seem like a gourmet experience.

NEARBY COMMUNITIES

C'EST SI BON ($$$), 23 Cedar Park Road, Port Angeles; east of town on US 101. ☎ (360) 452-8888. French cuisine. Port Angeles' most upscale restaurant, serving excellent French dishes in an attractive dining room and with a view of the Olympics.

EL AMIGO RESTAURANT ($-$$), 1017 E. 1st Street, Port Angeles; downtown. ☎ (360) 457-6477. Mexican food. Popular place for large servings of authentic traditional Mexican dishes (no Tex-Mex) in a colorful and festive dining room. Friendly service. Great for family dining.

THE NORTHWEST

SMOKEHOUSE RESTAURANT ($-$$), 193161 US 101, Forks; a mile north of town at the junction of State Highway 110. ☎ (360) 374-6258. American food. Good chow, mostly featuring steak and seafood. The salmon – an especially good choice – is caught locally and smoked on the premises . Nice salad bar.

TRAYLOR'S RESTAURANT ($$-$$$), 3256 US 101 East, Port Angeles; three miles east of town. ☎ (360) 452-3833. American food. Good selection of steak and seafood dishes along with several American favorites served in a pleasant atmosphere and in ample portions.

WHERE DO WE GO FROM HERE?

Olympic National Park is part of *Suggested Trip 9*, which includes several national parks throughout highly scenic western Washington. If you want an alternative, try taking the car/passenger ferry from Port Angeles to **Victoria**, British Columbia. There are many beautiful sights, both man-made and natural, on Vancouver Island. For ocean lovers there is another alternative: Rather than heading back inland towards Seattle, continue down the Washington coast and on into **Oregon**, where the coastal scenery is even more spectacular.

SAWTOOTH NATIONAL RECREATION AREA

This high mountain region sits at the convergence of three mountain ranges and provides some spectacular alpine scenery. In addition to dozens of perpetually snow-capped mountain peaks, there are countless lakes, thick forests and the Salmon River churning its away in an L-shape through the high country. As a recreation area, the Sawtooth is a great venue for almost any sort of outdoor recreation from fishing to skiing, and nature lovers will find great scenery. If you like cool weather, you're in for a special treat, as the Sawtooth rarely sees temperatures climb much above the mid 70s. So get your jacket and your camera and enjoy the greatest natural splendor that Idaho has to offer.

FACTS & FIGURES

Location/Gateways/Getting There: Located in the central portion of Idaho, the Sawtooth can be reached from Boise by taking SR 21 north. It is about 130 miles to the northern entrance of the recreation area, a drive of about 2½ hours. Alternatively, you can reach the Sawtooth by taking I-84 east to Bliss and then going east on US 26 to SR 75. The latter road travels north to the park's southern entrance about 180 miles away.

> ❖ **TIP**
>
> *If you're not going to be doing anything else in addition to the Sawtooth, a loop covering both access routes will be the fastest round-trip to Boise.*

Year Established: Administered by the US Forest Service, the Sawtooth was established in 1972.

Size: 729,322 acres (1,140 square miles), roughly two-thirds the size of Rhode Island.

Admission Fee: There is no charge.

Climate/When to Go: The town of Stanley, located centrally within the recreation area, is one of the coldest places in the country. If you're coming to take advantage of the skiing facilities, then winter is fine; otherwise, a visit should be limited to the middle of summer. Spring and fall can bring an unexpected snow and temperatures well below freezing.

Contact Information: Sawtooth National Recreation Area Headquarters, Star Route, Ketchum, ID 83340. ☎ (208) 727-5013.

AUTO TOUR/SHORT STOPS

The excellent road system, along with some short hikes, provides easy access to virtually all important sights within the huge Sawtooth National Recreation Area. There are three scenic byways – the Sawtooth, Salmon River and Ponderosa Pine Scenic Byways. The first two are portions of SR 75, which traverses most of the recreation area. The Ponderosa Pine is SR 21 and provides the most direct route to Boise. All three byways converge in the town of Stanley.

❖ SAWTOOTH SCENIC BYWAY

This route begins as soon as you enter the recreation area north of the resort towns of Ketchum and Sun Valley. It takes in about 55 miles of beautiful scenery. The recreation area headquarters and a visitor center are immediately inside the border. About a dozen miles after that the road will quickly start to climb and, after a series of turns and switchbacks, will reach the fabulous **Galena Overlook**, offering panoramic views of the Sawtooth Valley and the Salmon River. This is probably the single most dramatic view in the entire recreation area. Snow-capped peaks vie for your attention with rugged, rocky mountains and broad meadows. You'll also have a good view of the road ahead, which drops sharply into the river valley after you depart from the overlook. The headwaters of the Salmon River are just a few miles from this point. Once you reach the valley floor there are several more stops on this scenic byway. Pretty **Alturas and Pettit Lakes** are reached by a 2½-mile spur off the main road. Soon after, the **Sawtooth Fish Hatchery**, which raises salmon and steelhead trout, is an interesting stop. **Redfish and Little Redfish Lakes** are just a short drive off the main road. These attractive lakes have a magnificent mountain backdrop. There is also a visitor center at this point where you can take ranger-guided interpretive walks. Allow two to three hours for this byway.

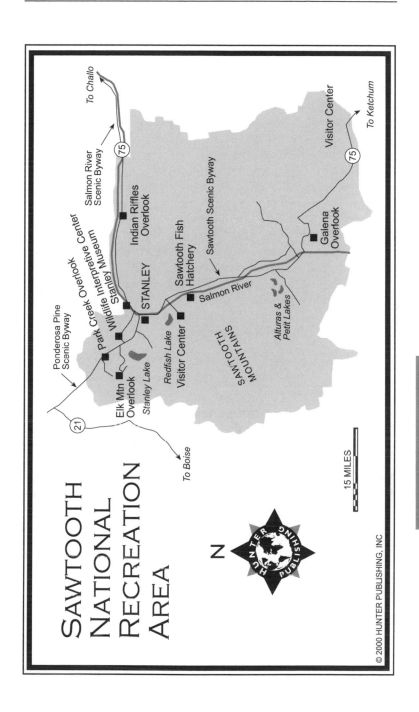

SAWTOOTH NATIONAL RECREATION AREA

To Challo

To Ketchum

Visitor Center

75

75

Salmon River
Scenic Byway

Indian Riffles
Overlook

Sawtooth Scenic Byway

Galena
Overlook

Sawtooth Fish
Hatchery

STANLEY

Salmon River

Park Creek Overlook Center
Wildlife Interpretive Museum
Stanley Museum

Ponderosa Pine
Scenic Byway

Redfish Lake
Visitor Center

Alturas &
Petit Lakes

SAWTOOTH MOUNTAINS

Elk Mtn
Overlook

Stanley Lake

21

To Boise

15 MILES

N

© 2000 HUNTER PUBLISHING, INC

THE NORTHWEST

❖ SALMON RIVER SCENIC BYWAY

Immediately after leaving the town of Stanley you should make a brief stop at the **Stanley Museum**, a mile past 190 on State Route 75. It's open daily 9-5, Memorial Day through Labor Day (no telephone). A former ranger station, it now documents the pioneer era in and around Stanley. From outside the log cabin museum there is a great view of the huge basin in which the town lies and a line of majestic mountains running in either direction as far as the eye can see. Along this byway are a couple of points of interest. The **Sunbeam Hot Springs** is where 170° water enters the chilly Salmon River. A little farther down the road is the **Indian Riffles Overlook**, which offers views of salmon spawning beds. After visiting Indian Riffles, turn around and make your way back to Stanley. The road runs alongside the river in a heavily forested area and makes for a most pleasant drive. The round-trip from Stanley to Indian Riffles and back covers 30 miles and you can do it in about an hour.

❖ PONDEROSA PINE SCENIC BYWAY

This trip covers less than 25 miles and, with the stops, should take you about 90 minutes. There's plenty of great scenery. The **Stanley Creek Wildlife Interpretive Area** has a short trail that traverses an area of wetlands and describes the flora and fauna. Beautiful **Stanley Lake** is four miles off the byway and is the loveliest of the many lakes in the recreation area. Nearby is the **Elk Mountain Overlook**, which looks down onto Stanley Lake. However, the most dramatic sight along the Ponderosa Pine Byway is the **Park Creek Overlook**, with close-up views of the perennially snow-capped Sawtooth Mountains. In the foreground is a tranquil meadow filled with wildflowers during the summer. It is often a good spot for seeing deer and other wildlife. Unless you're continuing on to Boise, this is where you should turn around. On the way back you have the option of taking a 30-minute detour on the **Nip & Tuck Road**. This dirt road was the original route through the Stanley Basin and is another great place for seeing wildflowers.

GETTING OUT/LONGER STOPS

❖ HIKING

While the Auto Tour has plenty of opportunity to stretch your legs, the Sawtooth has an abundance of longer trails extending from around 1½ miles to more than 10. They range from easy to difficult.

One of the easiest is the 1½-mile **Lilly Lake Trail**, near the Redfish Lake area. The trailhead is reached via a short boat ride from the end of the road at Redfish Lake (it's run by the NPS). Most of the longer and more difficult trails head up into the mountains from the basin.

SPECIAL ACTIVITIES

The Sawtooth is a great place for **ATVing, mountain biking** and, during the winter, **skiing** and **snowmobiling**. **Mountain climbing** on the Sawtooth Range is another option for the adventure traveler. **Rafting** on the calmer portions of the Salmon River and **river running** on the wilder portions are also staples of summer activity in the recreation area. The river season runs from April through December.

THE SALMON RIVER RAPIDS

The Salmon River Rapids drop an average of 15 feet every mile. While this may not seem like much to the uninitiated, it makes for some fierce whitewater in places. Most areas offer only Class I or II rapids, but some areas rise to Class III and IV, which requires experienced navigators.

Information on outfitters for all of these activities can be obtained from any recreation area visitor center or in the town of Stanley. Or you can try one of the following:

THE NORTHWEST

Whitewater Adventures. . . . . ☎ (800) 432-4611
Sawtooth Guide Service . . . . ☎ (208) 774-9947
Lost River Outfitters. . . . . ☎ (208) 726-1706
Redfish Corrals. . . . . ☎ (208) 774-3311
Valley Ranch Outfitters . . . . ☎ (208) 774-3470

ACCOMMODATIONS

❖ HOTELS & MOTELS

INSIDE THE RECREATION AREA

JERRY'S MOTEL ($$), State Highway 21, Stanley; a mile north of the junction with State Highway 75. ☎ (208) 774-3566. 9 rooms. Clean and comfortable rooms located along the picturesque Salmon River with views of Sawtooth's magnificent scenery. Restaurant within a short drive. General store on premises.

MOUNTAIN VILLAGE LODGE ($$), at the junction of State Highways 21 and 75, Stanley. ☎ (208) 774-3661. 63 rooms. In the heart of Stanley, a 100-person town right smack in the middle of the Sawtooth National Recreation Area. This is the biggest lodging establishment in the area and, while not fancy, is a couple of notches up from the other places in the vicinity. Restaurant on the premises. General store and other facilities adjacent.

STANLEY OUTPOST ($$-$$$), State Highway 21, Stanley; half a mile west from the junction of State Highway 75. ☎ (208) 774-3646. 6 rooms. Nice and comfortable log cabins with surprisingly modern interiors. All units (except for one) have full kitchen facilities, and there's a restaurant just a couple of minutes away by car.

NEARBY COMMUNITIES

CLARION INN ($$-$$$), 600 N. Main Street, Ketchum; on State Highway 75 in center of town, about nine miles south of the recreation area's southern entrance. ☎ (208) 726-5900 or (800) CLARION. Rate includes continental breakfast. 57 rooms. Although the exterior of this modern facility is rather drab, the guest rooms are spacious and wonderfully inviting, with beautiful furnishings and interesting decor. Swimming pool. Many restaurants within walking distance or a short drive away.

ELKHORN RESORT ($$-$$$), 100 Elkhorn Road, Sun Valley; in the Sun Valley Resort area, about two miles northeast of State Highway 75 in Ketchum and approximately 12 miles from the southern entrance to Sawtooth National Recreation Area. ☎ (208) 622-4511 or (800) ELKHORN. 132 rooms. First-rate accommodations in a lovely building set amid the natural splendors of the Sun Valley Resort, a little community in the style of a Tyrolean ski village that has loads of restaurants and shopping opportunities. A delightful place to stay.

Also within this resort is the SUN VALLEY LODGE ($$$$), which is more elegant and only an option for those without a budget.

HEIDELBERG INN ($$$), 1908 Warm Springs Road, Ketchum; 1¼ miles west of State Highway 75 and about 10 miles from the Sawtooth National Recreation Area. ☎ (208) 726-5361. Rate includes continental breakfast. 30 rooms. Large and attractive rooms in quiet location with good mountain views. Swimming pool and other recreational facilities. Restaurants nearby.

❖ CAMPING

Four campgrounds (Glacier View, Elk Creek, Point and Easley) accept reservations, ☎ (800) 280-CAMP. All others operate on a first-come, first-served basis. The Sawtooth has an abundance of campgrounds, so we've grouped them by area: **Stanley Lake** has nine campgrounds with 89 sites; **Redfish Lake** offers eight campgrounds with 196 sites; the **Alturas Lake** area has three campgrounds with 55 sites; **Salmon River Canyon** features eight campgrounds with 128 sites; and the **Wood River Corridor** has four campgrounds with 76 sites.

Daily rates vary from $6 to $16. Stay limitations may be imposed. RVs are allowed in many of the campgrounds. Call the recreation area's general number for specific information.

THE NORTHWEST

DINING

INSIDE THE RECREATION AREA

MOUNTAIN VILLAGE RESTAURANT ($-$$) is inside the Mountain Village Lodge (see listing above). ☎ (208) 774-3317. American food. Good selection of food in a friendly, family atmosphere (log-cabin style) with a great view of the Sawtooth Mountains.

NEARBY COMMUNITIES

DESPERADO'S ($), 4th and Washington Streets, Ketchum; one block west of State Highway 75 via 4th Street. ☎ (208) 726-3068. Mexican food. Authentic popular Mexican dishes served in a pleasant atmosphere. The chili rellenos are excellent.

KETCHUM GRILL ($$), East Avenue & Fifth Street, Ketchum; two blocks east of State Highway 75. ☎ (208) 726-4660. American food. Casual dining (indoor or outdoor) with good selection of items ranging from burgers and pizza to full dinners. Nice wine list.

The SUN VALLEY LODGE DINING ROOM ($$$) is inside the Sun Valley Lodge at 1 Sun Valley Road, about two miles east of State Highway 75 in Ketchum. ☎ (208) 622-2150. Continental cuisine. Fine dining with an extensive wine list. The surroundings are simply gorgeous, although the atmosphere is more on the casual side (no jackets, but no jeans). Superb presentation and service.

WHERE DO WE GO FROM HERE?

Centrally located in the middle of Idaho, the Sawtooth National Recreation Area is a focal point of *Suggested Trip 6*. It is also possible to combine a visit to Sawtooth with **Yellowstone** and **Grand Teton National Parks** to the west, or with **Glacier National Park** to the north. The extensive national forests to the immediate north of Sawtooth are an outdoor adventurer's paradise. However, there is a lack of paved roads in that region.

ALASKA

DENALI NATIONAL PARK & PRESERVE

Mt. McKinley is the highest point in North America at 20,320 feet. The almost-four-mile-high giant was known to the Native Americans of Alaska as Denali – "The Great One" – a fitting tribute to one of the world's best known mountains. But Denali National Park is more than just this single peak. Besides numerous other mountains (some of which are among America's highest), there are other features rarely or never seen in the Lower 48. Tundra, an arctic landscape, is one, and the underlying permafrost is another. Numerous glaciers, including the largest in the United States, are a part of the Denali scene, as is a diverse wildlife that encompasses about 200 different species. Despite all of these wonders it is, perhaps, the simple vastness of Denali that is most overpowering to the visitor; that, and the wilderness spirit which pervades the mountain and the area around it. So, come share that spirit.

FACTS & FIGURES

Location/Gateways/Getting There: The park occupies an immense tract of land in southcentral Alaska. Almost all park visitors will originate their trip in Anchorage. The 240-mile trip from there is an easy drive via SR 1 north to SR 3 north. (The latter road is also known as the George Parks Highway.) The entrance to Denali is 125 miles south of Fairbanks, also via SR 3.

417

The **Alaska Railroad**, ☎ (800) 544-0552, provides a pleasant alternative to the drive and is a popular combination with Alaska cruise passengers. The railroad has direct service from Anchorage and the Denali station is situated right at the park's entrance. Service is daily from late May through the middle of September, weekly at other times of the year.

Year Established: Denali was originally known as Mt. McKinley National Park when it was established way back in 1917. The current name was adopted in 1980.

Size: A huge 4,741,800 acres (7,409 square miles), Denali is not quite as large as New Jersey. It would be the 48th biggest state in the nation all by itself.

Admission Fees: $10 per vehicle or $5 per person for those not entering by private car. In addition, road transportation via shuttle bus beyond Savage River (except for those with campground reservations) costs from $12 to $26 per adult, depending upon the distance.

Climate/When to Go: Although road and rail access to Denali is maintained throughout the year, only the hardiest of souls are likely to be able to tolerate touring during the interior Alaskan winter. Even spring and fall can be extremely cold and snow can occur at any time. The best months to visit are June through August.

Contact Information: Superintendent, Denali National Park, PO Box 9, Denali Park, AK 99755. ☎ (907) 683-2294.

AUTO TOUR/SHORT STOPS

Of course you want to see **Mount McKinley**, but don't be disappointed if you don't get a clear view of the Great One during your visit. The peak is often shrouded in clouds – up to 70% of the time during the summer months – but the entire mountain is unlikely to be entirely blocked from vision. The often clearer lower slopes and the clouds at the top make for a most unusual sight and even add a little to the almost legendary magic of North America's premier mountain.

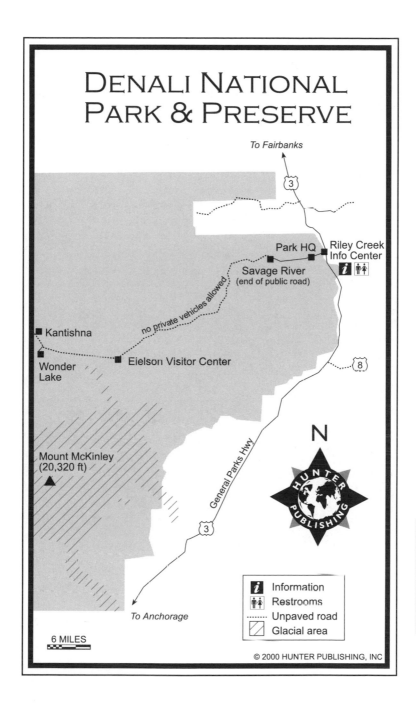

DENALI NATIONAL PARK & PRESERVE

To Fairbanks

(3)

Park HQ
Riley Creek
Info Center
i 👫

Savage River
(end of public road)

no private vehicles allowed

Kantishna

(8)

Wonder
Lake

Eielson Visitor Center

N

Mount McKinley
(20,320 ft)

General Parks Hwy

(3)

To Anchorage

i	Information
👫	Restrooms
··········	Unpaved road
▨	Glacial area

6 MILES

© 2000 HUNTER PUBLISHING, INC

ALASKA

419

Auto touring is quite limited in Denali. The portion of the road that is open to the public (those not having reserved camping reservations in the interior) goes only 15 miles from the Riley Creek entrance area to Savage River. Of course, your approach to Denali from the south via **AK 3** (which skirts the eastern edge of the park) is very scenic. Once inside, there is an information center at Riley Creek. Here, you can take the short **Horseshoe Lake Trail** near the railroad tracks. It leads to a vantage point above the pretty lake. The wild Nenana River is in the background. Along the road to Savage River you'll likely get some good shots of McKinley as well as see some wildlife. The unique land of Denali, consisting largely of taiga and tundra, is in evidence along this often windswept route. The many glaciers of Mt. McKinley and surrounding peaks are not distinguishable from this distance. Don't fret – just wait until you read about how to get closer in the *Special Activities* section.

Huge Denali National Park & Preserve is just smaller than the state of New Jersey.

GETTING OUT/LONGER STOPS

❖ HIKING

There are several longer trails in the Riley Creek/headquarters area. These include the **Rock Creek and Morino Loop Trails**. The latter has great views of the Alaska Railroad Bridge over Riley Creek. Denali is a great place for adventure hiking as few formal trails exist. You can do them on your own if you are experienced (that is, you won't get lost), or you can join one of the many ranger-led walks.

> NOTE: *Back-country permits are required for over-night hiking in Denali.*

❖ DOG KENNELS

An interesting stop is the dog kennels near the park headquarters. Rangers use sleds during the winter to get from one place to another (and to rescue stranded hikers), and these beautiful animals provide the fuel. Often, during the summer, sled demonstrations are given. Check at the kennel or the Riley Creek Information Center for the schedule. The demonstrations are free of charge.

SPECIAL ACTIVITIES

There are several ways to see the interior beyond Savage River without having to camp out in the wilderness. Those who wish to keep their feet planted on the ground can opt for either the park shuttle bus or one of several guided tours.

❖ ORGANIZED LAND TOURS

Shuttle buses run from Riley Creek to Wonder Lake, a distance of 85 miles. Buses depart every half-hour, beginning at 6 am. They stop to observe wildlife and to pick up and drop off passengers on a space-available basis. Reservations generally have

ALASKA

to be made in person and it is not uncommon for there to be a wait of two to three days.

> ### ❖ TIP
>
> *A limited number of seats on some shuttles can be reserved by phone,* ☎ *(800) 622-7275.*

Guided tours range from six to eight hours in length. Some include a box lunch. Fares range from $30-60. Contact **Natural History Tour**, ☎ (800) 276-7234, or **Tundra Wildlife Tours**, ☎ (907) 276-7234.

❖ FLIGHTSEEING

You can take a flightseeing trip over Denali either by airplane or helicopter. **ERA Helicopter Flightseeing Tours**, which offers frequent departures, is the most popular operator. Tours last either 50 or 75 minutes and cost $180-285. ☎ (800) 843-1947.

ACCOMMODATIONS

❖ HOTELS & MOTELS

INSIDE THE PARK

DENALI PARKS RESORTS ($$), just inside the park entrance off SR 3. ☎ (907) 276-7234 or (800) 276-7234. 534 rooms. A sprawling complex with varied accommodations and a good choice of dining facilities. Convenient for in-park tours, which can be arranged through the hotel's front desk staff.

NEARBY COMMUNITIES

DENALI BLUFFS HOTEL ($$$), George Parks Highway (SR 3), one mile north of park entrance. ☎ (907) 683-7000 or (800) 488-7002. 112 rooms. The newest facility in the vicinity of the park, the Bluffs features well-appointed and spacious rooms, as well as a tour desk.

DENALI PRINCESS LODGE ($$$), George Parks Highway (SR 3), 1½ miles north of the park entrance. ☎ (907) 683-2282 or (800) 426-0500. 280 rooms. Full-service luxury hotel owned and operated by Princess Cruise Line. Upscale atmosphere and accommodations.

DENALI RIVER CABINS ($$), George Parks Highway (SR 3), just south of the park entrance. ☎ (907) 683-2500. 50 rooms. Simple but clean and comfortable log cabin-style accommodations that fit nicely with the atmosphere of Denali.

DENALI WINDSOR LODGE ($$), George Parks Highway (SR 3), one mile north of the park entrance. ☎ (907) 683-1240 or (800) 208-0200. 48 rooms. A very attractive little property that nicely combines the look and feel of the wilderness with modern conveniences.

❖ CAMPING

CAMPGROUNDS AT A GLANCE			
NAME	LOCATION	SITES	COST
Riley Creek	By the entrance station.	102	$12 per day
Savage River	At end of the paved public access road.	34	$12 per day
Sanctuary River	Denali Park Rd (unpaved), past Savage River.	7	$12 per day
Teklanika	Denali Park Rd (unpaved), past Savage River.	50	$12 per day
Igloo Creek	Denali Park Rd (unpaved), past Savage River.	7	$12 per day
Wonder Lake	Denali Park Rd (unpaved), past Savage River.	20	$12 per day
Morino (walk-in)	West of Riley Creek.	67	$3 per day

ALASKA

No reservations are accepted. All campers must register at the Riley Creek Information Center. Road travel permits are required for RVs going beyond Savage River. RVs are allowed at Riley Creek, Savage River, Sanctuary River and Teklanika only.

Strict length restrictions apply at the latter two locations, so make advance inquiry before arriving in an RV. There is a 14-day limit at all areas.

DINING

INSIDE THE PARK

The DENALI PARKS RESORTS has several eating establishments ranging from snack bars/cafeterias to upscale full-service restaurants (price range $-$$$). These are described in the *Accommodations* section.

NEARBY COMMUNITIES

There aren't any towns with a recommended restaurant in the vicinity of the park entrance. However, the DENALI BLUFFS and the DENALI PRINCESS hotels both have a variety of food services (see above).

WHERE DO WE GO FROM HERE?

Denali isn't on any of our suggested itineraries because of its location. Many people visit Denali as an addition to an Alaskan cruise, arriving either by bus or via the Alaska Railroad.

If you're on your own in the Alaskan interior, there are a number of other sights that can be reached by car. These include **Wrangell-Saint Elias National Park** and the **Chugach State Park**. In addition, day-long boat tours from Anchorage and Seward can take you to **Kenai Fjords National Park, Prince William Sound, the Cook Inlet** and many other beautiful places.

HAWAII

HALEAKALA
NATIONAL PARK

Haleakala, or House of the Sun, is the crater of a dormant Hawaiian volcano (the last eruption in this vicinity was in 1790). It is one of the largest such craters in the world, measuring 7½ by 2½ miles, and more than 3,000 feet from the rim of the crater to its deepest recesses.

The many colors within the crater are highly unusual in a volcanic formation. Cinder cones throughout the crater give the appearance of a miniature mountain range, while other sections look like a desert. This, and the lack of vegetation in most of the crater, give it a moon-like appearance. Visibility within the crater varies greatly, practically from one minute to the next. Even on the sunniest days there are times when clouds will suddenly appear overhead and seem to become stuck in the crater. But wait a bit and they are likely to lift away, revealing the panoramic crater vista. It's an astonishing sight when cloud-filled as well. Vistas of the ocean and of the island of Maui below are also unforgettable from the House of the Sun.

FACTS & FIGURES

Location/Gateways/Getting There: Haleakala is in the eastern portion of the island of Maui, about 27 miles from the airport and town center of Kahului. It is, of course, just a short flight from Honolulu, if you are making your base there. From Kahului follow SRs 36, 37, 377 and 378 – in that sequence – to reach Haleakala.

Year Established: A part of the national park system since 1916 (as a section of Hawaii Volcanoes National Park), Haleakala was established as a separate national park in 1960.

Size: 28,655 acres (45 square miles).

Admission Fee: $10 for the main section. There is no admission fee at the Ohe'o Gulch.

Climate/When to Go: Although any time of the year is the right time to visit Hawaii in general, keep in mind that at the top of the crater it can be as much as 30° cooler than at sea level. So bring along a jacket, even if you are going to be in a bathing suit later in the day. If you are here in January or February you might even encounter a bit of snow. A sunny morning is the best time to visit the park throughout the year. In fact, for those willing to arise in the middle of the night, sunrise at Haleakala Crater is considered by many to be one of the most beautiful sights anywhere in the world!

Contact Information: Superintendent, Haleakala National Park, Box 369, Makawao, Maui, HI 96768. ☎ (808) 572-9306.

AUTO TOUR / SHORT STOPS

In the 27 miles from Kahului to the park you will climb from just above sea level to over 7,000 feet. Most of this altitude is gained during the second half of the trip. The road twists and turns constantly, with many switchbacks and steep grades. The drive is not as difficult as you might expect, but do keep your eyes on the road. There will be plenty of time for seeing the sights once you get there.

Just inside the entrance station, turn into **Hosmer Grove**. Here, a quarter-mile nature trail is surrounded by exotic plants with markers explaining the relationship of these plants to the surroundings.

> ❖ **DID YOU KNOW?**
>
> *The Silversword plant grows only at Haleakala. It can be seen in several parts of the park.*

Within the park itself, the road continues to climb until it reaches the summit of Puu Ulaula at 10,023 feet. Before getting there, however, there are two outstanding overlooks. The first is **Leleiwi Overlook**, which offers a good view of the crater. More significantly, if the cloud conditions are just right, your shadow will be projected onto the clouds in the crater. Rainbows are also frequently seen from this vantage point.

A bit farther up the road is **Kalahaku Overlook**, with a panoramic view of the crater and many of its cinder cones. Next is the visitor center, where there are numerous exhibits on the crater and the environment of Haleakala. Beyond the visitor center is the summit of **Puu Ulaula**, which provides vistas of the crater and dramatic views of the ocean and the valley of the isle of Maui far below.

The road ends at the summit. You should allocate half a day to see the main section of the park, including the round-trip drive from Kahului.

❖ KIPAHULU DISTRICT/OHE'O GULCH

This easternmost section of the park slopes downward to the ocean. In the Kipahulu District, also commonly referred to as the Ohe'o Gulch, you can see a fine example of a rain forest, several scenic pools and beautiful waterfalls, as well as a dramatic vista where the stream reaches the ocean in an area of rocky headlands.

The park road to the House of the Sun's crater does not connect with this section. To get there from Kahului or from the main portion of the park, it is a 70-mile drive each way. Fortunately, the bulk of the drive (via SR 36 from Kahului or 365 if you're on the way back from the House of the Sun; and then via SR 360) is on the spectacular and famous **Hana Road**. It has breathtaking vistas of the ocean and mountains, passing many beautiful attractions. This is definitely not among the straightest roads in the world; in fact, there are in excess of 600 turns. So, put on a recording of the *Long and Winding Road* and enjoy every single one of those turns.

Although Ohe'o Gulch is quite beautiful in its own right, it may seem anticlimactic to some visitors after the panorama seen along the Hana Road, which is surely one of the world's most beautiful drives. It isn't within the scope of this book to describe all the sights of the Hana Road, but all you have to do is stop, get out and look wherever you see something that interests you.

Allow a full day for the complete round-trip to Hana and the Gulch, including sightseeing.

GETTING OUT/LONGER STOPS

❖ HIKING

Back to the crater area for a few moments now. While most of the park's trails go into the crater and are long and difficult for the casual visitor, there is one trail that you should definitely consider. The fairly steep **White Hill Trail**, near the visitor center, is just over a quarter-mile long and will take about 45 minutes to complete. It provides some exceptional views that nicely juxtapose the barren crater with the color surrounding it.

There is also the **Rim Trail**, which extends around the rim of the crater and covers nearly 20 miles.

In the vicinity of O'heo Gulch are the five-mile **Kuloa Loop Trail**, an easy route along the stream that passes several different waterfalls; and the 1½-mile **Pipiwai Trail** that goes to two splendid waterfalls.

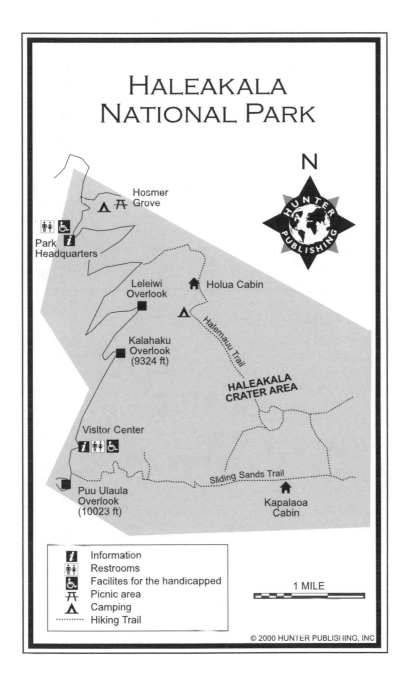

HALEAKALA
NATIONAL PARK

N

Hosmer Grove

Park Headquarters

Leleiwi Overlook

Holua Cabin

Kalahaku Overlook (9324 ft)

Halemauu Trail

HALEAKALA CRATER AREA

Visitor Center

Sliding Sands Trail

Puu Ulaula Overlook (10023 ft)

Kapalaoa Cabin

HAWAII

i Information
Restrooms
Facilites for the handicapped
Picnic area
Camping
.... Hiking Trail

1 MILE

© 2000 HUNTER PUBLISHING, INC

SPECIAL ACTIVITIES

❖ HORSEBACK RIDING

For those who want to venture into the crater but feel they won't be able to climb back out, there are guided horseback tours available. Contact **Pony Express Tours** at ☎ (808) 667-2200.

> NOTE: *If you are apprehensive about driving the road to and from the top, Gray Line, ☎ (888) 472-4729 of Hawaii offers numerous half- and full-day tours that include Haleakala National Park. (Remember, though, that you will see much more on your own.)*

❖ 4WD TRIP

We also have a suggestion for those who are making the trip on the Hana Road to O'heo Gulch. You can, of course, be like most people and just reverse your route to get back. Or, if you have a 4WD vehicle, you can return via a loop around the eastern half of Maui Island. From O'heo Gulch, continue on the Pulaui Highway (SR 31) through lava flows and rocky coastline all the way to where it meets up with SR 37, a "normal" road that will take you back to Kahului or other parts of Maui. The first 25 miles from O'heo Gulch are definitely difficult and not recommended for the novice driver.

> NOTE: *You can get into a lot of trouble taking your rental car on this excursion if the agency finds out what you did.*

ACCOMMODATIONS

❖ HOTELS & MOTELS

There are no overnight facilities inside the park.

NEARBY COMMUNITIES

The island of Maui has some of the world's most luxurious resort properties. Selections here have been chosen for their location close to the park. That is, listings include places in Kahului (the closest major community to the main section of the park), or in Hana for those going to O'heo Gulch. Most of the major resorts are in Kaanapali (65 miles from the park) or in the Wailea area (50 miles).

> NOTE: *Since all of Maui is a resort destination, decent lower-priced accommodations are hard to find.*

HANA KAI MAUI RESORT ($$$$), 1533 Uakea Road, Hana; a half-mile off State Highway 360; 10 miles north of O'heo Gulch. ☎ (808) 248-8426. 18 rooms. This is an older property with condominium-style accommodations that are attractively decorated and well maintained. All units have full cooking facilities and several have beautiful views of a secluded bay. Restaurants can be found in the main section of town, a short ride away.

MAUI SEASIDE MOTEL ($$$-$$$$), 100 W. Kaahumanu Avenue, Kahului; at the junction of State Highway 32, 37 miles from the main park entrance. ☎ (808) 877-3311 or (800) 367-7000. 195 rooms. This is not a spanking new property like the resorts in Kaanapali or Wailea, but it does have very comfortable, nicely decorated rooms set on attractive grounds. Restaurants are close by.

❖ CAMPING

The only fully developed campground is at HOSMER GROVE, just off the main road near the park's entrance station. It is small, accommodating a maximum of 25 persons. There is no stay limit or fee for its use.

There are also limited camping facilities within the Haleakala Crater. Contact the park superintendent's office for further information and reservations. A two-day limit is imposed on crater camping.

In the Kipahulu District, only a primitive campground exists. It is located near the ocean, reached via a rough dirt road.

DINING

There are no dining options within the park itself.

NEARBY COMMUNITIES

THE CAFE AT HANA GARDEN ($), on the Hana Highway at Kalo Road, Hana. ☎ (808) 248-8975. American food. Serves a large variety of vegetarian and light, health-conscious items in an informal setting. Local produce is used extensively, and even the coffee is a special Hana blend.

HANA RANCH RESTAURANT ($$-$$$), in the Hotel Hana-Maui, Hana Highway, Hana. ☎ (808) 248-8975. American food. Nice setting and dining room serving a good selection of entrées ranging from New York steak to Pacific Rim seafood selections. Maybe a little overpriced, but that's to be expected when you're at the end of the road!

MARCO'S GRILL & DELI ($$), 444 Hana Highway, Kahului; at the intersection of the main routes through town. ☎ (808) 877-4446. Italian cuisine. A popular place with the locals and for good reason. Friendly, unpretentious service and excellent food in ample portions at a reasonable price – a sure formula for success.

WHERE DO WE GO FROM HERE?

Obviously, any trip to Haleakala will be a part of a larger Hawaiian vacation. Therefore, see *Suggested Trip 13* for many ideas on developing a Hawaiian itinerary.

HAWAII VOLCANOES NATIONAL PARK

This is probably among the most active volcanic areas in the world. Here, you will not find the explosive, highly destructive type of volcano, but a more gently flowing lava that slowly builds up into relatively shallow craters known as calderas. Because of the type of volcanic activity here, Hawaii Volcanoes National Park has sometimes been referred to as the Drive-In Volcano. Don't let that nickname fool you. Its power is still awesome and there are occasions where sections of the park must be closed because of recurring volcanic activity. Some local residents can tell you how this gentle volcano has swallowed up their homes.

> NOTE: *If an area has temporarily been declared off-limits, do not attempt to circumvent that limitation – it is for your own safety.*

Most likely on your visit you will see only steam escaping from vents in the crater and, of course, evidence of past eruptions. But that alone is worth the visit, for the park is a highly unusual experience. The crater itself and past lava flows are both educational and impressive. It is a strange, eerie place.

FACTS & FIGURES

Location/Gateways/Getting There: On the Big Island of Hawaii, the park is 30 miles southwest of the island's largest city, Hilo. It is 96 miles from the Kailua-Kona resort coast on the western side of the island. SR 11 provides access to the park from either gateway, both of which have convenient inter-island air service.

Year Established: The park was established in 1916.

Size: 229,177 acres (350 square miles).

Admission Fee: $10.

Climate/When to Go: The park is open all year and is suitable for touring at any time, although up at the crater rim level the weather is substantially cooler than at sea level. Carry a sweater or light jacket at all times, especially for chilly mornings.

Contact Information: Superintendent, Hawaii Volcanoes National Park, PO Box 52, Hawaii National Park, HI 96178. ☎ (808) 967-7311 for general information; ☎ (808) 985-6000 for up-to-the-minute information on eruptions and road conditions.

AUTO TOUR/SHORT STOPS

Hawaii Volcanoes National Park has an excellent system of roads that bring you in close proximity to most points of interest, but there are substantial opportunities for more detailed exploration on foot as well. Our route assumes you will arrive from Hilo, and go clockwise around the crater. The **Crater Rim Road** encircles Kilauea Crater for 11 miles. The crater itself is 2½ miles across and there are many side craters and other craters within craters. The road elevation averages 4,000 feet. It's a well-maintained route and is easy to drive – even the portion that rises from near sea level up to the crater's rim.

NOTE: *Although the information contained herein was correct at press time, temporary road closures or detours may be necessary on occasion because of recent volcanic activity. This is especially true along the currently more active Chain of Craters Road as it approaches the sea. Call beforehand to check on road conditions, especially if you've heard about an eruption on TV or in your local newspaper.*

Start your tour at the **Kilauea Visitor Center**, where you can view films and exhibits on the park, some of which document past eruptions. (There are several trails here that will be discussed in the next section.)

LAVA TERMINOLOGY

At the visitor center you'll probably have your first exposure to two Hawaiian terms used to describe lava. These are **pahoehoe**, which has a smooth surface; and **a'a**, with a rough sharp surface. In fact, these terms have become commonly used throughout the world to differentiate the two main types of lava. Be aware that a'a is often sharp, so proper footwear is essential when walking on it.

Beginning the circle tour, you will come to the **Waldron Ledge Overlook** and then an overlook into **Kilauea Iki Crater**, a large side crater created in 1959. Just ahead is the short trail leading to the **Thurston Lava Tube**, a 500-foot tunnel created when the outer portion of a lava flow hardened, allowing lava on the inside to continue oozing out. The easy trail includes some stairs and totals just over a quarter-mile, including the cave-like tunnel of the tube itself.

Less than a mile farther along is the parking area for the **Devastation Trail**, which will be described in the next section. Also near this point is the interesting **Tree Fern Forest**. About a mile beyond here is the junction with the **Chain of Craters Road**, which leaves the rim and extends for 24 miles down to the coastal sec-

435

tion of the park. This road passes historic Hawaiian villages and temples, and also offers views of many small craters and other volcanic formations, including lava flows. There is ample evidence of volcanic activity which has occured during the past 15 years. The vista of the Pacific Ocean as you reach the coast is also spectacular. The road used to lead out of the park and connect back to Hilo, but lava flows in the 1980s (which continue sporadically today) will likely keep this section of the road closed for several years. Only a few miles along the coast are open. Still, Chain of Craters Road, the round-trip from Crater Rim Drive is a most worthwhile detour. After seeing this area, work your way back to the Crater Rim Road and stop at the **Keanakakoi Crater Overlook**.

After the road crosses a 1982 lava flow you'll come to the parking area for a short (10-minute), easy trail to an overlook facing the **Haleamaumau Crater**. This is one of the largest and most active vents in the Kilauea Caldera. It is one of the eeriest spots in the park, with steam coming from the ground, strange aromas, and a mostly barren, moon-like landscape.

Two miles ahead is the **Hawaii Volcano Observatory**. Although this research institute is closed to the public, you can get a spectacular view of the entire caldera from the adjacent overlook on the **Uwekahuna Bluff**, at an elevation of 4,077 feet and the highest point on the road. Next to the observatory is the **Jaggar Museum**, which has exhibits on seismology and volcanology. There are several working seismographs to study. The museum is open daily from 8:30 am until 5 pm.

Leave the Crater Rim Road once again to drive on **Mauna Loa Road**. This road extends for a few miles before ending at the trailhead to 13,677-foot **Mauna Loa**, where snow is common in winter. The drive to the end is worthwhile because the view of Mauna Loa is excellent from there.

❖ **DID YOU KNOW?**

Mauna Loa is the world's largest mountain in cubic mass. At a height of 30,000 feet from its base beneath the sea to the summit, it is even higher than Mt. Everest.

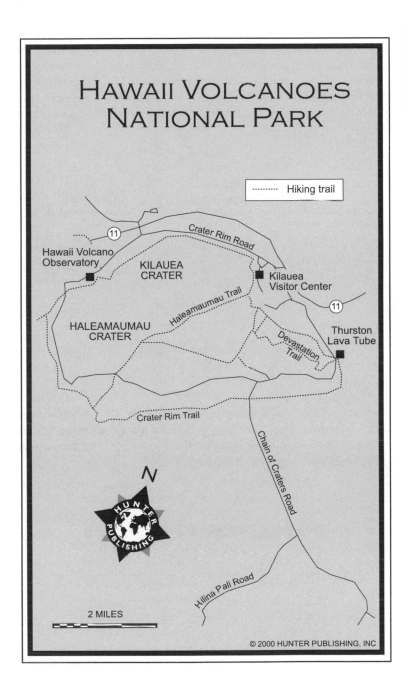

At the beginning of the road, close to Crater Rim Drive, are several points of interest. One is the **Tree Molds**, actual trees that were encased in lava. When the interior rotted away, what remained was a lava tree. The **Kipuka Puaulu Trail** (translation is Bird Park) is here as well and will be described in the next section.

Now return to the Crater Rim Road and you will shortly arrive back at the Kilauea Visitor Center, starting point for several other trails. Total distance (including the round-trip down the Chain of Craters and Mauna Loa Strip Roads) is 70 miles. With the many view stops and short trails, you should allow about four hours.

An additional short excursion can be made east on SR 11 to the vicinity of the Kilauea Volcano. Eruptions that began in 1983 continue to vent lava and steam. Access may be denied depending upon the level of activity. You should inquire at the visitor center before setting out to Kilauea Volcano.

GETTING OUT/LONGER STOPS

❖ HIKING

The casual visitor is not equipped to deal with the strenuous climb to Mauna Loa; the same is true for many of the trails that lead into and across the Kilauea Caldera. But there are many other trails that are easy and rewarding.

The 1¼-mile **Devastation Trail** is one of the most popular in the park. It takes a little more than a half-hour, one way.

> ❖ **TIP**
>
> *There is a parking area at either end, so if one member of your party is willing to skip the trail or to run back and get the car, it is not necessary for everyone to make the return trip. Otherwise, allow another half-hour.*

The trail consists of a boardwalk through an area that was completely devastated in an earlier eruption. Over the years, much vegetation has reappeared, but it is still a desolate place.

> NOTE: *The boardwalk has been constructed so that the natural regrowth of the area is not interfered with by visitors; so please, remain on the boardwalk in this living laboratory.*

The next trail of interest is **Kipuka Puaulu**. This is a one-mile nature trail that takes 30 minutes to complete. Many varieties of plants and flowers will be seen on this marked trail. The English name (Bird Park) comes from the many species of birds that make the area their home. Daytime visitors will likely encounter a few flying friends, but avid bird watchers may be disappointed.

Finally, two trails that originate at the visitor center are the **Sulfur Banks** and **Sandalwood Trails**. The former is only a quarter-mile-long and takes under a half-hour to complete. It passes numerous vents from which yellowish deposits of sulfur have accumulated over the years. The rotten-egg aroma of the sulfur is unmistakable. The other trail is much longer, taking an hour or more. It hugs the crater and provides excellent views. The two trails cross at one point, so you can combine them on a single walk rather than returning to the visitor center and starting over. The return climb on the Sandalwood Trail is fairly steep in places.

SPECIAL ACTIVITIES

❖ NIGHTTIME VOLCANO WATCHES

Nighttime viewing of current volcanic activity in the form of lava eruptions or flows is one of the most spectacular sights on the face of the earth. Inquire at the visitor center as to activity. If something is happening, the park service will likely designate areas from which you can view the movement in safety. They even have organized ranger programs. Helicopter flights over the area are another way to see it from a safe distance. You can find out about those at the visitor center as well.

Accommodations

❖ Hotels & Motels

Inside the Park

VOLCANO HOUSE ($$$-$$$$), off State Highway 11 at the park headquarters. ☎ (808) 967-7321. 42 rooms. This historic property will take you back to another era. The rooms are mostly small (although there are a few oversized units at the upper end of the price scale) and the furnishings are old fashioned. Some rooms overlook the Kilauea Crater. Attractive grounds. Evening educational programs about the park. Restaurant and cafeteria on the premises.

Nearby Communities

HILO BAY HOTEL ($$-$$$), 87 Banyan Drive, Hilo; bayfront near the junction of Highways 11 and 19, 28 miles from the park entrance. 142 rooms. ☎ (808) 935-0861. Also known as "Uncle Billy's hotel," this is an attractive motor inn decorated in island style. It has comfortable rooms that are maintained extremely well, which makes up for the fact that the place is a bit on the old side. However, it's a lot cheaper than the other hotels in Hilo. Restaurant adjacent and others nearby.

THE INN AT VOLCANO ($-$$$$), Dwight Road, Volcano; off State Highway 11, immediately outside the park entrance. ☎ (808) 967-7786 or (800) 937-7786. 24 rooms. This is the closest you can get to the park without actually staying at Volcano House. There is a wide selection of accommodations, hence the variety of rates. There are approximately equal numbers of chalets (highest price units with whirlpool and fireplace), lodges in two separate buildings (one at $$$ and the other at $$), and the budget-priced bed & breakfast facility. The latter has shared baths. Best bet for dining if staying here is to go into the park.

❖ CAMPING

All park campgrounds have a seven-day limit. Reservations are not required. Contact park headquarters for details.

CAMPGROUNDS AT A GLANCE			
NAME	LOCATION	SITES	COST
Namakani Paio	State Highway 11, southwest of the visitor center.	40	Free
Kipuka Nene	Hilina Pali Road, reached by the Chain of Craters Road.	12	Free
Kamoamoa	On the coast (Chain of Craters Road to State Highway 130).	11	Free

Kipuka and Kamoamoa campgrounds can be periodically closed due to lava flows in this portion of the park.

DINING

INSIDE THE PARK

THE DINING ROOM AT VOLCANO HOUSE ($$), inside the Volcano House Hotel (see above). ☎ (808) 967-7321. American food. Nothing to rave about, but this restaurant does have a good selection of decent food in a nice setting overlooking the crater.

For lower-priced dining you can try the adjacent cafeteria (good for lunch), but be prepared for cafeteria-style food.

NEARBY COMMUNITIES

KILAUEA LODGE RESTAURANT ($$-$$$), in the Kilauea Lodge, Volcano, off State Highway 11, just outside the park entrance. Continental cuisine. A wonderful dining experience where you'll get gourmet continental cuisine with a decidedly Asian in-fluence. The grounds are beautiful and the service is excellent. Scrumptious desserts top off a fine meal. Not inexpensive, but worth the price.

WHERE DO WE GO FROM HERE?

As was the case with visiting Haleakala National Park, anyone coming to Hawaii Volcanoes will certainly be incorporating it into an overall Hawaiian vacation. Once again, you are referred to *Suggested Trip 13* for further suggestions on a four-island tour.

SUGGESTED TRIPS

Combining national parks and other natural attractions can make for a great vacation. This section suggests a variety of tours that combine visits to the parks with other nearby scenic points of interest. You can, of course, extend any trip by adding in some time in cities.

All of these trips assume that you will either be driving from your home city to a gateway or flying to a gateway city and renting a car. The mileage and time allotment shown for each trip is from the gateway. All of the trips are loops that return to the same location as they began. All can be reworked into one-way itineraries. While this can often save a lot of mileage and time on a fly-drive vacation, remember that one-way car rentals (when they are possible) are significantly more expensive and often subject to exorbitant drop-off charges. It can also be difficult to get discounted airfares on flights that are not round-trips to and from the same city. Details on seeing the parks will not be repeated in this part of the book. Simply refer back to the chapter on the park in question.

Remember that these itineraries are merely suggestions, not fixed plans that must be followed to the letter. Change them to fit your individual tastes and to meet your time restrictions. The intent is to show how you can, with a little advance planning and imagination, create a memorable trip by stringing together several parks and nearby attractions.

The schedule for the first and last day of each trip makes another assumption that you are flying to and from the gateway and time to do this is built in. Therefore, the itinerary may seem sparse for the first day (because it allows time for a mid-day arrival) and the last day (so that you can return the car and catch a mid-afternoon flight back to your home city).

> NOTE: *It is especially important that you not plan too much for the first day. Even if the scheduled arrival should allow plenty of time for sightseeing or travel, you never know when there will be delays.*

SUGGESTED TRIP 1

ALONG THE BLUE RIDGE

❖ PARK HIGHLIGHTS: Great Smoky Mountains National Park (North Carolina/Tennessee); Shenandoah National Park (Virginia). Alternative Route/ Extension to Mammoth Cave National Park (Kentucky).

❖ GATEWAY: Washington, D.C.

❖ ESTIMATED MILES: 1,400 (2,050 for alternative/extension).

❖ TIME: 7 days (10 days for alternative/extension).

FIRST DAY

Leaving the nation's capital and crossing into Virginia, travel east on I-66 to the US 340 exit at Front Royal. Immediately to the south of the town is the entrance to **Shenandoah National Park** (page 47). You'll ride along the scenic ridgetop crest known as **Skyline Drive**, as was described on page 48. About

33 miles after entering the park, exit west on US 211 for the 10-mile drive to famous **Luray Caverns**, ☎ (540) 743-6551. The guided tours along well lighted pathways will take you past some amazing limestone formations. Return to Shenandoah and complete your tour of the park. The day will end at the park's southern terminus in **Waynesboro**.

SECOND DAY

This morning we head south on the **Blue Ridge Parkway**. This national parkway continues along the crest of the Blue Ridge for a total of 470 miles, all the way to the Great Smoky Mountains National Park. However, there are many interesting and beautiful sights along the way. Begin with stops at **Humpback Rocks Visitor Center** (Mile 5.8 from the beginning of the parkway), and the **Peaks of Otter Visitor Center** (Mile 86). Other worthwhile stops along or just adjacent to the parkway include **Rocky Knob** (Mile 169) and **Mabry Mill** (Mile 176). Overnight will be in **Fancy Gap**, just north of the Virginia-North Carolina line.

THIRD DAY

Continuing along the Blue Ridge, today's sights include **Grandfather Mountain**, an area of outstanding vistas and natural habitats for wildlife near Mile 306, and the **Linville Falls Recreation Area** (Mile 316). You will also pass many scenic overlooks where you might want to linger a few moments. As you near the southern portion of the parkway you'll reach the **Craggy Gardens** (Mile 365), set at an elevation of 6,000 feet. Here, trails lead to beautiful vistas. The gardens themselves are especially beautiful in mid-June when the rhododendrons are in full bloom. Overnight will be in the city of **Asheville**.

FOURTH DAY

Upon leaving Asheville, you can reach the Smoky Mountains by getting back on the **Blue Ridge Parkway**, which loops south and then westward through some of the Southern Highlands' best scenery. There are ample opportunities to get out and stretch your legs among the forested slopes. The parkway ends at the town of **Cherokee**, which is also the southern entrance to the **Great Smoky Mountains National Park** (page 31). The rest of the day will be spent exploring this most popular of scenic destinations. At the northern end of the park, in Tennessee, is the bustling town of **Gatlinburg**, your stopping place for tonight. The **Ober Gatlinburg aerial tramway**, ☎ (423) 436-5423, affords some wonderful views of the Smokies.

FIFTH DAY

US 441 leads out of Gatlinburg. A short distance north, at Sevierville, pick up SR 66 for the 10-mile ride to the junction with I-40. Take the Interstate east to I-81 and then proceed north on the latter route. At Bristol you'll reenter the state of Virginia and continue north. At the town of Wythville transfer to I-77 in a northerly direction and you'll soon cross into West Virginia. Exit at **Beckley**, which will serve as your home for tonight. However, there's lots to do before the end of the day. A scenic loop from Beckley consists of US routes 19 (north), 60 (east) and SR 41 west back into town. The tour will take you through the scenic **New River Gorge National River**. Stop at the **Canyon Rim Visitor Center** for a spectacular panorama as well as brochures that will guide you to more points of interest on or just off the loop.

SIXTH DAY

Travel east from Beckley on I-64 to Lewisburg and then head north on US 219. This road traverses the scenic **Monongahela National Forest**. Several state parks along the way provide restful breaks. At the town of Elkins turn east on US 33 and you'll soon enter one of the most beautiful parts of West Virginia – **Spruce Knob** and **Seneca Rocks National Recreation Areas**. After taking in the sights here (don't miss **Smoke Hole**), continue east on US 33 back into Virginia and the town of **Harrisonburg**.

SEVENTH DAY

Go north from Harrisonburg on I-81 to the junction with I-66. Go east on the latter road for the return trip to Washington. You should arrive by mid-day.

❖ EXTENSION TO MAMMOTH CAVE

This option diverges from the main itinerary early on Day 5, when you first reach I-40. Head west on the interstate, passing through Knoxville on your way to Louisville, where you'll pick up I-65 north. Soon after crossing into Kentucky you'll reach Bowling Green, before continuing on to the town of **Cave City**, where you will spend the night. This is a long day of driving, but it's on easy roads through mostly pleasant scenery. And tomorrow's activities will more than make up for it.

SIXTH DAY

The entire day will be devoted to unforgettable **Mammoth Cave National Park** (page 40).

SEVENTH DAY

I-65 north will take you to the **Blue Grass Parkway** at Elizabethtown. Take the parkway east to its end just before Lexington. US 60 east and Pisgah Road north will take you to I-64. A long easterly drive on that road will bring you to **Charleston**, West Virginia's capital city and your stopping point for tonight.

EIGHTH DAY

Take US 60 east to Ansted and the great views at the **Hawk's Nest State Park**. This park is on the edge of the New River Gorge area and, upon completing your visit, you'll be able to join the loop described on Day 5 of the main trip. You'll have a bit more time this way, so you can explore the New River in more detail. Overnight is in **Beckley**.

NINTH AND TENTH DAYS

These correspond to the Sixth and Seventh days of the original trip.

SUGGESTED TRIP 2

AMID THE BLACK HILLS

❖ PARK HIGHLIGHTS: Badlands National Monument (South Dakota); Devils Tower National Monument (Wyoming); Mount Rushmore National Memorial (South Dakota) Scotts Bluff National Monument (Nebraska).

❖ GATEWAY: Rapid City, South Dakota.

❖ ESTIMATED MILES: 1,060.

❖ TIME: 5 days.

FIRST DAY

From Rapid City head east on I-90 past the town of Wall to Exit 131. Immediately south of the interstate you'll enter **Badlands National Park** (see page 55). Allow the better part of the day to explore this area in detail. At the western end of the park, SR 240 will bring you into Wall and I-90. This time take it in a westerly direction to your overnight stopping place, the town of **Spearfish**.

SECOND DAY

Continue this morning for a little while on I-90 west into Wyoming and the town of Sundance. Then travel 30 miles via US 14 and SR 24 to the **Devils Tower National Monument** (see page 61). After completing your visit to this striking highlight, retrace your route back to Spearfish. Exit from the interstate and travel via ALT US 14, then US 85 north through Lead, and, finally, south on US 385. This route will take you through the northern part of the beautiful **Black Hills National Forest**, a region of incredible sights more commonly called, simply, The Black Hills. The northern part isn't as spectacular as the south, but on today's drive you'll see lovely **Spearfish Canyon** (along ALT 14) and **Pactola Reservoir**. The Forest Service maintains an interesting visitor center at this point.

About 10 miles south of the reservoir, turn left onto US 16 for five miles, and then right on ALT 16 for the short ride into **Keystone**. Accommodations are plentiful in this bustling little town. After dark you should take the mile or so ride from town to **Mount Rushmore National Memorial** (page 77) for the unforgettable spectacle of the four presidents.

THIRD DAY

Begin the day by exploring **Mount Rushmore National Memorial** in more detail. It looks completely different and the daylight will enable you to appreciate the surrounding scenery so much better. Then go back to ALT 16 and turn right. A dizzying series of turns will lead you to the **Norbeck Overlook**. From this point you'll have a dramatic view of the Black Hills as well as the distant Mt. Rushmore Memorial. Once you reach the end of the Norbeck Memorial Scenic Byway, with its many tunnels and spiraling turns that curve through the hills, you'll enter the huge **Custer State Park**. Two important attractions within the park are the interesting **Wildlife Loop Road** and the **Needles Highway**. The latter will take you through a fascinating landscape of rock pinnacles and other interesting formations. At one point you'll encounter a towering double spire with a narrow opening called the **Eye of the Needle**. In some places the road narrows so much that only a single car can pass through at one time. Within the park are hikes to several beautiful mountain lakes – pristine **Sylvan Lake** is the most impressive. You can also get a good view of **Harney Peak**, the highest point in the state of South Dakota.

Upon finishing the Needles Highway (SR 87), follow US 16 westbound to **Jewel Cave National Park**. There are several different tours of the beautiful caves available that range from simple to one for expert cave explorers. Then go back a little way on US 16 east to the town of **Custer**.

Fourth Day

Travel south from Custer on US 385. You'll soon reach the entrance to **Wind Cave National Park**. Whether this is nicer than Jewel Cave can be argued endlessly, but both are worthwhile attractions full of natural beauty. Continue south on US 385 to the town of **Hot Springs**. Here you can explore a site where ancient animals once roamed. Resume your southward trek on US 385. About 15 miles after you enter Nebraska, go west on US 20 to the town of Harrison and then south on SR 29. Approximately 20 miles south of Harrison is the **Agate Fossil Beds National Monument**, ☎ (308) 436-4340 . A mile-long nature trail leads to a place in the sedimentary rock where 20 million-year-old fossils are imbedded. After your visit, continue south on SR 29 to your stopping point for this evening, the town of **Scottsbluff**.

Fifth Day

A few pleasant hours will be spent this morning while you visit the **Scotts Bluff National Monument** (page 83), one of the park highlights of this trip. Note that the monument is two words while the town of the same name is a single word. Upon exiting the monument (which lies southwest of town off SR 71 via SR 92), head east on SR 92. This mildly scenic route follows the shoreline of the **North Platte River**. You'll see the next attraction miles before you reach it. The 500-foot-tall rock column in **Chimney Rock National Historic Site**, ☎ (308) 568-2581, was an important landmark for westbound pioneer travelers. This natural column is quite impressive. You can see it well from parking areas along SR 92 or you can get right up close by taking a short gravel road and a half-mile trail. About a quarter of an hour's drive past Chimney Rock is the town of Bridgeport and US 385, which you should take north all the way back into the Black Hills. At the junction of SR 44, turn right for the final short leg back into Rapid City.

NOTE: *Because this is a relatively short trip in terms of days, you might want to add a few more attractions. Some of the possibilities within the Black Hills are several privately operated caverns a short drive from Rapid City, and the 1880 Train that operates several times daily between Hill City and Keystone. The route passes through some lovely Black Hills scenery.*

Chimney Rock.

SUGGESTED TRIP 3

COLORADO CIRCLE

* ❖ PARK HIGHLIGHTS: Black Canyon of the Gunnison National Monument; Colorado National Monument; Great Sand Dunes National Monument; Mesa Verde National Park; Rocky Mountain National Park (all Colorado); Dinosaur National Monument (Colorado/Utah).
* ❖ GATEWAY: Denver.
* ❖ ESTIMATED MILES: 1,725.
* ❖ TIME: 11 days.

FIRST DAY

Spend some time exploring the mountain parks that are part of Denver's municipal park system and that lie just to the west of the city. **Red Rocks Park**, ☎ (303) 964-2500, is one such beautiful place, as is **Lookout Mountain Park**, ☎ (303) 526-0747. Then head west on I-70. This superhighway passes through some of the most beautiful mountain scenery in all of Colorado, on a road that makes it almost too easy! You don't have to go too far to take in some spectacular views. We suggest traveling only to Georgetown, less than a half-hour trip from the mountain parks that are closer to Denver. Then return east a bit on I-70 to Exit 244 and the town of **Black Hawk**. Pick up SR 119 and head north. At the town of Nederland follow SR 72 north until you reach SR 7, which you'll take north. All of these roads are part of the **Peak to Peak Scenic Byway**, one of the most gorgeous routes in the country. You'll have close-up views of towering snow-covered peaks and, in the northern section, will literally be surrounded by mountains on all sides as the road snakes its way past, among others, **Longs Peak** and the **Twin Sisters Peaks**. All are well over 14,000 feet high. The route ends at your overnight stopping point, the resort town of **Estes Park**.

SECOND DAY

All morning and part of the afternoon today should be devoted to the glorious splendors of **Rocky Mountain National Park** (page 260). The park is traversed by US 34, a route that will continue for a short time to the town of Granby near the southwest exit of the park. At Granby, take US 40 west through another portion of the scenic Rocky Mountains. The day will end in **Steamboat Springs**, a major winter sports center that is also quite busy with visitors during the summer touring months.

THIRD DAY

Prepare yourself for a long ride today on US 40. The scenery, although not nearly as spectacular as some you have seen in the past two days, will still be highly pleasing. Just before the town of Dinosaur, head north on the **Harpers Corner Scenic Drive** into the Colorado portion of **Dinosaur National Monument** (page 181). Upon completion of the Utah section of the monument, drive back east on US 40 to Dinosaur and then use SR 64 for the 18-mile drive into **Rangely**, your home for the evening.

FOURTH DAY

From Rangely, travel south on SR 139 for about 1½ hours to I-70. Go east eight miles to Exit 19. From this point you're only a couple of miles from the western entrance to the awesome wonders of the **Colorado National Monument** (page 174). After a few hours driving along the monument's rim, you'll leave through the east side at the city of Grand Junction. Take US 50 east and, about 15 miles out of town, turn left onto Lands End Road. A loop consisting of Lands End Road, SR 65 and SR 92 will bring you back to US 50 at the town of Delta. However, along this detour are some beautiful sights within the outstanding **Grand Mesa National Forest**. The highlight will be **Lands End** itself, which offers an endless panorama from high atop a rocky vantage point. From Delta, continue east on US 50 to **Montrose**.

FIFTH DAY

Leave Montrose this morning via US 50 eastbound. Travel to the **Curecanti National Recreation Area**, ☎ (970) 641-2337, a region of impressive mountains and gorges, as well as major lakes created by several dams. The road through the recreation area extends for some time and will, if you continue all the way, take you far off our main routing. Therefore, proceed only as far as the junction of SR 92 before retracing your route on US 50. Before you get back to Montrose, however, cut off on SR 347 for a short ride into the spectacular **Black Canyon of the Gunnison National Monument** (page 125). This is likely to be one of the most wonderful sights you'll ever encounter, regardless of where you travel. Once you return to Montrose, head south on US 550 to the town of **Ouray**. This little community, besides being your overnight stop, is known as the "Switzerland of America." There are some excellent sights in town, including the narrow **Box Canyon**, located in a municipal park of the same name, and waterfalls and rushing rivers at the south end of the town.

SIXTH DAY

South from Ouray, US 550 is called the **Million Dollar Highway**. The trip is worth that price as it must certainly rank with the most impressive auto routes anywhere. The narrow canyon offers excellent views of colorful mountains. South of the former mining town of Silverton, US 550 continues through the San Juan Mountains on into the town of Durango. While still pretty, the thick forest does block some of the scenery along this section. For the moment, we'll bypass Durango, taking instead US 160 west to **Mesa Verde National Park** (page 244). You'll have the entire afternoon to visit its many wonders, both natural and those made by the ancient Native American inhabitants. Return to **Durango** where you'll settle in for two evenings.

SEVENTH DAY

Today is a leisurely one, for you'll be taking an all-day ride on the famous **Durango & Silverton Narrow Gauge Railroad**, ☎ (888) 872-4607. Although the train's route parallels the highway that you took from Silverton to Durango, the view is completely different – and most extraordinary. Instead of being high up in the forests, the tracks are in the gorge and follow the turbulent course of the beautiful **Animas River**. At times the train will be along flat ground and at others it clings the edge of precipitous cliffs. It's an adventure that everyone will enjoy.

EIGHTH DAY

This morning you'll travel east for a scenic but lengthy distance on US 160 through the **San Juan Mountains**. Just past the town of Alamosa, turn left on SR 150. This road will take you into the **Great Sand Dunes National Monument** (page 230), another of the many park highlights on this trip. The night should be spent in **Alamosa**.

NINTH DAY

Travel north from Alamosa on SR 17. It will join US 385, which in turn meets US 50. Drive east on US 50 until you reach the town of Canon City. The eerie but beautiful **Royal Gorge of the Arkansas River** is the highlight here. Although it is privately operated and the surrounding "theme park" atmosphere may be too commercialized for some nature lovers, the gorge itself is a natural spectacle that should not be missed. You can see it from the suspension bridge or aerial tramway that crosses above, but nothing beats the experience of descending to the canyon bottom via the incline. Upon finishing your visit to the gorge, take US 50 east and SR 115 into **Colorado Springs**, your stopping point for the next two nights.

TENTH DAY

Even though Colorado Springs is the state's second largest *city*, you can spend an entire day exploring its numerous natural attractions. Located at the base of the mountains, few cities have as impressive a mountain backdrop as does Colorado Springs. Among the sights you should see are the **Pikes Peak Cog Railway**, ☎ (719) 685-5401, (the more adventurous may want to reach the summit via the hair-raising unpaved auto route); the weird and colorful formations in the **Garden of the Gods; Seven Falls; Cheyenne Canyon**; and the **Cave of the Winds**.

ELEVENTH DAY

The drive back to Denver is a relatively short and easy one via I-25 north. You might want to spend some more time in the Colorado Springs area (the United States Air Force Academy also has an excellent mountain setting here), or use the time to explore more of natural Denver.

SUGGESTED TRIP 4

SOUTHWEST SOJOURN

❖ PARK HIGHLIGHTS: Bandelier National Monument; Carlsbad Caverns National Park; White Sands National Monument (all New Mexico). Optional trip to Big Bend National Park (Texas).

❖ GATEWAY: Albuquerque, New Mexico.

❖ ESTIMATED MILES: 1,530 miles (2,130 with extension).

❖ TIME: 9 days (12 days with extension).

FIRST DAY

Immediately north of Albuquerque, just off I-25, is the **Sandia Peak Aerial Tramway,** ☎ (505) 856-6419. From the summit there is an absolutely gorgeous panorama of the surrounding area, including the city of Albuquerque. This is one of the longest single-tram ascents in the world and provides close-up views of the mountain's rocky crevices. The peak can also be reached by a paved road, but the trip isn't recommended for the novice mountain driver. After returning to earth, take I-25 north to Exit 242 at the town of Bernalillo and pick up SR 44. That road and SR 4 (which branches off about 25 miles from the Interstate) pass through several Indian reservations, by historic sites and through lovely scenery. The latter includes some impressive red rock formations. SR 4 rises gently into the forested slopes of New Mexico's highest mountain ranges and bring you to the entrance of the day's park highlight – **Bandelier National Monument** (page 112). Upon completion of your visit here, make your way via SRs 4 and 30 to your overnight stopping point for the next two nights, the town of **Espanola**.

SECOND DAY

A scenic adventure awaits you today. Head north towards **Taos** via SR 68. When you reach the famous town you may want to spend some time exploring the historic pueblo. However, our scenic destinations are out of town. So set out east on US 64, the beginning of a beautiful drive known as the **Enchanted Circle**. The route consists of, besides US 64 to Eagle Nest, SR 38 to Questa, and SR 522 back to Taos. The Enchanted Circle travels along mountains and through valleys, offering splendid views of lakes, forests and towering peaks – including 13,161-foot high **Wheeler Peak**, the highest point in New Mexico. An interesting stop just off the circle is the **New Mexico Wild Rivers Recreation Area**, ☎ (505) 758-8851. Before you get back into Taos you should also take a short detour west on US 64 to the bridge over the **Rio Grande**. The view of the deep, dark gorge from the overlooks is spectacular. Then it's time to return to Espanola for the night. You can retrace your route to Espanola along SR 68 or you can take an even more scenic route via SRs 518 and 76.

THIRD DAY

A southbound drive on US 285 will soon bring you into **Santa Fe**. Although the many historic attractions of this famous city are beyond the scope of this book, we would strongly recommend that you spend time exploring them. In fact, you could easily extend the trip by a full day if you wanted to discover Santa Fe, the "city different," in more detail. Either way, leave town via US 285 and SR 14, which will bring you back to I-25. Back in Albuquerque, head west on I-40 to **Grants**, where you'll spend the night. On the way, however, take a detour at Exit 108 to **Acoma Pueblo**, site of **Sky City**. Once you see the view from up here you may well understand why Native Americans consider this to be sacred ground. Sky City is accessible only via Indian-led tours.

FOURTH DAY

There will be a lot of driving today, but most of it will be via scenic roads that are lightly traveled, so you should find it quite pleasant. From Grants, briefly backtrack on I-40 to Exit 89. SR 117 will take you through the rugged and eerie terrain of **El Malpais National Monument**. Nearby is **La Ventana Natural Arch**. There are also ice caves and other unusual sights in this region of Badlands. SR 117 ends at SR 36. Turn left and continue to the town of Quemado, where you'll pick up SR 32. At Apache Creek take SR 12 to US 180 west. This last trio of roads travels through the beautiful lands of the **Apache-Sitgreaves** and **Gila National Forests**. The **Mogollon Mountains** are a highlight of the area. Stop at the **Catwalk**, near Glenwood, for an exciting walk over metal bridges that span a precipitous gorge. The walks were once used by miners but now are maintained by the Forest Service. You'll spend the evening in the town of **Silver City**.

FIFTH DAY

This morning you will continue heading east on US 180. About 30 miles from Silver City is a short cut-off leading to the **City of Rocks State Park**, ☎ (505) 536-2800. This grouping of large rocks does, from a distance (and seen from an overlook), resemble a city of stone buildings. You can walk around (and sometimes through) many of the rock formations. At Deming, US 180 will reach I-10. Take the interstate east to Las Cruces and then pick up I-25 north for seven miles to Exit 6. US 70 will then bring you 50 miles to the entrance of the fascinating **White Sands National Monument** (page 276). Overnight will be in **Alamogordo**, which is on US 70 about 15 miles past the monument.

SIXTH DAY

A couple of miles north of Alamogordo, take US 82 eastbound. The road rises steeply and passes through the pleasant scenery of the **Lincoln National Forest** before descending more gradually to wide open spaces where you'll encounter almost no traffic, towns, or much else. At Artesia, go south on US 285 to the town of Carlsbad and then west on US 62/180. (You'll pass the entrance to Carlsbad Caverns National Park, but skip it for now.) About 20 minutes later you'll cross into Texas and reach the **Guadalupe Mountains National Park**, ☎ (915) 828-3251. While we didn't include this as one of the scenic highlights of the previous section of this book, there's plenty to see here, including 8,751-foot-high **Guadalupe Peak**. Several canyons are within the confines of this national park and can be explored by trails ranging from easy to strenuous. Retrace your route on US 62/180 and spend tonight (and tomorrow night) at **Whites City**.

Seventh Day

You'll have the entire day to fully explore and appreciate the many scenic wonders of **Carlsbad Caverns National Park**, as was described on pages 166.

Eighth Day

Travel back to Carlsbad, stopping at the **Living Desert State Park**, ☎ (505) 887-5516, for an interesting lesson in desert flora and fauna. Then it's north on US 285 to Roswell, and east on US 70 and US 380. This route passes through another section of the **Lincoln National Forest** and has some lovely views.

Just past the town of Carrizozo on US 380 is the **Valley of Fires Recreation Area**, ☎ (505) 648-2241. This Bureau of Land Management facility encompasses a portion of a large ancient lava flow. The flow patterns are clearly visible in the black rock. It can be seen from a number of overlooks via a short road, or you can get out and walk on the flow itself.

> NOTE: *Be sure to wear sturdy boots, as the rocks can be sharp.*

Continue on US 380 until you reach I-25 and then go north a short distance to your stopping place for tonight, the town of **Socorro**.

Ninth Day

It's an easy 1½-hour drive north on I-25 from Socorro to Albuquerque, where you'll have time to do some exploration of New Mexico's largest city.

❖ Extension To Big Bend National Park

Sixth Day

The trip is the same as the main route through the Guadalupe Mountains National Park. After that, continue west for a short time on US 180 to the junction of SR 54. A southerly drive of 55 miles on that road will bring you to **Van Horn**, the Texas town where you'll be spending the night.

Seventh Day

Go east this morning on I-10 to Exit 176 and then drive south on SRs 118 and 166 to Fort Davis. Go north on SR 118 to the **W.J. MacDonald Observatory**, before returning to **Fort Davis** and then continuing south on SR 118 to Alpine. The loop around Fort Davis passes through some of the largest and most rugged of Texas' mountainous west and the view from the Observatory is excellent. From Alpine, go east on US 90 to **Marathon**, where you can spend the evening.

Eighth Day

South of Marathon via US 385 is **Big Bend National Park** (page 118). Except for the hour or so it takes you to reach the park from Marathon, you'll have the entire day to explore Big Bend. Overnight is in **Study Butte**, immediately outside the western entrance to the park.

Ninth Day

Use SR 118, US 90 west, SR 54 and, finally, US 180, to return to **Whites City**.

TENTH THROUGH TWELFTH DAYS

These are the same as the Seventh through Ninth Days of the basic itinerary.

SUGGESTED TRIP 5

THREE CROWN JEWELS

❖ PARK HIGHLIGHTS: Glacier National Park (Montana); Grand Teton National Park, and Yellowstone National Park (both Wyoming).

❖ GATEWAY: Jackson, Wyoming.

❖ ESTIMATED MILES: 1,580.

❖ TIME: 9 days.

FIRST DAY

Grand Teton National Park, surely one of the most majestic places to see alpine scenery in all the world, is just minutes north of the town of Jackson. You can spend the entire day exploring the park (and the adjacent Gros Ventre Slide area), which are fully described on page 66. Spend the night in the northern section of the park at **Moran Junction**.

SECOND DAY

Yellowstone National Park is so big and there is so much to see (refer to page 88 for details), that you can't do it justice in a single day. Today you'll use the park's **Grand Loop Road** to explore the Lake and Canyon areas, Old Faithful and the Upper Geyser Basin, and the Norris Geyser Basin, before ending the day in the park at **Mammoth Hot Springs**.

Third Day

The Mammoth Hot Springs area is filled with scenic wonders. A few hours this morning will let you see them before you leave the park via the northeastern entrance, which is US 212. The 70-mile drive from the park to the town of Red Lodge in Montana is called the **Bear Tooth Scenic Highway**. Few would dispute the claim that the Bear Tooth is one of the most dramatically beautiful roads in all the world. From Red Lodge, US 212 continues on into **Billing**s, where you'll spend the night.

Fourth Day

Having seen so much spectacular scenery during the past three days, you shouldn't mind a drive of just under 175 miles this morning. It's all via I-90 westbound and makes for easy travel. Use Exit 278 to access the **Missouri Headwaters State Park**, ☎ (406) 285-3198. Set amid lovely scenery, the park is the starting point of the wide **Missouri River**. Then get back on I-90 west for one exit and pick up US 287/SR 2 for the final few miles of the trip to the **Lewis & Clark Caverns State Park**, ☎ (406) 287-3541. The beautiful caves are reached via a long and fairly strenuous walk (uphill) that you'll probably welcome after all that driving. After completing your visit to the park, reverse your route via US 287. At the interstate, however, stay on US 287 and travel north to the capital city of **Helena**, your stopping point for the night.

Fifth Day

Leave town this morning by traveling north on I-15 for the short ride to Exit 209. This provides access to the **Gates of the Mountains Recreation Area**, ☎ (406) 458-5241. You'll take a boat ride on the Missouri River, flanked by high mountains on either side. At one bend in the river, the mountains appear to "open up" and let you pass through (hence, the name). Back on I-15 north, your next stop is in the city of Great Falls. **Giant Springs State Park** is of scenic interest in town. Then use I-15 for the short ride to Exit 290. US 89 north will bring you approximately 100 miles to Browning. From there it's a hop-skip-and-a-jump via US 2 to your overnight destination, **East Glacier Park**.

SIXTH DAY

Over the next two days you'll be encountering some of the most beautiful scenery in America as you explore **Glacier National Park** (see page 352). This morning our route, via SR 49 and US 89, skirts the eastern edge of the park and passes lower St. Mary's Lake before reaching SR 17. This route, known as the **Chief Joseph Highway**, will enter Canada so that you can explore **Waterton Lakes National Park**. The park was described along with Glacier on page 362. In fact, the two parks are together refered to as Waterton-Glacier International Peace Park. After Waterton, retrace your route as far as the town of Babb. A side road here will lead you into the spectacular **Many Glacier** section of Glacier National Park. Spend the night here.

SEVENTH DAY

At St. Mary we leave US 89 and travel along the **Going to the Sun Road**, which traverses the major portion of Glacier National Park and gives you access to most of the park's best known features. At West Glacier, travel west on US 2 to Kalispell and the junction of US 93. Go south on the latter, which hugs the shore of beautiful **Flathead Lake**. Your overnight stopping point for tonight is **Polson**. Cruises on Flathead Lake are available.

EIGHTH DAY

South of Ronan on US 93 is the **National Bison Range**. Either of two loop routes will enable you to see these huge creatures in their natural habitat. Then continue on US 93 to Missoula, where you'll pick up I-90 in an eastbound direction. Just west of Butte is the junction with I-15. Take that route south as far as **Dillon**, a good stopping point for the evening.

NINTH DAY

Today you'll return through some beautiful scenery to Jackson. Begin by continuing on I-15 to **Idaho Falls**. The falls that give the town its name aren't particularly striking, but it's worth a brief look. From Idaho Falls, US 26 will take you back to Jackson. The entire route is along the **Snake River** and there are some great views. This is especially true of the last leg of the trip (once you cross back into Wyoming) and the route traverses the **Grand Canyon of the Snake** through the **Targhee National Forest**. At many points the road is perched high above the river on a comfortingly wide ledge. You'll frequently see people on the river in rafts.

SUGGESTED TRIP 6

IDAHO ADVENTURE

❖ PARK HIGHLIGHTS: Craters of the Moon National Monument; Hell's Canyon National Recreation Area; Sawtooth National Recreation Area (all Idaho).

❖ GATEWAY: Boise, Idaho.

❖ ESTIMATED MILES: 1,300.

❖ TIME: 8 days.

FIRST DAY

The approximately 150-mile drive from Boise to Twin Falls is an easy one as it is all via I-84 in an eastbound direction. Along the way, however, there is one beautiful stop that is right off the highway: **Malad Gorge State Park**, ☎ (208) 837-4505, (Exit 147). Short trails lead to excellent views of a falls rushing through a narrow canyon. **Twin Falls** is your overnight stopping place. On the east side of the town is a municipal park from which you have an outstanding view of the spectacular falls of the **Snake River**. Also worthwhile is the view of the gorge from **Perrine Memorial Bridge**, just north of downtown on US 93.

SECOND DAY

Travel north this morning on US 93 to the town of Shoshone and then take SR 75 north. The **Shoshone Ice Caves**, ☎ (208) 886-2058, are of interest along the route. The temperature remains cool enough inside all year long that there is perpetual ice in portions of the small cavern. The surface trail to the main cave passes by several smaller caves that have collapsed and look more like craters. At the junction of US 20, turn east. The route will soon be joined by US 93 and 25 miles after the town of Carey is the entrance to the **Craters of the Moon National Monument**. One of the strangest looking places on earth, the monument's activities and sights are described on page 345-350. After you've finished touring the monument, reverse your route on US 20/93, but stay on US 20 westbound when the two routes split. Follow the road for Gannett back to SR 75 and head north on the latter road. In a short time you will reach the **Ketchum/Sun Valley** resort area. Once you've checked in for the evening at Idaho's most famous ski resort and year-round playground, there should be some time to explore the lovely scenery the area has to offer on one of many walking, hiking and biking trails.

THIRD DAY

A few miles north of Ketchum is the southern entrance to **Sawtooth National Recreation Area**, the agenda item for today (see page 408 for details of what to see). Your route through the recreation area will be via SR, backtracking after you've finished the northeastern section of the area, and then via SR 21 for the northwest corner of Sawtooth. That road will then turn toward the southwest and take you all the way into **Boise**, where you'll spend the night. The route between the Sawtooth and Boise is generally quite scenic as it traverses the mountainous **Boise National Forest**.

FOURTH DAY

The route today will carry you north, first on SR 55. This is another scenic road that offers good mountain views as it passes alternatively through forests and valleys. **Cascade Reservoir**, near the town of Cascade, and **Payette Lake** at McCall are especially worthy of at least a brief stop. SR 55 ends at New Meadows, where you should head north on US 95. Once again the route will be pleasing on the eyes. The narrow canyon of the Little Salmon River from a few miles north of New Meadows to

Riggins is the best part of the route. After Riggins the road travels along the broader Snake River, which converges with the Salmon at Riggins. Immediately after the tiny town of **White Bird**, US 95 rises sharply along an escarpment. At the top there is an overlook that gazes out upon the site of a battle during the **Indian Wars**. While the displays about troop movements are of interest, the panorama is superb and makes it a short but important stop on your itinerary for today. Then it's back to your northerly trek on US 95, arriving in Lewiston at the end of the day. However, before calling it quits, take a ride up to **Lewiston Hill** for a bird's eye view of the cities of Lewiston and Clarkston, the Snake River, and the entire surrounding area. It can be easily reached via US 95 (on the northern end of town). The more adventurous driver might like the dizzying ride on the old highway. Either way, the view is great. **Lewiston** will be your home for two nights.

FIFTH DAY

The entire day will be devoted to a water-borne exploration of the **Hells Canyon National Recreation Area** (page 364). Numerous jet-boat operators in the town offer trips to the deepest part of Hells Canyon. There are also overnight trips if you are so inclined.

SIXTH DAY

You will mostly be retracing your route southbound on US 95. However, along the way you will have the opportunity to take one or more side roads off the main route that will lead you to outstanding views from the top of Hells Canyon. These roads, are outlined in the Hells Canyon chapter, describing their difficulty and how to access them. You should have time to do at least two of them. Overnight will be in **New Meadows**.

SEVENTH DAY

Continue south on US 95 from New Meadows to the town of Cambridge. From there, SR 71 will lead you to the southern edge of Hells Canyon National Recreation Area at the Oxbow Dam. A private road (but open to the public) leads to the **Hells Canyon Dam**. At that point you can opt to take another boat ride on the **Snake River**. The ride from the point where SR 71 reaches the Snake at Brownlee Dam, all the way to the end at Hells Canyon Dam, is one of the most scenic in the Hells Canyon area. Make your way back to Cambridge and travel south again on US 95 to your stopping place for tonight, the town of **Weiser**.

EIGHTH DAY

One final short stretch of US 95 south will bring you to I-84. Travel east back to Boise, a trip of under an hour. There are several nature-related attractions in Boise that can fill up a few hours of your final day.

SUGGESTED TRIP 7

MARVELS OF ARIZONA

- ❖ PARK HIGHLIGHTS: Canyon de Chelly National Monument; Grand Canyon National Park; Glen Canyon National Recreation Area; Petrified Forest National Park; Saguaro National Park (all Arizona); Rainbow Bridge National Monument (Utah)
- ❖ GATEWAY: Phoenix, Arizona.
- ❖ ESTIMATED MILES: 1,850.
- ❖ TIME: 10 days.

FIRST DAY

From the Phoenix/Tempe area, drive east on US 60 (also called the Superstition Freeway) to the town of Apache Junction. Then get on SR 88, known to one and all in Arizona as the **Apache Trail**. The route follows an old trail that was used by Native Americans. Most of it is paved, but even the unpaved portion can be done in the family sedan without any difficulty. The sights en route are numerous and diverse. You'll encounter mountains and canyons, lakes and desert, dams and ancient Indian ruins, and more, all part of the beautiful **Tonto National Forest**. The 75-mile trail ends at Globe. From there, pick up SR 77 and take it all the way into your overnight stopping place – **Tucson**, Arizona's second largest city.

SECOND DAY

The **Saguaro National Park** is on tap for today and you can find all of the details on page 269. You'll be visiting both sections of the park. When in the western, or Tucson Mountain section, be sure to allow time for the adjacent **Tucson Mountain Park**, ☎ (520) 883-4200. Within the confines of this large municipal park is the outstanding **Arizona-Sonora Desert Museum**. There is no facility anywhere in the Southwest that provides more information on the flora and fauna of the desert than this one. The natural setting of the mostly outdoor museum is also attractive. Once you've seen the sights, leave Tucson via I-10 east. Take it to the town of **Willcox** (Exit 340), where you can spend the night.

THIRD DAY

Follow SR 186 for 34 miles to the junction of SR 181. The latter road will soon bring you to the unexpected wonders of the **Chiricahua National Monument**, ☎ (520) 824-3560. Certainly one of the lesser-known units of the national park system, the monument combines beautiful mountain scenery with strange rock formations. The drive to the summit is easy and the view from there is spectacular. There are also several places along the monument road where you can stop to get a better look at the formations. A series of trails, both easy and strenuous, originate at the summit for those seeking to explore in more depth. Then return to Willcox, pick up I-10 east for 12 miles (Exit 352) and take US 191 north to **Clifton**, where you can find accommodations.

FOURTH DAY

The approximately 80 miles of US 191 between Clifton and Alpine is known as the **Coronado Trail**. It traverses a part of the vast **Apache-Sitgreaves National Forest** and is one of the most scenic highways in all of Arizona. And that, considering the many wonderful roads in this state, is quite a compliment. At Alpine you'll turn west on US 180 for the half-hour ride to Eagar. Then take SR 260 west to Show Low. This scenic portion of Arizona is known as the **White Mountains** and the high altitude makes for a rather cool climate that is in sharp contrast to most of the state. From Show Low, travel north on SR 77 to your overnight destination of **Holbrook**. If you don't mind getting in a little later and doing some extra driving (not included in the estimated miles for this trip), you can extend your time in the White Mountains by continuing on SR 260 from Show Low to Heber. Then, SRs 277 and 377 will take you to Holbrook. The latter portion of SR 260 runs near the **Mogollon Rim,** a highly scenic area. There is access to the rim in a number of locations.

FIFTH DAY

Approximately 20 miles east of Holbrook via US 180 is the southern entrance to the fabulous **Petrified Forest National Park** (refer to page 253). You'll exit the northern end of the park at I-40 east for 22 miles (Exit 333) and then head north on US 191. It's a fairly lengthy ride through the huge **Navajo Indian Reservation** to the town of Chinle. Two miles east of town is the unforgettable **Canyon de Chelly National Monument**. This afternoon you'll have time to explore the two canyon rims via good paved roads. Details for this – as well as tomorrow morning's activities within the monument – can be found on page 142. You can spend the night either in **Chinle** or within the monument itself.

SIXTH DAY

Today begins with a Navajo-guided tour into the depths of Canyon de Chelly. After lunch you'll once again be traveling through the Navajo Reservation. Take US 191 north to Indian Route 59, and then US 180 west. Finally, branch off US 180 onto SR 98 for the final leg of today's journey. Overnight is in **Page**. This community is the headquarters for the **Glen Canyon Dam** and the surrounding national recreation area. The beautiful dark canyon walls surrounding the dam are of interest, even if the powerhouse doesn't strike your fancy. Regardless, you should go down to the bottom to get the great view looking up!

SEVENTH DAY

The best way to see the gorgeous blue waters and red sandstone cliffs of the Glen Canyon National Recreation Area is by boat. There are half- and full-day trips, but we suggest the half-day option. Either way, the ride will include a stop at **Rainbow Bridge National Monument**, so you get two park highlights for the price of one. Have some lunch upon your return to land and then set out on US 89 south. About 23 miles down the road, make a sharp right onto ALT 89. This will begin a highly scenic 50-mile stretch of road that will have you wondering which way to look. Chief among the sights are imposing **Marble Canyon**. You can stop there and walk on the old road bridge to get a better view. Afterwards, the road rises and at Jacobs Lake you will go south on SR 67. This road ends at the **North Rim of Grand Canyon National Park**. Besides spending the night at the rim you should have time to begin your explorations. They will continue tomorrow. See pages 196-215 for further information on both canyon rims.

EIGHTH DAY

Upon completing your North Rim visit, it's time to head toward the South Rim. Reverse your route all the way to the junction of US 89 and ALT 89. This time, however, continue south on US 89 to the town of Cameron. A right onto SR 64 will offer access to overlooks of the **Little Colorado River Gorge** before arriving at the western entrance to the South Rim of Grand Canyon National Park. You should be able to complete the sights of the **East Rim Drive** before ending the day. Overnight can be at **Grand Canyon Village** or in the nearby town of **Tusayan.**

NINTH DAY

This morning will be devoted to the most heavily visited portion of the Grand Canyon – the west side of the South Rim. Leave the Grand Canyon via SR 64/US 180 from Tusayan and follow US 180 towards Flagstaff. From Flagstaff head north for a short time on US 89 to the town of Antelope Hills. Then you'll begin a loop road that will take you through **Wupatki** and **Sunset Crater National Monuments**. A third, **Walnut Canyon National Monument**, is a few miles west of Flagstaff off I-40. While Walnut Canyon and Wupatki are of historic significance (ancient Indian dwellings), both are spectacular because of their beautiful natural settings. Sunset Crater is the remnant of a prehistoric volcanic eruption. Trails of varying difficulties and lengths can be found at all three monuments. Overnight is in **Flagstaff**.

TENTH DAY

The last day of this trip won't be lacking for great scenery. From Flagstaff, drive south on SR 89A. This road drops sharply into spectacular **Oak Creek Canyon**, whose fiery red sandstone walls and unusual formations have been made famous in many movies and television programs. There are several state parks in the area and a loop road at the southern end of the canyon at the town of Sedona will bring you to even more red rocks and strange shapes. Take SR 179 south from Sedona. It will soon run into I-17. In about 1½ hours you'll be back in the Phoenix area.

SUGGESTED TRIP 8

UNIQUE UTAH

- ❖ PARK HIGHLIGHTS: Arches National Park; Bryce Canyon National Park; Canyonlands National Park; Capitol Reef National Park; Grand Staircase-Escalante National Monument; Zion National Park (all Utah).
- ❖ GATEWAY: Salt Lake City, Utah.
- ❖ ESTIMATED MILES: 1,725.
- ❖ TIME: 10 days.

First Day

The state of Utah has some of the most beautiful, dramatic and unusual scenery in all the world – thus the name of this itinerary. The southwest section of the state is known as Color Country, while the equally wondrous southeast is a vast area of canyons. Today, however, is only an introduction. Travel south from Salt Lake City on I-15 to SR 92. This route is known as the **Alpine Scenic Loop** (closed during the winter) and will take you to **Timpanogos Cave National Monument** as well as through the beautiful scenery of the **Wasatch Mountains**. The loop reaches US 189, where you'll head south. **Bridal Veil Falls** is a brief but picturesque stop just outside Provo. Rejoin I-15 south for a short time until you reach US 6. Head east until you reach the town of **Price**, the stopping point for the evening.

Second Day

Continue east on US 6 (also US 191 south after Price) until you reach I-70 at Green River. Travel east on the interstate until US 191 south branches off. Follow US 191 to SR 313, the access point for the **Island in the Sky** section of **Canyonlands National Park**. Between the park and the magnificent **Dead Horse Point State Park** (adjacent to Canyonlands), you will have spent the entire afternoon (see pages 151-158 for details). Head back on SR 313 to US 191 and go south for the short ride into **Moab**, where you'll spend two nights.

Third Day

A few miles back north on US 191 will bring you to **Arches National Park**. Allow at least all morning for touring this spectacular region (described on pages 103-111). In the afternoon you can take a scenic ride through the **Manti-La Sal National Forest**. Follow SR 128 from Moab along the **Colorado River** and past colorful formations until you reach the **Manti-La Sal loop road**. Magnificent vistas await along this road, which will return to US 191 just south of **Moab**. Head back into town for the night.

FOURTH DAY

Today you'll travel south on US 191. About a half-hour south of Moab is **Wilson Arch**. While it isn't anything unusual compared to what you've already seen, it is one of the few big natural arches located right alongside a major through route. At SR 211 detour off US 191 for the 50-mile dead-end route into the **Needles section** of **Canyonlands National Park**. Upon returning to US 191, continue south once again. Just past the town of Bluff the road will divide and you should follow US 163 to the town of **Gouldings**, your stopping place for tonight.

FIFTH DAY

This morning you'll be visiting gorgeous **Monument Valley Navajo Tribal Park**, ☎ (435) 727-3287. The 17-mile loop road inside the park passes some remarkable sandstone monoliths, now world famous because of their frequent appearance in movies. You can drive through the valley on your own or use a Navajo guide. Monument Valley straddles the Utah/Arizona border, although most of the formations are actually in Arizona. After visiting Monument Valley retrace your route north on US 163 to SR 261 north. There are a few brief stops to be made via short spurs off this road. They include the **Goosenecks State Park** (no phone/facilities) and **Muley Point Overlook**. Both offer fantastic views of winding river canyons. Upon reaching SR 95, turn left and watch for the entrance to the **Natural Bridges National Monument**. Within the confines of this relatively small area are three of the most impressive natural bridge formations to be found anywhere. Nowhere else in the world are three bridges of such immense size found so close together. After visiting the monument, continue on SR 95. This long and lonely stretch of road passes through some awesome scenery, offering a view of Cataract Canyon as you traverse a remote portion of the **Glen Canyon National Recreation Area**. Overnight is in the small town of **Hanksville**.

SIXTH DAY

A little to the east of Hanksville via SR 24 is the remarkable **Capitol Reef National Park**, which will take up your morning (see page 159). The afternoon will be devoted to the scenic wonders of SR 12 (a left turn off SR 24 at Torrey, just after you leave Capitol Reef). Known as the **Boulder-Escalante Scenic Highway** or the Utah 12 Scenic Byway, among other names, no name can adequately describe the scenic splendors along the route. (Many sights are described under the **Grand Staircase-Escalante National Monument**, page 216, as SR 12 skirts the northern edge of this remote region.) Just before you reach your overnight destination of **Bryce**, take a short detour off SR 12 to **Kodachrome Basin State Park**, ☎ (435) 679-8562, a land of wonderful colors and formations.

SEVENTH DAY

Almost an entire day will be devoted to exploring the indescribable splendors of **Bryce Canyon National Park** (as discussed on pages 132-141). By mid-afternoon you can start making your way farther east on SR 12, passing through beautiful **Red Canyon** before reaching US 89. Go south to the town of **Mt. Carmel Junction**, your overnight stopping point.

EIGHTH DAY

Head east this morning on SR 9, known as the **Zion-Mount Carmel Highway** and an engineering wonder for its day. The scenery improves mile after mile and you'll soon enter **Zion National Park**, where you'll have the better part of the day to explore. You can find all of the details on pages 281-292. Spend the night in **St. George**, the "capital" of Utah's Dixie region.

NINTH DAY

Visit **Snow Canyon State Park**, ☎ (435) 628-2255, another place of remarkable colors and formations, and just a few minutes ride from town. Then work your way back into St. George and pick up I-15 in a northerly direction. A half-hour later you'll briefly leave the highway to visit the lesser-known **Kolob Canyons** section of Zion National Park. After that, another short ride on I-15 will bring you to Cedar City. Head west here on SR 14 and the road quickly climbs into the high plateau country. At SR 148 you'll turn left and enter the strange world of **Cedar Breaks National Monument**, which is often referred to as a miniature of

Bryce Canyon. Then continue north via SR 143, rejoining I-15 at the town of Parowan. Overnight will be in the town of **Beaver**, located right alongside the interstate. For a little more scenery you can explore the canyons to the east of Beaver via SR 153.

TENTH DAY

It's a four-hour drive, all via I-15, to return to Salt Lake City. The Salt Lake area has several scenic attractions of its own. You can explore **Big and Little Cottonwood Canyons** to the east of the city in the Wasatch Mountains; or you can go a little further north to **Antelope Island State Park**. This park is a wildlife refuge and the island is located in the Great Salt Lake.

SUGGESTED TRIP 9

THE CASCADES/OLYMPIC ODYSSEY

❖ PARK HIGHLIGHTS: Mount Rainier National Park; Mount St. Helens National Volcanic Monument; North Cascades National Park/Ross Lake National Recreation Area; Olympic National Park (all Washington).

❖ GATEWAY: Seattle, Washington.

❖ ESTIMATED MILES: 1,400.

❖ TIME: 9 days.

FIRST DAY

The beautiful setting of Seattle is one of the things that makes it among America's most livable cities. Explore "natural" Seattle today, including **Lakes Union** and **Washington**. Then head north for a short ride on I-5 to SR 525. At Mukilteo you'll cross the Saratoga Passage by ferry to **Whidbey Island**, largest of hundreds of islands big and small that are strung along the coast from Seattle all the way north to the Canadian border. There are many attractions of historic interest in the area, but we'll concentrate on enjoying the picturesque scenery of the islands and the water, and the forests and mountains on the mainland. SRs 525 and 20 will take you through the entire island. At the north end of the island in **Anacortes** you can get a good view of the many smaller **San Juan Islands**. Then take SR 20 east bound. It will cross back to the mainland via a bridge. Stay on this road to **Sedro Woolley**, your first night's stop.

SECOND DAY

The scenery along SR 20 will become increasingly dramatic as you rise into the **Cascades Mountain Range**. The road passes through the **Ross Lake National Recreation Area**. Access to **North Cascades National Park** is by boat from the recreation area. Activities, including the scenic sights on the Skagit/Seattle City Light tour, are detailed on pages 392-398. SR 20 leaves the park and recreation area on the east side. However, the next 60 miles continue to provide outstanding mountain and forest scenery as the road traverses the **Okanogan National Forest**. The views at the **Rainy** and **Washington Passes** are nothing short of spectacular. Just after the town of Twisp, follow SR 153 to the junction of US 97 and then go south on that road for the short final portion of today's drive. Overnight is in **Chelan** today and tomorrow.

THIRD DAY

Chelan sits at the southern edge of **Lake Chelan**. This long (almost 60 miles) and narrow lake (averaging only about 1½ miles), is in an almost pristine wilderness area that is not accessible by road. A relaxing day is in order as you'll take an all-day boat ride to the small town of **Stehekin** at the north end of the lake, and then return. You'll be ringed in by magnificent mountains and chances are you'll see plenty of wildlife, especially towards the northern part of the lake. That section is in the remote **Lake Chelan National Recreation Area**. Everywhere during your trip today, the primary features of the Cascades will be in evidence – towering mountain peaks, thick forests and the many lakes and rivers.

FOURTH DAY

The drive south this morning from Chelan on US 97 hugs the shore of the mighty **Columbia River**, providing great views during the approximately 40-mile drive to Wenatchee. About seven miles north of town you can visit the **Rocky Reach Dam** and watch migrating fish climb the fish ladders. A few miles farther on, at the junction of US 2 and 97 is the **Ohme Gardens County Park**, ☎ (509) 662-5783. The beautiful multi-level alpine-style gardens overlook the Wenatchee Valley and the Columbia, providing memorable vistas. After Wenatchee, continue on US 97 until you reach I-90 at Ellensburg. Go east to Exit 136 and the **Gingko Petrified Forest**. This large park contains numerous examples of fossilized trees that date back about 15 million years. Hiking some easy trails and a visit to the interpretive center will make your visit an enjoyable one. Now go back west on I-90 to I-82, which you should take to your overnight stopping place, the city of **Yakima**.

FIFTH DAY

Head 20 miles west of Yakima via US 12 to SR 410. Take that road for 50 miles and through the Chinook Pass to the northeastern entrance of **Mt. Rainier National Park**. This park has to rank among the greatest scenic wonders of America (see pages 374-383 for full touring details). You'll have virtually the entire day to explore the park, finally leaving via the southwest entrance and staying overnight in **Ashford** or within the park at **Paradise**.

SIXTH DAY

The park highlight for today is the east side of **Mount St. Helens National Volcanic Monument**. You can reach it from Ashford via SR 706 to SR 7 south and then east on US 12 to Randall. From Paradise, use the southwest (Stevens Canyon) entrance and pick up US 12 west to Randall. Either way, take SR 131 south from Randall to access the east side attractions from the monument. Refer to pages 383-391 for details. Once you've worked your way down to the south side of the monument, follow SR 503 through Cougar and on to I-5 at Woodland. Go north on the interstate to **Castle Rock** (Exit 49), where you'll spend the night.

SEVENTH DAY

Take SR 504 east for 50 miles from Castle Rock into the heart of the west side of the monument. Again, refer to the Mt. St. Helens chapter for complete information. Afterwards, work your way back to Castle Rock. Take I-5 north to Olympia (Exit 104) and pick up US 101 for the final 40 miles of the day's ride. Overnight is in **Aberdeen**.

> NOTE: *US 101 circles the Olympic Peninsula and, therefore, north and south designations can be quite confusing because you may actually, at times, be traveling in the opposite direction of the road's designation. Therefore, we'll point you towards geographic signed landmarks to make sure that you don't go the wrong way.*

EIGHTH DAY

You'll be traveling on US 101 towards Port Angeles this morning. Almost the entire day will be devoted to exploring the diverse features of immense **Olympic National Park**. (See pages 398-408 for sightseeing details. You'll read about several side roads that lead off US 101 and provide access to the park's interior and many of its best features.) Although the park occupies a good portion of the Olympic Peninsula, it is a little inland from the Pacific Ocean and the Juan de Fuca Strait, except for a small section along the coast between Queets and Ruby Beach. US 101 only traverses a small part of the park. Most of the time, however, you'll have good views of mountains, forest and sea. Overnight will be in **Port Angeles** after you've finished visiting the final section of the park at Hurricane Ridge.

NINTH DAY

This morning you'll continue along US 101, traveling in the direction towards Sequim. Just after the small town of Discovery

Bay, take SRs 104 and 3 to Bremerton. A scenic ferry ride among the many coves and islands will return you to Seattle, where you should have some time to take in a few of the sights.

SUGGESTED TRIP 10

HIGH SIERRA ADVENTURE

- ❖ PARK HIGHLIGHTS: Sequoia & Kings Canyon National Parks; Yosemite National Park (all California).
- ❖ GATEWAY: San Francisco, California.
- ❖ ESTIMATED MILES: 1,200.
- ❖ TIME: 7 days.

FIRST DAY

Since San Francisco is one of the most popular cities in the world, we're sure that even people who prefer nature will want to spend at least some time exploring the city's sights. Although this itinerary doesn't take city sights into account, you could easily add on a few days at the beginning or end to do so. The view of the city and San Francisco Bay from the overlook at the north end of the Golden Gate Bridge is spectacular. You'll be crossing the bridge to reach SR 1, which will provide access to the **Muir Woods National Monument**. The woods, on the slope of Mount Tamalpais, comprise a large grove of California coastal redwood trees, many of which stand over 250 feet tall. Upon conclusion of your visit here, most of the day will be spent getting to your next destination, but the drive will certainly be worth it. Reverse your route on SR 1 to US 101 and take the latter north for four exits to I-580. Follow that road past the town of Livermore and pick up I-205. Then follow SR 120 for a short time to the junction of SR 99 south. This highway will lead you to Merced. Exit there and take SR 140 for the final leg of today's drive. The road will soon begin gaining altitude as you enter the

Sierras. The last 30 miles to **El Portal** (where you should spend the next two nights), are especially scenic.

Second Day

Yosemite National Park is on tap for today. While Yosemite is justly one of America's most famous and heavily visited national parks, the portion of the park that you will be traveling through today is not seen by the majority of Yosemite visitors. This is the Tuolumne area, reached by the Tioga Pass Road. You'll travel that road as far as the Tuolumne Visitor Center before turning back and reversing the route to El Portal. Pages 322-338 provide the necessary details on this section of the park as well as those portions you'll be visiting tomorrow.

Third Day

Start your day with the breathtaking **Yosemite Valley**. This will be followed by a short side trip to **Glacier Point** and the southern (or **Mariposa Grove**) section. Leave Yosemite via the southern entrance gate and spend the night in the adjacent town of **Fish Camp**.

Fourth Day

SR 41 provides a pleasant but not overly scenic drive to Fresno, where you pick up SR 180 east. The 50-mile ride from Fresno to Grant Grove starts out with mostly flat farming country and a view of distant mountains. But soon you'll be rising through those mountains, the same Sierra Nevadas that dominate Yosemite, as you reach the northwest entrance of **Kings Canyon National Park**. This afternoon you'll visit the **Cedar Grove** section of the park before returning to **Grant Grove**, where you should plan on spending the evening. Refer to pages 309-321 for touring information on Kings Canyon as well as the adjacent **Sequoia National Park**.

Fifth Day

Begin by exploring the marvelous trees of the **Grant Grove** area before setting out on the **General's Highway**, which connects the two parks. Most of the day will be spent seeing the many sights within **Sequoia National Park**. SR 198 leads out the southern entrance of Sequoia and will bring you to your overnight stopping point of **Visalia** in about an hour. The scenery is somewhat anticlimactic after having toured the park, but the views on the stretch of road by Lake Kaweah are quite nice.

SIXTH DAY

Travel west this morning on SR 198, then south on SR 41 and west on SR 46. These roads will take you through a variety of terrain – from flat farmland to rolling hills and, finally, the coastal mountain range, before reaching the Pacific Ocean at Cambria. You'll then drive north on the famous **Pacific Coast Highway** (SR 1). There are numerous points where you can stop to take a better look at the excellent scenery – rocky headlands and precipitous drops to the sea. Several state parks en route are worthwhile stops as well. These include the **Julia-Pfeiffer Burns,** ☎ (831) 667-2315, and **Pfeiffer-Big Sur State Parks**, ☎ (831) 624-4909 . The most beautiful spot on the drive, however, is the **Point Lobos State Reserve**, just south of Monterey. A short road loops through the park and leads to many easy to moderate trails from which you can get great views of rocky coves, beaches, sea otters, lots of other wildlife, and much more. You should spend the night in **Monterey**.

SEVENTH DAY

Begin by taking the **Seventeen Mile Drive**, which loops through many golf courses and wealthy communities (it's a private toll road). The road looks out onto excellent coastal scenery, including the well-known **Lone Cypress Tree**. It's not as spectacular as Point Lobos, but is still well worth doing. From Monterey head north on SR 1. About seven miles north in Castroville, follow SR 156 for the short drive to the intersection with US 101. That road, in a northerly direction, will return you to San Francisco.

SUGGESTED TRIP 11

TRAIL OF THE VOLCANOES

❖ PARK HIGHLIGHTS: Crater Lake National Park (Oregon); Lassen National Park (California).

❖ GATEWAY: Portland, Oregon.

❖ ESTIMATED MILES: 2,080.

❖ TIME: 10 days.

FIRST DAY

This is the longest of the basic itineraries from a mileage standpoint and, with only two park highlights, you may well be wondering what the fuss is about. Although only two of the previously discussed parks are included on this journey, the number of other outstanding attractions is so great that this is as good as any of the other trips.

We set out from Portland, taking I-84 east. This interstate travels along the gorgeous **Columbia River Gorge**, where the Columbia River is hemmed in on both sides by sheer cliffs. Numerous exits along the highway provide easy access to excellent sights. These include the panorama from **Crown Point**, breathtaking **Multnomah Falls** and the many interesting exhibits and sights at the **Bonneville Dam**. At the latter, be sure to explore both the Oregon and Washington sides. At the town of **Hood River** (Exit 64), leave I-84 for the final time and head south on SR 35. There are numerous points from which you can get an outstanding view of **Mount Hood**, Oregon's tallest peak at 11,239 feet. Just before the town of Government Camp, take US 26 in an eastbound direction to Madras, where you'll pick up US 97 south for the final leg of your day's journey. Spend the next two nights in **Bend**.

SECOND DAY

Bend is in the middle of a scenic area of forests, mountains, lakes and even some unusual natural formations. Most of the sights are within state parks or the **Deschutes National Forest**. Your loop route from Bend (get a good map of the area because there are too many ins and outs to describe here) should include the following: the **Lava Butte Area** and **Lava Butte Cave**, and **Newberry Crater** (all within the national forest). Some of these, as well as numerous other sights, can be reached via the 87-mile **Cascade Lakes Highway**. **Pilot Butte State Park**, ☎ (800) 551-6949, is another worthy highlight.

THIRD DAY

About 80 miles south of Bend via US 97 is the cutoff for SR 138. A 15-mile drive west on that road will bring you to the north entrance of **Crater Lake National Park**. There is no word other than magnificent to describe the deep blue waters of this volcanic remnant. The drive around the lake is only the beginning, so refresh your memory by referring back to pages 339-344. You should be done with the park by late afternoon. Exit via SR 62 east, which runs into US 97 for the short stretch along picturesque **Klamath Lake** and to your overnight stop in **Klamath Falls**.

FOURTH DAY

There's a lot of riding on tap for today, but some gorgeous sights as well. Continue south on US 97 across into California, all the way to I-5 at the town of Weed. Go only two exits on the interstate and then drive south on SR 89. It's about 90 miles via this road from the interstate to the north entrance of **Lassen Volcanic National Park**. The route, however, is a scenic one. The road passes through thick forests with views of high mountain peaks. Lassen is the highlight for today and it is fully described on pages 301-308. Upon finishing your visit to the park, exit on the south side and follow SRs 89 south and 36 east to **Susanville**. There's a good choice of accommodations in this community.

FIFTH DAY

Drive south on US 395 (reached five miles east of Susanville) and take it into Nevada. Just south of Reno will be a cutoff for SR 431. This scenic but easy mountain route goes through the **Mt. Rose Summit**, from which there is a spectacular view, and then descends quickly to Incline Village on the north shore of lovely **Lake Tahoe**. There are many sights on the roads which encircle the lake.

> ### ❖ DID YOU KNOW?
>
> *The lake is 22 miles long and about 12 miles wide, with an average depth of almost 1,000 feet (the deepest point is more than 1,600 feet), and the water is extremely blue. About two-thirds of the lake's surface lies in California, the remainder in Nevada.*

Today you will explore the sights in Nevada, traveling from Incline Village via SR 28 south to US 50 and then west on the latter to your stopping place for tonight, **Stateline**. The California side of town has lots of small motels, while the Nevada side is a mini-Las Vegas. You should take **Heavenly Tram**, ☎ (775) 586-7000, to the mountaintop for an excellent overall view of the lake and surrounding area. It transports skiers during the winter months.

SIXTH DAY

Today begins with an exploration of the west side of the lake. The sights here are more diverse than those on the other side. Follow SR 89 north as it hugs the lake, sometimes in dramatic fashion from atop a rocky ridge, but more often down at the shore level. Among the places you should stop to explore are **Emerald Bay State Park** (great view of the lake as well as the inlet that goes by the name Emerald Bay), **D.L. Bliss State Park** and the **Sugar Pine State Park**. At Tahoe City the road splits, but continue on SR 89. If you want a different view from atop a mountain, there's another **aerial tramway**, ☎ (530) 583-6985, just off SR 89 at Olympic (Squaw) Valley. SR 89 will soon reach I-80. Head west (there will be outstanding views from the interstate as you cross the famous **Donner Pass**) for 24 miles and then drive west on SR 20 to Yuba City. Go north on SR 99 to your overnight stopping point in **Chico**.

SEVENTH DAY

Continue north on SR 99 this morning and you'll soon run into I-5. In the vicinity of Redding are the three separate units of the **Whiskeytown-Shasta-Trinity National Recreation Area**, ☎ (530) 241-6584. A short detour from the main route will take you via I-5 north of Redding to the best part – the two-hour tour of **Lake Shasta Caverns**. A short boat ride transports you across the lake to the cave entrance. Be warned, there are more than 600 steps to be climbed, but the sights both inside and outside the cave are wonderful. Then go back towards Redding and pick up SR 299 in a westbound direction. The scenery is pleasant as the road passes through the Whiskeytown unit of the recreation area. SR 299 will take you all the way to the northern California coast at the town of **Arcata**, where you should plan on spending the night.

EIGHTH DAY

The northern California coast, like the Oregon coast that follows it, is more spectacular than the coast in the southern portion of the state. Among the delightful sights on the 75-mile stretch of US 101 north from Arcata to Crescent City are (in the order you'll reach them) **Patricks Point** and **Humboldt Lagoons State Parks**, several scattered sections of the **Redwoods National Park** and the **Del Norte Coast Redwoods State Park**. It makes for a truly lovely drive with frequent short stops. After Crescent City, take US 199 north, which heads inland through the main section of Redwoods National Park and crosses into Oregon. At Cave Junction, detour 20 miles to the east via SR 46 to **Oregon Caves National Monument**. Tours of these spectacular caves (which feature such sights as the **Marble Pillars of Oregon**, huge flowstone formations, and a room that is 250 feet long) are quite strenuous, as they contain more than 500 steps. They last about 1¼ hours. Back to US 199 now, and north once again to

Grants Pass. Pick up I-5 for the final 65 miles of today's trek and your overnight accommodations in **Roseburg**.

Ninth Day

Go west on SR 42 for the drive to Coos Bay and the beginning of your travels on US 101 up the marvelous Oregon coast. Today you'll drive about 150 miles of coastline, all the way to your stopping point in **Lincoln City**. There are sights at every turn in the road and numerous stops along the way. Included in these should be the **Oregon Dunes National Recreation Area, Devil's Elbow State Park, Cape Perpetua, Seal Rock, Devil's Punchbowl, Depot Bay State Park** and the **"D" River** (reputedly the world's shortest). Most of these involve unusually sculpted rock formations created by wave action. There's also the commercially operated **Sea Lion Caves** at Florence that is worthwhile. Finally, at the previously mentioned Cape Perpetua, you should take the two-mile cutoff that rises sharply into the cliffs of the coastal **Siuslaw National Forest** for the breathtaking and unforgettable view at the **Cape Perpetua Overlook**.

Tenth Day

The final day of this adventure continues a while longer up the coast via US 101. Stops should be made at **Capes Lookout** and **Meares**, as well as at **Oswald West** and **Ecola State Parks**. The latter has one of the most famous offshore rocks in Oregon. Just north of Ecola and the town of Cannon Beach, take US 26 east for the trip back to Portland, a ride of less than two hours.

SUGGESTED TRIP 12

WONDERS OF THE DESERT

❖ PARK HIGHLIGHTS: Lake Mead National Recreation Area (Nevada/Arizona); Great Basin National Park (Nevada); Death Valley National Park (California/Nevada).

❖ GATEWAY: Las Vegas, Nevada.

❖ ESTIMATED MILES: 1,340.

❖ TIME: 7 days.

> NOTE: *Because of extreme weather conditions in all of the parks on this trip, we strongly recommend that this itinerary be undertaken only during the spring and fall. While hot summers in Lake Mead are tolerable, those in Death Valley can be dangerous. Winters in Great Basin are likely to have problems due to cold and snow. Mid-September through October and mid-March through early May are the suggested times. If you want to go in the middle of winter, omit Great Basin. Instead, you could head into the southern California desert and visit the Mojave National Preserve, Joshua Tree National Monument and the scenic sights in the Palm Springs area. Mojave Preserve, Joshua Tree and Death Valley should NOT be attempted during the summer.*

FIRST DAY

Las Vegas is not only the gateway city for this trip but is also the place to stay for the first two nights of the trip. Time is not allocated for daytime activities in Las Vegas, but you will probably want to see the sights of The Strip or take in a show or two during the evenings you spend in town. (You can also stay away from The Strip or in neighboring Henderson.) Today will have two separate short excursions, one to the southeast and one to the west, that can be done in a figure-eight loop.

Begin by taking I-515 (also US 93/95) to Lake Mead Drive in Henderson (also known as SR 146) and drive east. In a few miles you'll reach the **Lake Mead National Recreation Area**. You can refer to pages 234-243 for details on sightseeing. Today, however, we'll be concentrating on the most heavily visited section. Follow Lakeshore Road (SR 166) for access to the beach, lake and marina areas. Then take US 93 to **Hoover Dam**, a great place to view the lake and the gorge of the **Colorado River**. Further exploration can be done by taking a short cruise on Lake Mead, or you can take a raft trip down the river. (Doing the latter activity, however, won't allow time for our planned afternoon activities.) Reverse your route on US 93, taking it to I-515. Go all the way to Rainbow Boulevard and then south to Charleston Boulevard. A right on that street (which becomes SR 159) will take you to the entrance of the **Red Rock Canyon Natural Conservation Area**, ☎ (702) 363-1921. This beautiful area of desert shrubbery, high mountains, and colorful rock strata is a delight for nature enthusiasts. The fact that it's within 15 minutes of The Strip makes it all the more unusual. You can return to civilization via SR 160 (Blue Diamond Road) to I-15 north.

SECOND DAY

North of downtown Las Vegas, take Lake Mead Boulevard back into Lake Mead National Recreation Area. (This is SR 147, not to be confused with yesterday's Lake Mead Drive.) This time you'll follow SR 167, known as the **North Shore Drive**, all the way to **Overton Beach**. This part of the recreation area is picturesque and far less visited then the portion you saw yesterday. From Overton, proceed west on SR 169. This will provide access to the fantastic **Valley of Fire State Park**, ☎ (702) 397-2088. From the main road, as well as a spur that leads into even more beautiful areas, you can ride and walk to a number of amazing sculpted rock formations, many of which have dazzling colors. At certain times of the day it does, indeed, look like the rocks are on fire as they blaze in the glorious desert sun. SR 169 west will run back into I-15, where a short drive south will return you to Las Vegas.

THIRD DAY

Today, unfortunately, you have a 300-mile drive ahead, as there are few acceptable places to stay en route. The scenery along the way isn't bad and there are a few stops, mostly right in the middle of the trip, to break up the ride. Go north on I-15 to Exit 64 and then take US 93 north. This road will take you all the way to your overnight stopping place in **Ely**, where you'll spend two nights. The section of US 93 between Caliente and Pioche is especially scenic. Take some time to visit the beautiful **Cathedral Gorge State Park**, ☎ (775) 728-4460.

FOURTH DAY

The better part of the day will be spent exploring the wonders of the **Great Basin National Park**. See pages 224-229 for more information on discovering **Lehman Caves**, the sights along the drive to Wheeler Peak, and more. The route to the park from Ely is via US 93 south (also 6/50 west) for 26 miles to the junction of US 5 and 60, then 35 miles west on that route to Baker. SR 488 makes the final five miles into the park. Just reverse those directions to get back to Ely.

FIFTH DAY

Head west from Ely via US 6. The 170-mile drive to Tonopah crosses a major portion of the **Great Basin**, with good views of mountains both near and far. There are several summits that are traversed by US 6. From Tonopah, take US 95 south to **Beatty**, where you'll spend two nights. Along the route from Tonopah there are the remains of several **ghost towns**. One of the best is in **Goldfield**. Another, called **Rhyolite**, is right outside of Beatty.

SIXTH DAY

Take the entire day to explore the vast **Death Valley National Park** (see pages 293-300 for full description).

SEVENTH DAY

US 95 south will take you all the way back to Las Vegas. Just before your return to the Vegas area, there's an interesting scenic loop detour via SRs 156, 158 and 157. These three interconnected roads will take you through the pretty **Spring Mountains National Recreation Area** and the **Toiyabe National Forest**. Although less than an hour from the hot desert of Las Vegas, this forested area is actually the location for snow skiing during the winter months. Explore **Lee** and **Charleston Canyons** or, if you're more adventurous, try hiking up 11,918-foot-high **Mount Charleston**.

SUGGESTED TRIP 13

PARADISE FOUND

- ❖ PARK HIGHLIGHTS: Haleakala National Park; Hawaii Volcanoes National Park (both Hawaii).
- ❖ GATEWAY: Honolulu, Hawaii
- ❖ ESTIMATED MILES: 650 to 900.
- ❖ TIME: At least a week.

People differ as to how much time should be spent lying on the beach or taking in local entertainment and shopping (of which Hawaii has an abundance). For this reason, we will depart from our usual day-by-day itinerary and, instead, highlight what should be seen on four of the main islands of Oahu, Kauai, Maui and Hawaii. As usual, however, we'll only be mentioning scenic attractions. Many of Hawaii's scenic attractions are privately owned and operated, so you will have to put up with more than the usual amount of commercialization as well as more admission fees.

❖ HAWAII

A loop drive around the entire island is both feasible and desirable. The main city, **Hilo**, has a number of scenic attractions, including **Akaka Falls State Park, Liliuokalani Gardens Park** and **Rainbow Falls**. Hilo is also the island's orchid-growing center and several of these colorful facilities are open to the public. Nearby is the plantation and production center of **Mauna Loa Macadamia Nuts**.

A short drive south of Hilo is **Hawaii Volcanoes National Park**. As described on pages 433-443, you should allow the better part of a day to see it.

SRs 11 and 19 form a circle around the island. Among the sights are the **Punaluu Black Sand Beach** in Pahula, and miles and miles of wonderful coastal scenery. Hawaii's highest mountains – **Mauna Kea** (13,796 feet) and **Mauna Loa** (13,677 feet) – are visible from many points on the island. SR 200 leads near the top of Mauna Kea, but it is a rough drive.

Other points of interest include a guided trip into the isolated and spectacular **Waipo Valley** (reached via a short drive on SR 240 from Honokaa), and a scenic loop road off of SR 19 in the vicinity of **Pepeekeo Point**, north of Hilo.

Accommodations are concentrated in Kailua-Kona on the west coast and, to a lesser extent, Hilo, on the east coast.

❖ KAUAI

The Garden Isle's airport at Lihue is near the resort area of **Wailua**. A number of major attractions are also in this vicinity, including boat rides to the famous **Fern Grotto** and a rock formation known as the **Sleeping Giant**. But the island's major scenic attraction is spectacular **Waimea Canyon**, a state reserve which compares with the best of the national parks in its beauty. SRs 50 and 500 lead there (round-trip from Wailua is about 100 miles). The 10-mile gorge has a number of viewpoints, the best being **Canyon Lookout** at an elevation of 3,400 feet. **Kokee State Park** is next to Waimea Canyon and has an overlook which allows you to see the ruggedly spectacular **Na Pali Coast**. The only way to fully appreciate this magnificent coastal area is by helicopter tour or boat trip, the latter leaving from the town of Hanalei on Kauai's north coast.

The **Spouting Horn** and **Olu Pua Gardens** can be visited on the way to Waimea Canyon to break up the ride. The former is about five miles off SR 50 via SR 520 or 530.

❖ MAUI

The Valley Isle is the most scenic of the major islands. Most of the major resorts are in the **Kaanapali Beach** area, but numerous others are scattered throughout the island.

A half-day is necessary to visit **Haleakala National Park** properly (see pages 425-432), accessible by winding SRs 378 and 37.

Maui also has many other beautiful attractions. Among the most popular is the historic whaling town of **Lahaina** (near Kaanapali's resort area) and the **Iao Valley** in Wailuku. Within the valley is the famous **Iao Needle**, a vegetation-covered rock that rises about 1,300 feet above the floor of this tropical valley. **Maui Plantation** in Waikapu offers a guided tram tour of groves where some of the island's major crops are grown.

Two beautiful drives are also possible. One is SR 30 from **Lahaina to Maakea**. This 16-mile section of road presents dramatic views of sea and mountains. It is especially gorgeous at sunset. The other is the famous **Hana Road** (SR 360), which sports over 600 turns. The road offers innumerable rewarding vistas, waterfalls and supposedly sacred Hawaiian pools.

❖ OAHU

Site of Honolulu, Oahu is the Gathering Place. While the real Hawaii may be more readily found on the outer islands, Oahu does have many worthwhile scenic attractions.

Within greater **Honolulu** the best scenery can be found by driving through the tunnel leading to a trail that ascends the famous **Diamond Head**. If you want to avoid the strenuous climb, then an equally impressive panorama can be seen from atop the extinct volcanic crater of the **National Memorial Cemetery of the Pacific**, more commonly known as the Punchbowl. Further vis-las are available by taking the drive along **Round Top and Tantalus Drives**.

Just outside of Honolulu is the spectacular **Nuuanu Pali State Wayside Park** (one of the most dramatic vistas in all the islands). A loop from Honolulu can take you past the Nuuanu Pali and then around Oahu's eastern end via SR 72. There are many wonderful coastal landscapes and vistas along this drive. Among the most famous points are the **Spouting Horn** and **Haunama Bay Beach Park**. The unusually beautiful setting of the latter was where the famous beach scene of *From Here to Eternity* was filmed.

SUGGESTED TRIPS

For More Information

The listings that follow will help you to secure the information to make your plans, especially if you are following one of the preceding suggested trips. Addresses and telephone numbers for the national parks themselves are listed in the appropriate chapters.

National Park Service

You can obtain brochures and information from either the national or regional offices of the Park Service:

National Office

Office of Public Inquiries
1849 C Street NW
Washington, DC 20240
☎ (202) 208-4747

Regional Offices

Alaska Region
2525 Gambell Street
Anchorage, AK 99503-2892
☎ (907) 271-2737

Mid-Atlantic Region
143 South Third Street
Philadelphia, PA 19106-2818
☎ (215) 597-7018

Midwest Region
1709 Jackson Street
Omaha, NE 68102
☎ (402) 221-3471

North Atlantic Region
15 State Street
Boston, MA 02109
☎ (617) 223-5199

Pacific Northwest Region
909 First Avenue
Seattle, WA 98104-1060
☎ (206) 220-7450

Rocky Mountain Region
PO Box 25287
Denver, CO 80225-0287
☎ (303) 969-2000

Southeast Region
75 Spring Street SW
Atlanta, GA 30303
☎ (404) 331-5187

Southwest Region
PO Box 728
Santa Fe, NM 87504-0728
☎ (505) 988-6012

Western Region
600 Hamilton Street, Suite 600
San Francisco, CA 94107
☎ (415) 556-0560

The National Park Service maintains an impressive Website where you can explore the parks: www.nps.gov/parks.html. In addition to general information, you can use that site to link up with Websites for any National Park Service facility. Each has its own site address, but if you're planning a trip to more than one park, it is easy to use the main site as your "home page" for moving from one park to another.

A new site – www.recreation.gov – includes information on areas administered by eight different government agencies and has links to all of them.

CAMPING IN NATIONAL PARKS

For campground reservations in Acadia, Death Valley, Everglades, Glacier, Grand Canyon, Great Smoky Mountains, Mount Rainier, Rocky Mountain, Sequoia and Kings Canyon, Shenandoah, Yosemite and Zion, call the National Park Service Reservation Service, ☎ (800) 365-2267. For Yosemite, ☎ (800) 436-7275. Refer back to the *Using This Book* section, pages 7-8, for more information on camping.

STATE TOURISM OFFICES

NOTE: *Only states with parks mentioned in this book are included in this listing.*

APPENDIX

ALASKA

Division of Tourism
PO Box 110801
Juneau, AK 99811-0801
☎ (907) 465-2010
www.dced.state.ak.us/tourism/homenew.htm

ARIZONA

Office of Tourism
1100 W. Washington Street
Phoenix, AZ 85007
☎ (602) 255-3618
www.arizonaguide.com

CALIFORNIA

Office of Tourism
1121 L Street, Suite 103
Sacramento, CA 95814
☎ (916) 322-1396
www.gocalif.ca.gov

COLORADO

Colorado Tourism Board
PO Box 38700
Denver, CO 80238
☎ (800) 433-2656
www.colorado.com

FLORIDA

Florida Tourism Industry Marketing Corporation
661 East Jefferson Street, Suite 300
Tallahassee, FL 32301
☎ (888) 7FLA-USA
www.flausa.com

HAWAII

Hawaii Visitors Bureau
2270 Kalakaua Ave.
Honolulu, HI 96815
☎ (808) 923-1811
www.visit.hawaii.org

IDAHO

Idaho Travel Council
707 W. State Street
Boise, ID 83720
☎ (800) 635-7820
www.ohwy.com/id/i/itc.htm

KENTUCKY

Dept. of Tourism
2200 Capital Plaza Tower
Frankfort, KY 40601
☎ (800) 225-8747
www.state.ky.us/tour/tour.htm

MAINE

Maine Publicity
97 Winthrop Street
Hallowell, ME 04347
☎ (800) 533-9595
www.visitmaine.com

MONTANA

Travel Montana
1424 9th Ave.
Helena, MT 59620
☎ (800) 541-1447
http://travel.mt.gov

NEBRASKA

Travel & Tourism Division
301 Centennial Mall South
PO Box 94666
Lincoln, NE 68509
☎ (800) 228-4307
www.visitnebraska.org

NEVADA

Commission on Tourism
Capitol Complex
Carson City, NV 89710
☎ (702) 885-4322
www.travelnevada.com

APPENDIX

NEW MEXICO

New Mexico Travel Division
100 St. Francis Drive
Santa Fe, NM 87503
☎ (800) 545-2040
www.newmexico.org

OREGON

Oregon Tourism Division
Economic Development Dept.
595 Cottage Street N.E.
Salem, OR 97310
☎ (800) 547-7842
www.traveloregon.com

SOUTH DAKOTA

Division of Tourism
711 Wells Ave.
Pierre, SD 57501
☎ (800) 843-1930
www.state.sd.us

TENNESSEE

Dept. of Tourist Development
PO Box 23170
Nashville, TN 37202
☎ (615) 741-2158

TEXAS

Capitol Info Center
State Highways & Public Transportation Dept
11th & Brazos Streets
Austin, TX 78701
☎ (512) 462-9191
www.traveltex.com

UTAH

Utah Travel Council
Council Hall/Capitol Hill
Salt Lake City, UT 84114
☎ (801) 538-1030
www.utah.com

VIRGINIA

Division of Tourism
202 N. 9th Street, Suite 500
Richmond, VA 23219
☎ (800) 847-4882
www.virginia.org

WASHINGTON

Trade & Economic Development
Tourism Division
101 General Admin. Bldg.
Olympia, WA 98504
☎ (800) 544-1800
www.tourism.wa.gov

WYOMING

Wyoming Travel Commission
I-25 at College Drive
Cheyenne, WY 82002
☎ (800) 225-5996
www.state.wy.us/state/welcome.html

APPENDIX

INDEX

INDEX